COMPUTER CRIME, INVESTIGATION, AND THE LAW

CHUCK EASTTOM AND DET. JEFF TAYLOR

Course Technology PTR

A part of Cengage Learning

COURSE TECHNOLOGY
CENGAGE Learning

Australia • Brazil • Japan • Korea • Mexico • Singapore • Spain • United Kingdom • United States

COURSE TECHNOLOGY
CENGAGE Learning™

Computer Crime, Investigation, and the Law

Chuck Easttom and

Det. Jeff Taylor

Publisher and General Manager, Course Technology PTR:
Stacy L. Hiquet

Associate Director of Marketing:
Sarah Panella

Manager of Editorial Services:
Heather Talbot

Marketing Manager: Mark Hughes

Acquisitions Editor: Heather Hurley

Project Editor: Kate Shoup

Copy Editor: Heather Urschel

Interior Layout Tech: MPS Limited,
A Macmillan Company

Cover Designer: Mike Tanamachi

Indexer: Larry Sweazy

Proofreader: Kate Shoup

For product information and technology assistance, contact us at
Cengage Learning Customer & Sales Support, 1-800-354-9706

For permission to use material from this text or product, submit all requests online at **cengage.com/permissions**

Further permissions questions can be emailed to **permissionrequest@cengage.com**

All trademarks are the property of their respective owners.

All images © Cengage Learning unless otherwise noted.

Library of Congress Control Number: 2009942398

ISBN-13: 978-1-4354-5532-0

ISBN-10: 1-4354-5532-0

Course Technology, a part of Cengage Learning
20 Channel Center Street
Boston, MA 02210
USA

Cengage Learning is a leading provider of customized learning solutions with office locations around the globe, including Singapore, the United Kingdom, Australia, Mexico, Brazil, and Japan. Locate your local office at: **international.cengage.com/region**

Cengage Learning products are represented in Canada by Nelson Education, Ltd.

For your lifelong learning solutions, visit **courseptr.com**

Visit our corporate website at **cengage.com**

Printed in the United States of America
1 2 3 4 5 6 7 12 11 10

ACKNOWLEDGMENTS

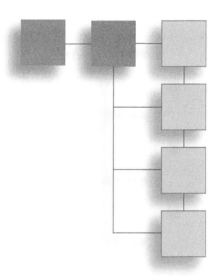

First and foremost, we would like to acknowledge the support of our families during this endeavor. Chuck Easttom's wife Misty and son A.J. have been supportive, as they always are when he is writing. Likewise, Detective Taylor's wife Vilma has been incredibly supportive as he worked on his first book. We would also like to thank the editorial staff that worked so hard on this book. Editors often go unnoticed, but they work as hard as the authors do on any book. Without them, no book could be a success.

About the Authors

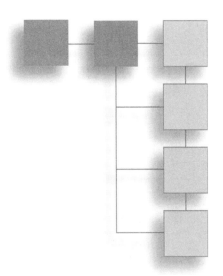

Chuck Easttom has 16+ years in the IT industry and has been an expert witness on several computer-related cases. He is the author of 10 other computer-science books, including two textbooks on computer security. He was also one of the subject-matter experts who helped to create CompTIA's Security+ certification test. He has been a frequent guest speaker on computer security at various computer groups and campuses, including Harvard and Columbia. He holds more than a dozen computer-industry certifications.

Jeff Taylor, a McKinney, Texas, police detective, began his law-enforcement career in 1982. He is currently assigned to the Criminal Investigations unit, where he specializes in white-collar crimes. In 2003, Detective Taylor became certified in the recovery of computer-forensic evidence. He uses various computer-software systems, including EnCase, Helix, and I-Look. He has received training and certifications from the FBI, Cyber Evidence Inc., the National White Collar Crime Center, and the High Intensity Drug Trafficking Area (HIDTA) task force. Detective Taylor is on the instructor staff at the Collin County Law Enforcement Academy, where he teaches a course on electronic crime scene investigations.

Contents

Introduction

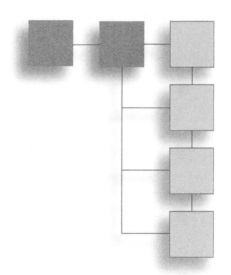

One can hardly open a newspaper or read news online without seeing another story about a computer-related crime. We are awash in identity theft, online child predators, and even cyber espionage. It seems overwhelming. And people in many different professions find themselves involved with computer-crime investigations. Obviously, law-enforcement officers are involved, but so are network administrators, technical-support personnel, and attorneys.

This book is for all of those groups, though each group will find different portions of the book of more interest than others. For example, we will discuss the various laws related to computer crime. That is important information that technical people probably know little about, and of which even law-enforcement officers may need more in-depth knowledge, but in which most attorneys would already be well versed. If any aspect of your work brings you into contact with computer crime, then this book is for you. It is also appropriate for college courses on computer crime.

Part 1, "Computer Crime," is a broad introduction to the field of computer crime. We will discuss the history of computer crime, basic criminal techniques, and the relevant laws.

In Part 2, "Computer Forensics," we walk you through the essentials of computer forensics. This section is a good introduction to forensic techniques and includes a great deal of specifics.

In Part 3, "Litigation," we discuss litigation related to computer crime. We will explore depositions, expert reports, trials, and even how one can select an appropriate expert witness.

Part 4, "Computer Crime and Individuals," is appropriate for almost anyone. It covers computer crimes that affect individuals. It discusses how you can ameliorate the dangers and how you should react if you become the victim of such a crime, and gives tips for investigating these specific crimes.

Part 5, "Techniques," is unique. In this part, we introduce you to the specific techniques that hackers use and even show you some of the tricks used to infiltrate computer systems. It is our belief that this knowledge will help you defend against such attacks. This part also includes a discussion of communication techniques used by computer criminals, with an overview of encryption, steganography, and even hacker slang language.

After you read this book, you should have a solid working knowledge of computer crimes and investigations. This book is meant to serve as your gateway into the world of investigating computer crimes.

PART 1

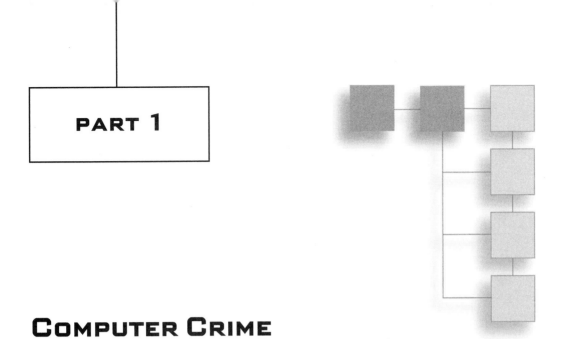

COMPUTER CRIME

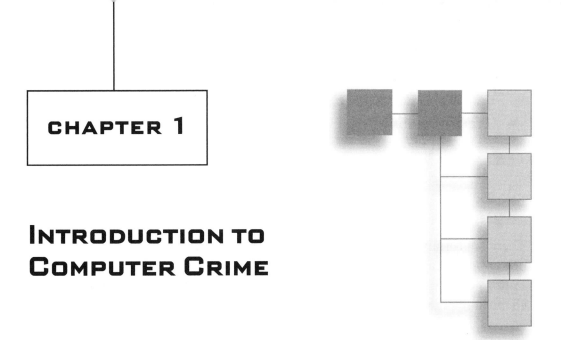

CHAPTER 1

INTRODUCTION TO COMPUTER CRIME

Introduction

One need not be a law-enforcement officer or a computer-security expert to realize that computer crime is on the rise. These crimes range from computer-network administrators hacking into the computers of current and/or former employees[1] to major credit-card theft and fraud rings[2]. Computer crimes can also include drug trafficking, harassment, sexual exploitation of minors, and a variety of types of theft. The increase of computer crime must be a significant concern for any law-enforcement agency or for anyone responsible for security on any network.

Computer crimes will always involve some type of computer-security breach. While this may seem obvious, let me explain: Contrary to some people's belief, "computer-security breach" and "computer crime" are not synonymous. They are related concepts, but not identical ones. When computer professionals begin working with computer crime and forensics, they often make the mistake of assuming the two terms mean the same thing. Let me illustrate the differences. Most computer-security books, certification tests, and courses discuss types of security breaches. Those breaches are typically categorized as follows (or something very similar):

- Privilege escalation

- Malware (Trojan horse, virus, worm, logic bomb, rootkit, etc.)

3

- Phishing

- Social engineering

- Session hijacking

- Password cracking

- Denial of service

There are certainly other ways to categorize network-security threats; indeed, if one consults different sources, their lists might be slightly different. All categorizations of security breaches are similar, however, in that they describe the mechanism by which the attack was perpetrated. From a preventative security point of view, this is entirely appropriate. Only by realizing how the attack is perpetrated can you take steps to prevent that type of attack. Put simply, network administrators are primarily concerned with the mechanisms for perpetrating an attack so that they may prevent that attack. They are less concerned with the legal aspects of the act.

In contrast, computer crime is generally broken into categories that emphasize the specific criminal activity taking place rather than the technological process used to execute the attack. Such lists would be similar to the following:

- Identity theft

- Cyber stalking/harassment

- Unauthorized access to computer systems or data

- Fraud

- Non-access computer crimes

These are rather broad categories and encompass a great many activities. This book looks at all of these areas, how to properly investigate computer crime, and computer-forensics procedures, and we examine specific computer-related laws. We will start with a brief overview of each of these categories in this chapter. But it is important for you to begin by realizing the difference between a computer-security breach and a computer crime. The difference is that a computer-security breach is a technique for circumventing normal computer operations, whereas a computer crime is the use of a computer in the furtherance of some criminal activity. A computer crime may be committed without circumventing the normal computer operations. In other words, it is entirely possible to have a computer crime that does not involve a security breach. A great example is cyber stalking. Cyber stalking, discussed in more detail momentarily, may not involve any actual security breach, but uses computers and computer systems in the furtherance of a crime.

Identity Theft

Identity theft is the process of obtaining personal information so that the perpetrator can pretend to be someone else. This is often done in order to obtain credit in the victim's name, leaving the victim with the debt. The U.S. Department of Justice defines identity theft in this manner:

> "*Identity theft* and *identity fraud* are terms used to refer to all types of crime in which someone wrongfully obtains and uses another person's personal data in some way that involves fraud or deception, typically for economic gain."[3]

Any attempt to use another person's personal data to commit any type of fraud or deception is identity theft. While identity theft is typically done for economic gain, it can be done for other, non-financially motivated reasons. One could also use personal data to impersonate another person in order to tarnish his or her reputation or to hide one's own actions. For example, the perpetrator might order pornographic materials using another person's identity to either embarrass the victim or hide the fact that the perpetrator is accessing such materials.

It is true, however, that most incidents of identity theft involve economic motivations. The Federal Trade Commission found that in 2005, 8.3 million Americans were the victims of some form of identity theft.[4] The majority of these identity-theft incidents were financial in nature, with 3.2 million involving the misuse of existing credit accounts and 1.8 million involving the use of the victim's information to open new accounts. Even if each of these cases were relatively small in scale (under $5,000), this would still amount to billions of dollars annually in losses due to identity theft. Clearly, this is a significant problem—and it seems to be growing each year.

Obviously, for most people and for law enforcement, of greatest concern is when identity theft is used to obtain funds or credit using the victim's identity. While diminishing one's reputation can be of great concern to the victim, identity theft of that type is often a civil matter, not a criminal one. Certainly under current law one can be prosecuted simply for stealing an identity, regardless of what one does with that identity. But, as we will see in later chapters, most penalties are tied to the economic damage. That means identity theft without a direct economic motive is a relatively minor crime. Thus it is often a matter handled via civil litigation rather than criminal prosecution. That said, many current laws make the simple act of stealing another's identity to be a crime in and of itself, even if no additional theft occurs. Indeed, many states have laws that make identity theft a crime. And in 1998, the Federal government passed 18 U.S.C. 1028, also known as The Identity Theft and Assumption Deterrence Act of 1998, making identity theft a Federal crime. All this is to say there is ample legislation to allow for the investigation and prosecution of identity theft. In Part 2, "Computer Forensics," this book explores in detail the forensics operations required to successfully gather evidence for such a prosecution. Chapters 3, "United States Computer Laws Part I," and 4 "United States Computer Laws Part II," examine the specifics of various computer crime laws relevant to identity theft.

It is important to consider the means by which identity theft occurs. The first and most crucial step for the perpetrator is to gain access to personal data so that it can be used in identity theft. There are four primary ways that one can gain access to personal information:

- Phishing

- Hacking or spyware

- Unauthorized access of data

- Discarded information

Let's briefly examine each of these.

Note

Regardless of how the identity is stolen, it can have devastating effects for the victim. Victims frequently spend months—even years—trying to clear up their credit after identity theft. And in some cases, the damages go beyond credit. In the late 1990s, one of the authors of this book had his identity stolen. The perpetrator only used the identity to obtain a fake driver's license (his was suspended), but he proceeded to receive a number of speeding tickets he did not bother to pay. The victim did not become aware of the crime until he was notified that his license had been suspended for failure to pay traffic tickets. It took several months to rectify the situation, and the perpetrator was eventually arrested, prosecuted, and convicted. This story illustrates the fact that no one is immune from identity theft, and that it is a growing problem for society in general and for law-enforcement in particular.

Phishing

Phishing is any process designed to elicit personal data from the targeted victim. This is often done via e-mail. A common scenario could involve the perpetrator setting up a fake Web site that is designed to look like the Web site of a legitimate financial institution (a bank, credit-card company, etc.). Then, the perpetrator sends e-mails to as many people as possible, informing them that their account needs verification and providing them with a link they can click to log on and verify their account. When someone clicks the link, he or she is taken to the fake Web site; when the victim enters his or her login information to "verify" the account, that person provides the perpetrator with his or her username and password. The perpetrator can then log on to the victim's real account and steal funds.

Note

To combat phishing, many banks and credit-card companies are adding mechanisms whereby consumers can verify that they are visiting the real site, not a fake one.

This tactic is becoming increasingly common, and its use is likely to continue to increase. Indeed, few people have escaped receiving such e-mails. In fact while writing this chapter, this author has received several obvious phishing messages, including the one shown in Figure 1.1.

This e-mail is a rather typical example of phishing. It first attempts to alarm the recipient; Certainly, most of us would be concerned if the IRS were accusing us of not paying our taxes. This e-mail also assumes that many recipients may have unreported income, thus increasing the stress they feel upon receiving the message. And of course, the e-mail directs recipients to click on the link provided. That being said, there are several things that should be noted by anyone reading such an e-mail. First, this is not how the IRS would send out such a notice. The IRS sends notices via traditional mail and on IRS letterhead. Second, the purported tax ID in the e-mail is clearly not valid, as any business owner can attest to. Figure 1.2 shows yet another common variation; in this case, the e-mail purports to be from Yahoo!, and informs the recipient that his or her e-mail

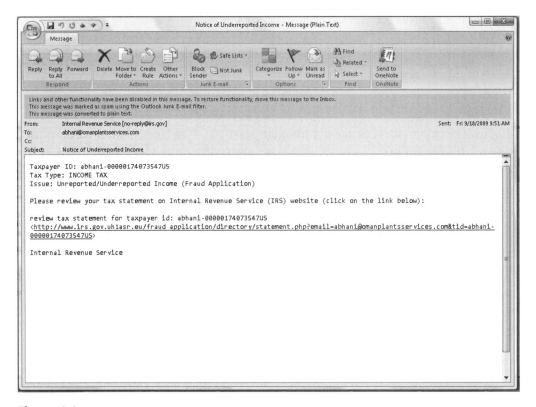

Figure 1.1
Phishing e-mail.

account may have been compromised. The recipient is then directed to click a link and confirm all of his or her information.

Note

Never follow links that have been e-mailed to you. If you receive an e-mail purporting to be from a financial institution, then either call the organization or manually enter the URL you normally use to access your account.

Phishing-related crimes can be particularly difficult to investigate for a number of reasons. First, victims are often unaware a crime has been committed until long after it has occurred. If someone steals your identity today, the financial ramifications are unlikely to come to your attention for several weeks. And as with any type of crime, the sooner after the incident that the investigation takes place, the easier it will be to collect forensics. Second, skilled identity thieves know how to hide their tracks. Moreover, they will conduct the phishing operation only for a

Dear member,

Due to recent activity, including possible unauthorized access in to your account, we will suspend any activity on your account in order to allow us to investigate this matter further. If you believe that this action may have been taken in error, or, if you feel that your account may have been tampered with, please respond to this message so that we can provide additional information and work with you to resolve this issue.

 1. Click on the link below. If nothing happens when you click on the link, copy and paste the link into the address bar of your web browser.

http://secure.yahoo.com/45499945004554-343-34-CsSersmmd-ConfirmYou+3URL/

The link will take you to our Verify Your Identity page.

2. On the Verify Your Identity page, answer ALL the questions, and click Submit. You will then be able to access your account.

If you received this notice and you are not the authorized account holder, please be aware that it is in violation of Yahoo policy to represent oneself as another Yahoo user. Such action may also be in violation of local, national, and/or international law. Yahoo is committed to assist law enforcement with any inquires related to attempts to misappropriate personal information with the intent to commit fraud or theft. Information will be provided at the request of law enforcement agencies to ensure that perpetrators are prosecuted to the fullest extent of the law.

Thank you for using Yahoo!
The Yahoo Team

Figure 1.2
Yahoo! phishing e-mail.

limited time and then shut it down. That means by the time the crime is reported and an investigation begins, it is very likely that the phishing operation has already been closed down for some time. Third, fake sites are often set up on off-shore public servers, sometimes even on an unwitting third-party server. Then, these Web sites are often dismantled as soon as the perpetrator has acquired a sufficient amount of personal data. These factors mean that investigations of this sort of crime must be initiated as soon as possible after the occurrence, and tracing the crime will require a high level of computer-forensic skill.

I do want to take a moment to elaborate on one aspect of this last scenario: when the phishing Web site is placed on a third-party server. This is not at all uncommon. The perpetrator finds a server that is not well secured, belonging to some business or even government entity. He or she then places the phishing Web site on that server and registers a domain name that routes to that server.

That means even if law enforcement is able to track down the phishing Web site, it is likely to be on a server belonging to an innocent and unwitting third party. This makes investigating such a crime even more difficult, though not impossible.

Hacking or Spyware

To some security professionals, it may seem strange to categorize hacking and spyware together, but when it comes to identity theft, both hacking and spyware have the same goal: to gain access to a computer system in order to obtain personal data. Obviously, hacking and spyware use different methods to achieve this goal, but the goal is the same.

Hacking

Hacking involves trying to compromise a system's security in order to gain unauthorized access. There are a number of ways this can be done, including finding some flaw in the operating system that can be exploited, hijacking a legitimate remote session to gain access to the target system, and others, most involving a fairly intimate knowledge of networking and operating systems. Whatever the method used, if the target system has personal data that the perpetrator wants, he or she can then get that data directly from the computer system.

Note

Hacking is an intensive task that requires a high level of technical expertise. The effort to hack into an individual home computer is usually not worth it. Typically, true hacking is only used on systems that are likely to have personal data for multiple people, such as schools, banks, hospitals, corporate databases, etc.

The term "hacking" is used quite frequently—in fact, overused. And a great many individuals call themselves hackers who are not. In the hacking world, the word "hacker" refers only to those individuals who are trying to find flaws in systems for research purposes. A "cracker" is one who attempts to exploit flaws in a system for malicious purposes. To the general public and most law-enforcement officials, however, this distinction is lost. For this reason, the terms "white-hat hacker," "gray-hat hacker," and "black-hat hacker" have evolved. A black-hat hacker is a hacker whose goal is malicious and usually illegal (what used to be called a cracker). A white-hat hacker has ethical and (usually) legal goals. For example, one who conducts penetration tests for companies would be a white-hat hacker. A gray-hat hacker is ethically in between the two, though frequently outside the law. A gray-hat hacker might attempt to find weaknesses in a system without the permission of the system's owners, but when the weaknesses are located, rather than exploit them, the gray-hat hacker notifies the system's owner. While this may seem ethical to many people, even noble to some, it is still criminal. Chapter 2, "A History of Computer Crime in America," elaborates on the history of hacking.

The most important point to understand about hacking is that it is not an easy task. Although many movies have made it seem that a hacker can gain access to highly secure systems in a matter of minutes, this simply is not true. Hacking is much like burglary: The more secure the target, the more skill and time it will take to infiltrate. And as with burglary, infiltrating secure systems requires a very high degree of skill and in-depth knowledge of many subjects. For example, a skilled burglar will need to understand locksmithing and alarm systems; similarly, a skilled hacker needs a thorough understanding of operating systems, networking, and security countermeasures. And just like with burglary, the vast majority of perpetrators are *not* highly skilled. Frankly, in the hacking community, there are vast numbers of individuals who grossly exaggerate their skill level. This does not mean that highly skilled hackers do not exist; they certainly do. But they make up a very small percentage of all hackers. What this means for law enforcement is that most perpetrators will be lower skilled—making it easier to conduct a successful investigation and prosecution.

Spyware

Spyware also has the goal of obtaining personal data directly from the target machine. Unlike hacking, however, spyware's *only* goal is to get data from the target machine. Spyware usually involves some piece of software that is loaded onto the target machine, without the knowledge of the machine's owner. That software might record any usernames and passwords entered, all keystrokes, Web sites visited, or other data. There are even spyware products that take periodic screen shots of the target computer, recording everything on the screen. Whatever the mechanisms of the spyware, the perpetrator then retrieves the data from the spyware. In some cases, this may be accomplished by the spyware periodically sending or uploading data to a particular Internet address, from which the perpetrator can access the data. If the perpetrator is particularly skilled, this address will be a third-party server belonging to someone totally unaware of the crime.

Spyware is very common for two reasons. First, it is quite easy to obtain. That's because many products made for legitimate purposes can be used as spyware. For example, products designed to monitor children's Web access, employees' productivity, or for other legal purposes can also be used as spyware. Second, it's easy to deliver. Frequently, spyware is delivered via a Trojan horse—that is, software that has some useful purpose but also delivers some malicious payload. For example, when one downloads a free game or stock ticker from the Internet, one might also be inadvertently downloading spyware. As long as people download items from the Internet, there is the potential for delivering spyware to their computers.

Both hacking and spyware can be easier to investigate than phishing. Spyware leaves a clear trace, and the data it collects must be transmitted somewhere. Similarly, hacking leaves definite traces that can be followed. That is not to say that investigating spyware or hacking is easy; it is not. But it can be less arduous than trying to track down phishing. The real issue with both spyware and hacking is the skill level of the perpetrator; in general, that skill level is likely to be low.

Unauthorized Access of Data

"Unauthorized access of data" refers to a scenario in which a person accesses data that he or she has not been given permission to access. A common scenario is when someone who has legitimate access to some particular source of data chooses either to access data he or she is *not* authorized to access or to use the data in a manner other than how he or she has been authorized. An example might be a hospital employee who accesses patient records to use the data to steal a patient's identity. Or it might be someone with no access at all who accesses records. An example of this would be a hacker breaking into a system to steal data.

How difficult it is to investigate these crimes depends a great deal on how robust the system is. Does it log the access of data and the source of that access? For example, most hospital systems record every single access of patient data, including what user accessed the data, from what terminal, and what date and time. If the system has such tracking capabilities, then investigating this sort of breach can be very simple. If the system lacks such controls, however, the problem becomes more difficult. Even so, it's still easier to investigate these types of cases than other forms of identity theft. If the perpetrator was an authorized member of the organization, then the pool of potential suspects is at least narrowed down to those employees who have access to the data that was compromised. If the perpetrator was an outside hacker, then there should be traces that can be followed to track down that individual.

This is actually a much greater problem than many people realize. Within an organization, information security is often more lax than it should be. Most people are concerned primarily with external security, so it is often rather easy to access data within an organization. One of the authors of this book has, in his consulting practice, seen networks in which sensitive data was simply placed on a shared drive with no limiting of access to it—meaning that anyone on the network could access that data. In such a case, no crime has been committed, but in other cases, employees purposefully circumvent security measures in order to access data they are not authorized to access. The most common method is to simply log in with someone else's password. That would enable the perpetrator to access any resources or data to which the person whose password was used has been granted access. Unfortunately, many people use weak passwords or, even worse, write their password down somewhere on their desk. It even happens that some users will share passwords—for example, if a sales manager is out sick but wants to check to see if a client has e-mailed her, she might call her assistant and give him her login so he can check her e-mail. This sort of behavior should be strictly prohibited by company security policies, but it still occurs. The problem is, now *two* people have that sales manager's login information; either one could use it or reveal it to someone else (accidentally or on purpose), meaning that there is now a greater chance of others using that manager's login to access data they have not been authorized to access.

Some readers might be wondering what the motive is behind such illicit data access. Why would one wish to peruse data in a company they work for? There can be several reasons, some more serious than others. One reason, which rarely leads to criminal conduct, is simple curiosity. Some people just want to know what they don't know. They are interested in finding out how much someone else gets paid, what was on someone else's performance review, or other picayune details. There are certainly more serious reasons people want to access data in a company environment, however. For example, one might wish to gather personal information such as Social Security numbers, addresses, maiden names, etc. from personnel files in order to conduct identity theft. (We discuss this in more detail later in this chapter.) Or one might retrieve a list of clients before leaving the company with the intent of stealing those clients, or sell sensitive corporate research to a competitor. (While many in the public are unaware of it, corporate espionage is actually quite common—and it is a growing problem.) Another serious motive would be stalking. If a person is stalking or harassing a co-worker, he or she may wish to access that person's files in order to gather more information. As you can see, there are a number of reasons why someone might want to access company data—some benign, some not. This is why unauthorized access of data should be taken quite seriously both by network security professionals and law enforcement.

The difficulty of investigating these crimes depends a great deal on how robust the system was. Does the system log the access of data and the source of that access? For example, most hospital systems record every single access of patient data, including what user accessed the data, from what terminal, and what date and time. If the system has such tracking capabilities, then investigating this sort of breach of data can be very simple. If the system lacks such controls, however, investigating these crimes becomes more difficult—although you still face an easier situation than with other forms of identity theft. If the perpetrator was an authorized member of the organization, then the pool of potential suspects is at least narrowed down to those employees who have access to the data that was compromised. If the perpetrator was an outside hacker, then, as mentioned, there should be traces that can be followed to track down that individual.

Discarded Information

Unfortunately, individuals as well as organizations often discard old data in a manner that makes it accessible to criminals. This can be anything from throwing old bills in the trash to a company's backup disks being discarded in a Dumpster. In either case, a person could obtain the data medium (paper, disk, drives, etc.) from the trash and then retrieve personal data. In 2004, a U.S. Army recruiting agency in the Dallas area was found to have discarded unshredded personnel records of new recruits in the Dumpster. Fortunately, the data was discovered by a reporter and not an identity thief! This episode is indicative of how such incidents occur.

From a law-enforcement perspective, investigating this sort of identity theft is of moderate difficulty. Identifying the source of the data and when it was discarded can be relatively simple, but identifying the actual perpetrator can be more difficult.

Cyber Stalking/Harassment

While cyber stalking and harassment are relatively new, real-world stalking has received a growing amount of attention in the past few years. The primary reason for this is that stalking has often been a prelude to violent acts, including sexual assault and homicide. Most states have long since passed a variety of anti-stalking laws; this movement has recently been expanded into cyberspace. This, of course, leads to the question, What exactly is cyber stalking or harassment?

Cyberstalking or harassment is using the Internet to harass or threaten another person. Or, as the U.S. Department of Justice puts it:

> "Although there is no universally accepted definition of cyber stalking, the term is used in this report to refer to the use of the Internet, e-mail, or other electronic communications devices to stalk another person. Stalking generally involves harassing or threatening behavior that an individual engages in repeatedly, such as following a person, appearing at a person's home or place of business, making harassing phone calls, leaving written messages or objects, or vandalizing a person's property. Most stalking laws require that the perpetrator make a credible threat of violence against the victim; others include threats against the victim's immediate family; and still others require only that the alleged stalker's course of conduct constitute an implied threat. While some conduct involving annoying or menacing behavior might fall short of illegal stalking, such behavior may be a prelude to stalking and violence and should be treated seriously."[5]

That means if a person utilizes the Internet to harass, threaten, or intimidate another person, then the perpetrator is guilty of cyber stalking. One obvious example of cyber stalking is the sending of threatening e-mail messages. But even the definitions of harass, threaten, or intimidate are somewhat vague. Obviously, if a person sends an e-mail to another person threatening to kill that person and provides photos of the recipient to demonstrate that the sender is familiar with the target's appearance and address, that would clearly be cyber stalking. But what about a situation in which a person is upset with a product and e-mails a harshly worded message to an executive at the product's manufacturer? If the e-mail has a vague threat, such as "You will get what you deserve," is that cyber stalking? This is not an easy question to answer, and no single answer applies to all jurisdictions and all situations. What constitutes threatening, harassing, or intimidating can vary a great deal from jurisdiction to jurisdiction. But a general guideline is that that if the e-mail's (or instant message's, newsgroup posting's, etc.) content would be considered threatening in normal speech, then it will probably be considered a threat if sent electronically.

The other element of a threat is viability—is the threat credible? On the Internet, people are frequently more vocal and often more hostile than they are in other venues. That means a law-enforcement officer will have to, to some extent, differentiate between someone simply spouting off or venting versus someone making a real, serious threat. So the question becomes, how do you determine whether to take a threat seriously? The key is to look for four factors:

- **Credibility.** This is rather easy to determine. For a threat to be credible, there must be some reasonable expectation that it could be carried out. For example, suppose a woman in Nebraska is on an Internet discussion board and receives a general threat from another user living in Bangkok in the course of a heated debate. In this scenario, the sender very likely has no idea where the recipient lives. Indeed, since many people use screen names on the Internet, the sender may not even know the recipient's real name, gender, age, or appearance. That means this threat has a very low level of credibility. If, however, the woman in Nebraska receives a threat from the user in Bangkok accompanied with personal information such as her address, place of work, or a photo, that is a very credible threat.

- **Frequency.** Unfortunately, people often make ill-advised comments on the Internet. Often, however, a single hostile comment is just a person reacting too emotionally and too quickly on the Internet. For this reason, this type of comment made in a chat room or on a bulletin board is less of a concern than a pattern of threats over a period of time. Frequently, stalkers escalate their comments and threats over time, gradually building up to point where they will act violently. While there certainly may be cases in which a single threat warrants investigation, as a general rule, isolated threats are of less concern than a pattern of harassment and threats.

- **Specificity.** Specificity refers to how specific the perpetrator is regarding the nature of the threat, the target of the threat, and the means of executing the threat. Of course, it is very important for law-enforcement officers to realize that real threats can sometimes be vague. Put another way, real threats won't always be specific. But specific threats are usually real. As an example, someone receiving an e-mail saying "You will pay for that" is less of a concern than an e-mail containing a specific threat of a very specific type of violence, such as "I will wait for you after work and shoot you in the head with my 9mm," along with a photo of the recipient leaving work. (Note that the photo also makes it very credible.) This threat is very specific and should be of much greater concern to law enforcement.

- **Intensity.** This refers to the general tone of the communications, the nature of the language, and the intensity of the threat. Graphic and particularly violent threats should always be taken very seriously by law enforcement. Often, when someone is simply venting or reacting emotionally he or she may make statements that could be considered threatening—but in these cases, most people make low-intensity statements, such as threatening to beat someone up. Threats such as these are of less concern than, say, a threat to dismember someone. This is because normal, non-violent people, can lose their temper and want to punch someone in the nose. But normal, non-violent people don't usually lose their temper and want to cut someone into pieces with a chainsaw. Anytime a threat raised to a level that is beyond what a reasonable person might say, even in a hostile situation, the threat becomes of greater concern.

Now, all four of these criteria need not be met in order for a cyber threat to be considered viable. Law-enforcement officers must always rely on their own judgment, and should always err on the side of caution. A particular officer may feel a given threat is very serious even if several of these criteria are not met. That officer should then treat the threat as a serious concern. And if one or more of these criteria *are* present, the officer should always treat the matter seriously, regardless of his or her personal inclinations. A credible, frequent, specific, and intense threat is very often a prelude to real-world violence.

Other examples of cyber stalking can be less clear. If you request that someone quit e-mailing you, yet they continue to do so, is that a crime? Unfortunately, there is no clear answer on that issue. The truth is, it may or may not be considered a crime, depending on such factors as the content of the e-mails, the frequency, the prior relationship between you and the sender, as well as your jurisdiction. It may be necessary for the recipient in this case to simply add that sender's e-mail address to his or her blocked list.

Real Cyber-Stalking Cases

The following real-world cases illustrate the problem of cyber stalking. Examining the facts in these cases might help you to get an idea of what legally constitutes cyber stalking:

- **Case 1:** An honors graduate from the University of San Diego terrorized five female university students over the Internet for more than a year. The victims received hundreds of violent and threatening e-mails, sometimes four or five a day. The graduate student, who has entered a guilty plea and faces up to six years in prison, told police he committed the crimes because he thought the women were laughing at him and causing others to ridicule him. In fact, the victims had never met.

- **Case 2:** A man in South Carolina allegedly fixated on news anchors at the WRAL TV station. He sent a large number of e-mails to the news anchors. Those e-mails contained sexually explicit material as well as references to cross burnings. The case was investigated by the South Carolina Bureau of Investigation.

- **Case 3:** Robert James Murphy was the first person charged under Federal law for cyber stalking. He was accused of violating Title 47 of U.S. Code 223, which prohibits the use of telecommunications to annoy, abuse, threaten, or harass anyone. Mr. Murphy was accused sending sexually explicit messages and photographs to his ex-girlfriend. This activity continued for a period of years. Mr. Murphy was charged and eventually pled guilty to two counts of cyber stalking

Of even more concern are cases where the cyber stalking involves minors. Pedophiles now use the Internet extensively to interact with minors and, in many cases, arrange in-person meetings with children. This must be a significant concern for all parents, law-enforcement officials, and computer-security professionals. Often, pedophiles use chat rooms, online discussion boards, and various other Internet media to meet with children. The discussions often turn more sexually explicit and eventually lead to an attempt to meet in person. Fortunately, this sort of activity is relatively easy to investigate. The pedophile normally wishes to continue communication with the victim and to escalate communication. This makes tracking and often capturing the pedophile an easier task once law enforcement becomes involved. The problem is that for law enforcement to become involved, the parents of the victim must first become aware of the situation; then, they must report the situation. Unfortunately, this sometimes occurs only after the online stalking has escalated to real-world sexual molestation.

There have been a number of well-publicized sting operations whose purpose has been to catch online predators by having adults (sometimes law-enforcement officers, sometimes not) pose as minors online and wait for a pedophile to approach them and attempt to engage in sexually explicit conversations. These attempts have been quite controversial. Given the nature of the activities, however, it seems unlikely that a non-pedophile adult could accidentally or mistakenly become involved in explicit sexual discussions with a minor. It is even less likely that a non-pedophile adult would attempt to meet in the physical world with a person they believed to be a minor. It would certainly seem that these programs, if conducted properly, can be an invaluable tool in combating online predators.

Unauthorized Access to Computer Systems or Data

We touched briefly on this area of computer crime in relation to identity theft. In the broader class of computer crimes, however, unauthorized access to computer systems or data can be for purposes other than identity theft. For example, the perpetrator might wish to steal confidential corporate data, sensitive financial documents, or other data. This information could be used to lure customers away from a competitor, released in order to damage a company's stock, or used for blackmail. In any case, the common factor is that the perpetrator is either not authorized to access the data or is not authorized to use the data in the manner in which he or she is using it.

The methods are similar regardless of the purpose of the unauthorized access. It can be executed via hacking or spyware, by employees accessing data, or through discarded data media. In particular, employee data theft is a significant problem, the primary reason being that is more difficult to block employees from accessing data. It is also sometimes difficult to differentiate between authorized access and unauthorized.

Fraud

Fraud is a broad category of crime that can encompass many different activities. A few of the more common Internet-based frauds include the following:

- Investment offers

- Auction fraud

- Check/money-order fraud

- Data piracy

We will briefly examine these classes of computer fraud here.

Investment Offers

Being presented with unsolicited investment offers is neither a new phenomenon nor necessarily a criminal activity. Even some legitimate stockbrokers make their living by "cold calling"—the process of simply calling people (perhaps from the phone book or some list of likely investors) and trying to get them to invest in a specific stock. But although this practice is sometimes employed by legitimate stock brokers, it should be noted that it is a very popular approach with people perpetrating fraud. The concept is often a "pump and dump": The perpetrators buy a significant amount of a very low-price, low-value stock. Then they use cold calling to increase the demand for the stock and thus drive the price up. Sometimes, they also give fake tips, indicating the company is about to secure a major government contract or a patent, or to release a ground-breaking new product. When the stock has been driven up to an artificial level, the perpetrators sell their stock; when the company fails to produce the indicated windfall (contract, patent, or product), the stock price then returns to its original level—and sometimes lower. This is only one example of an investment fraud, but it illustrates the problem.

Computers and the Internet have not changed the basic process of these fraud schemes; they have simply made them easier to perpetrate. They key to Internet-based fraud of this kind is, instead of cold-calling via the phone, to send an enticing e-mail to as many recipients as possible. Of course, the perpetrator realizes that most people will not respond to the e-mail enticement, but if even $1/10^{th}$ of 1 percent do, and the perpetrator sends out a million e-mails, he or she can still pull in a significant amount of money. This is one reason why e-mail spam is such a problem: So much of the spam one receives is actually part of some fraud scheme.

One of the more common schemes involves sending out an e-mail that suggests that you can make a large sum of money with a very minimal investment on your part. It may be a processing fee you must submit in order to receive some lottery winnings, or perhaps legal fees in order to receive some inheritance. Perhaps the most famous of these schemes has been the Nigerian Fraud. In this scenario, an e-mail is sent to a large number of random e-mail addresses. Each e-mail contains a message purporting to be from a relative of some deceased Nigerian doctor or government official, always of significant social standing. (It's more likely to convince victims that the arrangement is legitimate if it seems to involve people of social standing.) The offer goes like this: A person has a sum of money he wishes to transfer out of his country, and for security reasons, he cannot use normal channels. He wishes to use your bank account to "park" the funds temporarily. If you will allow him access to your account, you will receive a hefty fee. If you do agree to this arrangement, you will receive, via normal mail, a variety of very official-looking documents—enough to convince most casual observers that the arrangement is legitimate. You will then be asked to advance some money to cover items such as taxes and wire fees. Should you actually send any money, however, you will lose it—and you will never hear from these individuals again. The U.S. FBI has a bulletin issued detailing this particular fraud scheme.[6]

There are numerous variations on Internet fraud. One common example is for the victim to receive an e-mail purporting to be from a notable person in a foreign country. That person needs the recipient's help in transferring a large sum of money from his country to a bank in the United States. Now, the specific mechanisms beyond this point vary. In some scenarios, the sender requires the recipient's bank-account information in order to transfer money into that account. That, of course, ends with money being transferred *out* of the victim's account. This variation is actually less common, however, because it can be difficult to get money out of an account, as more than just an account number and routing number are required. A more common approach is to tell the victim that a small fee is needed to process that transfer. The perpetrator collects the fee, and is never heard from again.

Another scheme, personally encountered by one of this book's authors, is an investment fraud scam for new businesses. If you have a startup business and you list yourself in any of the many Web sites that allow startups to seek out investors, you may receive an e-mail purporting to be from an interested angel investor. In the scenario I encountered, the perpetrator had established a Web site for an investment capital firm that was allegedly based in Great Britain, and had even gone so far as to get a post-office box (in England) for this alleged firm. There were several telltale signs that this was a fraud, however. First, the Web site was based in Nigeria. It is hard to imagine a scenario where a reputable firm in England requires its Web hosting in Nigeria. Second, the offer mentioned a specific dollar amount they wanted to invest, but did not ask to see company financial data. No legitimate investor would invest money in a company without knowing some financial details. And of course, the final sign was a request for a small sum of money to "process required paperwork." One wonders how many other struggling startup companies, less savvy regarding matters of Internet fraud, had been duped by this or a similar scheme.

These types of schemes can be somewhat difficult to investigate. Often, tracing back the e-mail is not particularly useful as an investigative tool. The e-mails are usually sent from anonymous accounts that are difficult to trace to a given individual. The key is to trace the actual documents and checks sent via traditional mail to a real-world address. Usually, this address is a post-office box, not an office or residence. That at least provides a tangible, real-world place to further the investigation.

Auction Fraud

Online auctions are quite popular, and rightfully so. It is often the case that a legitimate user can either find some hard-to-locate item at a good price or unload items he or she no longer needs. As with many legitimate business venues, however, criminals do attempt to manipulate auctions to steal from their victims. The U.S. Federal Trade Commission (FTC) lists the following four categories of online auction fraud[7]:

- Failure to send the merchandise

- Sending something of lesser value than advertised

- Failure to deliver in a timely manner

- Failure to disclose all relevant information about a product or terms of the sale

The first, failure to send the merchandise, is relatively obvious. The victim sends funds for a given item and the seller never sends the item. This is the most obvious sort of auction fraud and usually the easiest to investigate and to prosecute.

The second category, sending something of lesser value, is much more difficult to investigate or prosecute. Let's say I buy an antique book on an online auction. I believe it to be a mint-condition, first-edition, signed copy. When I receive it, however, the item is instead in somewhat rough condition, a third-edition copy, but still signed. The seller can always claim the buyer misunderstood—and if the auction notice is worded vaguely enough, that will be a plausible story. In some cases, it would also take an expert in the given product (in this example, an expert in antique books) to verify that the item did not meet the advertisement. These factors make these cases very difficult to investigate or report. They are seldom even pursued by the victims unless the amount of money involved is very large.

The last two categories are often not even reported to law enforcement and in many cases do not constitute a crime to be investigated. Failure to deliver on time is obviously not a crime, but in extreme circumstances could be a matter for civil litigation. The failure to disclose all relevant information is very similar to sending something of lesser value—and can be just as hard to investigate or prosecute.

Check/Money-Order Fraud

A variety of scams on the Internet involve exchanging a fake money order or cashier's check for real money. These fraud schemes are quite common on the popular Craigslist Web site. In the first scenario, the victim has some item for sale on Craigslist—a nice watch, perhaps. The perpetrator contacts the victim and agrees to buy the item. However, the perpetrator claims to live outside of the area, and will have to have someone come pick up the item. The person who arrives to get the item brings a cashier's check or money order that happens to be for more than the amount the item sells for. The person apologizes for the "mistake" and suggests the victim just give him or her the difference in cash. The person then leaves with the item and a sum of cash. The victim later discovers that the money order or cashier's check is fake and worth nothing.

Data Piracy

The theft of intellectual property is rampant on the Internet. For decades, pirated software has been bought, sold, traded, and disseminated online. More recently, movies have been sold over the Internet. Whether it is software, songs, or movies, the common denominator is that the perpetrator does not have a legal right to the intellectual property. And whether the person is acquiring the intellectual property for personal use, giving it to friends, or selling it, it is still a crime. Often, these cases involve a civil component; lawsuits are used to both stop the perpetrator and extract significant monetary damages.

Although most people are familiar with the concept of pirated software and illegal music downloads, there is another growing class of data piracy that is related to identity theft. In some cases, individuals steal identities—not to use them, but rather to resell them. The buyer may be an illegal alien wanting documentation for employment or could be a fugitive wanting a different identity.

Whether we are talking about music, software, or identities, there is a growing black market for stolen data. Law-enforcement agencies must learn to check the Internet for stolen data in much the same way they check pawn shops for stolen jewelry.

Non-Access Computer Crimes

Although this may sound like an odd category for computer crimes, it encompasses a number of activities that can cause damage but do not involve the perpetrator actually gaining access to the target system. The two most common types of crime in this category are denial-of-service attacks and viruses; the most similar physical-world crime would be vandalism.

A denial-of-service attack is an attempt to prevent legitimate users from being able to access a given computer resource. The most common target would be a Web site. While there are a number of methods for executing this type of attack, they all come down to the simple fact that every technology can handle only a finite load. If you overload the capacity of a given technology, it ceases to function. With a Web site, if you flood it with fake connections, it will become overloaded and unable to respond to legitimate connection attempts. This is a classic example of a denial-of-service attack. While these attacks may not directly compromise data or seek to steal personal information, they can certainly cause serious economic damages. Imagine the cost incurred if a denial-of-service attack were to take eBay offline for a period of even four hours!

Denial-of-service attacks can be very difficult to investigate because they most often are executed via unwitting third-party computers. The perpetrator uses a Trojan horse to deliver a denial-of-service program to various computers. Then, at a specified date and time, each of these programs begins to initiate a denial-of-service attack on the predefined target. The situation will often have thousands of computers attacking the target computer, and most likely none of the owners of those computer systems had anything to do with the attack or are even aware they are participants. This is referred to as a distributed denial-of-service attack.

Another common computer crime that often does not involve the perpetrator directly accessing the target system is the dissemination of a virus. While a virus is technically any piece of software that can self replicate, many viruses do far more than that, from damaging system settings to deleting files. Even viruses without a malicious payload can disrupt network traffic simply by constantly self replicating.

Cybercrime Meets the Real World

One reason law-enforcement agencies are taking a much closer look at cyber crimes is the frequency with which they become real-world crimes with real consequences in the physical world. We have already mentioned cyber stalking that has, in some cases, escalated to real-world assaults and even homicides. We also mentioned online child predators who attempt to lure minors to real-world locations in order to assault them. Let's examine a few other ways that the cyber world can be connected to physical crimes.

- In 2006, Arizona resident Heather Kane was arrested for using MySpace to attempt to solicit a hit man to kill a woman whose picture had appeared on Ms. Kane's boyfriend's MySpace page[8]. After finding a person she thought was a hit man, she met with him and gave him a $400 down payment. The individual was in fact an undercover police officer.

- In February of 2009 in the United Kingdom, Edward Richardson stabbed his wife to death because she had changed her marital status on her Facebook page from married to single.[9]

- In July of 2008, Scott Knight of Aurora, Oregon was arrested on charges that he raped a 13-year-old girl he had met through MySpace[10]. A similar case occurred in 2009, when William Cox of Kentucky was charged with raping a 13-year-old girl that he, too, met on MySpace[11].

I could literally fill several volumes with similar cases. The common element is that in these crimes, the computer was used as either an agent or a catalyst for a real-world violent crime. These cases should make clear to the reader that computer crime is not just about hacking, fraud, and property crimes. It is becoming more common for law-enforcement officers to find a computer/Internet element in traditional crimes. And I am sure most readers have heard about Craigslist's "erotic services" ads, which are in reality advertisements for prostitution.

Hate Groups, Gangs, and the Internet

Federal law-enforcement groups have long been aware of the extent that hate groups use the Internet to organize, communicate, and in some cases plan criminal activities. This area is less clear for law enforcement, however. In many cases the actual Internet communication or Web page is itself not criminal, as it is protected as free speech. But being aware of these organizations and how they utilize the Internet can be a benefit for any law-enforcement officer who must interact with these groups.

First, let's define "hate group." A hate group is any organization that has as one of its primary purposes the degradation or diminution of some other group. Even that definition is a bit broad, however; a group might actively oppose another group without seeking the latter group's diminution or degradation. For example, political parties generally oppose other political parties, but they do not usually seek to circumscribe the rights (civil, human, or political) of their opponents. Skinhead groups, however, have as one of their primary goals the reduction in rights (civil and/or human) of various groups that they deem to be inferior to Caucasians.

While writing this book, I researched hate groups on the Web. Just a cursory search revealed the following:

- Seven different Web sites claiming to be Aryan Nations

- Six different Web sites claiming to be the Ku Klux Klan

- One skinhead Web site

- Three white-power Web sites

- Three neo-Nazi Web sites

- Three Web sites advocating black superiority

- Two Web sites devoted to Hispanic superiority

For the purposes of this search, I only considered organizational Web sites. I did not consider the Web sites of individuals or of groups that simply sold merchandise oriented toward a particular hate group. These organizational Web sites allow the various groups to achieve a number of goals. The first is to simply disseminate propaganda. Most of these Web sites have articles, essays, and in some cases news that is all slanted toward the group's particular world view. The second is to allow related groups to locate each other and to establish communications. Finally, the Web sites provide a very effective way for the groups to recruit new members.

Because these Web sites are not usually used directly in planning criminal activities, they are often outside of direct criminal investigations. But if a law-enforcement agency is seeking background information on a particular hate group or hate groups in a specific area, the Web sites for the various hate groups can be very helpful tools.

An interesting phenomenon has occurred recently. Whereas hate groups have been using the Web for some time, certain gangs have recently started building their own Web sites. A few of these include the following:

- The Bandidos (http://txbandidos.com/)

- Hells Angels (http://www.hells-angels.com/index.html)

- The Mongols (http://www.mongolsmc.com/)

- The Diablos (http://www.diablosmotorcycleclub.com/home.htm)

- The Reapers (http://reapersincmc.com/)

- The Warlocks (http://www.warlocksmc.net/)

- The Sons of Silence (http://www.sonsofsilence.com/)

- The Outlaws (http://www.outlawsmc.com/)

Note

Sometimes, these Web sites are transient. It is very possible that some may not be accessible when you attempt to visit them.

As of this writing, only motorcycle gangs are using Web pages. While most major motorcycle gangs have Web sites, so far, street gangs such as the Latin Kings, Bloods, Crips, and so on do not. It is also interesting to note that while some of these organizations might object to being listed as a gang, instead referring to themselves as "motorcycle clubs," several of them proudly refer to themselves on their Web sites as "1%ers." This comes from an old saying that 99 percent of people who ride motorcycles are law-abiding citizens, and only 1 percent are members of criminal gangs.

Why do motorcycle gangs use this medium? For some time, these groups have attempted to generate positive publicity through various charity activities. The groups' Web sites are just an extension of their public relations. Some, such as the Sons of Silence, use their Web site to claim that their members are innocent of any criminal wrongdoing, that any charges or convictions are fabricated by law enforcement, and that their members have been framed. These Web sites—both for hate groups and motorcycle gangs—clearly do not detail any criminal activities and won't directly affect criminal investigations. They can, however, be an excellent starting point for a law-enforcement agency or individual officer to begin gathering background information on a particular group.

Even terrorist groups are using the Internet for a number of purposes. First, terrorist groups, like the motorcycle gangs, use the Internet as a means to spread propaganda, trying to put their own slant on any given news story. They also use the Internet to raise money, recruit, and in some cases share operational information.

Another way terrorists use the Internet is to disseminate information and training. Potential terrorists can use the Internet to find explicit instructions on bomb manufacturing, circumventing security in buildings and airports, and a variety of other nefarious tasks. This is a serious problem; extremists who may not ordinarily move beyond being merely fascinated with terrorism are actually learning concrete ways to carry out attacks. They may not even have a direct connection with a specific terrorist group. But Internet instructions coupled with Web sites extolling the views of extremist groups can provide the motivation and means for lone attacks.

The Internet is also a valuable communication tool for terrorist groups. Internet chat rooms are perfect meeting places where terrorists can communicate and plan. One can readily set up a private chat room or bulletin board; members of a terrorist group can then use public terminals to log in to that chat room and discuss plans. The terror network in the Netherlands that was responsible for the killing of filmmaker Theo Van Gogh met regularly on Yahoo! to devise and discuss their plans. This is just one example of a terrorist group utilizing the Internet to plan attacks.

The Internet's ubiquitous nature allows terrorists who are geographically separated to communicate and coordinate. Web sites enable terrorist groups to spread propaganda, raise funds, and recruit new members. And, as we have discussed, the Internet enables extremist groups to inspire lone individuals to act on their own, but in the interests of the group.

Conclusion

While this book focuses on how to investigate computer crime, how to properly extract information, and understanding computer laws, the hope is that readers will understand that even non-computer crimes might still involve computer and Internet resources. Overlooking this deprives law-enforcement officers and agencies of a very valuable investigative tool. After reading this chapter, not only should you be aware of the scope of computer crimes, you should also be aware that even if a crime is not itself a computer crime, there could be a computer or Internet element to the crime. For example, a drug dealer might use e-mail to arrange sales and purchases, a prostitute and pimp might use Craigslist to facilitate their trade, and a social-networking site can provide clues as to the motive in a violent crime.

Note that this chapter focused on basic computer crimes. It did not discuss espionage and only mentioned terrorism briefly. Both areas are growing problems, particularly computer-based espionage. Chapter 6, "Organized Crime and Cyber Terrorism," discusses those issues in detail, as well as organized crime's growing role in computer-based criminal activity—particularly identity theft.

Endnotes

[1] United States Department of Justice. "Houston Computer Administrator Sentenced to Two Years in Prison for Hacking Former Employer's Computer Network." 2009. http://www.usdoj.gov/criminal/cybercrime/duannSent.pdf

[2] United States Attorney's Office. "'Iceman,' Founder of Online Credit Card Theft Ring, Pleads Guilty to Wire Fraud Charges." http://www.usdoj.gov/criminal/cybercrime/butlerPlea.pdf

[3] The U.S. Department of Justice Identity Theft Web page. http://www.usdoj.gov/criminal/fraud/idtheft.html

[4] Federal Trade Commission. "The Identity Theft and Assumption Deterrence Act." http://www.ftc.gov/os/statutes/itada/itadact.htm

5   The U.S. Department of Justice Cyber Stalking Web page. http://www.usdoj.gov/criminal/cybercrime/cyberstalking.htm

6   Federal Bureau of Investigation. "Nigerian Fraud Summary." http://www.fbi.gov/majcases/fraud/fraudschemes.htm

7   The U.S. Federal Trade Commission. "Auction Fraud." http://www.ftc.gov/bcp/conline/pubs/online/auctions.htm

8   The Smoking Gun. "MySpace Murder Plot Foiled." http://www.thesmokinggun.com/archive/0914061myspace1.html

9   BBC. http://news.bbc.co.uk/2/hi/uk_news/england/staffordshire/7845946.stm

10   MyCrimeSpace. "Brooklyn Man Charged with Having Sex with Upstate NY Teen He Met on Facebook." http://www.mycrimespace.com/2008/07/09/oregon-myspace-rape/

11   MyCrimeSpace. http://www.mycrimespace.com/2009/02/08/ky-man-charged-with-myspace-rape-of-teen/

CHAPTER 2

A HISTORY OF COMPUTER CRIME IN AMERICA

Introduction

In any subject area, having an historical perspective is critical for truly understanding the subject matter. It is difficult to fully understand what is occurring now without knowing what occurred in the past. In this chapter, we will examine the history and development of computer crime. We will see how computer crimes have evolved over the past few decades and take a look at what crimes are occurring now. This should help provide a background of knowledge that will assist you throughout the rest of the book. First, seeing how computer crime has developed will give you a better perspective on the current status of computer crime. Second, it will give you a good idea of how computer crime has changed, and how current criminal techniques have developed. Finally, only with an historical context will you be able to see likely future trends.

Some computer historians have included vandalism to buildings that damaged computer systems as part of the history such crime. For the purposes of this book, physical damage to a computer for the sake of vandalism won't be considered. We focus instead on crimes where the computer is either the vehicle for a crime or where the data on a computer system is the target of a crime. We are not concerned with situations where computer technology did not play a central role in the crime. We also won't be considering the theft of computer equipment. In those situations, the crime is not truly a computer crime. The computer was merely an item with monetary value and is no different from jewelry, art, or any other valuable item a thief might target.

Before we delve into the history of computer crime, there are a few terms we need to clarify. The first is the term *hacker,* which we used in Chapter 1, "Introduction to Computer Crime." Many in the hacking community object to the term hacker being used in the media to denote illegal intrusions onto systems. In the hacking community, a hacker is one who experiments with a system in order to learn more about it. This has led to a variety of terms being used to clarify the individual's actual motive and activities. Let us briefly define those terms, as it will help you throughout this chapter and this book.

A *hacker* is a person who wishes to understand a given system in depth, often through reverse-engineering techniques. A *cracker* is a person who uses those techniques to intrude on systems with malicious intent. A *phreaker* is a person who is hacking or cracking phone systems. In the past two decades, it has become more common to refer to white-hat, gray-hat, and black-hat hackers. A *white-hat hacker* is not conducting illegal activities, he is merely learning about systems. A white-hat hacker may actually be performing an authorized intrusion test of a system. A *black-hat hacker* is conducting illegal activities; these are the people traditionally associated with computer crimes. This term is synonymous with cracker. Usually, when the media discusses hacking, they are actually referring to black-hat hackers. A *gray-hat hacker* may break laws, but usually without malicious intent. For example, he or she may break into a target system, and then rather than wreak havoc on the system, will notify the system administrator of the flaw in the security. This person is still committing crimes, but usually without malicious intent.

The next term we need to define is the term attack. In computer-security parlance, an *attack* is any attempt to breach a system's security. This can be an attempt to crack a password, to get into a wireless network, or to execute a denial of service, just to name a few common examples. From an investigative point of view, we are only concerned with those crimes that violate a particular law. In Chapter 3, "United States Computer Laws Part I," we will examine federal laws and in Chapter 4, "United States Computer Laws Part II," we will look at state laws. It is possible that an attack may not violate a law, although most will.

Let's also define a few network terms that will be used in this chapter and throughout the book. Now, if your background in computer networks is lacking, you may want to refer to Appendix A, "Introduction to Computer Networks," for a more comprehensive tutorial, but for now we will just define a few terms. The first of those terms is node. A *node* is any device connected to any network that has an address. Computers use numerical addresses called IP addresses. These addresses take the form of four numbers, each between 0 and 255, separated by dots, such as 192.168.1.1. A *router* is a device that allows data packets to be transmitted between various networks. (That is a simplified definition; a more thorough one is given in Appendix A, but this will do for now.) A *server* is a computer set up to respond to requests from users. For example, a Web server responds to requests from clients and gives them Web pages. A *client* is a computer that connects to a server in order to request some sort of data. A *host* is similar to a node, except that a host refers to an actual computer (be it a client or server), whereas the term node can refer to other devices such as network printers and routers.

With these few terms defined, we can move forward with our discussion of the history of computer crime.

The "Prehistory" of Computer Crime

The earliest days of computer crime, the 1960s and 1970s, were very quiet from a computer-crime perspective. The majority of incidents were actually just pranks played on computer systems at universities by bright and inquisitive students. Not only did the incidents usually cause minimal if any damage, there were actually few laws against such activities, so they literally were not crimes. The entire purpose of hacking, in those days, was simply to understand a given system far better than any manual would allow.

A major reason for there being so little computer crime during this period was a lack of widespread access to computers and networks. In these "prehistoric" days of computer crime, there was no widespread public access to networks, no Internet, and no laws regarding computer activities. In fact, the only people who had any access to computers and networks tended to be university professors, students, and researchers.

To understand the history of computer crime, one needs to understand the history of the Internet. As the Internet grew and online communications became more commonplace, so did computer-based crimes. Before there could be any networks, much less the Internet, there had to be some method of moving a data packet from point A to point B. The first paper written on packet switching was by Leonard Kleinrock at MIT in 1961. Now, this may seem a somewhat arcane topic for book on computer crime. However, computer-crime forensics frequently involves tracking down packets to their source. Whether it be tracing an e-mail used in a phishing scam, tracking down someone who has hacked into a bank server, or proving the origins of harassing e-mails, the ability to track packets is key to investigating computer crime. In later chapters, as we discuss investigative techniques, you will see specifics on those issues. In Chapter 10, "Collecting Evidence from Other Sources," we will actually show you how to track down packets. But for now, it is important that you realize the critical nature of packet switching to all Internet communications, and ultimately to solving many if not most computer crimes. Packet switching allowed the creation of networks, and eventually the Internet itself. A *packet* is basically a unit of data. Packets will have a header that defines their point of origin, their destination, and what kind of packet they are (i.e., e-mail, Web page, etc.). Once packet-switching techniques were well established, widespread networks were the next logical step. Today, the Internet is ubiquitous. It is rare to find a business that does not have a Web page or an individual who does not have an e-mail account. The Internet permeates our lives. However, this is a relatively new phenomenon. Let's briefly look at the history of the Internet and how it grew to the massive global communication network it is today.

The Internet actually began as a research project called ARPANet (ARPA was the Advanced Research Projects Agency, part of the U.S. Defense Department). In 1969, the network consisted of just four nodes: the University of Utah, the University of California at Santa Barbara, the University of California at Los Angeles, and Stanford University. Twelve years later, in 1981, the network had grown to 213 nodes, still a paltry number compared to the millions of Internet users we have today. And in those days, those 213 nodes were simply research institutions, universities, and government entities. In those early days, computer crimes were quite rare. There was no Internet to utilize, and the nascent ARPANet was only accessible to a very small group of people, all of whom were engaged in research. In 1979, CompuServe became the first commercial e-mail service. But even then, e-mail was not widely used and no one had yet thought to use it for criminal purposes. However, the advent of commercial e-mail accounts is also a critical step in the history of computer crimes. It would not be an exaggeration to say that widespread access to e-mail was the impetus behind the early growth of the Internet. While hacking into computer networks was extremely rare during this time period, the same cannot be said of hacking into phone systems. The first incident of a phone system being hacked was in the early 1970s. John Draper, a former U.S. Air Force engineer, used a whistle that generated specific tones to place free phone calls. This technique is based on the way phones once worked. During this time, phones—particularly pay phones—used a different tone for each key pressed. Simulating the tones would actually send specific commands to the phone system via the phone. Mr. Draper used his engineering knowledge of phone systems in order to exploit this feature of the phone systems.

Note

As we discuss the history of computer crime, you may notice that computer-network crimes and phone-system crimes have some overlap. This should make sense if you recall that until rather recently, most people connected to the Internet via dial-up phone connections.

Mr. Draper was known in hacking circles as "Captain Crunch." He was repeatedly arrested throughout the 1970s on charges of phone tampering. This particular case is very interesting because it highlights the state of computer-related crimes prior to the Internet. In those early days, most of the incidents involved tampering with phone systems, a process colloquially referred to as phreaking. Phreaking is really the ancestor of later hacking, and not surprisingly many of the people involved in phreaking moved on to become hackers. John Draper is one of the more famous hackers, and has since become a computer-security consultant.

The case of John Draper also illustrates the nature of real hacking. To really hack a system, you have to have a solid understanding of that system. Mr. Draper was able to compromise the phone system because of his extensive knowledge of phone systems and how they worked. In modern times, one can often find a utility on the Internet that will execute some aspect of hacking for the user. This allows novices to attempt to execute some system exploits. Such people are generally derided by the computer-hacking community and given the unflattering moniker of *script kiddie*. To truly hack a system requires a depth and breadth of system knowledge. From a law-enforcement perspective, script kiddies are usually much easier to catch because they are generally novices and make many mistakes.

In the early days of hacking, it was not uncommon for someone who had been convicted of a computer crime to later become a computer-security consultant. The reasoning was that this person clearly knew how to compromise systems and could assist in securing them. The alternative viewpoint was that this person clearly had ethical issues, as they already proved their willingness to break the law. It has also been argued that perhaps these former criminals are not the most skilled; after all, they did get caught! Arguments for or against using former criminals are becoming less relevant in recent years. There are security experts, well versed in techniques for compromising systems, who have never used their knowledge to commit crimes. Having the technical expertise coupled with integrity and trustworthiness is essential for a computer-security professional. It is no longer likely that a former computer criminal will be given a position working in computer security.

Phone phreaking became quite widespread and was very popular among people who eschewed societal norms. Infamous counterculture icon Abbie Hoffman elaborated on John Draper's phone system phreaking. Mr. Hoffman took Mr. Draper's techniques and popularized them so that people with far less skill than Mr. Draper could exploit the phone-system weakness. Mr. Hoffman began a newsletter that showed people how to compromise phone systems and make free long-distance calls. He felt that making free long-distance calls was not stealing and should not be a crime. He claimed that the minutes being used were not a real resource being stolen, but an unlimited public resource that anyone should be able to access. He wanted to make sure that the techniques for accessing that resource were widely disseminated and clear enough that even technical neophytes could execute them.

Now, some readers might be surprised to find out that detailed instructions for exploiting phone systems were widely published. It is important to realize that publishing information is not illegal, even if that information can be used for malicious purposes. There are books and magazines today that provide rather explicit instructions on hacking computer systems. The knowledge is out there and readily accessible. Freedom of the press and freedom of speech both allow a person to publish such knowledge. Keep in mind that knowledge in itself is neither good nor evil, it is just a tool. For example, a network administrator might legitimately want to learn about hacking techniques in order to secure his or her own systems. One of the authors of this book teaches a course in ethical hacking, where students learn real techniques to compromise target systems—the goal is to be able to thwart criminals. But there is always the possibility that someone might misuse the knowledge they learn. To use an analogy, it is always possible that someone would use the chemistry knowledge they learned in college to produce illegal methamphetamines, but that does not lead to a public outcry that we quit teaching chemistry in college. As we move forward through these early days of computer history, it is important to understand the roots of the hacking community in order to understand modern computer crime. Certainly not all computer crime involves the hacking community; crimes such as cyber stalking and child pornography do not require any specialized computer knowledge and need not involve hacking. It is also true that not all members of the hacking community engage in criminal behavior. However, much of computer crime is rooted in the early hacker culture. These were counterculture people; they were usually quite intelligent, but suspicious of tradition and authority. They were smart, inquisitive people who just wanted to understand how these systems worked. They had no ill intent. At worst, many of them simply wanted to prove their own intelligence by outsmarting the network administrators. Today, a significant part of the hacker community still fits this mold. Law-enforcement efforts to catch computer criminals are unlikely to be successful unless law-enforcement officers can understand this segment of society. Put another way, most hackers are not criminals, but most hackers do not trust authority. You must also remember that many, if not most, hackers do not commit computer crimes, although many computer crimes will involve, at some level, hacking. When investigating any criminal activity, it is important to understand the community in which it occurs. For example, consider gang activity. Certainly not all the people living in a gang-controlled neighborhood are members of an illegal gang. However, law enforcement's anti-gang efforts will be hampered if they do not first attain an understanding of and rapport with that community. The same is true of the hacking community.

As time progressed and access to networks became more widespread, it was inevitable that this early curiosity would eventually lead to some individuals pursuing more nefarious goals. As hackers learned more and shared what they knew, less scrupulous individuals applied those skills to criminal ends. And as hacking skills became more widespread, it was inevitable that eventually there would be criminals who possessed hacking skills.

While phone phreaking grew in popularity in the 1970s, most of the computer-related crime was about physical damage to computer systems, such as the following examples:

- 1970—At the University of Wisconsin, a bomb is detonated, killing one person and injuring three more. The explosion also destroys $16 million of computer data stored on site.

- 1970—At New York University, a group of students place fire-bombs on top of an Atomic Energy Commission computer. This incident was connected with an attempt to free a jailed Black Panther.

- 1973—In Melbourne, Australia, protestors against the United States' involvement in Vietnam shoot an American firm's computer with a double-barreled shotgun.

- 1978—At Vandenberg Air Force Base in California, a protestor destroys an unused IBM computer using various tools as a protest against the NAVSTAR satellite navigation system. The protestor was concerned that the navigation system was designed to give the U.S. a first-strike capability.

Some sources consider all of these examples to be computer crimes. However, in each case, it was the computer hardware that was damaged; data was not the specific target, nor was a computer used to execute a crime. For the purposes of this book, these crimes constitute traditional property crimes; it is incidental that the property in question happens to be computer equipment. However, these examples are useful for illustrative purposes. They clearly show incidents of people targeting computers in order to make political statements. As we will see later in this chapter, such activities have grown more common with the spread of the Internet.

The Early Days

Figure 2.1 shows a timeline of the early days of computer crime. The year 1981 was a pivotal year in the history of computer crime. That year, Ian Murphy was arrested because he and three accomplices hacked into the AT&T systems and changed the systems' internal clocks. This change may seem trivial, but it had significant repercussions. People using the phone system suddenly received late-night discounts in the afternoon, while others who waited until midnight to use the phone received larger bills. For those readers who don't recall, during this time period, long-distance charges were significant and people frequently tried to find ways to make long-distance calls cheaper, such as calling during non-peak hours. Mr. Murphy has the distinction of being the first person convicted for a computer crime. His sentence was 1,000 hours of community service and 30 months probation. In addition to being the first person convicted of a computer crime, Ian Murphy's exploit is interesting for another reason: the way in which he accomplished his mission. His ultimate goal was to disrupt the normal operations of phone systems. Frequently, the most skilled computer hackers will use relatively

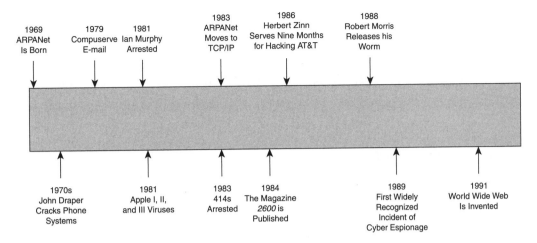

Figure 2.1
The early days of computer crime timeline.

simple techniques, but they are techniques that are based on a detailed understanding of how computer systems operate. In this case, the perpetrator realized the pivotal role the system clock played, and exploited that. This example illustrates that real hacking requires one to have a thorough knowledge of the target system. It also follows that one will be more successful at catching computer criminals if one is similarly well versed in computer hardware and software.

1981 was not only the year of the first arrest for a computer crime, it was also a pivotal year in the history of computer viruses. The first widely known viruses found "in the wild" (i.e., out in the public) were the Apple I, II, and III viruses, first discovered in 1981. These viruses targeted the Apple II operating system and spread initially in the Texas A&M University systems via pirated computer games. This incident is particularly interesting because it actually involved two crimes: The first crime was the actual release of the computer virus; the second was the fact that many victims of the virus became victims through their own criminal activity, theft of data via software piracy. It remains a fact to this day that pirated software, illegal music downloads, and illicit Web sites are hot spots for viruses and spyware. This is certainly not meant to imply that everyone who gets a virus is engaged in criminal activity themselves, of course. But like traditional crimes, when one frequents high-crime areas, one is just as likely to become a victim of a crime as a perpetrator.

The Apple viruses are also important because they illustrate a point regarding Apple products and about the goals of people who write viruses. Many Apple advocates tout the fact that viruses are quite rare in the Macintosh world. That is true today since PCs make up 90 percent of computers. It was not true in the early days, however, when Apple ruled the desktop-computer market and neither Microsoft nor Windows had never been heard of. This also should give you some insight into the mindset of virus writers, which is very similar to that of vandals and graffiti writers. There is a desire to affect the widest number of people, so virus writers tend to write their virus so that it will affect the largest number of users possible. Any platform that has a small market share is less likely to be targeted by virus writers.

In 1983, ARPANet moved to using only TCP/IP protocols for communication. This standardization paved the way for what would eventually become the Internet we know today. Without a standard protocol for communications, widespread global networks would simply not exist. The 1980s also marked a very rapid expansion of the nascent Internet. It was during this decade that the Internet first became accessible to large numbers of users. Without widespread Internet access, of course, many computer crimes would not be possible. Throughout the mid-1980s, additional nodes were being added to the Internet, including international sites such as the CERN laboratories in Europe. By 1987, there were around 10,000 hosts connected to the Internet. But the real turning point in widespread usage of the Internet came with the invention of the World Wide Web (WWW, or Web) by Tim Berners-Lee in 1991. Berners-Lee was the person who invented Web pages. Many people mistake the Internet for the Web, but while the Internet includes file transfers, e-mail, and many other activities, the World Wide Web refers specifically to Web pages that one can view. This new avenue of communication has become the focal point of Internet traffic. The ability for people to go to a specific Web address and access information and images made the Internet both desirable and accessible to the masses. Just as commercially available e-mail played a catalytic role in the growth of the Internet, so did the Web. Many would argue that without Web pages, the Internet would have never grown even close to its current size and widespread use. Unfortunately, as usage of the Internet grew, so did Internet-related crimes.

In 1983, we come to one of the earliest arrests for computer hacking. In this case, a group of teenagers, who referred to themselves as the 414s in reference to their area code (Milwaukee), were arrested by the FBI and accused of multiple incidents of breaking into computer systems. Among the systems they had broken into were the Sloan Kettering Cancer Center and the Los Alamos National Laboratories. One of the accused was given immunity from prosecution in return for cooperating with authorities, and the others received five years of probation. This case is fascinating for several reasons. First and foremost, it is one of the earliest arrests for hacking. In these early days, the laws regarding computer crime were still inadequate, and frankly most law-enforcement agencies lacked the expertise to pursue computer crimes. Second, this case is notable because of the high-profile targets the perpetrators hacked. In those days, it was common for network administrators to give little or even no thought to security measures. There had been so few incidents of hacking that even those in the IT community were not fully aware of the potential dangers. Finally, the relatively light sentence is worth noting. These individuals broke into very sensitive computer systems and risked causing a tremendous amount of damage to data, yet the criminal-justice system handled this case like a harmless, youthful prank. Unfortunately that is how early computer crimes were usually handled. The courts treated computer crimes very lightly. One can only speculate, but it seems reasonable to assume that such light sentences only encouraged more such crimes, and at the least did very little to discourage them.

This case is also very instructive for investigators. Note that the hackers left clues to their identities in the name of their group. In this case, it was their area code. It is not uncommon in these types of crimes for the perpetrator to leave clues behind. Investigators must look at all the nuances of a case to find such clues, but it is well worth the effort. It must also be noted that it is not uncommon for hackers, particularly neophyte hackers, to brag about their exploits on bulletin boards and chat rooms. Such venues can provide valuable leads.

The year 1984 can be thought of as the year the hacking community came into public light. This was the year the hacking magazine *2600* was first published. The magazine is still published on a quarterly basis and contains a great deal of useful information. As we previously pointed out, it is not a crime to publish information, even if that information might be used for nefarious purposes. The *2600* magazine is a mixture of ideological articles and hacking articles. It is not a "how to" guide to hacking, but it does provide valuable insight into the hacking community. The publication of this magazine brought the hacking community's existence and activities into public view. It would certainly be a good idea for anyone investigating computer crimes to read this magazine. While it is not a magazine specifically about computer crimes, it is an excellent source to learn the skills that can sometimes be used to perpetrate computer crimes.

In 1986, a 17-year-old New Jersey man named Herbert Zinn was accused of hacking into the AT&T computer systems. Mr. Zinn later confessed to the crime. What makes this crime interesting is that this incident took place after the passage of the Computer Fraud and Abuse Act of 1986. Mr. Zinn, operating under the screen name "Shadow Hawk," worked from his bedroom in his parents' house and stole more than 50 computer programs. He was eventually sentenced to nine months in jail. Clearly, a nine-month sentence is a very light sentence considering he admitted not only to hacking into the system, but also to actually stealing data. However, unlike earlier cases, the perpetrator did actually serve some time in jail. That is what makes this case important in the history of computer crime. We had previously seen computer criminals receive only community service and probation. Now the courts were beginning to recognize that computer crimes were indeed real crimes that warranted jail time.

We come to another interesting case in 1988. In this case, Cornell University graduate student Robert Morris launched a worm that spread to more than 6,000 computers, clogging networks with an overload of traffic. The purpose of the worm was to exploit security flaws/holes in the Unix operating system. Through its spread, it caused as much as $100 million in damages. Although the law at the time allowed for a sentence of up to five years of prison and a $250,000 fine, Mr. Morris actually received three years probation, 400 hours of community service, and $10,000 fine. As we previously noted, in the early days of computer crime, courts rarely gave out harsh sentences for computer crime. Most in the legal community still do not view computer crimes as serious criminal issues. This attitude permeated the courts, district attorneys' offices, and law-enforcement agencies.

1989 was a pivotal year in computer crime. This was the year of the first widely recognized incident of cyber espionage. Five individuals from West Germany were arrested for hacking into government and university systems and stealing data and programs. Three of the five were selling the data and software to the Soviet government. While there were undoubtedly incidents of cyber espionage prior to this, this incident was the first to become publicly known. Espionage, including cyber espionage, is difficult to document. One reason is that only the dramatic failures become public knowledge. Successful espionage never reaches the public. It is also problematic that intelligence agencies always make a policy of refusing to confirm or deny any alleged incident, while conspiracy theorists tend to blame everything on some nefarious government plot. Trying to find the truth between the two extremes is quite difficult. However, it is reasonable to assume that the use of computer systems for espionage purposes predated 1989, and undoubtedly continues today.

Also in 1989, Kevin Mitnick, a name that has become almost synonymous with hacking, was convicted of stealing software from DEC and stealing long-distance codes from MCI. His case was pivotal because he was the first person convicted under a law making interstate hacking a federal crime. He served just one year in prison, with parole requirements that he not use a computer or associate with hackers. Kevin Mitnick is perhaps the most widely known hacker. His life and exploits have been inspirational for several book and film characters. Today, Mr. Mitnick is an author and security consultant.

As you can see, the 1980s were a pivotal decade for computer crime. First and foremost, computer crimes became a lot more prevalent. Where viruses and hacking were once obscure phenomena relegated to university systems, they had now become serious threats to business networks and sensitive financial as well as government data. We also saw the courts begin to take on computer crimes, though the first sentences for such crimes were remarkably light. The 1980s also brought us the first incident of hacking in fictional media, in the movie *War Games*. This movie brought the concept of breaking into computer systems into the mainstream of public awareness.

The 1990s

Figure 2.2 shows a timeline of computer crime in the 1990s. If the 1980s were the decade of computer-crime growth, the 1990s were the decade of transition for computer crime. The 1990s marked a real change in computer crimes. The first change was on the side of the hackers. Basic hacking skills became more prevalent, and the Internet was more accessible to more people. This made attempted computer crimes more common. Also, the public began to become aware of hacking, viruses, and computer crimes. There were even fictional movies such as *Hackers* (1995) that seemed to glorify the hacking community. This popularization of hacking, combined with easy access to the Internet, led many younger people with basic computer skills to have an interest in computer hacking. At the same time, law enforcement began to take computer crime much more seriously.

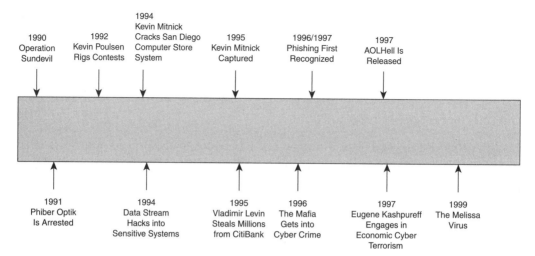

Figure 2.2
The 1990s computer crime timeline.

In 1990, the Secret Service launched "Operation Sundevil" with the express purpose of catching hackers. While this operation involved local law enforcement along with 150 Secret Service agents, raids in 15 states, and the seizure of a great deal of computer equipment, it only culminated in three arrests. Because of this, some feel the operation was a failure, or at least expended more resources than it was worth. That is a valid criticism. However, it was the first major federal operation directed at computer crime. It would take time for traditional law-enforcement officers to learn to properly investigate and combat computer based crime.

In 1991, Mark Abene, known online as "Phiber Optik," was arrested and charged under New York law with computer tampering and computer trespass in the first degree. The criminal investigation relied heavily on evidence collected by wiretaps of telephone conversations between members of a hacking group called Masters of Deception. That is one aspect of this case that makes it noteworthy: It was the first investigative use of wiretaps to record conversations and data transmissions of computer hackers. Wiretaps had long been used against various other types of criminals, most notably organized-crime figures, and now law-enforcement officials were turning this tool to computer crime. While Mark Abene was a minor at the time of the commission of his crimes, he was an adult when arrested, and he was still prosecuted and spent one year in jail. This sent a clear message that the courts were beginning to understand that, just as with other serious crimes, being a juvenile was not an excuse to commit computer crimes.

In 1992, a man named Kevin Poulsen was charged with hacking into systems to rig contests to garner himself two Porsches, $20,000 in cash, and a trip to Hawaii, among other prizes. Mr. Poulsen was already a fugitive due to hacking-related charges. He was accused of conspiring with two other hackers to take over incoming phone lines to a radio station so they could guarantee they would win the prizes. But Mr. Poulsen did not stop with rigging radio contests. He then began monitoring law enforcement and even military systems. Poulsen was arrested for charges stemming from his original contest-rigging scam, but he was also charged with the federal crime of espionage. This marked the first time in United States history that a defendant was accused of espionage for simply obtaining—rather than using or disclosing—classified information. Prior to this case, espionage charges were brought against a defendant only when he or she had disclosed, used, or transferred classified information. Mr. Poulsen spent three years in custody while awaiting trial. Eventually, the federal espionage charges were dropped and Poulsen pled guilty to computer fraud counts related to the original contest fraud. Poulsen received a 51-month sentence. This sentence was despite the fact that while awaiting trial, he had already spent more time in jail than any other hacker. He was released in June 1996 on probation terms forbidding the use of any computer for three years. This case is interesting for several reasons, the first being the espionage element. Clearly, the government was now taking very seriously the security of sensitive systems, and aggressively prosecuting those who trespass on such systems. The second interesting issue in this case was that Kevin Poulsen served more time in jail than any other computer criminal prior to this date. As we will see later in this chapter, longer sentences eventually became more commonplace, but prior to this case, most computer-crime convictions yielded only small, token sentences.

In 1994, a 16-year-old boy in the United Kingdom who used the screen name "Data Stream" broke into several sensitive systems, including Griffith Air Force Base, NASA, and the Korean Atomic Research Institute. This crime was investigated by Scotland Yard, which eventually found and arrested the perpetrator. This case is very interesting because of the sensitivity of the systems that he broke into. It also highlights the need for international cooperation in investigating computer crime. In this case, the perpetrator was in Europe and breaking into systems in North America and Asia. This case illustrates, as many other cases do, that law enforcement can only combat computer-based crime if there is clear cooperation between agencies—not just state, local, and federal, but on an international scale. It is my opinion that, particularly with regard to international cooperation, far too little has been done in this area and there is a great deal of room for improvement.

1994 was also the year that Kevin Mitnick was suspected of attempting to break into a computer at the San Diego Super Computer Center. That computer was operated by security expert Tsutomu Shimomura. Shimomura assisted the FBI in the investigation and in 1995, Mitnick was arrested. Mitnick eventually pleaded guilty to this offense along with a series of other computer-crime charges. This case is interesting because it involves a civilian computer expert assisting law-enforcement officers in investigating a computer crime. Clearly, many law-enforcement agencies are overburdened with cases and understaffed. At times, utilizing an outside consultant can be a great benefit. It is even better if the outside expert volunteers his time as a community service. However, law-enforcement officers must be careful in screening such outside experts. A standard background check would be a minimum. Beyond that, the law-enforcement agency should have a clear idea as to why this expert is volunteering his or her time. In some cases, the expert simply wishes to do some sort of service to the community. In others, the expert may feel the publicity is well worth the time. The expert may have a personal reason (i.e., they were once the victim of identity theft and now want to help catch identity thieves). Any of those are probably acceptable motives. But it is critical that the law-enforcement officials understand exactly why a particular expert is donating time. There is also always the possibility that the individual in question is either a perpetrator of computer crimes or an associate of such a perpetrator, in which case they may want to "help" the police in order to gain access to inside information.

1995 marked the capture of Vladimir Levin, a graduate of St. Petersburg Tekhnologichesky University. Mr. Levin was the alleged ring leader of an organized group of Russian hackers. This group was purported to have absconded with approximately $10 million from Citibank. Mr. Levin was arrested by Interpol at Heathrow Airport in 1995. He was eventually extradited to the United States, convicted, and sentenced to three years in prison and ordered to pay Citibank $240,015, which was his share of the theft from Citibank. This case is important because it clearly demonstrates both the need for international cooperation and the effectiveness said cooperation can have. Without international cooperation, this perpetrator would never have been captured. This case is also interesting because it involves an organized computer-based gang. As we will see later in this chapter, this has since become far more common.

The year 1995 was also the year that the FBI created its Innocent Images National Initiative (IINI). The goal of this program was to investigate and prosecute groups of online pedophiles. At that time, most of the public was still not aware of the serious dangers to children on the Internet, but pedophiles had already discovered that the Internet was a way they could traffic in child pornography. Years later, with the advent of social networks, chat rooms, and many juveniles having their own e-mail accounts, pedophiles would escalate to stalking children online.

N o t e

> It is important for all readers to understand the extent of pedophiles utilizing the Internet to perpetrate their crimes. We devote Chapter 14, "Protecting Children on the Internet," to this topic. However, it is important to note that starting in the 1990s and continuing until today, pedophiles have been making increasing use of the Internet to find victims. Chat rooms, bulletin boards, social-network sites, or any aspect of the Internet that can be used for individuals to meet is a potential hunting ground for pedophiles.

In 1996, a computer hacker associated with a white-supremacist group temporarily disabled a Massachusetts ISP and damaged part of the ISP's record-keeping system. The ISP had attempted to stop the hacker from sending out worldwide racist messages under the ISP's name. The hacker signed off with the threat, "You have yet to see true electronic terrorism. This is a promise." This particular attacked caused very little damage. However, this was clearly an incident of an ideologically based attack, and technically speaking constituted cyber terrorism. We saw as early as the 1970s radical advocates for a particular cause using damage to computer equipment to make their point. By the mid 1990s, we began to see defacing Web sites as a growing means for radicals to spread their message. By the 21st century, Web-site defacements had become almost commonplace.

The 1990s also brought much more clear-cut examples of cyber terrorism. In 1998, ethnic Tamil guerrillas swamped Sri Lankan embassies with 800 e-mails a day over a two-week period. The messages read, "We are the Internet Black Tigers and we're doing this to disrupt your communications." Intelligence authorities characterized it as the first known attack by terrorists against a country's computer systems. Obviously, one can argue what is the first real cyber terrorist attack, but this incident certainly has all the requirements. First, it was a purely

cyber attack, not merely a traditional physical attack aided by computer resources. Second, it was clearly carried out for political purposes. Finally, it was
part of an ongoing conflict.

As the 1990s continued, cyber terrorism grew. During the Kosovo conflict in
1999, NATO computers were flooded with e-mail bombs and were also targeted
with denial-of-service attacks by hackers protesting the NATO bombings. In
addition, businesses, public organizations, and academic institutions received
highly politicized virus-laden e-mails from a range of eastern European countries. Web defacements were also common. After the Chinese embassy was accidentally bombed in Belgrade, Chinese hackers posted messages such as "We
won't stop attacking until the war stops!" on U.S. government Web sites. What is
clear in both of these incidents is that the damage was relatively minor. However,
these examples were simply harbingers of what was to come.

The middle to late 1990s saw a new trend. The traditional organized-crime
groups, such as the New York Italian mafia, began to see cyberspace as a rich new
field they could plunder. By 1996, New York mafia families were involved in
"pump and dump" schemes (described in Chapter 1), using the Internet to help
inflate and sell stock. In the mid 1990s, Sovereign Equity Management Corp., a
firm based in Boca Raton, Florida, was used as a vehicle for various pump and
dump schemes. The details of the company and the process were detailed in 1996
by *Business Week*[1]. The essentials are this: The company was a front to take the
money of original investors, put it into low-performing stocks, artificially inflate
those stocks, then sell the stocks.

In the 1990s, specifically 1996 and 1997, the world became aware of a new cyber
threat: phishing. The first known incident of the term *phishing* being used involved America Online accounts, and was somewhat different from what we
think of as phishing today. Initially, AOL did not verify credit-card numbers
when you first created an account. This allowed hackers to create fake accounts
using a credit-card generator. In 1996, these accounts were being called "phish,"
and by 1997 they were actually being traded online by hackers.

The earliest media reference to phishing was made in March 1997. It was in a
quote from an AOL executive, "The scam was called 'phishing'—as in fishing for
your password, but spelled differently." The next reference to phishing in the
media came in 1997 by Ed Stansel, who in a report for the *Florida Times Union*
said, "Don't get caught by online 'phishers' angling for account information." In

this case, the word "phishing" was a play on the word "fishing." By this time, the word "phishing" took on the meaning we ascribe to it today: to attempt to get personal information, particularly financial or password data, from a target by luring them into giving it to you. As of this writing, some 13 years after the 1997 incident, it is not uncommon for a person to receive multiple phishing e-mails every single day. The Internet is replete with attempts to gather personal information in order to facilitate identity theft.

In 1997, Network Solutions Internet domain registry was hacked by a business rival. Eugene Kashpureff, owner of AlterNic, eventually pleaded guilty in this case. This case is fascinating for two reasons: First, it caused a significant amount of havoc on the Internet; second, this is a clear case of economic terrorism between corporate entities. One company used hacking to subvert the business practices of a rival. This was clearly a case of corporate warfare being waged via the Internet. It is reasonable to assume that in the future we will be seeing more of these types of cases.

1997 also brought the advent of tools being made widely available that would allow unskilled people to engage in computer crimes. Such tools existed before 1997, but it was then that they began to be used on a widespread basis. That year a utility called AOLHell was released. It was a free application that allowed virtually anyone to launch attacks on America Online (AOL). For days, AOL chat rooms were clogged with spam, and the e-mail boxes of AOL users were overwhelmed with spam. Since that year, many more tools have been released on the Internet. Now it is a trivial matter to find utilities to crack passwords, conduct denial-of-service attacks, or aid in hacking into a network.

1999 was the year of the Melissa virus. New Jersey-based programmer David Smith created this worm, which was purported to have caused as much as $500 million in damages. Mr. Smith was convicted and received five years in prison. This case is pivotal in the history of computer crime for several reasons, the first being the severe damage caused by the Melissa virus and the second being the sentence he received. This showed that courts were beginning to take computer crime more seriously and to sentence perpetrators accordingly.

The 1990s marked an explosion in computer crime. We saw attacks become far more prevalent and far more devastating. Terrorist groups and organized crime began to move into the realm of cyberspace.

The 21st Century

Figure 2.3 shows a timeline of computer crime in the 21st century. While it began in the late 1990s, it was the early part of the 21st century that saw organized crime embrace the cyber world in a significant way. The Internet has become a hotbed of organized criminal activities, and criminal groups are using cyberspace in every way conceivable. We have already mentioned online pump and dump scams, and in Chapter 1 we discussed biker gangs using the Web for public relations. We also see organized criminal groups using the Internet for money laundering and identity theft. And it does not take a very computer-savvy person to find prescription painkillers on the Internet, or to find ads for "escort services." Drug dealing and prostitution now have an Internet component. The 21st century has brought us an Internet that is replete with all manner of computer crimes.

We are now even seeing organized groups of hackers utilize their skills to provide services for other criminals[2], such as stolen identities, money laundering, and assistance with computer-based crimes. These are essentially groups of computer mercenaries.

In June of 2002, Russian authorities arrested a man they accused of being a cyber spy for the CIA. They accused him of hacking into systems of the Russian Domestic Security Service (FSB) and gathering secrets, which he then passed on to

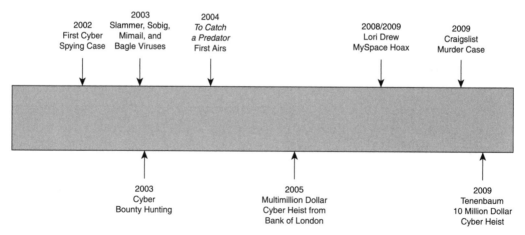

Figure 2.3
The 21st century computer crime timeline.

the CIA. While it is likely that computer-based espionage was going on long before 2002, this is one of the first publicized cases of it.

In January of 2003, the Slammer worm infected hundreds of thousands of computers in less than three hours. This made it, as of that date, the fastest-spreading worm ever. And this virus caused significant problems. It wreaked havoc on businesses worldwide, disrupting cash machines and even delaying airline flights. This virus, once on a given machine, would scan the network for any computers running the Microsoft SQL Server Desktop Engine. Then it used a flaw in that application to infect the target machine. It would continually scan every computer connected to the infected machine, seeking one with Microsoft SQL Server Desktop Engine. This virus is very interesting from an historical perspective for three reasons, the first being the speed at which it spread, and the second reason being the extensive damage it caused. The third reason was that the effect of the virus was to initiate a denial-of-service attack on any network it was installed on. This virus literally initiated a denial of service launched from inside the network. This virus clearly showed the damage viruses could cause, and should serve as a wake-up call to anyone who might still feel viruses are just an annoyance.

Another significant virus of the year 2003 was the sobig virus. This virus was particularly virulent. It utilized a multi-modal approach to spreading. This means that it used more than one mechanism to spread and infect new machines, unlike single-modal methodologies. One of its more straightforward methods of spreading was simply to copy itself to any shared drives on the network and then e-mail itself out to everyone in the infected machines' address book. This multi-modal method of spreading showed that sophisticated programming was clearly utilized in creating this virus.

The year 2003 also brought us the mimail and bagle viruses. Each of these viruses spread via e-mail, though their specific methodology was different. For example, the mimail virus was able to extract e-mail addresses not just from the infected computer's address book, but also from any document on that infected machine's hard drive. This allowed it to spread farther and faster. The bagle virus also scanned the infected hard drive looking for e-mail addresses. While neither of these was as damaging as the Slammer or sobig viruses, the fact that we can easily find four major viruses in just the year 2003 should illustrate the point that by the beginning of the 21st century, viruses had become just a point of life on the Internet.

2003 was an explosive year for computer crime. This year, in addition to some massive virus outbreaks, phishers began a new tactic. Rather than send e-mails that led their victims to fake bank Web sites, the e-mail link would instead take the user to the real bank's Web site, but add a pop-up window in front of it that had the phisher's fake logon screen. This tactic demonstrates an escalation in both the technical sophistication and the creativity of phishers.

2003 brought us yet another interesting chapter in the history of computer crime. This was the year Microsoft began announcing "bounties" for aid in capturing hackers, virus writers, and various other computer criminals. So far, there is no indication that cyber bounty hunting has been very successful, but it was an interesting way to combat computer crime. It remains to be seen if free-lance "cyber bounty hunters" will be useful in tracking down computer criminals, in much the same way bounty hunters of the Old West helped to capture various outlaws of their time.

In 2004, the general public became aware of online predators. While many in law enforcement were aware of the problem, and the FBI had had a task force in place since 1995, many in the public did not realize this new threat. The *Dateline NBC* program *To Catch a Predator* first aired in 2004. A great deal of controversy surrounded this program, and some have accused its producers of having a conflict of interest and even entrapment. But the fact remains that, whatever one thinks of the program itself, it made parents around the United States and even the world keenly aware of the very real dangers of pedophiles on the Internet. The program continued until 2007, and through its three years on the air allowed the general public to see exactly how online predators operate and how they lure children. For that reason, this program earns its place in the history of computer crime.

In 2005, hackers attempted to transfer $420 million from a bank in London[3]. This would have been the largest electronic heist in history. What makes this case most interesting is that police were able to stop the theft. The perpetrators had managed to get keyloggers on the computers of bank employees, and thus gain usernames and passwords, allowing them to access bank systems. A *keylogger* is a program that resides on a computer and simply records key strokes. That data is then either retrieved directly by the perpetrator, or the keylogger can be configured to automatically send the data to some predetermined IP address. In a typical scheme, the culprits will mask the keylogger in some other software, thus creating a Trojan horse. A *Trojan horse* is software that appears to have some useful purpose but really delivers some malicious payload. When users download what they believe is a useful program or utility, the keylogger is also delivered. The people committing this crime have already established an IP address to send the data to. Often, this is an unsecure server belonging to some unsuspecting third party that has been hacked and subverted for this purpose. Then, as the data comes streaming into the server, the person responsible for creating the keylogger can scan the data for useful information. Spyware is a growing problem on the Internet. It is becoming one of the most serious threats to computer security. This case illustrates just how damaging spyware can be.

2008 brought us the now infamous case of Lori Drew, the mother who set up a fake MySpace page in order to taunt a rival of her teenage daughter. Federal prosecutors attempted to prosecute Mrs. Drew under the Federal Computer Fraud and Abuse Statute. That statute does not cover cyber bullying, but prosecutors claimed that since Mrs. Drew used a fake identity on MySpace, she was fraudulently accessing the MySpace network. In September of 2009, U.S. District Judge George Wu dismissed the case. What made this particular case such a focus of public attention was that the target of the MySpace hoax, teenager Megan Meier, committed suicide in response to things Lori Drew posted on the fake MySpace account. Law-enforcement officials clearly wanted to hold someone accountable. While most people familiar with the case find Mrs. Drew's activities deplorable, this case shows the folly of trying to stretch existing laws into areas they are not intended for. Had the prosecutors prevailed, this would have set a precedent making it illegal to lie on a social network. I would suspect that a great many people exaggerate or outright lie about themselves on the Internet. It is impractical to attempt to make self aggrandizement and exaggeration a federal crime.

In 2009, Brian Hurt used Craigslist to locate a prostitute to come to his residence. He then subsequently shot the prostitute. This case brought to light the various dangers of advertising on Craigslist. Regular posters on that Web site have long been aware that many ads are actually part of some fraud scheme, and that the "erotic services" section was simply a euphemism for prostitution. But the link between Craigslist advertising and murder brought public scrutiny to the Web site.

In 2009, an Israeli hacker named Ehud Tenenbaum[4] was suspected of stealing approximately $10 million from banks in the United States. The shocking part of this case is that Mr. Tenenbaum had been arrested in Canada for stealing

$1.5 million in 2008. This case shows that the criminal-justice community still does not effectively deal with computer crime. It also shows that computer crime is just as real and just as damaging as traditional crime. Certainly Mr. Tenenbaum's thefts exceeded that of most armed bank robbers.

2009 was also an important year in the history of computer crime due to the guilty plea and subsequent conviction of Albert Gonzales. Mr. Gonzales, of Miami, Florida, was accused of stealing credit-card numbers from a wide array of retailers, including Office Max, The Sports Authority, Boston Market, and Barnes and Noble. Mr. Gonzales pleaded guilty to a total of 19 federal crimes including conspiracy, computer fraud, wire fraud, access device fraud, and aggravated identity theft[5]. He also pleaded guilty to a New York state charge of conspiracy to commit wire fraud for hacking into Dave and Busters. As of this writing, sentencing is still pending, but Mr. Gonzales faces up to 25 years in prison. What makes this case interesting are two facts. The first is the very significant sentence he seems likely to receive. This is a far cry from the minor penalties handed out by courts in the 1980s. It is also interesting because Mr. Gonzales' crimes continued for quite some time while he lived a lavish lifestyle, spending more than $2.8 million in stolen funds. This case makes it abundantly clear that computer crime is a very serious matter, and it shows that courts are taking it quite seriously in the 21st century.

Modern Attacks

We have already made the point that not all hacking involves criminal activity, and not all computer-related criminal activity involves hacking. However, it is important that you have a good understanding of what types of attacks are used today to compromise systems. In Chapter 1 we identified types of security threats and types of computer crimes. We focused, in that chapter, on describing the types of crimes. In this chapter, you have seen a history of computer crime. In many cases, those crimes utilized one or more types of security breaches. In order to give you a fuller understanding of these computer crimes, we will now discuss the various areas of computer security breach and how they are executed. These areas include the following:

- Privilege escalation

- Malware (Trojan horse, virus, worm, logic bomb, rootkit, etc.)

- Phishing

- Social engineering

- Session hijacking

- Password cracking

- Denial of service

This book's focus is on how to investigate computer crimes, so as we discuss various types of security breaches, we will touch on countermeasures to those security breaches, but only briefly. In Chapter 3, when we discuss computer-related laws, we will tie those laws to specific computer attacks mentioned here.

Privilege Escalation

Privilege escalation is a relatively simple process. One obtains access to a system with fewer rights than one wants, and then tries to force escalation of rights. This can be done by legitimate users of a system or outside attackers. In the former case, perhaps the user has general user rights and attempts to escalate those to administrative rights. This can be done for any number of reasons, ranging from idle curiosity to corporate espionage. In the latter case, an intruder finds access to an account that has minimal privileges and then attempts to escalate privileges to a point at which he or she can access sensitive files. This is a common method of intrusion because accounts with fewer privileges (such as guest accounts) are often less secure and easier to compromise. The goal is to take an account that has a certain set of privileges and give it access to other resources it currently cannot access. The most common scenario is an attempt to escalate to administrator-level privileges. However, in some cases, the goal is more ambitious. The goal is to achieve system level privileges. That means having the same access and privileges that the operating system itself has.

There are two common types of privilege escalation:

- *Vertical privilege escalation* is a scenario in which an account with a lower-privilege user attempts to access resources reserved for higher privileges. This is often referred to as privilege elevation.

- *Horizontal privilege escalation* is a scenario in which an account is used to access resources reserved for a different account of the same level. For example, one user attempts to access another user's documents.

The mechanism by which this works is usually based on exploiting some flaw in the system, often the operating system itself. While the particulars of a given method of privilege escalation are specific to that attack, there are two underlying concepts that all privilege-escalation attacks depend on. The first underlying concept is simply that any given system must allow for users of various levels of privilege. That means that within the system itself, there is some mechanism for determining what level of privilege a user should have when the user logs in, and granting him or her only that level of privilege. The second concept is that systems, particularly operating systems, are quite complex and there are sometimes flaws, loopholes, and alternative ways to accomplish some goal. Privilege escalation depends on using that second fact in order to trick the system into giving you more or different privileges than you have been assigned.

From a security point of view, the countermeasures to privilege escalation are twofold. The first is to ensure the system in question is updated, patched, and as secure as possible. When vendors discover such flaws, they usually release some patch for that vulnerability. The second countermeasure is to ensure all access is logged. This allows you to at least be aware if someone is using privilege escalation. For example, if a user from a given IP is suddenly logged accessing resources that he or she should not have privileges for, you likely have found an incident of privilege escalation.

Privilege escalation is one of the most common hacking techniques. The reason for this is that it is often relatively easy to obtain access to a system under a less-secure login such as the Windows guest login account. Once an intruder has gained access, he or she will then seek to escalate that account's privileges.

This leads us to the law-enforcement perspective on privilege escalation. The primary evidence in a case involving privilege escalation is going to come from system logs. Those logs should clearly record what entity is accessing what resource at what time and from what machine/IP address. Beginning in Chapter 7, "Observing, Collecting, Documenting, and Storing Electronic Evidence," we will discuss the details of computer forensics, so you will learn how to properly gather and handle such logs. For now, it is important that you realize that those logs are the primary evidence for privilege escalation as well as many other computer crimes.

Malware

Malware is a generic term for any software that effects, or attempts to effect, some malicious purpose. This encompasses a variety of specific software types, as you'll see in the following sections.

Viruses

The most well-known malware is the virus. Technically speaking, a *virus* is any software that self replicates. That means that a virus need not actually cause direct harm to a target machine in order to be classified as a virus. It merely has to self replicate. Now, there are cases where simply the massive amount of copying a virus does cause problems for networks. In 2000, the I Love You virus copied itself to everyone in one's address book. When this virus was released on a corporate network, it could start a sort of feedback loop. After one user opened the virus, it copied itself to everyone in his or her address book. Then, if one of those people opened the virus, it would again copy itself to everyone in that address book, likely including the original person who first opened the virus. Even on a small network, this quickly led to thousands of messages, slowing down the network and flooding the mail server. While self replication is the hallmark of a virus, many viruses also seek to cause some direct damage such as deleting some file or files, disabling some system security setting, or some other malicious goal.

Viruses are often sent in e-mails. The perpetrator attempts to word the e-mail in such a manner as to entice the victim to open an attachment in the e-mail. If the victim does so, the virus is launched and the victim's computer is infected. Figure 2.4 shows an example of a typical virus e-mail.

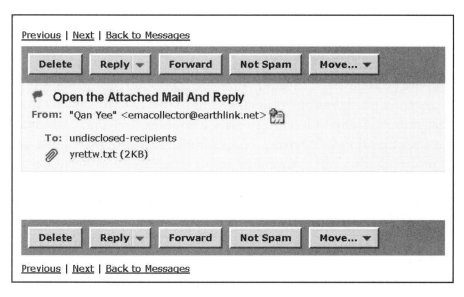

Figure 2.4
Example of a virus e-mail.

From a security point of view, the countermeasure for viruses is to run updated and properly configured antivirus software. It is also important to educate end users on the need to be very cautious about attachments. From a law-enforcement perspective, the investigation of a crime involving spyware would involve a forensic scan of the computer hard drive looking for the virus itself. Unfortunately, it will usually be the case that the virus has been sent from one victim's machine to another, and that tracing it back to the original machine is an onerous task.

Worms

The computer worm is related to a virus. Some experts consider the worm separate from a virus, while others (including this author) consider it a special case of a virus. A *worm* is essentially a virus that can replicate without direct human intervention. With a virus, the user must take some action, such as opening an e-mail attachment, to spread the virus. If the user does not take the action, then the virus is not launched and does not spread. A worm does not require this element. Once on a computer, it will seek out methods to copy itself. Those methods include looking for shared network drives to copy itself to, seeking open ports on nearby machines to attempt to send itself to, and other methods as well. Once on the target machine, the worm will usually have some additional malicious purpose.

Spyware

Spyware is becoming one of the most pervasive computer-security threats. At one time, the virus was the most common threat to home and business computer users, but spyware is quickly supplanting the virus in this regard. *Spyware* is any software that monitors any aspect of a user's computer use. There are many perfectly legal applications for spyware—for example, software that allows parents to monitor their children's computer and Internet usage or software that allows an employer to monitor employee computer usage. Because there are viable, in fact common, legal uses for spyware, spyware is very easy to acquire. Once spyware is on a target machine, there exist a variety of ways for the information gathered to get to the person who placed the spyware. In some cases, a hidden file that records data is kept on the target machine, and must be retrieved at some later time/date. In other cases, the spyware periodically sends data to some predetermined IP address or e-mail address, usually in the background without the user being aware.

This spyware can be used to collect personal information, bank passwords, sensitive financial or medical information, or any other information that is accessed by the computer that has the spyware on it. From a security point of view, the countermeasure for spyware is to run updated and properly configured antivirus/anti-spyware software. From a law-enforcement perspective, the investigation of a crime involving spyware would involve a forensic scan of the computer hard drive looking for the spyware itself. Once you have located the spyware, the next step will be to find out how the attacker got information from the machine once the spyware had collected it. This will allow you to track down the attacker.

The Trojan Horse

Trojan horses are an important classification of malware. A Trojan horse gets its name from the historical Trojan horse. Like the historical Trojan horse, a computer Trojan horse appears to be a legitimate item the recipient wants. It may appear to be some useful utility or game. Once the user loads it on the machine, the Trojan horse will then either deliver a second program, such as a virus or worm, or simply take some malicious action itself. Trojan horses are a very common way to deliver spyware to target machines. What makes them so insidious is that they are purposefully installed on the user's machine by the user himself of herself. This allows them to frequently circumvent system security measures.

Since Trojan horses are usually installed by users themselves, the security countermeasure for this attack is to prevent downloads and installations by end users. From a law-enforcement perspective, the investigation of a crime involving a Trojan horse would involve a forensic scan of the computer hard drive looking for the Trojan horse itself.

Logic Bomb

A *logic bomb* is a program that lies dormant until a specific logical criterion is met. That criterion could be a certain date, a certain user logging onto the system, or a certain threshold being reached (a certain number of files or number of users being reached). A logic bomb could also be programmed to wait for a certain message from the perpetrator. For example, it could periodically check a given IP address for some condition or the lack of the condition. When this condition occurs, the logic bomb activates and executes its code.

Certain malware programs contain logic bombs that execute their payload when a given condition is met. This makes logic bombs very insidious. They can lie dormant for a period of time before executing. The security countermeasure is the same as with viruses and Trojan horses: that is, to keep antivirus software running and to educate end users about downloads.

A good example of a logic bomb is the case of Michael Lauffenburger. In June 1992, Mr. Lauffenburger, who was an employee of defense contractor General Dynamics, was arrested for inserting a logic bomb into the company's systems. This logic bomb was designed to delete sensitive project data. Mr. Lauffenburger hoped the cause of the missing data would go unnoticed, and he could return as a consultant to "fix" the problem. Fortunately, another employee of General Dynamics uncovered the logic bomb before it was triggered, and a thorough investigation ensued. Lauffenburger was charged with computer tampering and attempted fraud. While statutes allowed for fines of up to $500,000, as well as incarceration, he was only fined $5,000 and given no jail time.

Another, more recent example occurred at the mortgage company Fannie Mae. On October 29, 2008, a logic bomb was discovered in the company's systems. This logic bomb had been planted by a former contractor, Rajendrasinh Makwana, who had been terminated. The bomb was set to activate on January 31, 2009, and completely wipe all of the company's servers. Makwana was indicted in a Maryland court on January 27, 2009 for unauthorized computer access. As of this writing, the case has not been resolved. What is most interesting about this case is that Mr. Makwana planted the logic bomb between the time he was terminated and the time the network administrators cancelled his network access. This illustrates the importance of ensuring that the accounts of former employees are terminated immediately when their employment is terminated. That applies whether it is an involuntary termination, retirement, or voluntary quit.

Logic bombs involve some skill at programming. This can be an important fact when investigating such crimes. You should begin by focusing on those people with adequate programming skill who have a motive. The other route your investigation should take is to track down the logic bomb itself. It had to be placed on the computer somehow. Was it delivered via a Trojan horse? Via an e-mail attachment? Or by someone with physical access to the machine? Finding out how the software was put on the target machine will help in determining who perpetrated the crime.

Rootkit

A *rootkit* derives its name from the Unix operating system where the administrator is referred to as the "root" user. A rootkit will usually attempt to gain root or administrator access. But the name has come to mean any program that works to hide the fact that the infected machine has been infected. That means any virus, worm, logic bomb, or Trojan horse that hides its presence and covers its tracks could be considered a rootkit. Rootkits are rather sophisticated pieces of software and require some very extensive knowledge of the target operating system to create. However, it is possible that a less-skilled perpetrator could download a pre-made rootkit from the Internet.

As with all malware, the main focus when investigating rootkits is to find out how the software was placed on the target machine. It will also be important to determine if this was a custom-made rootkit or a tool downloaded off the Internet. This information could also be quite useful in determining who committed the crime.

Phishing

Phishing is the process of attempting to get a user to give you personal information that can then be used to access resources to which that user has access or to perpetrate identity theft. Let's take a moment to look at a common scenario. A perpetrator carefully studies the Web site for bank XYZ. He then creates a Web site that looks as close to the real one as possible. The perpetrator then either hosts that Web site with some anonymous Web hosting company using a pre-paid Visa or in many cases actually hosts it on a server belonging to an unwitting third party, the perpetrator having previously hacked into that server. Once the fake Web site is up, the perpetrator sends out an e-mail blast to tens of thousands of e-mail addresses at random. The e-mail purports to be from bank XYZ and warns customers that for security reasons they need to log on to their account, and the e-mail provides them a link. The link is actually to the fake Web site. Once there, the user logs on, and the system records his or her username and password. The perpetrator now has that user's username and password, which he can use to access the person's real bank Web site.

Obviously, many of the recipients won't be customers of bank XYZ and will ignore the e-mail. And many of those recipients who are customers of bank XYZ will be suspicious enough to not follow the e-mail's directions. But all it takes is a small percentage to believe the e-mail and to follow the link and the perpetrator will have access to a number of bank accounts. A typical phishing e-mail is shown in Figure 2.5.

A good example of phishing occurred in 2006, when phishers targeted MySpace users, particularly youthful users. A message was sent to random MySpace users promising a free $500 Macy's gift card. In order to receive the card, the MySpace user had to give over various items of personal information, allowing the perpetrators to steal the member's identity. It also involved sending the victim's MySpace friends e-mails and posting comments on their profiles that would recommend they also sign up for this free gift card. This is a classic example of a phishing scheme.

From a security perspective, the only answer to this attack is to educate end users. There is no antivirus, firewall, or other technological method to stop this attack. From a law-enforcement perspective, the investigation of these crimes can be quite complex. The obvious first step is tracing the e-mail link, but that will frequently lead to a server that has been compromised, and the owners of which are unaware of the crime. Phishing is complex to investigate and an insidious problem.

WOODFOREST

Our Valued Customer,

For your security, Woodforest Helpdesk has safeguard your account when there is a possibility that someone other than you is attempting to sign on. You now need to verify your Identity.

To verify your identity, kindly follow reference below and take the directions to instant activation.

http://online.woodforest.com/

Thank you for helping us to protect you.

Security Advisor
WOODFOREST Online Helpdesk

Figure 2.5
An example of a phishing e-mail.

Social Engineering

Social engineering can be associated with almost any computer crime or attack. *Social engineering* is a phrase used to describe old-fashioned conning. It is the use of various social salesman skills to get sensitive information from a target, including passwords. A good social engineer will first investigate the target organization in order to find information to use in a social-engineering attack. For example, a perpetrator might study a company's Web site and public documents in order to get names of managers and then call a receptionist pretending to be a new IT technician. He might tell the receptionist he needs to update his computer remotely but lost the password, and ask if she could please give him her password. Now, if you add to this ruse by dropping the name of the real IT manager and you are a good salesman, you have a good chance of this succeeding.

Unfortunately, the only countermeasure to this is educating employees. From a law-enforcement perspective, investigating this sort of intrusion is more akin to investigating traditional, non-computer-based crimes. Simply interview all relevant parties. But be aware that you must ask them about any phone calls, messages, or any sort of relevant data, such as access methods and passwords.

In case you are inclined to minimize the efficacy of social engineering, consider the following quote from infamous hacker Kevin Mitnick:

> "The Weakest Link in the security chain is the human element. I obtained confidential information in the same way government employees did, and I did it all without even touching a computer. ... I was so successful with this line of attack that I rarely had to go towards a technical attack."

From a security point of view, social engineering can only be countered by educating users of a system. It is important that all users be aware of social-engineering tactics and avoid falling for them. From an investigative point of view, crimes involving social engineering are much like traditional crimes. The investigation will have to focus on witness interviews and finding out who was compromised and how.

Session Hijacking

Session hijacking is one of the more technical methods of computer attacks. It involves finding a legitimate remote connection, such as a salesman using a VPN to connect to his office, and literally hijacking that session. There are a number of methods for doing this. All require a high level of computer-hacking skill, with in-depth knowledge of networks, operating systems, and security. The skill level required to execute this is one reason this attack is far less common than other attacks. Given the complex nature of these attacks, the specific technical details of this sort of attack are beyond the scope of this book.

One of the more common methods of executing a session hijacking is referred to as the man-in-the-middle attack. In this particular attack, the perpetrator uses some sort of packet-sniffing program to listen in on the transmissions between two computers, taking whatever information he or she wants, but not actually disrupting the conversation. A common component of such an attack is to execute a denial-of-service attack against one end point to stop it from responding. Since that end point is no longer responding, the hacker can now interject his own machine to stand in for that end point. There are many variations of the man-in-the-middle attack, and the some would not be considered a session hijacking by some experts. However, this should illustrate the general concept of hijacking a session.

The point of hijacking a connection is to exploit trust and to gain access to a system that one would not otherwise have access to.

The security countermeasures for this attack involve hardening operating systems and ensuring reliable encrypted remote sessions. From an investigative point of view, a law-enforcement officer should check logs for incidents of the following:

- A login credential being resent when the user is already logged in and there is no need to resend.

- A legitimate login session being initiated at times when it is certain that user was not logging in.

Also be aware that this attack requires significant skill on the part of the attacker. Your suspects should be those people with at least a working knowledge of computer networks, network logins, and some programming skill.

Password Cracking

Password cracking is often an element in other computer crimes. The basic premise is to attempt to compromise a user's password so that the perpetrator can log on as that user. There are a variety of methods for doing this. Even a quick

Web search for "password cracker" will give you a number of utilities that purport to crack passwords.

From a security perspective, the countermeasures for this are as follows:

- Strong passwords, as they are harder for password crackers to break.

- Login limits. For example, the account locks after three failed attempts.

From an investigative point of view, a law-enforcement officer should check for repeated failed attempts to log on. This is often a sign that someone is using a password cracker to try to break the password. Then, of course, tracking down the source of those break-in attempts would be the next step.

Denial of Service

Denial-of-service attacks are the cyber equivalent of vandalism. Rather than seek to break into the target system, the perpetrator simply wishes to render the target system unusable. These sorts of attacks require a great deal less technical skill and are consequently quite common. While there are a number of methods for executing a denial of service (commonly called a DoS), they are all based on the fact that computers, like all technology, have finite limits. If you exceed any technology's limits, it can no longer respond to legitimate requests for service.

Let's consider one common method of executing a denial-of-service attack, called a SYN flood. First, we need to briefly describe how a standard TCP connection works with a server. Basically it works like this:

1. Computer A sends a TCP SYNchronize packet to Computer B.

2. Computer B receives A's SYN.

3. Computer B sends a SYNchronize-ACKnowledgment.

4. Computer A receives B's SYN-ACK.

5. Computer A sends an ACKnowledgment.

6. Computer B receives the ACK. The TCP connection is established. This is called a TCP handshake. The packets being sent back and forth are called SYN packets or ACK packets. A SYN flood takes advantage of this.

7. Computer A sends a TCP SYNchronize packet to Computer B.

8. Computer B receives A's SYN.

9. Computer B sends a SYNchronize-ACKnowledgement.

10. Computer A receives B's SYN-ACK.

11. Computer A does not respond to B's SYN-ACK but rather sends another TCP SYNchronize packet.

This process continues, and each time the target computer leaves another connection open. In a very short time, the target computer has so many open connections waiting to receive the connecting computer's ACK packet that it can no longer respond to legitimate connection requests. You can see a diagram of the DoS attack in Figure 2.6.

This is only one method of executing a denial-of-service attack, and it is an older one at that. However, it helps illustrate the concept of DoS. And that is simply to overload the target machine so that legitimate users cannot access it. One would think this would be very easy to investigate, since all the packets come from the perpetrator's machine and can easily be traced back. However, over the past several years, a variation on this, one that is very hard

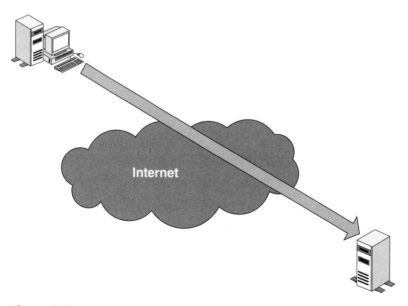

Figure 2.6
Denial-of-service attack.

to trace, has become popular. This is the distributed denial of service (or DDoS). In this scenario, the perpetrator gets software onto a large number of machines belonging to unwitting third parties. At a predetermined date and time, all of these machines begin attacking the target. The trick is to get the software onto the third-party machines. Frequently, Trojan horses or viruses are used to accomplish this. You can see a diagram of the DDoS attack in Figure 2.7.

One can demonstrate a simple denial-of-service attack in a lab setting. Be aware that the method we are about to discuss would not be adequate to bring down a real-world Web server, but it does give one a good understanding of how denial-of-service attacks work. To execute this simple experiment, you must first start a Web server service running on one machine. It is better if you use an older machine so that its capacity is more limited. You can then use any Web server software you feel comfortable with: Microsoft's Internet Information Server, Apache Web Server, or some other brand. Then, on a different machine,

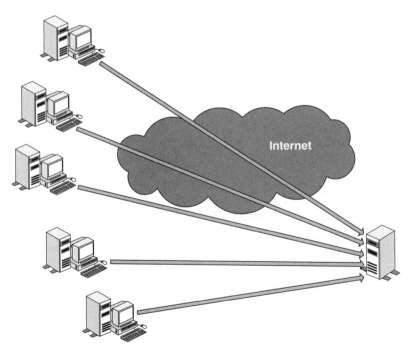

Figure 2.7
Distributed denial-of-service attack.

open a Web browser and type the IP address of that machine in the address bar. You should see the default Web site for that Web server. Now you are ready to execute a rather primitive denial-of-service attack on it. For this experiment, you just need to use the `ping` command line command. The `ping` options we will use are `-w` and `-t`. The `-l` option changes the size of the packet you can send. The `-w` option determines how many milliseconds the ping utility will wait for a response from the target. We are going to use `-0`, so it does not wait at all, thus sending one packet after the other without any delay. Then the `-t` instructs the ping utility to keep sending packets until explicitly told to stop. Then, at the command prompt, we type in ping *<address of target machine goes here>*`-l 65000 -w 0 -t`. If you continue, adding more machines all pinging the Web server without pause or delay, you will reach a point at which the Web server no longer responds to Web requests. This is the concept behind a denial-of-service attack.

From a security point of view, the countermeasure involves sophisticated measures such as intrusion-detection systems that look for signs of DoS attacks and then block any communication from that IP address and alert the network administrator. For law-enforcement personnel investigating DoS and DDoS attacks, you will frequently find your trail leads to a number of unwitting third-party computers. You then need to try to track down how the attacking software was loaded onto their computers. This can be a very difficult thing to investigate.

Before moving on, let's briefly summarize the main types of attacks, their usual targets, and the level of technical skill required to perpetrate them.

Table 2.1 Categorization of Attack Methods

Attack	Technical Proficiency	Usual Targets
Privilege escalation	Moderate to high.	Organization systems.
Virus	Moderate to high to create a virus, low to use an existing virus.	Any.
Trojan horse	Moderate to high to create a Trojan horse, low to use an existing Trojan horse.	Any.
Spyware	Moderate to high to create spyware, low to use an existing spyware program.	Any, but more prevalent on home computers.

Attack	Technical Proficiency	Usual Targets
Logic bomb	Moderate to high to create a logic bomb, low to use an existing logic bomb.	Any, but more prevalent on organizational networks.
Rootkit	Moderate to high to create a rootkit, low to use an existing rootkit.	Any.
Phishing	Low to high, depending on the sophistication of the phishing scheme.	Any, but more prevalent on home computers.
Social engineering	Low.	Any, but usually organizational networks.
Session hijacking	Moderate to high.	Any, but usually organizational networks.
Password cracking	Low to moderate. Many utilities exist to aid a technical novice in cracking passwords.	Any.
Denial of service	Low to moderate.	Organization networks, particularly Web servers.

Issues

A fundamental question that should come to mind is simply why? Why is the Internet such a focal point for criminal activity? One reason is the ease of communication. Traditionally, criminal activities such as drug sales and prostitution have been concentrated in specific areas of cities.

One major problem with computer crime is that the computer-security community is often reactive, sometimes to the point of absurdity. As we mentioned earlier, the first viruses were found in the wild in 1981. It was seven years later before a commercial antivirus program was released, and then that program was only for one specific virus, the Brain virus. It was not until 1991 that Symantec released the first version of Norton AntiVirus. As we will see, this failure to think proactively still hampers computer-security efforts today, and it makes the tasks of computer criminals just a bit easier.

Conclusion

A complete review of all events in the history of computer crime could occupy a rather large book in and of itself. The purpose of this brief review is to give the reader a sense of how computer crime has developed and evolved over the past few decades. It is also important that the reader have a basic conceptual understanding of the major methods used in computer attacks. You must have at least a general knowledge of computer attacks in order to successfully investigate computer crimes.

Endnotes

1   *Business Week.* "The Mob on Wall Street." http://www.businessweek.com/1996/51/b35061.htm

2   *Security Baseline.* "Geekfathers: CyberCrime Mobs Revealed" http://www.baselinemag.com/c/a/Projects-Security/Geekfathers-CyberCrime-Mobs-Revealed/

3   *E-Week.* "Police Foil $420 Million Keylogger Scam" http://www.eweek.com/c/a/Security/Police-Foil-420-Million-Keylogger-Scam/

4   *Wired Magazine.* "'The Analyzer' Hack Probe Widens; $10 Million Allegedly Stolen From U.S. Banks." http://www.wired.com/threatlevel/2009/03/the-analyzer-ha/+

5   Yahoo! Tech News. "Hacker pleads guilty to huge theft of card numbers." http://tech.yahoo.com/news/ap/20090911/ap_on_hi_te/us_retailer_hacker

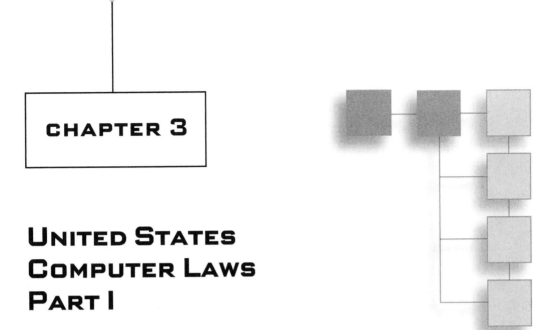

CHAPTER 3

UNITED STATES COMPUTER LAWS PART I

Introduction

In the previous chapter, we examined the history of computer crime over the past several decades. You should now be familiar with how computer crimes have developed and changed, and you should also have a good understanding of common computer crimes. We also introduced you to the different types of computer attacks, so you should have a basic understanding of the methods used by computer criminals. The next step is to study the laws pertinent to computer crimes. In this chapter, we will examine federal legislation and specific court cases that have arisen due to that federal legislation. After reading this chapter, you should have a basic familiarity with federal computer-related laws. In the next chapter we will discuss specific state legislation.

In this chapter we will also relate how these particular laws affect the commission of specific crimes we mentioned in Chapters 1, "Introduction to Computer Crime," and 2, "A History of Computer Crime in America." It is very important to understand what laws are applicable in a given situation. In addition to providing a summary and analysis of relevant laws in this chapter, we will also provide the text of each law. This will allow the reader to see the actual language of the law in question for themselves. This will be in a separate subsection under each law so that readers who wish to, can skip that section. In some cases, the text of the law is too large to present here in its entirety. If that is the case, then the most relevant portions will be presented. It may seem cumbersome to include such lengthy citations in the text of a book, however it is critical that the reader have a fundamental understanding of these laws. There is one notable exception: The Digital Millennium Copyright Act is simply too large to put within the confines of this chapter. Furthermore, it is complex legislation and omitting part of it is not practical. So instead, none of it is reproduced here.

The Ribicoff Bill

The Ribicoff Bill was the first proposal for federal computer-crime legislation in the United States that would specifically prohibit the misuse of computers. The bill was referred to as Federal Computer Systems Protection Act of 1977. While this bill did not pass, it set the stage for future computer-related legislation, and it showed that at least some members of Congress were contemplating the dangers of computer crime as early as the 1970s.

In presenting the bill, Senator Ribicoff stated:

> "Our committee investigation revealed that the government has been hampered in its ability to prosecute computer crime. The reason is that our laws, primarily as embodied in title 18, have not kept current with the rapidly growing and changing computer technology.

> "Consequently, while prosecutors could, and often did, win convictions in crime by computer cases, they were forced to base their charges on laws that were written for purposes other than computer crime. Prosecutors are forced to 'shoe horn' their cases into already existing laws, when it is more appropriate for them to have a statute relating directly to computer abuses."

While that particular bill did not pass and become law, the statement by Senator Ribicoff is still true today. The fact is that legislation is frequently reactive rather than proactive, and it will often be the case that laws will need amending and changing to keep up with more modern crimes.

The Computer Fraud and Abuse Act of 1986

This law is perhaps one of the most fundamental computer-crime laws, and merits careful study by anyone interested in the field of computer crime. The primary reason to consider this legislation as pivotal is that it was the first significant federal legislation designed to provide some protection against computer-based crimes. Prior to this legislation, courts relied on common-law definitions and adaptations of legislation concerning traditional, non-computer crimes in order to prosecute computer crimes.

Throughout the 1970s and early 1980s, the frequency and severity of computer crimes increased, as we have seen in the preceding two chapters. In response to this growing problem, the Comprehensive Crime Control Act of 1984 was amended to include provisions to specifically address the unauthorized access and use of computers and computer networks. These provisions made it a felony offense to access classified information in a computer without authorization. They also made it a misdemeanor offense to access financial records in a computer system.

However, these amendments were not considered in and of themselves to be adequate. Thus during 1985, both the House and the Senate held hearings on potential computer-crime bills. These hearings eventually culminated in the Computer Fraud and Abuse Act (CFAA)[1], enacted by Congress in 1986, which amended 18 U.S.C. § 1030. The original goal of this act was to provide legal protection for computers and computer systems that were in one of the following categories:

- Under direct control of some federal entity

- Part of a financial institution

- Involved in interstate or foreign commerce

As you can see, this law was aimed at protecting computer systems that came within the federal purview. This act made several activities explicitly criminal. First and foremost was accessing a computer without authorization in order to obtain any of the following types of information:

- National security information

- Financial records

- Information from a consumer reporting agency

- Information from any department or agency of the United States

This is a crucial piece of legislation. It is true that outside of cyber spying or terrorism, which we will discuss later in this book in Chapter 6, "Organized Crime and Cyber Terrorism," few computer crimes involve the theft of national security information. However, financial records are often the primary target of sophisticated hackers. In fact even today, 25 years after the passage of this law, financial records are a primary target in many computer crimes. This legislation provides the legal framework for prosecuting such crimes at the federal level.

Also note that obtaining information from a consumer reporting agency or *any* federal agency or department without authorization is a crime. This element of the act is crucial because those activities are often an element in identity-theft cases. Specifically, one can relate the prohibition of fraudulently obtaining records with financial information to cases of identity theft, phishing, and any attempt to breach a bank or other financial entity's computer systems.

Beyond those provisions, the act made it a crime to simply access a federal government computer without authorization, even if you cause no damage or access any confidential data. Since some hackers attempt to breach the security of target systems as merely an intellectual exercise rather than with a specific criminal intent, this provision of this law is very important. It means that if an individual obtains unauthorized access to any federal or financial-institution computer system, he or she is guilty of a federal crime regardless of what further action the individual may or may not take.

Obviously, some in the hacking community might take exception to this provision. But it is clearly prudent and necessary for two reasons. The first reason is that when a person intrudes on a system, it is entirely possible that he or she might accidentally cause damage, even without any malicious intent on his or her part. The second reason is that it could be the case that a perpetrator is caught before he or she can effect damages or theft of information. If the act of intruding on a system is not a crime in and of itself, then that perpetrator is essentially rewarded for being caught before he or she could complete his or her plan. This is why, for example, breaking and entering is a crime in and of itself, even without the commission of an actual theft.

This law also made it a criminal offense to traffic in information, such as passwords, that might be used to access computer systems without authorization. This means that compromising passwords and distributing them on the Internet is a federal crime. Some readers may be unaware that there are places on the Internet where individuals do indeed traffic in stolen passwords, stolen credit-card numbers, and utilities that allow one to compromise systems. The black market for information, specifically cyber information, is a growing problem.

Perhaps the broadest-reaching aspect of this act was the portion that made it a crime to:

> knowingly cause the transmission of a program, information, code, or command that causes damage or intentionally accessing a computer

without authorization, and as a result of such conduct, causes damage that results in:

- Loss to one or more persons during any one-year period aggregating at least $5,000 in value

- The modification or impairment, or potential modification or impairment, of the medical examination, diagnosis, treatment, or care of one or more individuals.

- Physical injury to any person

- A threat to public health or safety

- Damage affecting a government computer system

This broad-reaching language made virtually all forms of hacking, viruses, denial-of-service attacks, and session hijacking a federal crime. The first clause requires damages of $5,000. Now, obviously, some attacks do not cause direct economic damages. However, one must keep in mind that the cost of repairing the damage (i.e., removing a virus, getting the system functioning normally, etc.) is considered a part of this damage. This means that indirectly, most computer attacks will involve damages. The second area, involving medical records, was expressly designed to provide legal protection to medical-information systems. The next one is far less common, as it is rare that a computer attack involves physical harm. The fourth category is one that deserves some consideration. This essentially means that any computer attack that represents a threat to public health or safety is a crime. This is very broad language and could very readily be applied to any range of computer attacks. A creative prosecuting attorney could certainly expand this into new areas. For example, would a court consider a person who deliberately spread false information via computer systems to have constituted a threat to public safety if said information was actually harmful or caused unnecessary panic? I would suspect that this aspect of the Computer Fraud and Abuse Act will be the subject of future computer decisions.

Of course, the final case is simply criminalizing damage affecting government computer systems. This would include defacing Web sites of government agencies. This is particularly important because attacks on government or military systems are often launched against the agencies' public Web sites. These attacks can cause significant inconvenience for the agency in question, and in some cases can lead to disinformation being given to the public via a defaced Web site. It is also true that it is simply easier to compromise a Web server than to intrude into a secure network. The reason for this is that the Web server must, by its very nature, interact with the public. Budding computer criminals often begin by attacking Web sites. Once they have honed their skills, they may then attempt to compromise more secure systems. Making the first steps a federal crime gives law enforcement a very useful tool.

The Patriot Act, passed in 2001, further expanded the Computer Fraud and Abuse Act of 1984 by including expanded sentencing:

- Maximum prison term went from five years to 10 years for the first offense.

- Maximum prison term went from 10 years to 20 years for the second offense.

- The previous threshold had been $5,000 in damages; now the threshold could be $5,000 aggregate in damages.

The Identity Theft Enforcement and Restitution Act of 2007 further expanded the Computer Fraud and Abuse Act. The first—and some would say most important—change was the elimination of the requirement for $5,000 in damages. This means that a computer offense may indeed cause no physical damage and still be a prosecutable offense. Next, this act made it a felony to threaten to damage a computer, computer system, or steal data. Therefore, merely threatening a computer attack is now a felony. This act also expanded the law, making any hacking of a system or even conspiring to hack a system a felony.

The specific penalties given by the Computer Fraud and Abuse Act are shown in Table 3.1.

Table 3.1 Penalties under the Computer Fraud and Abuse Act

Offense	Minimum/Maximum Sentence
Obtaining national security information	10 years/20 years
Trespassing in a government computer	1 year/10 years
Intentional access and damage	1 year/10 years
Intentional access and reckless damage	5 years/20 years
Trafficking in passwords	1 year/10 years
Extortion involving threats to damage computer	5 years/10 years

As you can see, this piece of legislation treated computer crimes quite seriously, and provided federal courts the ability to give out significant sentences for computer-based crimes. This particular bill addresses a number of the attacks we discussed in Chapter 2. It could easily apply to virtually all forms of computer attack, provided the target of the attack was within the scope of this legislation.

Amendments to the Legislation

While this law was a pivotal piece of legislation when it was originally enacted, it had some weak points. Prior to 1996, this law did not clearly define what a protected computer was. In 1996, the law was amended to define this term. The term "protected computer" now includes any computer used in interstate or foreign commerce, computers of the federal government, and financial institutions. Consider briefly the part concerning "any computer used in interstate or foreign commerce." In many, if not most cases, this includes virtually any computer involved in Internet commerce. This would include large scale e-commerce sites such as Amazon.com and eBay.com, but also any Web site that is involved in commercial transactions that cross state lines or international boundaries.

Related Cases

In January of 1989, Herbert Zinn gained the distinction of being the first person to be convicted under the Computer Fraud and Abuse Act[2]. If you will recall from Chapter 2, Mr. Zinn had broken into computer systems at the Department of Defense as well as other sensitive systems. Zinn was sentenced to nine months in prison and fined. Many feel he would have received a much harsher sentence except for the fact that he was a minor when he committed his crimes, although he was an adult when charged and convicted.

Another early conviction stemming from the Computer Fraud and Abuse Act was Robert Morris[3]. Mr. Morris was a Cornell student. He wrote a worm that was designed to be harmless: It simply checked computers to see how many were connected to the Internet. This was in 1988, and there were not so many machines on the Internet as we have today. However, the computer worm's massive self replication caused losses in productivity on the networks it infected. He received no jail time, even though the law did allow for jail time. Instead, he received community service and probation. A few oddities about this case: Robert Morris was the son of the chief scientist at the National Computer Security Center when he committed his crime. He has since gone on to become an associate professor at M.I.T. You should note that some sources mistakenly claim

Robert Morris was the first person convicted under the Computer Fraud and Abuse Act. This is incorrect, it was Herbert Zinn. However, Robert Morris was a very early conviction under this law, and an important case.

Theofel v. Farey-Jones, in 2003, is a case that illustrates the breadth of the Computer Fraud and Abuse Act. This case began as a civil matter between Alwyn Farey-Jones and Integrated Capital Associates[4]. Farey-Jones' attorney subpoenaed ICA's Internet service provider, demanding access to e-mails from ICA, and the Internet service provider complied without notifying ICA. Furthermore, the subpoena itself was very broad and included personal e-mails from ICA employees. The ICA employees whose e-mail had been compromised filed a civil lawsuit against Farey-Jones and his attorney, claiming they had violated three federal statutes: the Stored Communications Act, the Computer Fraud and Abuse Act, and the Wiretap Act. The initial court rejected those claims, but the Ninth Circuit Court of Appeals upheld them. The appeals court ruled that "using a civil subpoena which is patently unlawful, bad faith and at least gross negligence" to gain access to stored e-mail is a breach of the Computer Fraud and Abuse Act. This case is interesting because it involves the improper use of subpoenas. Attorneys, as well as law-enforcement officials, must always be wary to ensure that their gathering of evidence is done in a legal and proper manner. If they do not, not only can the evidence be rejected by a court, it can lead to even more legal difficulties, as it did in this case.

The Actual Law

(1) knowingly accesses a computer without authorization or exceeds authorized access, and by means of such conduct obtains information that has been determined by the United States Government pursuant to an Executive order or statute to require protection against unauthorized disclosure for reasons of national defense or foreign relations, or any restricted data, as defined in paragraph y. of section 11 of the Atomic Energy Act of 1954, with the intent or reason to believe that such information so obtained is to be used to the injury of the United States, or to the advantage of any foreign nation;

(2) intentionally accesses a computer without authorization or exceeds authorized access, and thereby obtains information contained in a financial record of a financial institution, or of a card issuer as defined in section 1602(n) of title 15, or contained in a file of a consumer reporting agency on a consumer, as such terms are defined in the Fair Credit Reporting Act (15 U.S.C. 1681 et seq.);

(3) intentionally, without authorization to access any computer of a department or agency of the United States, accesses such a computer of that department or agency that is exclusively for the use of the Government of the United States or, in the case of a computer not exclusively for such use, is used by or for the Government of the United States and such conduct affects the use of the Government's operation of such computer;

(4) knowingly and with intent to defraud, accesses a Federal interest computer without authorization, or exceeds authorized access, and by means of such conduct furthers the intended fraud and obtains anything of value, unless the object of the fraud and the thing obtained consists only of the use of the computer; shall be punished as provided in subsection (c) of this section.

(5) intentionally accesses a Federal interest computer without authorization, and by means of one or more instances of such conduct alters, damages, or destroys information in any such Federal interest computer, or prevents authorized use of any such computer or information, and thereby

(A) causes loss to one or more others of a value aggregating $1,000 or more during any one year period; or

(B) modifies or impairs, or potentially modifies or impairs, the medical examination, medical diagnosis, medical treatment, or medical care of one or more individuals; or

(6) knowingly and with intent to defraud traffics (as defined in section 1029) in any password or similar information through which a computer may be accessed without authorization, if

(A) such trafficking affects interstate or foreign commerce; or

(B) such computer is used by or for the Government of the United States;

(b) Whoever attempts to commit an offense under subsection (a) of this section shall be punished as provided in subsection (c) of this section.

(c) The punishment for an offense under subsection (a) or (b) of this section is

(1)(A) a fine under this title or imprisonment for not more than ten years, or both, in the case of an offense under subsection (a)(1) of this section which does not occur after a conviction for another offense under such subsection, or an attempt to commit an offense punishable under this subparagraph; and

(B) a fine under this title or imprisonment for not more than twenty years, or both, in the case of an offense under subsection (a)(1) of this section which occurs after a conviction for another offense under such subsection, or an attempt to commit an offense punishable under this subparagraph; and

(2)(A) a fine under this title or imprisonment for not more than one year, or both, in the case of an offense under subsection (a)(2), (a)(3) or (a)(1) of this section which does not occur after a conviction for another offense under such subsection, or an attempt to commit an offense punishable under this subparagraph; and

(B) a fine under this title or imprisonment for not more than ten years, or both, in the case of an offense under subsection (a)(2), (a)(3) or (a)(6) of this section which occurs after a conviction for another offense under such subsection, or an attempt to commit an offense punishable under this subparagraph; and

(3)(A) a fine under this title or imprisonment for not more than five years, or both, in the case of an offense under subsection (a)(4) or (a)(5) of this section which does not occur after a conviction for another offense under such subsection, or an attempt to commit an offense punishable under this subparagraph; and

(B) a fine under this title or imprisonment for not more than ten years, or both, in the case of an offense under subsection (a)(4) or (a)(5) of this section which occurs after a conviction for another offense under such subsection, or an attempt to commit an offense punishable under this subparagraph.

(d) The United States Secret Service shall, in addition to any other agency having such authority, have the authority to investigate offenses under this section. Such authority of the United States Secret Service shall be exercised in accordance with an agreement which shall be entered into by the Secretary of the Treasury and the Attorney General.

(e) As used in this section

(1) the term "computer" means an electronic, magnetic, optical, electrochemical, or other high speed data processing device performing logical, arithmetic, or storage functions, and includes any data storage facility or communications facility directly related to or operating in conjunction with such device, but such term does not include an automated typewriter or typesetter, a portable hand held calculator, or other similar device;

(2) the term "federal interest computer" means a computer

(A) exclusively for the use of a financial institution or the United States Government, or, in the case of a computer not exclusively for such use, used by or for a financial institution or the United States Government and the conduct constituting the offense affects the use of the financial institution's operation or the Government's operation of such computer; or

(B) which is one of two or more computers used in committing the offense, not all of which are located in the same State;

(3) the term "State" includes the District of Columbia, the Commonwealth of Puerto Rico, and any other commonwealth, possession or territory of the United States;

(4) the term "financial institution" means

(A) an institution with deposits insured by the Federal Deposit Insurance Corporation;

(B) the Federal Reserve or a member of the Federal Reserve including any Federal Reserve Bank;

(C) a credit union with accounts insured by the National Credit Union Administration;

(D) a member of the Federal home loan bank system and any home loan bank;

(E) any institution of the Farm Credit System under the Farm Credit Act of 1971;

(F) a broker-dealer registered with the Securities and Exchange Commission pursuant to section 15 of the Securities Exchange Act of 1934;

(G) the Securities Investor Protection Corporation;

(H) a branch or agency of a foreign bank (as such terms are defined in paragraphs (1) and (3) of section l (b) of the International Banking Act of 1978); and

(I) an organization operating under section 25 or section 25(a) of the Federal Reserve Act.

(5) the term "financial record" means information derived from any record held by a financial institution pertaining to a customer's relationship with the financial institution;

(6) the term "exceeds authorized access" means to access a computer with authorization and to use such access to obtain or alter information in the computer that the accesser is not entitled so to obtain or alter; and

(7) the term "department of the United States" means the legislative or judicial branch of the Government or one of the executive departments enumerated in section 101 of title 5.

(f) This section does not prohibit any lawfully authorized investigative, protective, or intelligence activity of a law enforcement agency of the United States, a State, or a political subdivision of a State, or of an intelligence agency of the United States.

The Electronic Communications Privacy Act of 1986

This piece of legislation is a critical one in regard to computer crimes. One reason for this is because it was one of the earliest laws to specifically address computer crimes. Prior to this act there were few laws at state or federal levels that specifically addressed computer crime. The most obvious and notable exception is the Computer Fraud and Abuse Act of 1984. The fact that these two laws were enacted within a period of two years marks a turning point in computer crime. Legislative bodies were beginning to take computer crime seriously and to address those crimes by passing relevant legislation.

A second reason that the Electronic Communications Privacy Act is so important is that it covers how evidence can be gathered. The purpose of the act was to extend federal wiretap laws into the domain of the newer electronic communications medium[5]. Specifically, it was an amendment to Title III of the Omnibus Crime Control and Safe Streets Act of 1968, also called the "wiretap statute." Anyone investigating computer crimes should be familiar with the Electronic Communications Privacy Act and make certain that any investigations are conducted in compliance with this act.

As with many laws, this one has been challenged in court. Specifically, the question has been raised as to whether or not this law applies to e-mail that is stored for transit, such as on an e-mail server. In United States v. Councilman, a United States District Court ruled that e-mail in storage for transit was not protected under this law. The crux of the case was essentially a claim that an e-mail that was found on an e-mail server, rather than on an individual's computer, was not protected by privacy laws. However in 2005, the United States Court of Appeals for the First Circuit reversed this opinion. In this author's opinion, that was absolutely the right thing to do. Many computer users are not aware that their e-mail might be on an e-mail server and not simply on their computers. An end user who happens to be a computer novice would have an expectation of privacy in e-mail, and this was what the appellate court found. This means that e-mail on an e-mail server is considered private communication just like phone conversations, and law enforcement officers are under the same burden to seek a warrant for accessing such data.

The Federal Wiretap Statute, as amended by the Electronic Communications Privacy Act, affects the recording of phone conversations. The two statutes (the Federal Wiretap Statute and ECPA) make it illegal to intercept or disclose intercepted telephone communications unless certain exceptions apply. The law creates civil and criminal liability for anyone who "intentionally intercepts, endeavors to intercept, or procures any other person to intercept or endeavor to intercept, any wire, oral or electronic communication."

There are two exceptions to this law that must be met before one can legally monitor phone calls:

- **The consent exception.** This simply means that both parties to a conversation must give consent. If you will recall the last time you called a customer-service phone number, it is likely that an automated voice informed you the call was being recorded, and the person you spoke to may have even asked your consent to record the call.

- **The business extension exemption.** This does not mean that a business can monitor and record all employee calls. The business extension exemption can only be claimed for monitoring performed by certain types of equipment, and the recording must occur in the ordinary course of business.

With the Electronic Communications Privacy Act, these same guidelines are now extended to e-mail communications, with a few minor adjustments. The most obvious difference is that e-mail is a written message that when sent to a recipient is automatically "recorded" by the recipient. The recipient has the e-mail and may choose to keep it or delete it. This is obviously different from a phone conversation where special steps must be taken to record a phone call. This is important for investigators as well as business owners, or anyone who might feel a need to intercept any form of electronic communications.

Related Cases

The case of United States v. Councilman, which we briefly mentioned earlier, is important in the history of the Electronic Communications Privacy Act. The defendant in this case was a vice president of Interloc and Alibris. Interloc was a book service that also provided e-mail accounts to book dealers[6]. Mr. Councilman had an employee write a program that took all of the e-mails from Amazon.com to these book dealers and copied them to his own e-mail box, which allowed him to intercept literally thousands of e-mails.

The case became interesting because the defendant's attorneys claimed that since the messages were still on an e-mail server, and had not yet been delivered to the recipient, that this did not constitute a wiretap. The court agreed with the defendant. This has lead to ambiguities regarding the interception of e-mails, when it is legal and when it is not. As we have already stated, the appellate court overturned this decision. This case is also noteworthy because the individual intercepting the e-mails was not a law-enforcement official, but rather a private citizen, and the interception of the e-mails was not part of a criminal investigation.

The Actual Law

Section 2511. Interception and disclosure of wire, oral, or electronic communications prohibited

Except as otherwise specifically provided in this chapter any person who intentionally intercepts any wire oral or electronic communication; intentionally uses any electronic, mechanical or other device to intercept any oral communication when

(ii) such device transmits communications by radio, or interferes with the transmission of such communication; intentionally discloses...the contents of any wire, oral or electronic communication...; or intentionally uses...the contents of any wire, oral or electronic communication...; shall be punished as provided in subsection (4) or shall be subject to suit as provided in subsection (5).

(g) It shall not be unlawful under this chapter or chapter 121 of this title for any person -

(i) to intercept or access any electronic communication made through an electronic communication system that is configured so that such electronic communication is readily accessible to the general public;

(ii) to intercept any radio communication that is transmitted -

by any station for the use of the general public, or that relates to ships, aircraft, vehicles, or persons in distress; by any governmental, law enforcement, civil defense, private land mobile, or public safety communications system, including police and fire, readily accessible to the general public; by any station operating on an authorized frequency within the bands allocated to the amateur, citizens band, or general mobile radio services; or by any marine or aeronautical communications system;

(iv) to intercept any wire or electronic communication the transmission of which is causing harmful interference to any lawfully operating station or consumer electronic equipment, to the extent necessary to identify the source of such interference; or

(v) for other users of the same frequency to intercept any radio communication made through a system that utilizes frequencies monitored by individuals engaged in the provision or the use of such system, if such communication is not scrambled or encrypted. (Paragraph (4)(b)(ii) is where ECPA specifically mentions cellular and cordless telephones, public land mobile radio system and paging services as being prohibited from monitoring, subject to a $500 fine.)

Section 2512. Manufacture, distribution, possession, and advertising of wire, oral or electronic communication intercepting devices prohibited

(1) Except as otherwise specifically provided in this chapter, any person who intentionally -

(a) sends through the mail, or sends or carries in interstate or foreign commerce, any electronic, mechanical, or other device, knowing or having reason to know that the design of such device renders it primarily useful for the purpose of the surreptitious interception of wire, oral, or electronic communications;

(b) manufactures, assembles, possesses, or sells any electronic, mechanical, or other device, knowing or having reason to know that the design of such device renders it primarily useful for the purpose of the surreptitious interception of wire, oral, or electronic communications, and that such device or any component thereof has been or will be sent through the mail or transported in interstate or foreign commerce; or

(c) places in any newspaper, magazine, handbill, or other publication or disseminates by electronic means any advertisement of -

(i) any electronic, mechanical, or other device knowing or having reason to know that the design of such device renders it primarily useful for the purpose of the surreptitious interception of wire, oral, or electronic communications; or

(ii) any other electronic, mechanical, or other device, where such advertisement promotes the use of such device for the purpose of the surreptitious interception of wire, oral, or electronic communications, knowing the content of the advertisement and knowing or having reason to know that such advertisement will be sent through the mail or transported in interstate or foreign commerce, shall be fined under this title or imprisoned not more than five years, or both.

(2) It shall not be unlawful under this section for -

(a) a provider of wire or electronic communication service or an officer, agent, or employee of, or a person under contract with, such a provider, in the normal course of the business of providing that wire or electronic communication service, or

(b) an officer, agent, or employee of, or a person under contract with, the United States, a State, or a political subdivision thereof, in the normal course of the activities of the United States, a State, or a political subdivision thereof, to send through the mail, send or carry in interstate or foreign commerce, or manufacture, assemble, possess, or sell any electronic, mechanical, or other device knowing or having reason to know that the design of such device renders it primarily useful for the purpose of the surreptitious interception of wire, oral, or electronic communications.

(3) It shall not be unlawful under this section to advertise for sale a device described in subsection (1) of this section if the advertisement is mailed, sent, or carried in interstate or foreign commerce solely to a domestic provider of wire or electronic communication service or to an agency of the United States, a State, or a political subdivision thereof which is duly authorized to use such device.

Section 2515. Prohibition of use as evidence of intercepted wire or oral communications

Whenever any wire or oral communication has been intercepted, no part of the contents of such communication and no evidence derived therefrom may be received in evidence in any trial, hearing, or other proceeding in or before any court, grand jury, department, officer, agency, regulatory body, legislative committee, or other authority of the United States, a State, or a political subdivision thereof if the disclosure of that information would be in violation of this chapter.

The Communications Decency Act of 1996

This was the first legislative attempt to curtail Internet pornography. The Communications Decency Act was actually part of the Telecommunications Act of 1996, specifically title V. One of the main focuses of the act was to reduce children's access to pornography[7]. To quote from the act itself, any person who:

> knowingly (A) uses an interactive computer service to send to a specific person or persons under 18 years of age, or (B) uses any interactive computer service to display in a manner available to a person under 18 years of age, any comment, request, suggestion, proposal, image, or other communication that, in context, depicts or describes, in terms patently offensive as measured by contemporary community standards, sexual or excretory activities or organs

In July of 1996, a U.S. federal court in New York struck down the portion of the act which was intended to protect children from indecent speech on the grounds that it was too broad[8]. Almost a year later, on June 26, 1997, the Supreme Court upheld another court's decision in Reno v. American Civil Liberties Union, thus striking down significant portions of the Communications Decency Act. The court stated that the indecency provisions were an unconstitutional abridgement of the First Amendment right to free speech because they did not permit parents to decide for themselves what material was acceptable for their children. The court also opined that the CDA's provisions were overly broad in that they extended to non-commercial speech, and did not define "patently offensive," a term with no prior legal meaning.

In 2003, Congress amended the Communications Decency Act and removed the indecency provisions that the Supreme Court had struck down in Reno v. ACLU. In the case of Nitke v. Gonzales, additional and separate challenges were made to those provisions of the act, but they were rejected by a federal court in New York in 2005. In 2006, the Supreme Court affirmed that New York court's 2005 decision. What this means for law-enforcement agencies is that the Communications Decency Act, as it was amended in 2003, is current federal law, not the original act that was passed by Congress in 1996.

Section 230 of the Communications Decency Act is particularly important in a law-enforcement context. This section states that "No provider or user of an interactive computer service shall be treated as the publisher or speaker of any information provided by another information content provider." This means that Internet service providers and Web hosting companies cannot be held liable for the content their users may post on their services.

Related Cases

The most obvious related case would be the case that struck down significant portions of this act. In the case of Reno v. ACLU, the American Civil Liberties Union sued then attorney general Janet Reno, challenging the constitutionality of this law[9]. A three-judge federal district court ruled that certain provisions of the Communications Decency Act violate the first amendment of the U.S. Constitution. On June 26, 1997, the Supreme Court affirmed that ruling. This is important for the obvious reason that it rendered portions of the law null and void.

The case of Zango Inc. v. Kaspersky Lab[10] dealt with the immunity clause in the Communications Decency Act. That clause holds Internet service providers immune from prosecution for activities in which their subscribers may engage that violate the Communications Decency Act. In this case, the issue was whether that immunity applied to the makers of antivirus and anti-spyware programs.

The plaintiff in the case, Zango, Inc., was a company that provided access to a catalog of online videos, games, and music to users who agreed to view advertisements while surfing the Internet. Kaspersky's software classified Zango as adware, a type of malware. Zango sued Kaspersky, seeking an injunction against its blocking activities.

In 2009, the Ninth Federal Circuit Court of Appeals held that Kaspersky was entitled to immunity as a "provider" of an "interactive computer service." The court concluded that a provider of filtering software or services may not be held liable for any action taken to make its filtering software available "so long as the provider enables access by multiple users to a computer service."

This case is important not only because the appeals court clarified what a service provider was, but also because this was an interesting application of the act itself. The protections in the Communications Decency Act were meant to protect Internet service providers from being convicted should one of their subscribers use their service to publish pornography. However, the defendants in this litigation, Kaspersky Labs, utilized the law to defend themselves against a matter not directly related to the provisions of the law. The lesson to be learned here is that the law is not static, but rather malleable. Creative attorneys on either side of any case can often make novel applications of the law to suit their clients' needs.

The Actual Law

Section 223 (47 U.S.C. 223) is amended

(1) by striking subsection (a) and inserting in lieu thereof:

(a) Whoever

(1) in interstate or foreign communications -

(A) by means of a telecommunications device knowingly -

(i) makes, creates, or solicits, and

(ii) initiates the transmission of, any comment, request, suggestion, proposal, image, or other communication which is obscene, lewd, lascivious, filthy, or indecent, with intent to annoy, abuse, threaten, or harass another person;

(B) by means of a telecommunications device knowingly -

(i) makes, creates, or solicits, and

(ii) initiates the transmission of, any comment, request, suggestion, proposal, image, or other communication which is obscene or indecent, knowing that the recipient of the communication is under 18 years of age, regardless of whether the maker of such communication placed the call or initiated the communication;

(C) makes a telephone call or utilizes a telecommunications device, whether or not conversation or communication ensues, without disclosing his identity and with intent to annoy, abuse, threaten, or harass any person at the called number or who receives the communications;

(D) makes or causes the telephone of another repeatedly or continuously to ring, with intent to harass any person at the called number; or

(E) makes repeated telephone calls or repeatedly initiates communication with a telecommunications device, during which conversation or communication ensues, solely to harass any person at the called number or who receives the communication; or

(2) knowingly permits any telecommunications facility under his control to be used for any activity prohibited by paragraph (1) with the intent that it be used for such activity,

shall be fined under title 18, United States Code, or imprisoned not more than two years, or both.”; and

(2) by adding at the end the following new subsections:

(d) Whoever -

(1) in interstate or foreign communications knowingly -

(A) uses an interactive computer service to send to a specific person or persons under 18 years of age, or

(B) uses any interactive computer service to display in a manner available to a person under 18 years of age, any comment, request, suggestion, proposal, image, or other communication that, in context, depicts or describes, in terms patently offensive as measured by contemporary community standards, sexual or excretory activities or organs, regardless of whether the user of such service placed the call or initiated the communication; or

(2) knowingly permits any telecommunications facility under such person’s control to be used for an activity prohibited by paragraph (1) with the intent that it be used for such activity, shall be fined under title 18, United States Code, or imprisoned not more than two years, or both.

(e) In addition to any other defenses available by law:

(1) No person shall be held to have violated subsection (a) or (d) solely for providing access or connection to or from a facility, system, or network not under that person’s control, including transmission, downloading, intermediate storage, access software, or other related capabilities that are incidental to providing such access or connection that does not include the creation of the content of the communication.

(2) The defenses provided by paragraph (1) of this subsection shall not be applicable to a person who is a conspirator with an entity actively involved in the creation or knowing distribution of communications that violate this section, or who knowingly advertises the availability of such communications.

(3) The defenses provided in paragraph (1) of this subsection shall not be applicable to a person who provides access or connection to a facility, system, or

network engaged in the violation of this section that is owned or controlled by such person.

(4) No employer shall be held liable under this section for the actions of an employee or agent unless the employee's or agent's conduct is within the scope of his or her employment or agency and the employer (A) having knowledge of such conduct, authorizes or ratifies such conduct, or (B) recklessly disregards such conduct.

(5) It is a defense to a prosecution under subsection (a)(1)(B) or (d), or under subsection (a)(2) with respect to the use of a facility for an activity under subsection (a)(1)(B) that a person -

(A) has taken, in good faith, reasonable, effective, and appropriate actions under the circumstances to restrict or prevent access by minors to a communication specified in such subsections, which may involve any appropriate measures to restrict minors from such communications, including any method which is feasible under available technology; or

(B) has restricted access to such communication by requiring use of a verified credit card, debit account, adult access code, or adult personal identification number.

(6) The Commission may describe measures which are reasonable, effective, and appropriate to restrict access to prohibited communications under subsection (d). Nothing in this section authorizes the Commission to enforce, or is intended to provide the Commission with the authority to approve, sanction, or permit, the use of such measures. The Commission shall have no enforcement authority over the failure to utilize such measures. The Commission shall not endorse specific products relating to such measures. The use of such measures shall be admitted as evidence of good faith efforts for purposes of paragraph (5) in any action arising under subsection (d). Nothing in this section shall be construed to treat interactive computer services as common carriers or telecommunications carriers.

(f)(1) No cause of action may be brought in any court or administrative agency against any person on account of any activity that is not in violation of any law punishable by criminal or civil penalty, and that the person has taken in good faith to implement a defense authorized under this section or otherwise to restrict or prevent the transmission of, or access to, a communication specified in this section.

(2) No State or local government may impose any liability for commercial activities or actions by commercial entities, nonprofit libraries, or institutions of higher education in connection with an activity or action described in subsection (a)(2) or (d) that is inconsistent with the treatment of those activities or actions under this section: Provided, however, That nothing herein shall preclude any State or local government from enacting and enforcing complementary oversight, liability, and regulatory systems, procedures, and requirements, so long as such systems, procedures, and requirements govern only intrastate services and do not result in the imposition of inconsistent rights, duties or obligations on the provision of interstate services. Nothing in this subsection shall preclude any State or local government from governing conduct not covered by this section.

(g) Nothing in subsection (a), (d), (e), or (f) or in the defenses to prosecution under (a) or (d) shall be construed to affect or limit the application or enforcement of any other Federal law.

(h) For purposes of this section -

(1) The use of the term "telecommunications device" in this section -

(A) shall not impose new obligations on broadcasting station licensees and cable operators covered by obscenity and indecency provisions elsewhere in this Act; and

(B) does not include an interactive computer service.

(2) The term "interactive computer service" has the meaning provided in section 230(e)(2).

(3) The term "access software" means software (including client or server software) or enabling tools that do not create or provide the content of the communication but that allow a user to do any one or more of the following:

(A) filter, screen, allow, or disallow content;

(B) pick, choose, analyze, or digest content; or

(C) transmit, receive, display, forward, cache, search, subset, organize, reorganize, or translate content.

(4) The term "institution of higher education" has the meaning provided in section 1201 of the Higher Education Act of 1965 (20 U.S.C. 1141).

(5) The term "library" means a library eligible for participation in State-based plans for funds under title III of the Library Services and Construction Act (20 U.S.C. 355e et seq.).

No Electronic Theft Act of 1997

What is commonly called the No Electronic Theft Act of 1997[11], known also as the NET Act, was House Resolution 2265 signed into law by President Clinton on December 16, 1997. The purpose of this law is to provide law enforcement and prosecutors with the tools to fight copyright violations on the Internet. Under this law, electronic copyright infringement can carry a maximum penalty of three years in prison and a $250,000 fine. This law made it a federal crime to reproduce, distribute, or share copies of electronic copyrighted works. This means not only software, but also music, videos, or electronic versions of printed material. Under this law, it is a crime to distribute such copyrighted material, even if the distributor does so without any financial gain.

The law does require that the distribution be willful, and that the retail value of the copyrighted material exceed $1,000. It is important for law enforcement and prosecutors to keep in mind that this law comes with a five-year statute of limitations. In other words, the crime must be charged and prosecuted within five years of its commission.

While the distribution of copyrighted material is the key focus of this act and the portion most often discussed in legal circles, it is not the only thing this law did. It also made it a criminal act to:

- Remove a copyright notice from an electronic product.

- Knowingly place a false copyright notice (in other words, to claim a copyright on something someone else already had copyright to).

Furthermore, the NET Act specifically addressed violation of copyrights on live musical or video performances. This means that it is a federal crime to record live performances without permission and then distribute such recordings.

Related Cases

The case of United States v. LaMacchia[12] involved an M.I.T. student named David LaMacchia. Mr. LaMacchia created and operated electronic bulletin boards on the Internet and encouraged users to upload and download copies of popular copyrighted commercial software. The illegal copying that took place on the bulletin boards resulted in alleged losses to the copyright owners of more than $1 million. However, LaMacchia himself did not have any financial interest in the copyright violations; he did not have any monetary gain, he merely encouraged the acts and provided a bulletin board. Because of this issue, prosecutors charged him with wire fraud rather than criminal copyright infringement. The court dismissed the indictment, holding that copyright infringement can only be prosecuted under the Copyright Act. This case is important because it demonstrates the care law enforcement and prosecutors must take in charging a client. Sometimes one can creatively apply the law to prosecute a criminal who might not exactly fit into a particular law's definitions. However, this is always fraught with problems and, as happened in this case, can be completely dismissed by the court.

The Actual Law

SEC. 2. CRIMINAL INFRINGEMENT OF COPYRIGHTS.

(a) DEFINITION OF FINANCIAL GAIN. Section 101 of title 17, United States Code, is amended by inserting after the undesignated paragraph relating to the term "display," the following new paragraph: "The term 'financial gain' includes receipt, or expectation of receipt, of anything of value, including the receipt of other copyrighted works."

(b) CRIMINAL OFFENSES. Section 506(a) of title 17, United States Code, is amended to read as follows:

(a) CRIMINAL INFRINGEMENT. Any person who infringes a copyright willfully either -

(1) for purposes of commercial advantage or private financial gain, or

(2) by the reproduction or distribution, including by electronic means, during any 180-day period, of 1 or more copies or phonorecords of 1 or more copyrighted works, which have a total retail value of more than $1,000 shall be punished as provided under section 2319 of title 18, United States Code. For purposes of this subsection, evidence of reproduction or distribution of a copyrighted work, by itself, shall not be sufficient to establish willful infringement.

(c) LIMITATION ON CRIMINAL PROCEEDINGS. Section 507(a) of title 17, United States Code, is amended by striking "three" and inserting "5."

(d) CRIMINAL INFRINGEMENT OF A COPYRIGHT. Section 2319 of title 18, United States Code, is amended -

(1) in subsection (a), by striking "subsection (b)" and inserting "subsections (b) and (c)";

(2) in subsection (b) -

(A) in the matter preceding paragraph (1), by striking "subsection (a) of this section" and inserting "section 506(a)(1) of title 17" and

(B) in paragraph (1) -

(i) by inserting "including by electronic means," after "if the offense consists of the reproduction or distribution,"; and

(ii) by striking "with a retail value of more than $2,500" and inserting "which have a total retail value of more than $2,500"; and

(3) by redesignating subsection (c) as subsection (e) and inserting after subsection (b) the following:

(c) Any person who commits an offense under section 506(a)(2) of title 17, United States Code

(1) shall be imprisoned not more than 3 years, or fined in the amount set forth in this title, or both, if the offense consists of the reproduction or distribution of 10 or more copies or phonorecords of 1 or more copyrighted works, which have a total retail value of $2,500 or more;

(2) shall be imprisoned not more than 6 years, or fined in the amount set forth in this title, or both, if the offense is a second or subsequent offense under paragraph (1); and

(3) shall be imprisoned not more than 1 year, or fined in the amount set forth in this title, or both, if the offense consists of the reproduction or distribution of 1 or more copies or phonorecords of 1 or more copyrighted works, which have a total retail value of more than $1,000.

(d) (1) During preparation of the pre-sentence report pursuant to Rule 32(c) of the Federal Rules of Criminal Procedure, victims of the offense shall be permitted to submit, and the probation officer shall receive, a victim impact statement that identifies the victim of the offense and the extent and scope of the injury and loss suffered by the victim, including the estimated economic impact of the offense on that victim.

(2) Persons permitted to submit victim impact statements shall include -

(A) producers and sellers of legitimate works affected by conduct involved in the offense;

(B) holders of intellectual property rights in such works; and

(C) the legal representatives of such producers, sellers, and holders.

(e) UNAUTHORIZED FIXATION AND TRAFFICKING OF LIVE MUSICAL PERFORMANCES -

Section 2319A of title 18, United States Code, is amended -

(1) by redesignating subsections (d) and (e) as subsections (e) and (f), respectively; and

(2) by inserting after subsection (c) the following:

(d) VICTIM IMPACT STATEMENT-

(1) During preparation of the pre-sentence report pursuant to Rule 32(c) of the Federal Rules of Criminal Procedure, victims of the offense shall be permitted to submit, and the probation officer shall receive, a victim impact statement that identifies the victim of the offense and the extent and scope of the injury and loss suffered by the victim, including the estimated economic impact of the offense on that victim.

(2) Persons permitted to submit victim impact statements shall include -

(A) producers and sellers of legitimate works affected by conduct involved in the offense;

(B) holders of intellectual property rights in such works; and

(C) the legal representatives of such producers, sellers, and holders.

(f) TRAFFICKING IN COUNTERFEIT GOODS OR SERVICES. Section 2320 of title 18, United States Code, is amended -

(1) by redesignating subsections (d) and (e) as subsections (e) and (f), respectively; and

(2) by inserting after subsection (c) the following:

(d) (1) During preparation of the pre-sentence report pursuant to Rule 32(c) of the Federal Rules of Criminal Procedure, victims of the offense shall be permitted to submit, and the probation officer shall receive, a victim impact statement that identifies the victim of the offense and the extent and scope of the injury and loss suffered by the victim, including the estimated economic impact of the offense on that victim.

(2) Persons permitted to submit victim impact statements shall include -

(A) producers and sellers of legitimate goods or services affected by conduct involved in the offense;

(B) holders of intellectual property rights in such goods or services; and

(C) the legal representatives of such producers, sellers, and holders.

Digital Millennium Copyright Act

This act, signed into law on October 28, 1998[13], frequently called the DMCA, focused primarily on methods for circumventing access control. Basically, this law made it illegal to attempt to circumvent copy-protection technologies. Manufacturers of CDs, DVDs, and other media frequently introduce technological measures that prevent unauthorized copying of the media in order to protect their copyrighted material.

This law did provide protection from prosecution for online providers, including Internet service providers, if they adhered to certain measures. In other words, an ISP is not liable if one of its customers is using the ISP's service to violate the DMCA.

In addition to the protections for ISPs and other online providers, the law allows for the Library of Congress to issue specific and explicit exceptions to DCMA. Usually, these exemptions are granted when it is shown that a particular access-control technology has had a significant adverse effect on the ability of individuals to make non-infringing uses of copyrighted works. The specific exemption rules are revised every three years. A proposal for an exemption can be submitted by anyone to the Registrar of Copyrights.

Related Cases

In the case of IO Group Inc. v. Veoh Networks Inc.[14], IO Group alleged that Veoh was responsible for copyright infringement by allowing videos owned by

IO Group to be accessed through Veoh's online service without permission. According to IO Group, this had occurred more than 40,000 times in a period of less than one month. IO Group argued that since Veoh translated the uploaded videos from users to a Flash format that Veoh was a direct violator of the law, not merely an Internet service provider. The IO Group argued that this prevented Veoh from using the DMCA safe harbor provisions granted to Internet service providers whose customers violated the act. However, the court granted Veoh's motion for summary judgment and held that Veoh was entitled to the protection of the DMCA safe-harbor provisions.

Children's Internet Protection Act

This bill was first introduced into Congress in 1999, and was signed into law on December 21, 2000[15]. The primary purpose of this bill was to require libraries and schools to filter content that children have access to. The law does require that libraries turn off the filter for adult patrons should they request it. The intent is simply to ensure that children are not exposed to pornographic or indecent material on computer systems supplied by the taxpayer.

Schools and libraries subject to CIPA may not receive the discounts offered by the E-rate program unless they certify that they have an Internet safety policy and technology-protection measures in place. An Internet safety policy must include technology-protection measures to block or filter Internet access to pictures that are obscene, child pornography, or harmful to minors (for computers that are accessed by minors).

Schools and libraries must also certify that, as part of their Internet safety policy, they are educating minors about appropriate online behavior, including cyber-bullying awareness and response and interacting with other individuals on social-networking sites and in chat rooms.

Schools subject to CIPA are required to adopt and enforce a policy to monitor online activities of minors. Specifically, schools and libraries subject to CIPA are required to adopt and implement a policy addressing access by minors to in-appropriate matter on the Internet; the safety and security of minors when using electronic mail, chat rooms, and other forms of direct electronic communications; unauthorized access, including so-called "hacking," and other unlawful activities by minors online; unauthorized disclosure, use, and dissemination of personal information regarding minors; and restricting minors' access to materials harmful to them.

The Actual Law

SEC. 1703. STUDY OF TECHNOLOGY PROTECTION MEASURES.

(a) IN GENERAL. Not later than 18 months after the date of the enactment of this Act, the National Telecommunications and Information Administration shall initiate a notice and comment proceeding for purposes of -

(1) evaluating whether or not currently available technology protection measures, including commercial Internet blocking and filtering software, adequately addresses the needs of educational institutions;

(2) making recommendations on how to foster the development of measures that meet such needs; and

(3) evaluating the development and effectiveness of local Internet safety policies that are currently in operation after community input.

(b) DEFINITIONS. In this section:

(1) TECHNOLOGY PROTECTION MEASURE. The term "technology protection measure" means a specific technology that blocks or filters Internet access to visual depictions that are -

(A) obscene, as that term is defined in section 1460 of title 18, United States Code;

(B) child pornography, as that term is defined in section 2256 of title 18, United States Code; or

(C) harmful to minors.

(2) HARMFUL TO MINORS. The term "harmful to minors" means any picture, image, graphic image file, or other visual depiction that -

(A) taken as a whole and with respect to minors, appeals to a prurient interest in nudity, sex, or excretion;

(B) depicts, describes, or represents, in a patently offensive way with respect to what is suitable for minors, an actual or simulated sexual act or sexual contact, actual or simulated normal or perverted sexual acts, or a lewd exhibition of the genitals; and

(C) taken as a whole, lacks serious literary, artistic, political, or scientific value as to minors.

(3) SEXUAL ACT; SEXUAL CONTACT. The terms "sexual act" and "sexual contact" have the meanings given such terms in section 2246 of title 18, United States Code.

Subtitle A. Federal Funding for Educational Institution Computers

SEC. 1711. LIMITATION ON AVAILABILITY OF CERTAIN FUNDS FOR SCHOOLS.

Title III of the Elementary and Secondary Education Act of 1965 (20 U.S.C. 6801 et seq.) is amended by adding at the end the following:

PART F. LIMITATION ON AVAILABILITY OF CERTAIN FUNDS FOR SCHOOLS.

SEC. 3601. LIMITATION ON AVAILABILITY OF CERTAIN FUNDS FOR SCHOOLS.

(a) INTERNET SAFETY.

(1) IN GENERAL. No funds made available under this title to a local educational agency for an elementary or secondary school that does not receive services at discount rates under section 254(h)(5) of the Communications Act of 1934, as added by section 1721 of Children's Internet Protection Act, may be used to purchase computers used to access the Internet, or to pay for direct costs associated with accessing the Internet, for such school unless the school, school board, local educational agency, or other authority with responsibility for administration of such school both -

(A)(i) has in place a policy of Internet safety for minors that includes the operation of a technology protection measure with respect to any of its computers with Internet access that protects against access through such computers to visual depictions that are -

(I) obscene;

(II) child pornography; or

(III) harmful to minors; and

(ii) is enforcing the operation of such technology protection measure during any use of such computers by minors; and

(B)(i) has in place a policy of Internet safety that includes the operation of a technology protection measure with respect to any of its computers with Internet access that protects against access through such computers to visual depictions that are -

(I) obscene; or

(II) child pornography; and

(ii) is enforcing the operation of such technology protection measure during any use of such computers.

(2) TIMING AND APPLICABILITY OF IMPLEMENTATION.

(A) IN GENERAL. The local educational agency with responsibility for a school covered by paragraph (1) shall certify the compliance of such school with the requirements of paragraph (1) as part of the application process for the next program funding year under this Act following the effective date of this section, and for each subsequent program funding year thereafter.

(B) PROCESS.

(i) SCHOOLS WITH INTERNET SAFETY POLICIES AND TECHNOLOGY PROTECTION MEASURES IN PLACE. A local educational agency with responsibility for a school covered by paragraph (1) that has in place an Internet safety policy meeting the requirements of paragraph (1) shall certify its compliance with paragraph (1) during each annual program application cycle under this Act.

(ii) SCHOOLS WITHOUT INTERNET SAFETY POLICIES AND TECHNOLOGY PROTECTION MEASURES IN PLACE. A local educational agency with responsibility for a school covered by paragraph (1) that does not have in place an Internet safety policy meeting the requirements of paragraph (1) -

(I) for the first program year after the effective date of this section in which the local educational agency is applying for funds for such school under this Act, shall certify that it is undertaking such actions, including any necessary procurement procedures, to put in place an Internet safety policy that meets such requirements; and

(II) for the second program year after the effective date of this section in which the local educational agency is applying for funds for such school under this Act, shall certify that such school is in compliance with such requirements.

Any school covered by paragraph (1) for which the local educational agency concerned is unable to certify compliance with such requirements in such second program year shall be ineligible for all funding under this title for such second program year and all subsequent program years until such time as such school comes into compliance with such requirements.

(iii) WAIVERS. Any school subject to a certification under clause (ii)(II) for which the local educational agency concerned cannot make the certification otherwise required by that clause may seek a waiver of that clause if State or local procurement rules or regulations or competitive bidding requirements prevent the making of the certification otherwise required by that clause. The local educational agency concerned shall notify the Secretary of the applicability of that clause to the school. Such notice shall certify that the school will be brought into compliance with the requirements in paragraph (1) before the start of the third program year after the effective date of this section in which the school is applying for funds under this title.

(3) DISABLING DURING CERTAIN USE. An administrator, supervisor, or person authorized by the responsible authority under paragraph (1) may disable the technology protection measure concerned to enable access for bona fide research or other lawful purposes.

(4) NONCOMPLIANCE.

(A) USE OF GENERAL EDUCATION PROVISIONS ACT REMEDIES. Whenever the Secretary has reason to believe that any recipient of funds under this title is failing to comply substantially with the requirements of this subsection, the Secretary may -

(i) withhold further payments to the recipient under this title,

(ii) issue a complaint to compel compliance of the recipient through a cease and desist order, or

(iii) enter into a compliance agreement with a recipient to bring it into compliance with such requirements, in same manner as the Secretary is authorized to take such actions under sections 455, 456, and 457, respectively, of the General Education Provisions Act (20 U.S.C. 1234d).

(B) RECOVERY OF FUNDS PROHIBITED. The actions authorized by subparagraph (A) are the exclusive remedies available with respect to the failure of a school to comply substantially with a provision of this subsection, and the Secretary shall not seek a recovery of funds from the recipient for such failure.

(C) RECOMMENCEMENT OF PAYMENTS. Whenever the Secretary determines (whether by certification or other appropriate evidence) that a recipient of funds who is subject to the withholding of payments under subparagraph (A) (i) has cured the failure providing the basis for the withholding of payments, the Secretary shall cease the withholding of payments to the recipient under that subparagraph.

(5) DEFINITIONS. In this section:

(A) COMPUTER. The term "computer" includes any hardware, software, or other technology attached or connected to, installed in, or otherwise used in connection with a computer.

(B) ACCESS TO INTERNET. An computer shall be considered to have access to the Internet if such computer is equipped with a modem or is connected to a computer network which has access to the Internet.

(C) ACQUISITION OR OPERATION. An elementary or secondary school shall be considered to have received funds under this title for the acquisition or operation of any computer if such funds are used in any manner, directly or indirectly -

(i) to purchase, lease, or otherwise acquire or obtain the use of such computer; or

(ii) to obtain services, supplies, software, or other actions or materials to support, or in connection with, the operation of such computer.

(D) MINOR. The term "minor" means an individual who has not attained the age of 17.

(E) CHILD PORNOGRAPHY. The term "child pornography" has the meaning given such term in section 2256 of title 18, United States Code.

(F) HARMFUL TO MINORS. The term "harmful to minors" means any picture, image, graphic image file, or other visual depiction that -

(i) taken as a whole and with respect to minors, appeals to a prurient interest in nudity, sex, or excretion;

(ii) depicts, describes, or represents, in a patently offensive way with respect to what is suitable for minors, an actual or simulated sexual act or sexual contact, actual or simulated normal or perverted sexual acts, or a lewd exhibition of the genitals; and

(iii) taken as a whole, lacks serious literary, artistic, political, or scientific value as to minors.

(G) OBSCENE. The term "obscene" has the meaning given such term in section 1460 of title 18, United States Code.

(H) SEXUAL ACT; SEXUAL CONTACT. The terms "sexual act" and "sexual contact" have the meanings given such terms in section 2246 of title 18, United States Code.

(b) EFFECTIVE DATE. This section shall take effect 120 days after the date of the enactment of the Children's Internet Protection Act.

(c) SEPARABILITY. If any provision of this section is held invalid, the remainder of this section shall not be affected thereby.

CAN-SPAM Act of 2003

The CAN-SPAM Act of 2003[16] was pivotal because it was the first law concerning the transmission of commercial e-mail. However, critics have claimed the law has too many loopholes. For example, one does not need permission before sending e-mail, which means unsolicited e-mail—what most people consider spam—is not prohibited. It also means mass e-mailings for political, religious, or ideological purposes that do not represent a commercial interest are exempt.

The only requirement is that the sender must provide a method whereby the receiver can opt out, and that method cannot require the receiver to pay a fee to opt out.

The law defines commercial e-mail as "any electronic mail message the primary purpose of which is the commercial advertisement or promotion of a commercial product or service (including content on an Internet Web site operated for a commercial purpose)." This means mass mailings that have no commercial purpose are not covered by this law.

All commercial e-mail is required to offer ways for the recipient to opt out. Those methods must meet the following guidelines:

- A visible and operable unsubscribe mechanism is present in all e-mails.

- Consumer opt-out requests are honored within 10 days.

- Opt-out lists, also known as suppression lists, can only used for compliance purposes, not to be sold to other vendors/senders

There are also restrictions on how the sender can acquire the recipient's e-mail address and how the sender can actually transmit the e-mail. Those requirements are as follows:

- A message cannot be sent through an open relay.

- A message cannot be sent to a harvested e-mail address.

- A message cannot contain a false header.

Perhaps the most controversial portion of this law is the fact that it supersedes all other state and local ordinances. To quote from the law itself:

> This chapter supersedes any statute, regulation, or rule of a State or political subdivision of a State that expressly regulates the use of electronic mail to send commercial messages, except to the extent that any such statute, regulation, or rule prohibits falsity or deception in any portion of a commercial electronic mail message or information attached thereto.

Related Cases

On February 16, 2004, Anthony Greco, 18, of Cheektowaga, New York was the first person to be arrested under the CAN-SPAM Act of 2003, a charge to which he pleaded guilty. Mr. Greco allegedly sent more than 1.5 million messages promoting mortgage refinancing and adult pornography to MySpace users in October and November 2004[17]. The final disposition of his case is unknown.

On September 27, 2004, Nicholas Tombros pleaded guilty to charges and became the first person to be convicted under the CAN-SPAM Act of 2003[18]. Note that

Anthony Greco was the first person arrested, but Mr. Tombros was the first convicted. Mr. Tombros was sentenced in July 2007 to three years of probation, six months of house arrest, and a fine $10,000.

The Actual Law

SECTION 3. DEFINITIONS.

In this Act:

(1) AFFIRMATIVE CONSENT. The term "affirmative consent," when used with respect to a commercial electronic mail message, means that -

(A) the recipient expressly consented to receive the message, either in response to a clear and conspicuous request for such consent or at the recipient's own initiative; and

(B) if the message is from a party other than the party to which the recipient communicated such consent, the recipient was given clear and conspicuous notice at the time the consent was communicated that the recipient's electronic mail address could be transferred to such other party for the purpose of initiating commercial electronic mail messages.

(2) Commercial electronic mail message -

(A) IN GENERAL. The term "commercial electronic mail message" means any electronic mail message the primary purpose of which is the commercial advertisement or promotion of a commercial product or service (including content on an Internet Web site operated for a commercial purpose).

(B) TRANSACTIONAL OR RELATIONSHIP MESSAGES. The term "commercial electronic mail message" does not include a transactional or relationship message.

(C) REGULATIONS REGARDING PRIMARY PURPOSE. Not later than 12 months after the date of the enactment of this Act, the Commission shall issue regulations pursuant to section 13 defining the relevant criteria to facilitate the determination of the primary purpose of an electronic mail message.

(D) REFERENCE TO COMPANY OR WEB SITE. The inclusion of a reference to a commercial entity or a link to the Web site of a commercial entity in an electronic mail message does not, by itself, cause such message to be treated as a commercial electronic mail message for purposes of this Act if the contents or circumstances of the message indicate a primary purpose other than commercial advertisement or promotion of a commercial product or service.

(3) COMMISSION. The term "Commission" means the Federal Trade Commission.

(4) DOMAIN NAME. The term "domain name" means any alphanumeric designation which is registered with or assigned by any domain name registrar, domain name registry, or other domain name registration authority as part of an electronic address on the Internet.

(5) ELECTRONIC MAIL ADDRESS. The term "electronic mail address" means a destination, commonly expressed as a string of characters, consisting of a unique user name or mailbox (commonly referred to as the "local part") and a reference to an Internet domain (commonly referred to as the "domain part"), whether or not displayed, to which an electronic mail message can be sent or delivered.

(6) ELECTRONIC MAIL MESSAGE. The term "electronic mail message" means a message sent to a unique electronic mail address.

(7) FTC ACT. The term "FTC Act" means the Federal Trade Commission Act (15 U.S.C. 41 et seq.).

(8) HEADER INFORMATION. The term "header information" means the source, destination, and routing information attached to an electronic mail message, including the originating domain name and originating electronic mail address, and any other information that appears in the line identifying, or purporting to identify, a person initiating the message.

(9) INITIATE. The term "initiate," when used with respect to a commercial electronic mail message, means to originate or transmit such message or to procure the origination or transmission of such message, but shall not include actions that constitute routine conveyance of such message. For purposes of this paragraph, more than one person may be considered to have initiated a message.

(10) INTERNET. The term "Internet" has the meaning given that term in the Internet Tax Freedom Act (47 U.S.C. 151 nt).

(11) INTERNET ACCESS SERVICE. The term "Internet access service" has the meaning given that term in section 231(e)(4) of the Communications Act of 1934 (47 U.S.C. 231(e)(4)).

(12) PROCURE. The term "procure," when used with respect to the initiation of a commercial electronic mail message, means intentionally to pay or provide other consideration to, or induce, another person to initiate such a message on one's behalf.

(13) PROTECTED COMPUTER. The term "protected computer" has the meaning given that term in section 1030(e)(2)(B) of title 18, United States Code.

(14) RECIPIENT. The term "recipient," when used with respect to a commercial electronic mail message, means an authorized user of the electronic mail address to which the message was sent or delivered. If a recipient of a commercial electronic mail message has one or more electronic mail addresses in addition to the address to which the message was sent or delivered, the recipient shall be treated as a separate recipient with respect to each such address. If an electronic mail address is reassigned to a new user, the new user shall not be treated as a recipient of any commercial electronic mail message sent or delivered to that address before it was reassigned.

(15) ROUTINE CONVEYANCE. The term "routine conveyance" means the transmission, routing, relaying, handling, or storing, through an automatic technical process, of an electronic mail message for which another person has identified the recipients or provided the recipient addresses.

(16) SENDER -

(A) IN GENERAL. Except as provided in subparagraph (B), the term "sender," when used with respect to a commercial electronic mail message, means a person who initiates such a message and whose product, service, or Internet Web site is advertised or promoted by the message.

(B) SEPARATE LINES OF BUSINESS OR DIVISIONS. If an entity operates through separate lines of business or divisions and holds itself out to the recipient throughout the message as that particular line of business or division rather than as the entity of which such line of business or division is a part, then the line of business or the division shall be treated as the sender of such message for purposes of this Act.

(17) Transactional or relationship message -

(A) IN GENERAL. The term "transactional or relationship message" means an electronic mail message the primary purpose of which is -

(i) to facilitate, complete, or confirm a commercial transaction that the recipient has previously agreed to enter into with the sender;

(ii) to provide warranty information, product recall information, or safety or security information with respect to a commercial product or service used or purchased by the recipient;

(iii) to provide -

(I) notification concerning a change in the terms or features of;

(II) notification of a change in the recipient's standing or status with respect to; or

(III) at regular periodic intervals, account balance information or other type of account statement with respect to a subscription, membership, account, loan, or comparable ongoing commercial relationship involving the ongoing purchase or use by the recipient of products or services offered by the sender;

(iv) to provide information directly related to an employment relationship or related benefit plan in which the recipient is currently involved, participating, or enrolled; or

(v) to deliver goods or services, including product updates or upgrades, that the recipient is entitled to receive under the terms of a transaction that the recipient has previously agreed to enter into with the sender.

(B) MODIFICATION OF DEFINITION. The Commission by regulation pursuant to section 13 may modify the definition in subparagraph (A) to expand or contract the categories of messages that are treated as transactional or relationship messages for purposes of this Act to the extent that such modification is necessary to accommodate changes in electronic mail technology or practices and accomplish the purposes of this Act.

SECTION 4. PROHIBITION AGAINST PREDATORY AND ABUSIVE COMMERCIAL E-MAIL.

(a) OFFENSE -

(1) IN GENERAL. Chapter 47 of title 18, United States Code, is amended by adding at the end the following new section:

Sec. 1037. Fraud and related activity in connection with electronic mail

(a) IN GENERAL. Whoever, in or affecting interstate or foreign commerce, knowingly -

(1) accesses a protected computer without authorization, and intentionally initiates the transmission of multiple commercial electronic mail messages from or through such computer,

(2) uses a protected computer to relay or retransmit multiple commercial electronic mail messages, with the intent to deceive or mislead recipients, or any Internet access service, as to the origin of such messages,

(3) materially falsifies header information in multiple commercial electronic mail messages and intentionally initiates the transmission of such messages,

(4) registers, using information that materially falsifies the identity of the actual registrant, for five or more electronic mail accounts or online user accounts or two or more domain names, and intentionally initiates the transmission of multiple commercial electronic mail messages from any combination of such accounts or domain names, or

(5) falsely represents oneself to be the registrant or the legitimate successor in interest to the registrant of five or more Internet Protocol addresses, and intentionally initiates the transmission of multiple commercial electronic mail messages from such addresses, or conspires to do so, shall be punished as provided in subsection (b).

(b) PENALTIES. The punishment for an offense under subsection (a) is -

(1) a fine under this title, imprisonment for not more than five years, or both, if -

(A) the offense is committed in furtherance of any felony under the laws of the United States or of any State; or

(B) the defendant has previously been convicted under this section or section 1030, or under the law of any State for conduct involving the transmission of multiple commercial electronic mail messages or unauthorized access to a computer system;

(2) a fine under this title, imprisonment for not more than three years, or both, if -

(A) the offense is an offense under subsection (a)(1);

(B) the offense is an offense under subsection (a)(4) and involved 20 or more falsified electronic mail or online user account registrations, or 10 or more falsified domain name registrations;

(C) the volume of electronic mail messages transmitted in furtherance of the offense exceeded 2,500 during any 24-hour period, 25,000 during any 30-day period, or 250,000 during any one-year period;

(D) the offense caused loss to one or more persons aggregating $5,000 or more in value during any one-year period;

(E) as a result of the offense any individual committing the offense obtained anything of value aggregating $5,000 or more during any one-year period; or

(F) the offense was undertaken by the defendant in concert with three or more other persons with respect to whom the defendant occupied a position of organizer or leader; and

(3) a fine under this title or imprisonment for not more than one year, or both, in any other case.

(c) FORFEITURE -

(1) IN GENERAL. The court, in imposing sentence on a person who is convicted of an offense under this section, shall order that the defendant forfeit to the United States -

(A) any property, real or personal, constituting or traceable to gross proceeds obtained from such offense; and

(B) any equipment, software, or other technology used or intended to be used to commit or to facilitate the commission of such offense.

(2) PROCEDURES. The procedures set forth in section 413 of the Controlled Substances Act (21 U.S.C. 853), other than subsection (d) of that section, and in Rule 32.2 of the Federal Rules of Criminal Procedure, shall apply to all stages of a criminal forfeiture proceeding under this section.

(d) DEFINITIONS. In this section:

(1) LOSS. The term "loss" has the meaning given that term in section 1030(e) of this title.

(2) MATERIALLY. For purposes of paragraphs (3) and (4) of subsection (a), header information or registration information is materially falsified if it is altered or concealed in a manner that would impair the ability of a recipient of the message, an Internet access service processing the message on behalf of a recipient, a person alleging a violation of this section, or a law enforcement agency

to identify, locate, or respond to a person who initiated the electronic mail message or to investigate the alleged violation.

(3) MULTIPLE. The term "multiple" means more than 100 electronic mail messages during a 24-hour period, more than 1,000 electronic mail messages during a 30-day period, or more than 10,000 electronic mail messages during a one-year period.

(4) OTHER TERMS. Any other term has the meaning given that term by section 3 of the CAN-SPAM Act of 2003.

(2) CONFORMING AMENDMENT. The chapter analysis for chapter 47 of title 18, United States Code, is amended by adding at the end the following:

Sec. 1037. Fraud and related activity in connection with electronic mail.

(b) UNITED STATES SENTENCING COMMISSION -

(1) DIRECTIVE. Pursuant to its authority under section 994(p) of title 28, United States Code, and in accordance with this section, the United States Sentencing Commission shall review and, as appropriate, amend the sentencing guidelines and policy statements to provide appropriate penalties for violations of section 1037 of title 18, United States Code, as added by this section, and other offenses that may be facilitated by the sending of large quantities of unsolicited electronic mail.

(2) REQUIREMENTS. In carrying out this subsection, the Sentencing Commission shall consider providing sentencing enhancements for -

(A) those convicted under section 1037 of title 18, United States Code, who -

(i) obtained electronic mail addresses through improper means, including -

(I) harvesting electronic mail addresses of the users of a Web site, proprietary service, or other online public forum operated by another person, without the authorization of such person; and

(II) randomly generating electronic mail addresses by computer; or

(ii) knew that the commercial electronic mail messages involved in the offense contained or advertised an Internet domain for which the registrant of the domain had provided false registration information; and

(B) those convicted of other offenses, including offenses involving fraud, identity theft, obscenity, child pornography, and the sexual exploitation of children, if such offenses involved the sending of large quantities of electronic mail.

(c) SENSE OF CONGRESS. It is the sense of Congress that -

(1) Spam has become the method of choice for those who distribute pornography, perpetrate fraudulent schemes, and introduce viruses, worms, and Trojan horses into personal and business computer systems; and

(2) the Department of Justice should use all existing law enforcement tools to investigate and prosecute those who send bulk commercial e-mail to facilitate the commission of Federal crimes, including the tools contained in chapters 47 and 63 of title 18, United States Code (relating to fraud and false statements); chapter 71 of title 18, United States Code (relating to obscenity); chapter 110 of title 18, United States Code (relating to the sexual exploitation of children); and chapter 95 of title 18, United States Code (relating to racketeering), as appropriate.

SECTION 5. OTHER PROTECTIONS FOR USERS OF COMMERCIAL ELECTRONIC MAIL.

(a) REQUIREMENTS FOR TRANSMISSION OF MESSAGES -

(1) PROHIBITION OF FALSE OR MISLEADING TRANSMISSION INFORMATION. It is unlawful for any person to initiate the transmission, to a protected computer, of a commercial electronic mail message, or a transactional or relationship message, that contains, or is accompanied by, header information that is materially false or materially misleading. For purposes of this paragraph -

(A) header information that is technically accurate but includes an originating electronic mail address, domain name, or Internet Protocol address the access to which for purposes of initiating the message was obtained by means of false or fraudulent pretenses or representations shall be considered materially misleading;

(B) a "from" line (the line identifying or purporting to identify a person initiating the message) that accurately identifies any person who initiated the message shall not be considered materially false or materially misleading; and

(C) header information shall be considered materially misleading if it fails to identify accurately a protected computer used to initiate the message because the person initiating the message knowingly uses another protected computer to relay or retransmit the message for purposes of disguising its origin.

(2) PROHIBITION OF DECEPTIVE SUBJECT HEADINGS. It is unlawful for any person to initiate the transmission to a protected computer of a commercial electronic mail message if such person has actual knowledge, or knowledge fairly implied on the basis of objective circumstances, that a subject heading of the message would be likely to mislead a recipient, acting reasonably under the circumstances, about a material fact regarding the contents or subject matter of the message (consistent with the criteria used in enforcement of section 5 of the Federal Trade Commission Act (15 U.S.C. 45)).

(3) Inclusion of return address or comparable mechanism in commercial electronic mail -

(A) IN GENERAL. It is unlawful for any person to initiate the transmission to a protected computer of a commercial electronic mail message that does not contain a functioning return electronic mail address or other Internet-based mechanism, clearly and conspicuously displayed, that -

(i) a recipient may use to submit, in a manner specified in the message, a reply electronic mail message or other form of Internet-based communication requesting not to receive future commercial electronic mail messages from that sender at the electronic mail address where the message was received; and

(ii) remains capable of receiving such messages or communications for no less than 30 days after the transmission of the original message.

(B) MORE DETAILED OPTIONS POSSIBLE. The person initiating a commercial electronic mail message may comply with subparagraph (A)(i) by providing the recipient a list or menu from which the recipient may choose the specific types of commercial electronic mail messages the recipient wants to receive or does not want to receive from the sender, if the list or menu includes an option under which the recipient may choose not to receive any commercial electronic mail messages from the sender.

(C) TEMPORARY INABILITY TO RECEIVE MESSAGES OR PROCESS REQUESTS. A return electronic mail address or other mechanism does not fail to satisfy the requirements of subparagraph (A) if it is unexpectedly and temporarily unable to receive messages or process requests due to a technical problem beyond the control of the sender if the problem is corrected within a reasonable time period.

(4) PROHIBITION OF TRANSMISSION OF COMMERCIAL ELECTRONIC MAIL AFTER OBJECTION -

(A) IN GENERAL. If a recipient makes a request using a mechanism provided pursuant to paragraph (3) not to receive some or any commercial electronic mail messages from such sender, then it is unlawful -

(i) for the sender to initiate the transmission to the recipient, more than 10 business days after the receipt of such request, of a commercial electronic mail message that falls within the scope of the request;

(ii) for any person acting on behalf of the sender to initiate the transmission to the recipient, more than 10 business days after the receipt of such request, of a commercial electronic mail message with actual knowledge, or knowledge fairly implied on the basis of objective circumstances, that such message falls within the scope of the request;

(iii) for any person acting on behalf of the sender to assist in initiating the transmission to the recipient, through the provision or selection of addresses to which the message will be sent, of a commercial electronic mail message with actual knowledge, or knowledge fairly implied on the basis of objective circumstances, that such message would violate clause (i) or (ii); or

(iv) for the sender, or any other person who knows that the recipient has made such a request, to sell, lease, exchange, or otherwise transfer or release the electronic mail address of the recipient (including through any transaction or other transfer involving mailing lists bearing the electronic mail address of the recipient) for any purpose other than compliance with this Act or other provision of law.

(B) SUBSEQUENT AFFIRMATIVE CONSENT. A prohibition in subparagraph (A) does not apply if there is affirmative consent by the recipient subsequent to the request under subparagraph (A).

(5) INCLUSION OF IDENTIFIER, OPT-OUT, AND PHYSICAL ADDRESS IN COMMERCIAL ELECTRONIC MAIL. (A) It is unlawful for any person to initiate the transmission of any commercial electronic mail message to a protected computer unless the message provides -

(i) clear and conspicuous identification that the message is an advertisement or solicitation;

(ii) clear and conspicuous notice of the opportunity under paragraph (3) to decline to receive further commercial electronic mail messages from the sender; and

(iii) a valid physical postal address of the sender.

(B) Subparagraph (A)(i) does not apply to the transmission of a commercial electronic mail message if the recipient has given prior affirmative consent to receipt of the message.

(6) MATERIALLY. For purposes of paragraph (1), the term "materially," when used with respect to false or misleading header information, includes the alteration or concealment of header information in a manner that would impair the ability of an Internet access service processing the message on behalf of a recipient, a person alleging a violation of this section, or a law enforcement agency to identify, locate, or respond to a person who initiated the electronic mail message or to investigate the alleged violation, or the ability of a recipient of the message to respond to a person who initiated the electronic message.

(b) Aggravated Violations Relating to Commercial Electronic Mail -

(1) Address harvesting and dictionary attacks -

(A) IN GENERAL. It is unlawful for any person to initiate the transmission, to a protected computer, of a commercial electronic mail message that is unlawful under subsection (a), or to assist in the origination of such message through the provision or selection of addresses to which the message will be transmitted, if such person had actual knowledge, or knowledge fairly implied on the basis of objective circumstances, that -

(i) the electronic mail address of the recipient was obtained using an automated means from an Internet Web site or proprietary online service operated by another person, and such Web site or online service included, at the time the address was obtained, a notice stating that the operator of such Web site or online service will not give, sell, or otherwise transfer addresses maintained by such Web site or online service to any other party for the purposes of initiating, or enabling others to initiate, electronic mail messages; or

(ii) the electronic mail address of the recipient was obtained using an automated means that generates possible electronic mail addresses by combining names, letters, or numbers into numerous permutations.

(B) DISCLAIMER. Nothing in this paragraph creates an ownership or proprietary interest in such electronic mail addresses.

(2) AUTOMATED CREATION OF MULTIPLE ELECTRONIC MAIL ACCOUNTS. It is unlawful for any person to use scripts or other automated means to register for multiple electronic mail accounts or online user accounts from which to transmit to a protected computer, or enable another person to transmit to a protected computer, a commercial electronic mail message that is unlawful under subsection (a).

(3) RELAY OR RETRANSMISSION THROUGH UNAUTHORIZED ACCESS. It is unlawful for any person knowingly to relay or retransmit a commercial electronic mail message that is unlawful under subsection (a) from a protected computer or computer network that such person has accessed without authorization.

(c) SUPPLEMENTARY RULEMAKING AUTHORITY. The Commission shall by regulation, pursuant to section 13 -

(1) modify the 10-business-day period under subsection (a)(4)(A) or subsection (a)(4)(B), or both, if the Commission determines that a different period would be more reasonable after taking into account -

(A) the purposes of subsection (a);

(B) the interests of recipients of commercial electronic mail; and

(C) the burdens imposed on senders of lawful commercial electronic mail; and

(2) specify additional activities or practices to which subsection (b) applies if the Commission determines that those activities or practices are contributing substantially to the proliferation of commercial electronic mail messages that are unlawful under subsection (a).

(d) REQUIREMENT TO PLACE WARNING LABELS ON COMMERCIAL ELECTRONIC MAIL CONTAINING SEXUALLY ORIENTED MATERIAL -

(1) IN GENERAL. No person may initiate in or affecting interstate commerce the transmission, to a protected computer, of any commercial electronic mail message that includes sexually oriented material and -

(A) fail to include in subject heading for the electronic mail message the marks or notices prescribed by the Commission under this subsection; or

(B) fail to provide that the matter in the message that is initially viewable to the recipient, when the message is opened by any recipient and absent any further actions by the recipient, includes only -

(i) to the extent required or authorized pursuant to paragraph (2), any such marks or notices;

(ii) the information required to be included in the message pursuant to subsection (a)(5); and

(iii) instructions on how to access, or a mechanism to access, the sexually oriented material.

(2) PRIOR AFFIRMATIVE CONSENT. Paragraph (1) does not apply to the transmission of an electronic mail message if the recipient has given prior affirmative consent to receipt of the message.

(3) PRESCRIPTION OF MARKS AND NOTICES. Not later than 120 days after the date of the enactment of this Act, the Commission in consultation with the Attorney General shall prescribe clearly identifiable marks or notices to be included in or associated with commercial electronic mail that contains sexually oriented material, in order to inform the recipient of that fact and to facilitate filtering of such electronic mail. The Commission shall publish in the Federal Register and provide notice to the public of the marks or notices prescribed under this paragraph.

(4) DEFINITION. In this subsection, the term "sexually oriented material" means any material that depicts sexually explicit conduct (as that term is defined in section 2256 of title 18, United States Code), unless the depiction constitutes a small and insignificant part of the whole, the remainder of which is not primarily devoted to sexual matters.

(5) PENALTY. Whoever knowingly violates paragraph (1) shall be fined under title 18, United States Code, or imprisoned not more than five years, or both.

SECTION 6. BUSINESSES KNOWINGLY PROMOTED BY ELECTRONIC MAIL WITH FALSE OR MISLEADING TRANSMISSION INFORMATION.

(a) IN GENERAL. It is unlawful for a person to promote, or allow the promotion of, that person's trade or business, or goods, products, property, or services sold, offered for sale, leased or offered for lease, or otherwise made available through that trade or business, in a commercial electronic mail message the transmission of which is in violation of section 5(a)(1) if that person -

(1) knows, or should have known in the ordinary course of that person's trade or business, that the goods, products, property, or services sold, offered for sale, leased or offered for lease, or otherwise made available through that trade or business were being promoted in such a message;

(2) received or expected to receive an economic benefit from such promotion; and

(3) took no reasonable action -

(A) to prevent the transmission; or

(B) to detect the transmission and report it to the Commission.

(b) Limited Enforcement Against Third Parties -

(1) IN GENERAL. Except as provided in paragraph (2), a person (hereinafter referred to as the "third party") that provides goods, products, property, or services to another person that violates subsection (a) shall not be held liable for such violation.

(2) EXCEPTION. Liability for a violation of subsection (a) shall be imputed to a third party that provides goods, products, property, or services to another person that violates subsection (a) if that third party -

(A) owns, or has a greater than 50 percent ownership or economic interest in, the trade or business of the person that violated subsection (a); or

(B)(i) has actual knowledge that goods, products, property, or services are promoted in a commercial electronic mail message the transmission of which is in violation of section 5(a)(1); and

(ii) receives, or expects to receive, an economic benefit from such promotion.

(c) EXCLUSIVE ENFORCEMENT BY FTC. Subsections (f) and (g) of section 7 do not apply to violations of this section.

(d) SAVINGS PROVISION. Except as provided in section 7(f)(8), nothing in this section may be construed to limit or prevent any action that may be taken under this Act with respect to any violation of any other section of this Act.

SECTION 7. ENFORCEMENT GENERALLY.

(a) VIOLATION IS UNFAIR OR DECEPTIVE ACT OR PRACTICE. Except as provided in subsection (b), this Act shall be enforced by the Commission as if the violation of this Act were an unfair or deceptive act or practice proscribed under section 18(a)(1)(B) of the Federal Trade Commission Act (15 U.S.C. 57a(a)(1)(B)).

(b) ENFORCEMENT BY CERTAIN OTHER AGENCIES. Compliance with this Act shall be enforced -

(1) under section 8 of the Federal Deposit Insurance Act (12 U.S.C. 1818), in the case of -

(A) national banks, and Federal branches and Federal agencies of foreign banks, by the Office of the Comptroller of the Currency;

(B) member banks of the Federal Reserve System (other than national banks), branches and agencies of foreign banks (other than Federal branches, Federal agencies, and insured State branches of foreign banks), commercial lending companies owned or controlled by foreign banks, organizations operating under section 25 or 25A of the Federal Reserve Act (12 U.S.C. 601 and 611), and bank holding companies, by the Board;

(C) banks insured by the Federal Deposit Insurance Corporation (other than members of the Federal Reserve System) and insured State branches of foreign banks, by the Board of Directors of the Federal Deposit Insurance Corporation; and

(D) savings associations the deposits of which are insured by the Federal Deposit Insurance Corporation, by the Director of the Office of Thrift Supervision;

(2) under the Federal Credit Union Act (12 U.S.C. 1751 et seq.) by the Board of the National Credit Union Administration with respect to any Federally insured credit union;

(3) under the Securities Exchange Act of 1934 (15 U.S.C. 78a et seq.) by the Securities and Exchange Commission with respect to any broker or dealer;

(4) under the Investment Company Act of 1940 (15 U.S.C. 80a-1 et seq.) by the Securities and Exchange Commission with respect to investment companies;

(5) under the Investment Advisers Act of 1940 (15 U.S.C. 80b-1 et seq.) by the Securities and Exchange Commission with respect to investment advisers registered under that Act;

(6) under State insurance law in the case of any person engaged in providing insurance, by the applicable State insurance authority of the State in which the person is domiciled, subject to section 104 of the Gramm-Bliley-Leach Act (15 U.S.C. 6701), except that in any State in which the State insurance authority elects not to exercise this power, the enforcement authority pursuant to this Act shall be exercised by the Commission in accordance with subsection (a);

(7) under part A of subtitle VII of title 49, United States Code, by the Secretary of Transportation with respect to any air carrier or foreign air carrier subject to that part;

(8) under the Packers and Stockyards Act, 1921 (7 U.S.C. 181 et seq.) (except as provided in section 406 of that Act (7 U.S.C. 226, 227)), by the Secretary of Agriculture with respect to any activities subject to that Act;

(9) under the Farm Credit Act of 1971 (12 U.S.C. 2001 et seq.) by the Farm Credit Administration with respect to any Federal land bank, Federal land bank association, Federal intermediate credit bank, or production credit association; and

(10) under the Communications Act of 1934 (47 U.S.C. 151 et seq.) by the Federal Communications Commission with respect to any person subject to the provisions of that Act.

(c) EXERCISE OF CERTAIN POWERS. For the purpose of the exercise by any agency referred to in subsection (b) of its powers under any Act referred to in that subsection, a violation of this Act is deemed to be a violation of a Federal Trade Commission trade regulation rule. In addition to its powers under any provision of law specifically referred to in subsection (b), each of the agencies referred to in that subsection may exercise, for the purpose of enforcing compliance with any requirement imposed under this Act, any other authority conferred on it by law.

(d) ACTIONS BY THE COMMISSION. The Commission shall prevent any person from violating this Act in the same manner, by the same means, and with the same jurisdiction, powers, and duties as though all applicable terms and provisions of the Federal Trade Commission Act (15 U.S.C. 41 et seq.) were incorporated into and made a part of this Act. Any entity that violates any provision of that subtitle is subject to the penalties and entitled to the privileges and immunities provided in the Federal Trade Commission Act in the same manner, by the same means, and with the same jurisdiction, power, and duties as though all applicable terms and provisions of the Federal Trade Commission Act were incorporated into and made a part of that subtitle.

(e) AVAILABILITY OF CEASE-AND-DESIST ORDERS AND INJUNCTIVE RELIEF WITHOUT SHOWING OF KNOWLEDGE. Notwithstanding any other provision of this Act, in any proceeding or action pursuant to subsection (a), (b), (c), or (d) of this section to enforce compliance, through an order to cease and desist or an injunction, with section 5(a)(1)(C), section 5(a)(2), clause (ii), (iii), or (iv) of section 5(a)(4)(A), section 5(b)(1)(A), or section 5(b)(3), neither the Commission nor the Federal Communications Commission shall be required to allege or prove the state of mind required by such section or subparagraph.

(f) Enforcement by States -

(1) CIVIL ACTION. In any case in which the attorney general of a State, or an official or agency of a State, has reason to believe that an interest of the residents of that State has been or is threatened or adversely affected by any person who violates paragraph (1) or (2) of section 5(a), who violates section 5(d), or who engages in a pattern or practice that violates paragraph (3), (4), or (5) of section 5(a), of this Act, the attorney general, official, or agency of the State, as parens patriae, may bring a civil action on behalf of the residents of the State in a district court of the United States of appropriate jurisdiction -

(A) to enjoin further violation of section 5 of this Act by the defendant; or

(B) to obtain damages on behalf of residents of the State, in an amount equal to the greater of -

(i) the actual monetary loss suffered by such residents; or

(ii) the amount determined under paragraph (3).

Identity Theft Enforcement and Restitution Act of 2008

This act was actually an extension of the 1984 Computer Fraud and Abuse Act[19]. It was written in response to the growing threat of identity theft and the perceived inadequacy of existing laws. One of its most important provisions was to allow prosecution of computer fraud offenses for conduct not involving an interstate or foreign communication. This meant that purely domestic incidents occurring completely within one state were now prosecutable under federal law.

Beyond that important provision, this act expanded the definition of cyber extortion to include threats to damage computer systems or steal data.

Another important aspect of this legislation was that it expanded identity-theft laws to organizations. Prior to this, only natural persons could legally be considered victims of identity theft. Under this act, organizations can also legally be considered victims of identity theft and fraud. This law also made it a criminal offense to conspire to commit computer fraud.

The Actual Law

SEC. 2. CRIMINAL RESTITUTION.

Section 3663(b) of title 18, United States Code, is amended -

(1) in paragraph (4), by striking "; and" and inserting a semicolon;

(2) in paragraph (5), by striking the period at the end and inserting "; and"; and

(3) by adding at the end the following:

(6) in the case of an offense under sections 1028(a)(7) or 1028A(a) of this title, pay an amount equal to the value of the time reasonably spent by the victim in an attempt to remediate the intended or actual harm incurred by the victim from the offense.

SEC. 3. PREDICATE OFFENSES FOR AGGRAVATED IDENTITY THEFT AND MISUSE OF IDENTIFYING INFORMATION OF ORGANIZATIONS.

(a) Identity Theft. Section 1028 of title 18, United States Code, is amended -

(1) in subsection (a)(7), by inserting "(including an organization as defined in section 18 of this title)" after "person"; and

(2) in subsection (d)(7), by inserting "or other person" after "specific individual."

(b) Aggravated Identity Theft. Section 1028A of title 18, United States Code, is amended -

(1) in subsection (a)(1), by inserting "(including an organization as defined in section 18 of this title)" after "person"; and

(2) in subsection (c) -

(A) in the matter preceding paragraph (1), by inserting ", or a conspiracy to commit such a felony violation," after "any offense that is a felony violation";

(B) by redesignating -

(i) paragraph (11) as paragraph (14);

(ii) paragraphs (8) through (10) as paragraphs (10) through (12), respectively; and

(iii) paragraphs (1) through (7) as paragraphs (2) through (8), respectively;

(C) by inserting prior to paragraph (2), as so redesignated, the following:

(1) section 513 (relating to making, uttering, or possessing counterfeited securities);

(D) by inserting after paragraph (8), as so redesignated, the following:

(9) section 1708 (relating to mail theft);

(E) in paragraph (12), as so redesignated, by striking "; or" and inserting a semicolon; and

(F) by inserting after paragraph (12), as so redesignated, the following:

(13) section 7201, 7206, or 7207 of title 26 (relating to tax fraud); or.

SEC. 4. ENSURING JURISDICTION OVER THE THEFT OF SENSITIVE IDENTITY INFORMATION.

Section 1030(a)(2)(C) of title 18, United States Code, is amended by striking "if the conduct involved an interstate or foreign communication."

SEC. 5. MALICIOUS SPYWARE, HACKING AND KEYLOGGERS.

(a) In General. Section 1030 of title 18, United States Code, is amended -

(1) in subsection (a)(5) -

(A) by striking subparagraph (B); and

(B) in subparagraph (A) -

(i) by striking "(A)(i) knowingly" and inserting "(A) knowingly";

(ii) by redesignating clauses (ii) and (iii) as subparagraphs (B) and (C), respectively; and

(iii) in subparagraph (C), as so redesignated -

(I) by inserting "and loss" after "damage"; and

(II) by striking "; and" and inserting a period;

(2) in subsection (c) -

(A) in paragraph (2)(A), by striking "(a)(5)(A)(iii),";

(B) in paragraph (3)(B), by striking "(a)(5)(A)(iii),";

(C) by amending paragraph (4) to read as follows:

(4)(A) except as provided in subparagraphs (E) and (F), a fine under this title, imprisonment for not more than five years, or both, in the case of -

(i) an offense under subsection (a)(5)(B), which does not occur after a conviction for another offense under this section, if the offense caused (or, in the case of an attempted offense, would, if completed, have caused) -

(I) loss to one or more persons during any one-year period (and, for purposes of an investigation, prosecution, or other proceeding brought by the United States only, loss resulting from a related course of conduct affecting one or more other protected computers) aggregating at least $5,000 in value;

(II) the modification or impairment, or potential modification or impairment, of the medical examination, diagnosis, treatment, or care of one or more individuals;

(III) physical injury to any person;

(IV) a threat to public health or safety;

(V) damage affecting a computer used by or for an entity of the United States Government in furtherance of the administration of justice, national defense, or national security; or

(VI) damage affecting 10 or more protected computers during any one-year period; or

(ii) an attempt to commit an offense punishable under this subparagraph;

(B) except as provided in subparagraphs (E) and (F), a fine under this title, imprisonment for not more than 10 years, or both, in the case of -

(i) an offense under subsection (a)(5)(A), which does not occur after a conviction for another offense under this section, if the offense caused (or, in the case of an attempted offense, would, if completed, have caused) a harm provided in subclauses (I) through (VI) of subparagraph (A)(i); or

(ii) an attempt to commit an offense punishable under this subparagraph;

(C) except as provided in subparagraphs (E) and (F), a fine under this title, imprisonment for not more than 20 years, or both, in the case of -

(i) an offense or an attempt to commit an offense under subparagraphs (A) or (B) of subsection (a)(5) that occurs after a conviction for another offense under this section; or

(ii) an attempt to commit an offense punishable under this subparagraph;

(D) a fine under this title, imprisonment for not more than 10 years, or both, in the case of -

(i) an offense or an attempt to commit an offense under subsection (a)(5)(C) that occurs after a conviction for another offense under this section; or

(ii) an attempt to commit an offense punishable under this subparagraph;

(E) if the offender attempts to cause or knowingly or recklessly causes serious bodily injury from conduct in violation of subsection (a)(5)(A), a fine under this title, imprisonment for not more than 20 years, or both;

(F) if the offender attempts to cause or knowingly or recklessly causes death from conduct in violation of subsection (a)(5)(A), a fine under this title, imprisonment for any term of years or for life, or both; or

(G) a fine under this title, imprisonment for not more than one year, or both, for -

(i) any other offense under subsection (a)(5); or

(ii) an attempt to commit an offense punishable under this subparagraph; and

(D) by striking paragraph (5); and

(3) in subsection (g) -

(A) in the second sentence, by striking "in clauses (i), (ii), (iii), (iv), or (v) of subsection (a)(5)(B)" and inserting "in subclauses (I), (II), (III), (IV), or (V) of subsection (c)(4)(A)(i)"; and

(B) in the third sentence, by striking "subsection (a)(5)(B)(i)" and inserting "subsection (c)(4)(A)(i)(I)."

(b) Conforming Changes. Section 2332b(g)(5)(B)(i) of title 18, United States Code, is amended by striking "1030(a)(5)(A)(i) resulting in damage as defined in 1030(a)(5)(B)(ii) through (v)" and inserting "1030(a)(5)(A) resulting in damage as defined in 1030(c)(4)(A)(i)(II) through (VI)."

SEC. 6. CYBER-EXTORTION.

Section 1030(a)(7) of title 18, United States Code, is amended to read as follows:

(7) with intent to extort from any person any money or other thing of value, transmits in interstate or foreign commerce any communication containing any -

(A) threat to cause damage to a protected computer;

(B) threat to obtain information from a protected computer without authorization or in excess of authorization or to impair the confidentiality of information obtained from a protected computer without authorization or by exceeding authorized access; or

(C) demand or request for money or other thing of value in relation to damage to a protected computer, where such damage was caused to facilitate the extortion.

SEC. 7. CONSPIRACY TO COMMIT CYBER-CRIMES.

Section 1030(b) of title 18, United States Code, is amended by inserting "conspires to commit or" after "Whoever."

SEC. 8. USE OF FULL INTERSTATE AND FOREIGN COMMERCE POWER FOR CRIMINAL PENALTIES.

Section 1030(e)(2)(B) of title 18, United States Code, is amended by inserting "or affecting" after "which is used in."

Conclusion

Since 1984, the United States federal government has enacted several laws in an effort to fight computer-based crimes. Most recently, issues of identity theft have become a target of legislation. It is critical that the person interested in computer-crime investigation be familiar with these federal laws. While not all crimes will be investigated and prosecuted under federal jurisdiction, many will. And in many cases, state laws have been modeled after one or more of these federal statutes. That means that a fundamental understanding of the key pieces of federal legislation will provide the framework for understanding computer crime laws, even at the state level. In Chapter 4, "United States Computer Laws Part II," we will examine those state laws.

Endnotes

[1] U.S. Department of Justice. Computer Fraud and Abuse Act. http://www.usdoj.gov/criminal/cybercrime/ccmanual/01ccma.html

[2] Answers.com. Computer Fraud and Abuse Act. http://www.answers.com/topic/computer-fraud-and-abuse-act

[3] Answers.com. The Morris Worm. http://www.answers.com/topic/morris-computer-worm

[4] FindLaw.com http://caselaw.lp.findlaw.com/data2/circs/9th/0215742p.pdf

[5] Computer Professionals for Social Responsibility. Electronic Communications Privacy Act of 1986. http://cpsr.org/issues/privacy/ecpa86/

[6] The Catholic University of America. Electronic Communications Privacy Act of 1986 (ECPA). http://counsel.cua.edu/FEDLAW/Ecpa.htm

[7] Federal Communications Commission. The Communications Decency Act. http://www.fcc.gov/Reports/tcom1996.txt

[8] The Center for Democracy and Technology. The Communications Decency Act. http://www.cdt.org/speech/cda/

[9] Cornell Law School. RENO, ATTORNEY GENERAL OF THE UNITED STATES, et al. v. AMERICAN CIVIL LIBERTIES UNION et al. http://www.law.cornell.edu/supct/html/96-511.ZS.html

[10] California Courts. Zango v. Kaspersky Labs. http://www.ca9.uscourts.gov/datastore/opinions/2009/06/25/07-35800.pdf

[11] United States Copyright Office. No Electronic Theft Act of 1997. http://www.copyright.gov/docs/2265_stat.html

[12] Kent State Law School. The United States v. David LaMacchia. http://www.kentlaw.edu/faculty/rstaudt/classes/oldclasses/internetlaw/casebook/us_v_lamacchia.html

[13] The United States Copyright Office. The Digital Millennium Copyright Act. http://www.copyright.gov/legislation/dmca.pdf

[14] Law.com. "DMCA: A Safe Harbor for Video Sharing?" http://www.law.com/jsp/legaltechnology/pubArticleLT.jsp?id=1202425323100

15 Federal Communications Commission. Children's Internet Protection Act. http://www.fcc.gov/cgb/consumerfacts/cipa.html

16 Federal Trade Commission. The CAN-SPAM Act: Requirements for Commercial E-mailers. http://www.ftc.gov/bcp/edu/pubs/business/ecommerce/bus61.shtm

17 *The U.K. Register.* "NY Teen Charged Over IM Spam Attack." http://www.theregister.co.uk/2005/02/22/spim_arrest/print.html

18 Federal Bureau of Investigation. The Case of the Not-So-Friendly Neighborhood Spammer. http://www.fbi.gov/page2/nov04/warspammer111004.htm

19 Open Congress. H.R. 6060. http://www.opencongress.org/bill/110-h6060/show

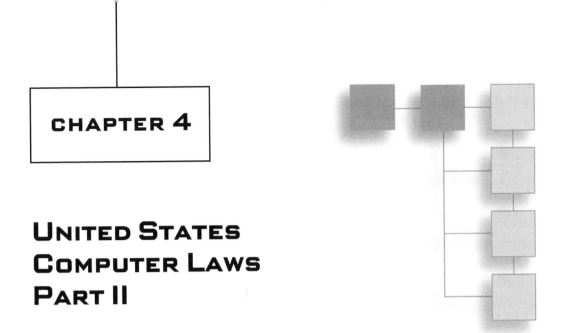

CHAPTER 4

UNITED STATES COMPUTER LAWS PART II

Introduction

In Chapter 3, "United States Computer Laws Part I," we reviewed the major federal statutes that have the most impact on investigating and prosecuting computer crime. In this chapter, we will examine various state laws. With 50 states, it is obviously too large a task to attempt to cover every statute in every single state. Instead, we will take a sampling of these statutes in order to give the reader a good overview of the state laws pertinent to computer crime. We will, of course, include certain state laws that are considered key developments/milestones on the evolution of computer-related laws. In each section, we will examine state laws that are laudable for one reason or another. We will also examine laws that have significant flaws or omissions. It is important for you to keep in mind that you should make certain you are familiar with your state's specific laws and the laws of any state in which you may conduct investigations.

Cyber-Stalking Laws

As we have pointed out in previous chapters, cyber stalking is a very serious crime primarily because it can, and often does, lead to crimes in the real world. Cyber stalking can frequently be a prelude to assault, rape, or even homicide. Any law-enforcement officer or prosecutor should take these crimes very seriously. Unlike crimes such as identity theft or stealing financial information, cyber stalking is often a local crime. The perpetrator is often within a reasonable driving distance of the victim, sometimes in the same town. This makes the state statutes on these crimes far more serious, as they are usually investigated and prosecuted by local law enforcement.

California Cyber-Stalking Law

In 1991, California became the first state to pass a cyber-stalking law[1], and in 2009 they expanded their law[2]. One of the additions to the law is that it is now a misdemeanor to publish information about an academic researcher or that researcher's family with the intent of eliciting someone else to harass or harm that individual. This new law allows for up to one year in jail and/or $1,000 fine per violation. This law is in California penal code 422.4.

The first and perhaps most famous conviction under California anti-stalking laws occurred in 1999. In 1999, Gary S. Dellapenta[3], a 50-year-old security guard, had been making advances toward a woman at his church, which she rejected. He reacted aggressively and his behavior became such a concern that church elders asked him to leave the church. To retaliate against the woman, Mr. Dellapenta took out fake ads on the Internet, purporting to be from the woman in question, claiming she enjoyed rape fantasies. When men contacted the e-mail address in the ad, it went to Mr. Dellapenta, who responded with the address and phone number of the victim. On at least six separate occasions, men actually showed up at the victim's home. Mr. Dellapenta was arrested, convicted, and received a six-year prison sentence.

Texas Cyber-Stalking Law

Texas penal code section 42.07[4] covers all types of stalking and harassment, including acts done via electronic means. There are two factors about this law that make it interesting to study. First, it is not a new law written for Internet stalking; the Texas legislature simply expanded existing stalking and harassment laws to include Internet stalking. This is often a very efficient way for any legislative body to handle computer crime: simply to expand existing laws. It is also interesting due to the fact that it is very explicit about what is covered:

- Sending obscene material

- Sending threats of violence

- Sending threats to commit any felony

- Falsely claiming a third party has suffered death or severe bodily harm

- Sending repeated electronic communications in a manner reasonably likely to harass, annoy, alarm, abuse, torment, embarrass, or offend another

Even more intriguing is the fact that this law explicitly defines what it means by "electronic communication." It specifically mentions any communication by e-mail, instant message, or across any network. It even includes communications to a pager. Frequently, when legislation is enacted, the legislative body fails to clarify the intent and scope of the law, leading to legal complexities and loopholes. The Texas statute is quite explicit. The only vague area is the prohibition against "Sends repeated electronic communications in a manner reasonably likely to harass, annoy, alarm, abuse, torment, embarrass, or offend another." The legal community frequently uses the term "reasonably"; unfortunately, that is an ill-defined and subjective term. What one person finds reasonable, another may not. However, it seems clear that this clause was intended as a catch-all to cover any items not covered by the more explicit prohibitions.

Utah Cyber-Stalking Laws

Utah took a similar approach to Texas in that they simply expanded existing anti-stalking laws so that those laws would also cover cyber stalking. Utah penal code 76-5-106 covers all types of harassment and stalking[5] and has simply been expanded to include computer-based crimes.

The original law enumerates a number of ways one might be guilty of stalking or harassment, and so the law was simply expanded with the addition of one small clause to include cyber crimes: "uses a computer, the Internet, text messaging, or any other electronic means to commit an act that is a part of the course of conduct." It is usually better for a legislative body to specifically address the issue of computer crime. However, both Texas and Utah statutes show that it is a relatively easy matter for any legislative body to simply amend current laws so that they encompass computer-based crimes. For that reason it is incumbent on all legislative bodies to ensure their legislation appropriately covers computer crimes.

Louisiana Cyber-Stalking Laws

Louisiana statute RS 14:40.36[6] is very explicit in defining exactly what cyber stalking is:

B. Cyberstalking is action of any person to accomplish any of the following:

(1) Use in electronic mail or electronic communication of any words or language threatening to inflict bodily harm to any person or to such person's child, sibling, spouse, or dependent, or physical injury to the property of any person, or for the purpose of extorting money or other things of value from any person.

(2) Electronically mail or electronically communicate to another repeatedly, whether or not conversation ensues, for the purpose of threatening, terrifying, or harassing any person.

(3) Electronically mail or electronically communicate to another and to knowingly make any false statement concerning death, injury, illness, disfigurement, indecent conduct, or criminal conduct of the person electronically mailed or of any member of the person's family or household with the intent to threaten, terrify, or harass.

(4) Knowingly permit an electronic communication device under the person's control to be used for the taking of an action in Paragraph (1), (2), or (3) of this Subsection.

C. (1) Whoever commits the crime of cyberstalking shall be fined not more than two thousand dollars, or imprisoned for not more than one year, or both.

Notice that the law targets two areas of conduct. The first is any overt threats: Regardless of whether the threat is to the person or a family member, whether it is a threat of physical harm or an attempt at extortion, if it is done via electronic communication, it is cyber stalking. The second area that the law deals with is basic harassment. Notice that the law states threatening, terrifying, or *harassing*. This means that under Louisiana law, constantly badgering someone with electronic communication—even if the communication does not involve any sort of threat—can be construed as cyber stalking. Obviously, this is an area that will be up to individual prosecutors, law-enforcement officers, and ultimately juries to decide. Fortunately, the legislature took some action to attempt to avoid the abuse of this law. They added a class to the law to attempt to prevent this law from being applied too broadly:

This Section does not apply to any peaceable, nonviolent, or nonthreatening activity intended to express political views or to provide lawful information to others.

This means that simply because you might not like the content of an e-mail or text message, it does not mean that message constitutes cyber stalking. This is an important element that not all state legislatures have had the foresight to include. Even in the case of Louisiana, this short clause may prove to be insufficient. The fact is that sometimes, individuals in civil litigation or overzealous law-enforcement officers and prosecutors can attempt to stretch a law into areas it was not intended. Previously in this book, we discussed the famous case of the mother using a fictitious account on MySpace to harass a rival of her teenage daughter. While it is clear this mother's actions were deplorable and the outcome tragic, it is also clear that the laws against unauthorized access of a computer system were not intended to address people using a fictitious identity on the Internet. But prosecutors, in their zeal to hold this woman accountable for actions that ultimately led to a young girl's suicide, tried to apply this law inappropriately. Ultimately, a judge threw out the case. But it is the legislature's responsibility to ensure that any laws they write are clear and unambiguous. And with laws relating to computer crimes, the issues can be complex as well as new. This puts an even greater onus on the legislature to clarify their intent. Louisiana is to be commended for taking a step in that direction.

Also of note in this law is that it includes increasing penalties for future offenses:

> (2) Upon a second conviction occurring within seven years of the prior conviction for cyberstalking, the offender shall be imprisoned for not less than one hundred and eighty days and not more than three years, and may be fined not more than five thousand dollars, or both.

> (3) Upon a third or subsequent conviction occurring within seven years of a prior conviction for stalking, the offender shall be imprisoned for not less than two years and not more than five years and may be fined not more than five thousand dollars, or both.

This means that if a person is convicted of one count of cyber stalking and persists in the activity, even with a new target, that person can incur substantially increased penalties. This is an important aspect of this legislation. It is surprising that many state laws do not include a similar provision.

Miscellaneous States

Several states, in fact most of them, have laws regarding cyber stalking and harassment. However, most of those don't expand one's understanding of the law beyond what has already been exemplified in the preceding examples. As a brief sampling of some other state laws on cyber stalking, we present the following list:

- Arizona statute 13-2921[7] simply expands the existing state statute regarding stalking by adding the clause "Anonymously or otherwise contacts, communicates or causes a communication with another person by verbal, electronic, mechanical, telegraphic, telephonic or written means in a manner that harasses."

- Indiana also simply expands existing law (Statute 35-45-2-2)[8] with the addition of the following clause: "uses a computer network (as defined in IC35-43-2-3(a)) or other form of electronic communication."

- Oklahoma statute 21-1173[9] probably does less to address cyber stalking than most states. This legislation simply adds the clause "sending mail or electronic communications to that individual" to existing stalking legislation. Notice that this clause is less verbose than the others. It certainly shows the Oklahoma legislature intended to address the issue of computer-based stalking, but it may not be explicit enough.

It is important to realize that any time a law is not absolutely clear, it leaves a loophole that can be exploited by a criminal to avoid punishment for his or her actions. It can also be misapplied to punish people who were never intended to be penalized. It is important that state legislative bodies strive to make clear and unambiguous legislation regarding cyber stalking. However, as we have seen here, it is a small matter for any legislative body to at least expand current stalking and harassment laws to encompass cyber stalking. This gives law-enforcement agencies the legal framework to investigate such activities. Table 4.1 lists the cyber-stalking statutes for all states that have specific anti–cyber-stalking laws. Some states do not have specific statutes and simply use existing stalking and harassment laws to apply to cyber stalking as well.

Table 4.1 Cyber Stalking Statutes

State	Statute
Alabama	Ala. Code 13A-11-8
Alaska	Alaska Stat. 11.41.260, 11.41.270, 11.61.120
Arizona	Ariz. Rev. Stat. 13-2921
Arkansas	Ark. Code 5-41-108, 5-27-306
California	Cal. Civil Code 1708.7, Cal. Penal Code 422, 646.9, 653m
Colorado	Colo. Rev. Stat. 18-9-111
Connecticut	Conn. Gen. Stat. 53a-182b, 53a-183
Delaware	Del. Code title 11 1311
Florida	Fla. Stat. 817.568, 784.048
Georgia	Georgia Code 16-5-90
Hawaii	Hawaii Rev. Stat. 711-1106
Idaho	Idaho Statutes 18-7905, 18-7906
Illinois	720 Ill. Comp. Stat. 5/12-7.5, 135/1-2, 135/1-3, 135/2
Indiana	Ind. Code 35-45-2-2
Iowa	Iowa Code 708.7
Kansas	Kan. Stat. 21-3438
Louisiana	La. Rev. Stat. 14:40.2, La. Rev. Stat. 14:40.3
Maine	Me. Rev. Stat. title 17A 210-A
Maryland	Md. Code title 3 3-805
Massachusetts	Mass. Gen. Laws ch. 265 43 and 43A
Michigan	Mich. Comp. Laws 750.411h, l, and s
Minnesota	Minn. Stat. 609.749
Mississippi	Miss. Code 97-29-45, 97-45-15
Missouri	Mo. Rev. Stat. 565.225, 565.090
Montana	Mont. Code Ann. 45-8-213, 45-5-220
Nevada	Nev. Rev. Stat. 200.575
New Hampshire	N.H. Rev. Stat. 644:4
New York	New York Penal Law 240.30
North Carolina	N.C. Gen. Stat. 14-196 and 14-196.3
North Dakota	N.D. Cent. Code 12.1-17-07
Ohio	Ohio Rev. Code 2903.211, 2913.01(Y), 2917.21(A)
Oklahoma	Okla. Stat. title 21 1173
Oregon	Or. Rev. Stat. 163.730-732, 166.065
Pennsylvania	Pa. Cons. Stat. title 18 2709, 2709.1
Rhode Island	R.I. Gen. Laws 11-52-4.2, 11-52-4.3

State	Statute
South Carolina	S.C. Code 16-3-1700(B), -1700(C), -1700(F)
South Dakota	S.D. Code Laws 22-19A-1, 49-31-31
Tennessee	Tenn. Code 39-17-308, 39-17-315
Texas	Texas Penal Code 42.07
Utah	Utah Code 76-5-106.5
Vermont	13 V.S.A. 1027, 1061, 1062, 1063
Virginia	Va. Code 18.2-60 18.2-152.7:1
Washington	Wash. Rev. Code 9A.46.020, 9A.46.110, 9.61.260, 10.14.020
West Virginia	W. Va. Code 61-3C-14a
Wisconsin	Wis. Stat. 947.0125
Wyoming	Wyo. Stat. 6-2-506

Identity-Theft Laws

As with other computer-related crimes, the specific laws regarding identity theft vary from state to state. Some states have created legislation specifically to address this issue, while others have modified existing laws, and still others have done surprisingly little on the issue. Identity theft, unlike cyber stalking, frequently falls under federal jurisdiction because it is often done across state lines or involves financial institutions. But this does not mean there is no need for state laws on this issue. While identity theft within federal jurisdiction is more common, there are still many instances of identity theft that fall within state jurisdictions. This is why it is important to be familiar with the state legislation. Let us look at a few examples of state laws.

Alabama Consumer Identity Protection Act

The Alabama Consumer Identity Protection Act[10] is a very comprehensive piece of legislation. In fact, it is so extensive that it was split into several portions covering Alabama statues 13A-8-190 to 13A-8-201. The first thing this act did was to elevate the crime of identity theft from a misdemeanor to a class C felony. The classification of any crime is often a gauge of how seriously the legislature believes that crime is affecting society. In the case of identity theft, it would be difficult to argue that it does not have a very serious and growing impact on society. The Alabama legislature realized this and increased the legal severity with which this crime is treated.

The second interesting thing this law does is that it clearly defines what constitutes a violation of the statute. Let's look at the actual wording of this law:

(a) A person commits the crime of identity theft if, without the authorization, consent, or permission of the victim, and with the intent to defraud for his or her own benefit or the benefit of a third person, he or she does any of the following:

    (1) Obtains, records, or accesses identifying information that would assist in accessing financial resources, obtaining identification documents, or obtaining benefits of the victim.

    (2) Obtains goods or services through the use of identifying information of the victim.

    (3) Obtains identification documents in the victim's name.

(b) Identity theft is a Class C felony.

(c) This section shall not apply when a person obtains the identity of another person to misrepresent his or her age for the sole purpose of obtaining alcoholic beverages, tobacco, or another privilege denied to minors.

(d) Any prosecution brought pursuant to this article shall be commenced within seven years after the commission of the offense.

This is very clear and unambiguous, and identifies exactly what actions violate this statute. This is a good example of a law against identity theft.

Florida Criminal Use of Personal Identification Information

The Florida statute 817.568 is an exemplary piece of legislation. The act does a very good job of clearly defining its scope, the terms used, and the consequences. More importantly, the law makes abundantly clear that the purpose of using someone's personal information is irrelevant. To quote the statute[11]:

Any person who willfully and without authorization fraudulently uses personal identification information concerning an individual without first obtaining that individual's consent commits a felony of the second degree.

What this means is that even if one does not use the personal identification information for financial purposes, it is still a felony. This is a very important point that not all identity-theft laws address. As we discussed in Chapters 1, "Introduction to Computer Crime," and 2, "A History of Computer Crime in America," while identity theft is often associated with economic crimes, it does not have to be. A perpetrator can use someone else's identity to discredit that person, to embarrass him or her, or to simply hide the perpetrator's own actions.

Of course, the law goes on to address identity theft for financial gain. In fact, it divides punishments based on the scope of the crime:

- For crimes with damages between $5,000 and $50,000 and/or affecting between 10 and 20 people, the penalty is a minimum of three years imprisonment.

- For crimes with damages between $50,000 and $100,000 and/or affecting between 20 and 30 people, the penalty is a minimum of five years imprisonment.

- For crimes with damages in excess of $100,000 and/or affecting more than 30 people, the penalty is a minimum of 10 years imprisonment.

The wording in the law then explicitly states that these are minimum sentences and nothing in this law should be construed as prohibiting a court from imposing a greater sentence. These facts alone make the Florida statute worthy of examination. However, they have added an interesting item. Under this law, using personal identification information in the furtherance of harassment carries, in and of itself, additional penalties. The law states the following:

> Any person who willfully and without authorization possesses, uses, or attempts to use personal identification information concerning an individual without first obtaining that individual's consent, and who does so for the purpose of harassing that individual, commits the offense of harassment by use of personal identification information, which is a misdemeanor of the first degree.

The statute then continues on and specifies additional penalties and damages based on specific modifiers to the underlying crime. Specifically, the law states that if the identity information was gleaned from a public record, the crime just became elevated, as follows:

- A misdemeanor of the first degree is reclassified as a felony of the third degree.

- A felony of the third degree is reclassified as a felony of the second degree.

- A felony of the second degree is reclassified as a felony of the first degree.

I find this segment of this legislation particularly interesting and would hope all state legislatures would contemplate adding something similar to their own laws. Clearly, a great deal of information is available online via public records, and to some extent this is quite helpful and useful. For example, if one is about to go into business with a partner, it is good to be able to easily find out if that partner has been involved in business litigation in the past, has filed bankruptcy, and so on. However, the Florida legislature, with this clause in the statute, is taking a rather harsh stance on those who misuse that information either in the course of identity theft or in the course of harassing someone.

Idaho Identity-Theft Laws

Idaho took a slightly different approach to identity theft. Their legislature passed a series of separate laws, each targeting a specific aspect of identity theft[12]. Let's look at some of the specific items addressed in the Idaho legislation:

- State law 18-3125 makes it a crime to possess or obtain an FTC number that "is fictitious, counterfeit, revoked, expired or fraudulently obtained FTC or any FTC account number."

- Statute 18-3126 specifically addresses what is usually considered identity theft. The law states, "It is unlawful for any person to obtain or record personal identifying information of another person without the authorization of that person, with the intent that the information be used to obtain, or attempt to obtain, credit, money, goods or services without the consent of that person."

- Statute 18-3126A addresses the act of obtaining personal information fraudulently. The law specifically states, "It is unlawful for any person to falsely assume or pretend to be a member of the armed forces of the United States or an officer or employee acting under authority of the United States or any department, agency or office thereof or of the state of Idaho or any department, agency or office thereof, and in such pretended character, seek, demand, obtain or attempt to obtain personal identifying information of another person."

- Then, in statute 18-3127, the law makes receiving goods purchased through fraud to be a crime: "It is unlawful for any person to receive, retain, conceal, possess or dispose of personal property, cash or other representative of value, who knows or has reason to believe the property, cash or other representative of value has been obtained by fraud."

The approach the Idaho legislature used—enumerating each potential aspect of identity theft and making each aspect a crime in and of itself—is important for many reasons. First, it allows investigation and prosecution even when the perpetrator may only be in the process of identity theft and may not have completed the crime. It also allows criminal conspirators who engage in ongoing identity theft scams to be charged with a number of crimes related to their activities. For example, if one poses as an agent of some government agency to acquire personal identification information and then uses that information to acquire goods, then at least four different statutes are violated. This gives law-enforcement agencies a wide array of tools to utilize in combating identity theft. For this reason, the Idaho statutes are worthy of study and should be contemplated by other state legislative bodies.

New York Identity-Theft Laws

The state of New York addresses identity theft via penal code 190.77-190.84[13], which covers identity theft and related charges. Statutes 190.77 through 190.80 define a variety of levels of identity-theft crimes, including identity theft in the second and third degrees as well as aggravated identity theft. Identity theft in the third degree, the least serious offense under New York law, is defined as follows:

> A person is guilty of identity theft in the third degree when he or she knowingly and with intent to defraud assumes the identity of another person by presenting himself or herself as that other person, or by acting as that other person or by using personal identifying information of that other person, and thereby:

1. obtains goods, money, property or services or uses credit in the name of such other person or causes financial loss to such person or to another person or persons.

Identity theft in the third degree is considered a class A misdemeanor. If the offense involves loss in excess of $2,000, New York statute 190.80 classifies that as identity theft in the first degree, which is a class D felony. 190.80-A further classifies identity theft wherein the victim is a member of the armed services who is deployed outside the continental United States with damages in excess of $500 as aggravated identity theft, which is also a class D felony. This fine tuning of identity-theft laws is very interesting as it demonstrates that the New York legislature put some time and thought into these laws. It also demonstrates recognition on the part of New York that, like other crimes, identity theft can occur in varying degrees of severity.

The New York penal code 190.81 through 190.9-83 goes on to list three levels (first through third degree) of crimes for possession of personal identifying information without authorization. The law states:

> A person is guilty of unlawful possession of personal identification information in the third degree when he or she knowingly possesses a person's financial services account number or code, savings account number or code, checking account number or code, brokerage account number or code, credit card account number or code, debit card number or code, automated teller machine number or code, personal identification number, mother's maiden name, computer system password, electronic signature or unique biometric data that is a fingerprint, voice print, retinal image or iris image of another person knowing such information is intended to be used in furtherance of the commission of a crime defined in this chapter.

This is important because it makes it a crime to simply possess information that one could use to commit fraud. This has a similar effect to Idaho's legislation in that it makes various aspects of identity theft individual crimes. It also gives law enforcement the opportunity to prosecute a case in which the fraud aspect may not be provable, but the possession of personal identification information is. For example, if in the course of an investigation a law-enforcement officer discovers a suspect's computer has personal identifying information for 20 people, that suspect can be charged with 20 counts under this law. This holds true even if any use of this information in the commission of a fraud cannot be proven.

Maryland Identity-Theft Laws

The Maryland statute has some interesting language that is worthy of examination. It states the following:

> A person may not knowingly, willfully, and with fraudulent intent possess, obtain, or help another to possess or obtain any personal identifying information of an individual, without the consent of the individual, in order to

use, sell, or transfer the information to get a benefit, credit, good, service, or other thing of value in the name of the individual[14].

Note that this language states that possessing, obtaining, or helping someone else to obtain personal identifying information is a crime. Like the previously mentioned New York statute, this law allows investigation and prosecution even before financial damages have been incurred. This is an important tool for any law-enforcement officer. The law goes on to address the devices that are often used to gather information from credit cards for the purpose of identity theft:

A person may not knowingly, willfully, and with fraudulent intent to obtain a benefit, credit, good, service, or other thing of value, use:

1. a re–encoder to place information encoded on the magnetic strip or stripe of a credit card onto the magnetic strip or stripe of a different credit card or use any other electronic medium that allows such a transaction to occur without the consent of the individual authorized to use the credit card from which the personal identifying information or payment device number is being re–encoded; or

2. a skimming device to access, read, scan, obtain, memorize, or store personal identifying information or a payment device number on the magnetic strip or stripe of a credit card without the consent of the individual authorized to use the credit card.

It is an important aspect of this law that it addresses the tools used in identity theft, but it should be a concern that the legislation, as it is written, provides no exception for such devices that may be possessed for legitimate purposes. The legislature depends on reasonable people interpreting this law in a reasonable manner. It would have been preferable for them to specifically exclude such devices being used for legitimate retail, research, or software-development purposes in situations where the person whose card is being swiped or scanned is fully aware of the scanning and agrees to it. As this law is written, it would be possible to charge a computer programmer who is working on new card-scanning software with a crime. So far no law-enforcement agency or prosecutor has tried to bring such charges, and it is likely that none will. However, it is always better for the legislative bodies that create such laws to be perfectly clear on the issues involved.

Table 4.2 lists the identity-theft–related statutes for all states.

Table 4.2 Identity-Theft Statutes

State	Statute	Title/Specific Items Addressed
Alabama	13A-8-190 to 13A-8-201	The Consumer Identity Protection Act
Alaska	11.46.180	Theft by deception
	11.46.565	Criminal impersonation in the first degree
	11.46.570	Criminal impersonation in the second degree
Arizona	13-2008	Taking identity of another person
	13-2009	Aggravated taking identity of another person or entity
	13-2010	Trafficking in the identity of another person or entity
Arkansas	5-37-227	Financial identity fraud and non-financial identity fraud
	5-37-228	Identity theft passport
California	Penal Code 530.5 to 530.8	Personal Information Trafficking and Mail Theft Prevention Act
Colorado	18-5-901 *et seq.*	Identity theft
		Criminal possession of a financial device
		Gathering identity information by deception
		Possession of identity-theft tools
Connecticut	53a-129a *et seq.*	Identity theft in the first degree
		Identity theft in the second degree
		Identity theft in the third degree
		Trafficking in personal identifying information
Delaware	11828	Possession of burglar's tools or instruments facilitating theft; class F felony
	11854	Identity theft
	11854a	Identity theft passport; application; issuance
District of Columbia	22-3227.01 to 3227.08	Identity theft in the first degree
		Identity theft in the second degree
		Enhanced penalty
Florida	817.568	Criminal use of personal identification information
Georgia	16-9-121 to 16-9-128	Financial identity fraud
Hawaii	708-839.6	Identity theft in the first degree
	708-839.7	Identity theft in the second degree
	708-839.8	Identity theft in the third degree
	708-839.55	Unauthorized possession of confidential personal information

State	Statute	Title/Specific Items Addressed
	708-893	Use of a computer in the commission of a separate crime
Idaho	18-3124	Fraudulent use of a financial transaction card or number
	18-3125	Criminal possession of financial transaction card, financial transaction number, and FTC forgery devices
	18-3125A	Unauthorized factoring of credit-card sales drafts
	18-3126	Misappropriation of personal identifying information
	18-3126A	Acquisition of personal identifying information by false authority
	18-3127	Receiving or possessing fraudulently obtained goods or services
	18-3128	Penalty for violation
Illinois	720 ILCS	Identity Theft Law
	5/16G-1 to	Facilitating identity theft
	720 ILCS	Transmission of personal identifying information
	5/16G-40	Identity theft
	2007 P.A. 95-60	Aggravated identity theft
Indiana	35-43-5-1	Definitions
	34-43-5-3.5	Identity deception
Iowa	715A-8 *et seq.*	Identity theft
	715A.9A	Identity theft passport
Kansas	21-3830	Vital records identity fraud
	21-4018	Identity theft, identity fraud
	21-4603d	
Kentucky	514.160	Theft of identity
	514.170	Trafficking in stolen identities
Louisiana	RS 14:67.16	Identity theft
Maine	17-A905-A	Misuse of identification
Maryland	Criminal Law	Identity fraud
	8-301 to 8-305	Intent to manufacture, distribute, or dispense identities
		Assuming identity of another/representation without authorization
		Identity theft passport
Massachusetts	26637E	Use of personal identification of another; identity fraud; penalty
Michigan	445.61 *et seq.*	Identity Theft Protection Act
Minnesota	609.527	Identity theft
		Crime of electronic use of false pretense to obtain identity
Mississippi	97-19-85	Fraudulent use of identity, Social Security number, credit card, or debit-card number, or other identifying information to obtain thing of value

State	Statute	Title/Specific Items Addressed
	97-45-1 *et seq.*	Computer crimes and identity theft
	97-45-29	Identity theft passport
Missouri	570.223	Identity theft; penalty
		Trafficking in stolen identities, crime of possession of documents, exemptions violations, penalty
Montana	45-6-332	Theft of identity
	46-24-220	Identity theft passport
Nebraska	28-608	Criminal impersonation
Nevada	205.461 *et seq.*	Obtaining and using personal identifying information of another person to harm person or impersonate person
	205.464	Obtaining, using, possessing, or selling personal identifying information for unlawful purpose by public officer or public employee.
	205.465	Possession or sale of document or personal identifying information to establish false status or identity.
	205.4651	Identity theft passport
New Hampshire	638:25 to 638:27	Identity fraud
New Jersey	2C:21-17 to 2C:21-17.6	Impersonation; theft of identity; crime
		Use of personal identifying information of another, certain; second-degree crime
		Trafficking in personal identifying information pertaining to another person, certain; crime degrees; terms defined
New Mexico	30-16-24.1	Theft of identity
		Obtaining identity by electronic fraud
New York	Penal Code 190.77 to 190.84	Identity theft in the third degree
		Identity theft in the second degree
		Identity theft in the first degree
		Unlawful possession of personal identifying information in the third degree
		Unlawful possession of personal identifying information in the second degree
		Unlawful possession of personal identifying information in the first degree
North Carolina	14-113.20 to 14-113.23	Identity theft
		Trafficking in stolen identities
North Dakota	12.1-23-11	Unauthorized use of personal identifying information; penalty
Ohio	2913.49	Identity fraud
	109.94	Identity fraud against an elderly person or disabled adult

State	Statute	Title/Specific Items Addressed
		Identity theft passport
Oklahoma	211533.1	Identity theft
	2007	Identity theft passport
	Chapter 167	
	22-19b	
Oregon	165.800 2007	Identity theft
	Chapter 184	Aggravated identity theft
Pennsylvania	Pa. Cons. Stat. title 18, 4120	Identity theft
Rhode Island	11-49.1-1 to 11-49.1-5	Impersonation and Identity Fraud Act
South Carolina	16-13-500 to 16-13-530	Personal Financial Security Act
South Dakota	22-40-1 *et seq.*	Identity theft
Tennessee	39-14-150	Identity theft
	39-16-303	Identity theft trafficking
		Using a false identification
Texas	Penal Code 32.51	Fraudulent Use or Possession of Identifying Information
	2007 Chapter 1163	Identity Theft Enforcement and Protection Act
Utah	76-6-1101 to 76-6-1104	Identity fraud
		Unlawful possession of another's identification documents
Vermont	13 2030	Identity theft
Virginia	18.2-152.5:1	Using a computer to gather identifying information
	18.2-186.3	Identity fraud; consumer reporting agencies; police reports
	18.2-186.3:1	Expungement of false identity information from police and court records
	18.2-186.5	Identity theft passport
Washington	9.35.001 to 9.35-902	Improperly obtaining financial information
		Identity theft
West Virginia	61-3-54	Taking identity of another person; penalty
Wisconsin	943.201	Misappropriation of personal identifying information or personal identification documents
	943.203	Unauthorized use of an entity's identifying information or documents
Wyoming	6-3-901	Unauthorized use of personal identifying information

Child-Pornography Laws

It is unfortunate that the technology that gives us instant access to information and news has become a hunting ground for pedophiles. However distasteful this subject might be, no one can work in computer-related crimes for long and not encounter it. Every state has some law addressing child pornography. Some states even have laws requiring IT workers to report child pornography should they find it. Other states may not yet have specific legislation dealing with IT workers who discover child pornography but do have laws requiring anyone who sees evidence of child abuse to report it. Let's look at a few examples of state laws regarding child pornography.

Arkansas Legislation

Arkansas bills 5-27-602 and 603 deal with child pornography. These bills are quite explicit and comprehensive[15]. They clearly refer to any person who:

1. Knowingly receives for the purpose of selling or knowingly sells, procures, manufactures, gives, provides, lends, trades, mails, delivers, transfers, publishes, distributes, circulates, disseminates, presents, exhibits, advertises, offers, or agrees to offer, through any means, including the Internet, any photograph, film, videotape, computer program or file, computer-generated image, video game, or any other reproduction or reconstruction which depicts a child engaging in sexually explicit conduct; or

2. Knowingly possesses or views through any means, including on the Internet, any photograph, film, videotape, computer program or file, computer-generated image, video game, or any other reproduction, which depicts a child engaging in sexually explicit conduct.

This legislation is commendable in that it explicitly defines any number of means of disseminating child pornography as well as addresses anyone who simply possesses or views such material. However it falls short in one regard. The law states, "which depicts a child engaging in sexually explicit conduct"—this could be construed by some to not include simple pictures of nude children if they are not engaged in any activity. The law would be clearer if it addressed this issue.

What makes the Arkansas legislation even more interesting is section 604. This section addresses employees and Internet service providers who may discover child pornography. Any person who:

1. Is the owner, operator, or employee of a computer online service, Internet service, or bulletin board service; and

2. The person knowingly fails to notify law-enforcement officials that a subscriber is using the service to commit a violation of 5-27-603.

While this legislation is laudable for addressing this issue, it is still incomplete. It does not expressly deal with technicians who may be repairing a computer and discover child pornography. When teaching classes to IT professionals, I have encountered questions about this scenario more than once. There are few state laws that explicitly address this issue. My response to students is always that they are ethically bound to report such material, even if their state imposes no legal obligation on them to do so.

Illinois Laws

The state of Illinois, in its Abused and Neglected Child Reporting Act[16], covers all forms of child abuse, including child pornography. And unlike most state laws, it covers the obligation of a computer technician to report child pornography. The law states:

> If an electronic and information technology equipment worker discovers any depiction of child pornography while installing, repairing, or otherwise servicing an item of electronic and information technology equipment, that worker or the worker's employer shall immediately report the discovery to the local law enforcement agency or to the Cyber Tipline at the National Center for Missing & Exploited Children.

The law goes further and protects that technician from any reprisals for reporting the pornography and provides for fines should the technician knowingly fail to report it:

> (d) An electronic and information technology equipment worker or electronic and information technology equipment worker's employer who reports a discovery of child pornography as required under this Section is immune from any criminal, civil, or administrative liability in connection with making the report, except for willful or wanton misconduct.

> (e) Failure to report a discovery of child pornography as required under this Section is a business offense subject to a fine of $1,001.

This is an important area that too many state legislatures have overlooked. Computer technicians, particularly in retail environments, routinely examine a variety of computers. It is in fact quite likely that at some point in their career, every technician may indeed discover illicit material on a customer's computer. This law is critical not only because it compels the technician to report the crime, but it provides blanket protection for that technician. That is an important element. Any law that compels a citizen to any action should also protect that citizen from liability for that action.

California Laws

California laws regarding obscenity and child pornography are contained within California penal code 311[17]. It can be a difficult task to define obscenity in general, but when dealing with child pornography the issue is a bit clearer. The main issue with child pornography is defining the medium by which something is transmitted. California penal code does an excellent job of this.

(a) Every person who knowingly sends or causes to be sent, or brings or causes to be brought, into this state for sale or distribution, or in this state possesses, prepares, publishes, produces, develops, duplicates, or prints any representation of information, data, or image, including, but not limited to, any film, filmstrip, photograph, negative, slide, photocopy, videotape, video laser disc, computer hardware, computer software, computer floppy disc, data-storage media, CD-ROM, or computer-generated equipment or any other computer-generated image that contains or incorporates in any manner, any film or filmstrip, with intent to distribute or to exhibit to, or to exchange with, others, or who offers to distribute, distributes, or exhibits to, or exchanges with, others, any obscene matter, knowing that the matter depicts a person under the age of 18 years personally engaging in or personally simulating sexual conduct, as defined in Section 311.4, shall be punished either by imprisonment in the county jail for up to one year, by a fine not to exceed one thousand dollars ($1,000), or by both the fine and imprisonment, or by imprisonment in the state prison, by a fine not to exceed ten thousand dollars ($10,000), or by the fine and imprisonment.

The wording of this legislation is notable for several reasons. Aside from the fact that it clearly delineates an extensive list of possible media by which pornographic materials might be transmitted, it also clearly defines the criminal aspect with the clause "knowing that the matter depicts a person under the age of

18 years." This is fascinating because of the word "knowing." Under California law, if you did not know (or reasonably should have known) that the person depicted in the images was under 18, or you did not know the media contained pornographic images, you are not guilty of trafficking in child pornography. Throughout the California penal code regarding child pornography, the words "knowing" and "knowingly" are repeated several times. It is clear that the intent of the legislature was to make certain that someone who unwittingly transmits child pornography is not punished for it. The law goes on to clearly and in detail describe what is meant by sexual conduct, what is meant by distribution, and other related terms. All legislation will attempt to define its terms, but the California penal code on child pornography is noteworthy due to how extensively it clarifies the meaning of terms in the law.

Connecticut Laws

The state of Connecticut codifies its obscenity laws in statute 53-A 196[18] (parts A through D). For the most part, this legislation faces the same tough challenge that all legislation faces: defining exactly what is obscene. However, this legislation attempts to define what obscenity is not:

> it depicts or describes in a patently offensive way a prohibited sexual act, and (C) **taken as a whole, it lacks serious literary, artistic, educational, political or scientific value.**

Note the last clause (emphasis added). This is designed to exempt medical imagery, legitimate art, and other types of images. It is important that child pornography laws take steps to ensure that non-pornographic material does not inadvertently fall under the law.

This legislation attempts to define child pornography in the following way:

> "Child pornography" means any material involving a live performance or photographic or other visual reproduction of a live performance which depicts a minor in a prohibited sexual act . . .

The flaw with this wording is that it does not address the issue of still photos of nude children not engaged in any sexual acts at all. It also does not attempt to address simulated child pornography. For those readers not aware, simulated child pornography is when adult actors and actresses are used because they appear particularly young and can pass for minors.

The Connecticut law has another very serious flaw when addressing the transfer of pornographic material to minors. In 53a -196, it states, "A person is guilty of obscenity as to minors when he knowingly promotes to a minor, for monetary consideration, any material or performance which is obscene as to minors."

The phrase "for monetary consideration" is potentially problematic. Taken literally (as it is certain some defense attorney will), this means that if the material is given away free of charge, it does not fall under this particular clause of this law. However, this law does provide exemptions to individuals who unwittingly sell pornography to minors:

> In any prosecution for obscenity as to minors, it shall be an affirmative defense that the defendant made (1) a reasonable mistake as to age, and (2) a reasonable bona fide attempt to ascertain the true age of such minor, by examining a draft card, driver's license, birth certificate or other official or apparently official document, exhibited by such minor, purporting to establish that such minor was seventeen years of age or older.

All obscenity and pornography laws must make very clear that a person cannot be guilty of a crime if he or she did not realize (or reasonably should have realized) the person was a minor. Taken as a whole, the Connecticut law falls short on several elements.

Delaware Laws

Title 11 section 1103 of the Delaware Code[19] deals with child pornography. As with all laws regarding pornography, this law uses some terms that may not have a clear-cut meaning for all people. For example, the Delaware law makes frequent use of the term "lascivious." However, this piece of legislation does address two issues that, as we have already seen, many state laws fail to address.

The first area that Delaware law addresses is simulated child pornography. As we have already mentioned, some distributors of child pornography use actors and actresses who are quite young (often around 18 years of age) who naturally appear much younger. These actors and actresses will then be made to look even younger. Unfortunately this phenomenon has escaped the attention of many state legislatures. However, it is clear that even though the actors themselves are not actually minors, the pornographic product is meant to appeal to pedophiles. Therefore, the Delaware legislature addressed this with the following clause:

> For the purposes of 1108, 1109, 1110, 1111 and 1112A of this Title, "child" shall also mean any individual who is intended by the defendant to appear to be 14 years of age or less.

This is a very important distinction that other state legislative bodies would do well to consider and emulate. Based on this clause, it does not matter what the actual age of the person depicted is. If the imagery is intended to make that person appear to be 14 years old or younger, then the image can be treated as child pornography.

We have also mentioned previously in this chapter that many state laws only expressly address child pornography as imagery depicting minors in actual sexual acts. Delaware has gone further and addressed the issue of nude photos of children not engaged in any acts:

> Lascivious exhibition of the genitals or pubic area of any child . . . .

Note that this clause is meant to address the gaps found in other laws; however, it is dependent upon the definition of the word lascivious. The intent is to prevent innocent family photographs from being classified as child pornography—for example, a picture of a baby in a bath tub. This is a laudable goal, but the term "lascivious" is too easily challenged and open to interpretation. It might have been more clear if they had borrowed language from California and used the term "sexually provocative."

Delaware also followed the example of other states and amended its code to insert the word "knowingly." This was done for the express purpose of exempting people who might unwittingly be in possession of or transport child pornography. This is an important item and many states include such clauses.

Oregon Laws

As most readers are no doubt aware, online predators are a growing problem. The TV documentary series *To Catch a Predator* documented numerous online predators who used their online activities as a prelude to attempts to meet with a child in person. Unfortunately, many state laws have not yet addressed the online activity itself. In many states, it is only illegal if the person actually attempts to engage in sexual activity with the child or sends pornographic imagery to the child. Oregon statutes 163.432 and 433[20] have taken a step forward and made the online sexual discussions with a minor a criminal offense in and of itself:

(a) For the purpose of arousing or gratifying the sexual desire of the person or another person, knowingly uses an online communication to solicit a child to engage in sexual contact or sexually explicit conduct; and

(b) Offers or agrees to physically meet with the child.

163.433 goes further and states that trying to escalate the online activity into a physical meeting is, in and of itself, yet another offense:

1. A person commits the crime of online sexual corruption of a child in the first degree if the person violates ORS 163.432 and intentionally takes a substantial step toward physically meeting with or encountering the child.

These are important provisions that many state laws have not added to their own penal code.

While the state of Oregon has been very proactive in addressing this issue, they have also done a very good job of protecting innocent parties from being accused under this law. It is not uncommon for teenagers to engage in explicit online dialogue with one another. The purpose of this law is not to address that issue, but to address adults attempting to exploit minors. In order to prevent the prosecution of minors who are engaged in online conversation with other minors, the Oregon statute has added this clause:

It is an affirmative defense to a prosecution for online sexual corruption of a child in the first or second degree that the person was not more than three years older than the person reasonably believed the child to be.

The Oregon legislation also explicitly approves of decoys working online to catch predators, and does so with the following language:

It is not a defense to a prosecution for online sexual corruption of a child in the first or second degree that the person was in fact communicating with a law-enforcement officer, as defined in ORS 163.730, or a person working under the direction of a law-enforcement officer, who is 16 years of age or older.

This clause is critical as it paves the way for undercover sting operations by law-enforcement agencies. The Oregon legislation is very thorough and commendable.

Sexting

Any discussion of laws regarding child pornography would be incomplete if it did not include the topic of sexting. *Sexting* is the use of the text-messaging feature of cell phones to send sexually explicit material. The news throughout 2009 was replete with stories of teenagers sexting and being arrested for it. In most cases, both the person sending the images and the person in the images were minors, and usually the sender was charged under existing child pornography laws. A few notable cases would include the following:

- August 26, 2009, a 17-year-old from Middletown, New York[21] was arrested for sending pictures involving his 15-year-old girlfriend either nude and/or engaged in sexual acts.

- In October of 2009, Whitnall, Wisconsin saw a single incident of a teenager sending nude pictures of his 14-year-old girlfriend expand into an investigation of sexting throughout the high school[22]. Multiple students could face charges of child pornography.

- In October of 2009, seven teenagers, including three females, from Susquenita High School[23] in Perry County, Pennsylvania, were charged with child pornography in relation to sexting. It began with some of the accused using a cell phone to video themselves engaged in a sex act and then sending that video on to friends.

Clearly, this is a controversial topic. On one side, many parents and law-enforcement officials feel this is an appropriate application of the law and that teenagers should be aware of the consequences of distributing pornography. On the other side are parents, citizens, and legal experts who feel this is a perversion of the entire intent of child pornography laws. Whatever one's personal opinion on the matter, it is clear that this is a very difficult area for law enforcement. As of this writing, most states have not written any legislation to clarify this situation.

While most states have not enacted any laws related specifically to sexting, in June 2009 New Jersey introduced a law regarding minors accused of sexting[24]. This bill set up an alternative educational program for juveniles convicted of sexting. This was a compromise position that did not de-criminalize the act of sexting, but did avoid sending juveniles to jail for the offense.

Vermont, in State Bill 125[25], added provisions to their pornography laws to address minors sexting. However, the Vermont law expressly sends such issues to family court as a matter of juvenile delinquency rather than a serious criminal activity. The law states

> No minor shall knowingly and voluntarily and without threat or coercion use a computer or electronic communication device to transmit an indecent visual depiction of himself or herself to another person.

and

> Except as provided in subdivision (3) of this subsection, a minor who violates subsection (a) of this section shall be adjudicated delinquent. An action brought under this subdivision (1) shall be filed in family court and treated as a juvenile proceeding pursuant to Chapter 52 of Title 33, and may be referred to the juvenile diversion program of the district in which the action is filed.

Ohio took a different approach[26]. With house bill 132, the Ohio legislature chose to directly treat sexting as a criminal act. Their statute is very clear:

> Sec. 2907.324. (A) No minor, by use of a telecommunications device, shall recklessly create, receive, exchange, send, or possess a photograph, video, or other material that shows a minor in a state of nudity.

> (B) It is no defense to a charge under this section that the minor creates, receives, exchanges, sends, or possesses a photograph, video, or other material that shows themselves in a state of nudity.

> (C) Whoever violates this section is guilty of illegal use of a telecommunications device involving a minor in a state of nudity, a delinquent act that would be a misdemeanor of the first degree if it could be committed as an adult.

This legislation is clear and unambiguous. It expressly targets juveniles who might be in any way engaged in the process of sending, possessing, or receiving sexually explicit images.

Clearly the matter of sexting remains a sensitive and controversial issue. Many state legislatures have still not addressed this matter, and those who have seem to have very diverse approaches to the issue.

As you can see, there is quite a bit of variation from state to state regarding both child-pornography laws and sexting. It is critical for any law-enforcement officer to be intimately familiar with the laws in his or her state. Table 4.3 summarizes the child pornography laws in all 50 states.

Table 4.3 Child-Pornography Laws

State	Relevant Laws
Alabama	Code 13 A 12 190–198
Alaska	Statute 11.61.123, 125,127, and 128
Arizona	Statute 13-3551–3553
Arkansas	Code 5-27-302–306 and 5-17.602-607
California	Penal Code 311
Colorado	Statute 8-16-403 and 404
Connecticut	Statute 53A-196
Delaware	Code 1108-1111
District of Columbia	Code 22-3101–3104
Florida	Statute 827.071 and 847
Georgia	Code 16-12-100
Hawaii	Statute 707-750–753
Idaho	Code 1801707
Illinois	Statute 5 11-20.1
Indiana	Code 35-42-4-4 and 35-49-3-2 and -3
Iowa	Code 728.1
Kansas	Statute 21-3516
Kentucky	Statute 531-300, 310, 320, 330, 335, 340, and 350
Louisiana	Statute 14:81.1 and 14:91.11
Maine	Statute 281-284
Maryland	Code 11-207 and 208
Massachusetts	General Law 272 29-30
Michigan	Law 750-145c
Minnesota	Statute 647.245–247
Mississippi	Code 97-5-31, 33, 35, and 37
Missouri	Statute 573.010, .023, .025, .030, .035, .037, .050, and .052
Montana	Code 45-5-625
Nebraska	Statute 28-1463.02–.05
Nevada	Statute 200.700, 710, 720, 725, 730, 735, 740, and 750
New Hampshire	Statute 649-A:2, 3, 5, 6, and 7
New Jersey	Statute 2C:34-3 and 2C:24-4
New Mexico	Statute 30-6A
New York	Penal Law 263
North Carolina	Statute 14-190

State	Relevant Laws
North Dakota	Code 12.1-27.2
Ohio	Code 2907-321, 322, and 323
Oklahoma	Title 12 1021 and Statute 1021-1024
Oregon	Statute 163.665 to 693
Pennsylvania	Statute 6312
Rhode Island	General Law 11-9-1.2 and 1.3
South Carolina	Code 16-15-395, 405, and 410
South Dakota	Law 22-24A-3
Tennessee	Code 39-17-1003-1005
Texas	Code 43.25 and 43.26
Utah	Code 75-51-2, 3, and 4
Vermont	Title 13 2821, 2825, 2826, and 2827
Virginia	Code 18.2-374
Washington	Code 9.68A.040, 050, 060, 070, 080, 110
West Virginia	Code 61-8c
Wisconsin	Statute 948-.05 and .12
Wyoming	Statute 6-4-303

Hacking Laws

While many hackers are ultimately tried and convicted under federal statutes, most states do have laws regarding hacking into systems. This is necessary for scenarios in which there is no federal jurisdiction. For example, if a student hacks into a school system, this is likely to be state jurisdiction.

Maine Laws

The Maine statute is of note primarily because it is rather limited. The law simply states

> A person is guilty of criminal invasion of computer privacy if the person intentionally accesses any computer resource knowing that the person is not authorized to do so.[27]

Now prior to this, the legislation does define key terms:

1. "Access" means to gain logical entry into, instruct, communicate with, store data in or retrieve data from any computer resource. [1989, c. 620, (NEW).]

2. "Computer" means an electronic, magnetic, optical, electrochemical, or other high-speed data processing device performing logical, arithmetic, or storage functions, and includes any data-storage facility or communications facility directly related to or operating in conjunction with such device.

Now the definition of access is actually quite good. Logical entry has a well-defined meaning in the computer profession: It means the person need not be physically present. For example, when you log on to your bank Web site to check your balance, you have gained logical entry into the system. The problem here is the definition of computer and the fact that there are various types of unauthorized access. For example, purposefully using a password cracker to break into someone's bank account is one type of unauthorized access; accidentally getting into someone's Yahoo! e-mail account because they forgot to log off when on a public terminal is quite another. This is the weakness of this particular legislation. It does cover all types of unauthorized access but provides no differentiation.

Montana Laws

Montana has what is essentially a slightly expanded but similar legislation to what we have seen in Maine. Their law[28] states that any person who

(a) obtains the use of any computer, computer system, or computer network without consent of the owner;

(b) alters or destroys or causes another to alter or destroy a computer program or computer software without consent of the owner; or

(c) obtains the use of or alters or destroys a computer, computer system, computer network, or any part thereof as part of a deception for the purpose of obtaining money, property, or computer services from the owner of the computer, computer system, computer network, or part thereof or from any other person.

(2) A person convicted of the offense of unlawful use of a computer involving property not exceeding $1,500 in value shall be fined not to exceed $1,500 or be imprisoned in the county jail for a term not to exceed 6 months, or both. A person convicted of the offense of unlawful use of a computer involving property exceeding $1,500 in value shall be fined not more than 2½ times the value of the property used, altered, destroyed, or obtained or be imprisoned in the state prison for a term not to exceed 10 years, or both.

This law differentiates sentencing based on the amount of damage done. It also includes a clause wherein the dollar value of any property obtained can be a basis for sentencing. This is important for cases in which nothing is damaged, but intellectual property is stolen. This law is also interesting in that it includes prison terms of up to 10 years in addition to fines. It is important that prosecutors have at their discretion the option of significant criminal penalties for computer-related offenses.

North Carolina Laws

The North Carolina laws are much more extensive in regard to hacking. Statute 14-454[29] deals with unauthorized access of computers.

(a) It is unlawful to willfully, directly or indirectly, access or cause to be accessed any computer, computer program, computer system, computer network, or any part thereof, for the purpose of:

    (1) Devising or executing any scheme or artifice to defraud, unless the object of the scheme or artifice is to obtain educational testing material, a false educational testing score, or a false academic or vocational grade, or

    (2) Obtaining property or services other than educational testing material, a false educational testing score, or a false academic or vocational grade for a person, by means of false or fraudulent pretenses, representations or promises.

    (3) A violation of this subsection is a Class G felony if the fraudulent scheme or artifice results in damage of more than one thousand dollars ($1,000), or if the property or services obtained are worth more than one thousand dollars ($1,000). Any other violation of this subsection is a Class 1 misdemeanor.

(b) Any person who willfully and without authorization, directly or indirectly, accesses or causes to be accessed any computer, computer program, computer system, or computer network for any purpose other than those set forth in subsection (a) above, is guilty of a Class 1 misdemeanor.

(c) For the purpose of this section, the phrase "access or cause to be accessed" includes introducing, directly or indirectly, a computer program (including a self-replicating or a self-propagating computer program) into a computer, computer program, computer system, or computer network.

Notice that this law is quite explicit on exactly what is meant by unauthorized access. Also note that this law addresses self-replicating programs such as worms and viruses. Now on your first read it might seem this law has limited applicability, only to hacking for the purposes listed. But note the class that states "Any person who willfully and without authorization, directly or indirectly, accesses or causes to be accessed any computer, computer program, computer system, or computer network for any purpose other than those set forth in subsection (a) above." This language allows the prosecution of individuals who may have obtained unauthorized access to a computer system for a purpose not listed.

Then statute 14-451 expands upon this for the special case of accessing government computers. 14-455 deals with damage to computer systems as a separate issue.

(a) It is unlawful to willfully and without authorization alter, damage, or destroy a computer, computer program, computer system, computer network, or any part thereof. A violation of this subsection is a Class G felony if the damage caused by the alteration, damage, or destruction is more than one thousand dollars ($1,000). Any other violation of this subsection is a Class 1 misdemeanor.

(a1) It is unlawful to willfully and without authorization alter, damage, or destroy a government computer. A violation of this subsection is a Class F felony.

(b) This section applies to alteration, damage, or destruction effectuated by introducing, directly or indirectly, a computer program (including a self-replicating or a self-propagating computer program) into a computer, computer program, computer system, or computer network.

Notice that like the legislation regarding unauthorized access, this law also addresses viruses and worms. This is an important addition that some state laws fail to address.

Section 14-456 adds language that is often overlooked in legislation. This section states that:

Any person who willfully and without authorization denies or causes the denial of computer, computer program, computer system, or computer network services to an authorized user of the computer, computer program, computer system, or computer network services is guilty of a Class 1 misdemeanor.

This expressly addresses denial-of-service (DoS) attacks. As we discussed in Chapters 1 and 2, this is a very common sort of attack. Unfortunately, many state laws fail to address this particular issue directly. Other state legislative bodies would be well advised to emulate North Carolina in its addressing of denial-of-service attacks.

Rhode Island Laws

The state of Rhode Island has addressed a wide array of computer crimes via subsections of law 11-52. 11-52-3[30] addresses unauthorized access:

> Whoever, intentionally, without authorization, and for fraudulent or other illegal purposes, directly or indirectly, accesses, alters, damages, or destroys any computer, computer system, computer network, computer software, computer program, or data contained in a computer, computer system, computer program, or computer network shall be guilty of a felony....

The first thing of note in this law is that it makes these acts a felony. Under many state laws, unauthorized access is merely a misdemeanor. The other item of note is the broad language used. Phrases such as "directly or indirectly" and "or other illegal purposes" give prosecutors and law-enforcement officials wide latitude.

11-52-4-1 deals with computer trespass and does so quite thoroughly.

(a) It shall be unlawful for any person to use a computer or computer network without authority and with the intent to:

  (1) Temporarily or permanently remove, halt, or otherwise disable any computer data, computer programs, or computer software from a computer or computer network;

  (2) Cause a computer to malfunction regardless of how long the malfunction persists;

  (3) Alter or erase any computer data, computer programs, or computer software;

  (4) Effect the creation or alteration of a financial instrument or of an electronic transfer of funds;

  (5) Cause physical injury to the property of another;

(6) Make or cause to be made an unauthorized copy, in any form, including, but not limited to, any printed or electronic form of computer data, computer programs, or computer software residing in, communicated by, or produced by a computer or computer network;

(7) Forge e-mail header information or other Internet routine information for the purpose of sending unsolicited bulk electronic mail through or into the facilities of an electronic mail service provider or its subscribers; or

(8) To sell, give or otherwise distribute or possess with the intent to sell, give or distribute software which is designed to facilitate or enable the forgery of electronic mail header information or other Internet routing information for the purpose of sending unsolicited bulk electronic mail through or into the facilities of an electronic mail service provider or its subscribers.

(b) Nothing in this section shall be construed to interfere with or prohibit terms or conditions in a contract or license related to computers, computer data, computer networks, computer operations, computer programs, computer services, or computer software or to create any liability by reason of terms or conditions adopted by, or technical measures implemented by, a Rhode Island–based electronic mail service provider to prevent the transmission of unsolicited bulk electronic mail in violation of this chapter. Whoever violates this section shall be guilty of a felony and shall be subject to the penalties set forth in § 11-52-2. If the value is five hundred dollars ($500) or less, then the person shall be guilty of a misdemeanor and may be punishable by imprisonment for a term not exceeding one year or by a fine of not more than one thousand dollars ($1,000) or both.

Under this law, even temporarily disabling a computer program running on a system without authorization is a crime. Also listed as crimes in this law are altering or erasing any data or program, forging an e-mail header, and distributing software that would facilitate the forging of an e-mail header. This broad and thorough language is important because many times, these techniques are used as part of a skillful hacker's process of compromising a target system. Rhode Island is one of the few states that address these issues directly and specifically.

Table 4.4 lists the state laws related to unauthorized computer access.

Table 4.4 Unauthorized Access Laws

State	Relevant Law(s)
Alabama	Code 13A-8-102, 13A-8-103
Alaska	Statute 11.46.740
Arizona	Rev. Statute Ann. 13-2316
Arkansas	Statute 5-41-103, -104, -203
California	Penal Code 502
Colorado	Rev. Statute 18-5.5-102
Connecticut	Gen. Statute 53a-251
Delaware	Code title 11, 932, 933, 934, 935, 936
Florida	Statute Ann. 815.01 to 815.07
Georgia	Code 16-9-93, 16-9-152, 16-9-153
Hawaii	Statute 708-892, 708-891.5, 708-895.5, 708-892.5
Idaho	Code 18-2202
Illinois	Statute. 720, 5/16D-3, 5/16D-4
Indiana	Code 35-43-1-4, 35-43-2-3
Iowa	Code 716A.1 to 716A.16
Kansas	Statute Ann. 21-3755
Kentucky	Statute 434.845, 434.850, 434.851, 434.853
Louisiana	Statute Ann. 14:73.3, 14:73.5, 14:73.7
Maine	Statute Ann. title 17-A, 432 to 433
Maryland	Criminal Code Ann. 7-302
Massachusetts	General Law 266, 33A
Michigan	Law 752.794, 752.795
Minnesota	Statute 609.87, 609.88, 609.89, 609.891
Mississippi	Code Ann. 97-45-1 to 97-45-13
Missouri	Statute 537.525, 569.095, 569.097, 569.099
Montana	Code 45-2-101, 45-6-310, 45-6-311
Nebraska	Statute 28-1343, 28-1343.01, 28-1344, 28-1345, 28-1346, 28-1347
Nevada	Statute 205.473 to 205.492
New Hampshire	Statute Ann. 638:17, 638:18
New Jersey	Statute 2A:38A-3
New Mexico	Statute 30-45-3, 30-45-4, 30-45-5
New York	Penal Law 156.00 to 156.50
North Carolina	General Statute 14-453 to 14-458
North Dakota	Code 12.1-06.1-08

State	Relevant Law(s)
Ohio	Code 2909.01, 2909.07(A)(6), 2913.01, 2913.04
Oklahoma	Statute . 21, 1951, 1952, 1953, 1954, 1955, 1957, 1958
Oregon	Statute 164.377
Pennsylvania	7601 - 7616
Rhode Island	11-52-1 to 11-52-8
South Carolina	Code 16-16-10 to 16-16-30
South Dakota	Codified Laws 43-43B-1 to 43-43B-8
Tennessee	Code 39-14-601, 39-14-602
Texas	Penal Code 33.02
Utah	Code 76-6-702, 76-6-703
Vermont	Statute 13, 4101 to 4107
Virginia	Code 18.2-152.2, -152.3, -152.4, -152.5, -152.5:1, -152.6, -152.7, -152.8, -152.12, 19.2-249.2
Washington	Code 9A.52.110, 9A.52.120, 9A.52.130
West Virginia	Code 61-3C-3, -4, -5, -6, -7, -8, -9, -10, -11, -12
Wisconsin	Statute 943.70
Wyoming	Statute 6-3-501 to 6-3-505

State Spyware Laws

Spyware and adware have become a bigger problem than viruses , and many state legislative bodies have realized that. Several states have enacted laws specifically against spyware and adware; let's take a look at a few of those.

Arizona Laws

Arizona statute 44-7301[31] addresses the issue of spyware and adware. A major emphasis in this legislation is the use of spyware to perpetrate identity theft. That is a common occurrence, so it is natural for lawmakers to have this in mind when drafting legislation. This law does a very good job of defining what exactly personal identifying information is and specifically prohibits any type of software designed to get that information.

This law also does a good job of addressing phishing. According to this statute, it is a class 5 felony to use a Web page or an e-mail message or to solicit or induce another person to provide identifying information by representing or implying that the person is an online business without the authority or approval of the online business. In other words, sending an e-mail claiming to be from Bank of America and asking people to go to a Web page and enter their username and password is a class 5 felony.

Furthermore, this law explicitly addresses spyware. It bans any person from transmitting computer software if:

> That software will change Internet control settings, collect personally identifiable information, prevent the operator's efforts to block the installation or execution of the software, falsely claims that software will be disabled by the operator's actions; remove or disable security software installed on the computer; or take control of the computer.

The wording of the law is quite explicit and comprehensive.

Just as important as addressing spyware and phishing, this law also defines how businesses should dispose of customer information that could be used in identity theft.

Texas Laws

Texas legislation regarding spyware and phishing is quite comprehensive and includes some items that many other laws overlook. First, the Texas State Bill 28[32] specifically exempts legitimate entities such as Internet service providers who monitor Internet activity in order to maintain quality of service. If one reads the exact wording of the bill, it is clear that well-informed people wrote this bill; there are technical nuances sometimes missed in other laws. For example, the legislation explicitly addresses botnets and zombies. According to the bill, a *zombie* is a computer that is being controlled by another person without the computer's owner being aware, and a *botnet* is a network of two or more zombies. The Texas bill explicitly makes the creation of zombies or botnets illegal. The law allows the victim to recover actual damages or up to $100,000 for each zombie used. This is a very stiff financial penalty and shows that the Texas legislature is taking these crimes seriously. Table 4.5 summarizes the state anti-spyware and anti-adware laws, for those states that have such laws.

Table 4.5 State Spyware/Adware Laws

State	Relevant Laws
Alaska	Alaska Stat. 45.45.792, .794, .798;45.50.471(51)
Arizona	Ariz. Rev. Stat. Ann. 44-7301 to 44-7304
Arkansas	Ark. Code 4-11-101, -102, -103, -104, -105, 19-6-301, 19-6-804
California	Cal. Bus. & Prof. Code D. 8 22947 to 22947.6
Georgia	Ga. Code 16-9-152 to -157
Illinois	720 ILCS 5/16D-5.5
Indiana	Ind. Code 24-4.8-1 *et seq.*; Ind. Code 24-4.8-2 *et seq.*; Ind. Code 24-4.8-3 *et seq.*
Iowa	Iowa Code 715.1 to 715.8
Louisiana	La. Rev. Stat. Ann. 51:2006 to 51:2014
Nevada	Nev. Rev. Stat. 205.4737
New Hampshire	N.H. Rev. Stat. Ann. 359-H:1 to 359-H:6
Rhode Island	R.I. Gen. Laws §11-52.2-2, -3, -4, -5, -6, -7
Texas	Tex. Business & Commerce Code Ann. 324.001 to 324.102, 2009 S.B. 28
Utah	Utah Code Ann. 13-40-101 to 13-40-401
Washington	Wash. Rev. Code 19.270.101 to 19.270.900

Conclusion

As we have seen in this chapter, the various computer-crime laws vary greatly from state to state. Obviously, it is critical for anyone involved in the investigation of computer crimes to be familiar with the laws in their own state, but beyond that it is important for those involved in the legislative process to examine the laws in all states. As we have seen, some states have done an excellent job in one area, but perhaps not as well in other areas. Legislative bodies should examine and, when appropriate, borrow the language from the legislation in other states. Remember that gaps in the law can cause tremendous problems for law-enforcement agencies and prosecutors.

Endnotes

[1] Beverly Police Department. http://www.beverlypd.org/pdf/ PERSONAL%20SAFETY/CYBERSTALKING.pdf

2   Robert Bernstein, Defense Attorney. http://blog.california-law.org/2009/04/new-california-law-makes-cyber-stalking-a-crime.html

3   *Time Magazine.* "First California Cyber Stalking Case to Go to Trial." http://www.time.com/time/nation/article/0,8599,18789,00.html?iid=digg_share

4   Texas Penal Code. http://www.statutes.legis.state.tx.us/SOTWDocs/PE/htm/PE.42.htm#42.07

5   Utah Penal Code. http://www.le.utah.gov/UtahCode/getCodeSection?code=76-5-106.5

6   Louisiana Statutes. http://www.youtube.com/watch?v=ExF976UNuA8&feature=PlayList&p=98434276A12F9BE4&playnext=1&playnext_from=PL&index=4

7   Arizona Statute. http://www.azleg.state.az.us/ars/13/02921.htm

8   Indiana Statute. http://www.ai.org/legislative/ic/code/title35/ar45/ch2.html#IC35-45-2-2

9   Oklahoma Statute 21-1173. http://oklegal.onenet.net/oklegal-cgi/get_statute?98/Title.21/21-1173.html

10 Alabama Consumer Identity Protection Act. http://www.icje.org/id101.htm

11 Florida Statute 817.568. http://www.leg.state.fl.us/statutes/index.cfm?App_mode=Display_Statute&Search_String=&URL=Ch0817/SEC568.HTM&Title=-%3E2000-%3ECh0817-%3ESection+568

12 Idaho Identity Theft Center. http://www.idtheftcenter.org/artman2/publish/states/Idaho.shtml

13 New York Identity Theft Center. http://codes.lp.findlaw.com/nycode/PEN/K/190

14 Maryland Identity Theft Statutes. http://mlis.state.md.us/asp/web_statutes.asp?gcr&8-301

15 Arkansas Bill 5-27-602-604. http://www.accardv.uams.edu/SB975.asp

16 Illinois Abused and Neglected Child Reporting Act. http://www.ilga.gov/legislation/ilcs/ilcs3.asp?ActID=1460&ChapAct=325%26nbsp%3BILCS%26nbsp%3B5%2F&ChapterID=32&ChapterName=CHILDREN&ActName=Abused+and+Neglected+Child+Reporting+Act%2E

[17] California Penal Code 311. http://www.leginfo.ca.gov/cgi-bin/displaycode?section=pen&group=00001-01000&file=311-312.7

[18] Connecticut Obscenity Laws. http://www.moralityinmedia.org/nolc/stateObscLaws/connecticut.pdf

[19] Delaware Obscenity Laws. http://delcode.delaware.gov/sessionlaws/ga140/chp480.shtml

[20] Oregon Code. http://www.leg.state.or.us/ors/163.html

[21] *The Straus News Chronicle.* "Teen Charged with Sexting." http://www.straus-news .com/articles/2009/10/11/the_chronicle/news/14.txt

[22] WISN News. "Whitnall Sexting Investigation Expands." http://www.wisn.com/news/21233385/detail.html

[23] Newport Pennsylvania sexting case. http://blog.perrycountytimes.com/?p=1788

[24] New Jersey Sexting Law. http://www.njleg.state.nj.us/2008/Bills/A4500/4069_I1.HTM

[25] Ohio House Bill 132. http://www.legislature.state.oh.us/bills.cfm?ID=128_HB_132

[26] Vermont State Bill 125. http://www.leg.state.vt.us/docs/2010/Acts/ACT058.pdf

[27] Maine Unauthorized Access Statutes. http://www.mainelegislature.org/legis/statutes/17-A/title17-Asec432.html

[28] Montana code 45-6-311. http://data.opi.state.mt.us/bills/mca/45/6/45-6-311.htm

[29] North Carolina Hacking Statutes. http://www.ncga.state.nc.us/EnactedLegislation/Statutes/HTML/ByArticle/Chapter_14/Article_60.html

[30] Rhode Island Statutes http://www.rilin.state.ri.us/Statutes/TITLE11/11-52/INDEX.HTM

[31] Arizona Anti Spyware laws. http://www.azleg.state.az.us/FormatDocument.asp?inDoc=/ars/44/07301.htm&Title=44&DocType=ARS

[32] Texas Phishing Laws. http://www.capitol.state.tx.us/tlodocs/81R/billtext/html/SB00028F.htm

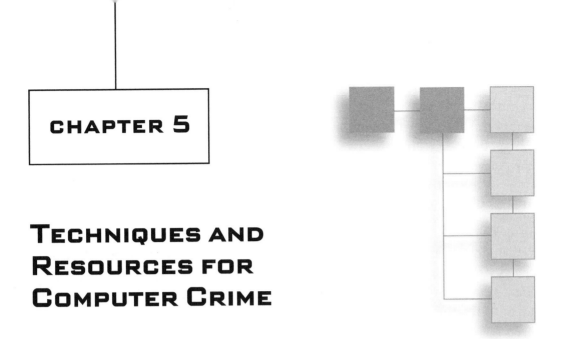

CHAPTER 5

TECHNIQUES AND RESOURCES FOR COMPUTER CRIME

Introduction

In this chapter, we will examine some of the techniques used by computer criminals. We will look at how they gather information, how they exploit system flaws, typical identity theft techniques, and various scenarios. The purpose of this chapter is to familiarize you with the techniques that criminals use to commit cyber crimes. Obviously, one chapter won't make you a hacker, and that is not our intent. But we should be able to make you familiar with the essential techniques used by cyber criminals.

It is important to keep in mind that "studying the enemy" is a good tactic in any conflict. One of the authors of this book teaches a course in hacking techniques for network administrators, IT professionals, and law enforcement. The idea is to make sure these individuals are familiar with the tactics that criminals employ. In this chapter we will be discussing general principles, not specific techniques.

Identity-Theft Techniques

To properly understand the techniques used in identity theft, one must keep in mind the goal of identity theft. The purpose is to gather enough information about an individual that the perpetrator can successfully pretend to be that individual. Often, the goal is to obtain credit cards, access to bank accounts, or some other financial goal. However, as we have previously discussed, there certainly are circumstances where the goal of identity theft is not monetary. It is also

important to differentiate identity-theft techniques based on the target. A perpetrator may have an undifferentiated target, which means he or she simply wants to steal identities—usually several—and has no specific target in mind. This is the case with phishing scams. Another far less common scenario is when the perpetrator is attempting to steal a specific person's identity. This is usually done in conjunction with some other crime, such as cyber stalking. We will look at both scenarios and the techniques used in each.

Identity theft is a growing problem and a very troubling one. The concept is rather simple, although the process can be complex, and the consequences for the victim can be quite severe. The idea is simply for one person to take on the identity of another. This is usually for the purpose of making purchases, but identity theft can be done for other reasons, such as obtaining credit cards or even driver's licenses in the victim's name. If the perpetrator obtains a credit card in someone else's name, then he can purchase products and the victim of this fraud is left with debts he or she was not aware of and did not authorize.

In the case of getting a driver's license in the victim's name, this fraud might be attempted to shield the perpetrator from the consequences of his or her own poor driving record. For example, a person might steal your personal information to create a license with his or her own picture. Perhaps the criminal in this case has a very bad driving record and even warrants out for immediate arrest. Should the person be stopped by law-enforcement officers, he or she can then show the fake license. When the police officer checks the license, it is legitimate and has no outstanding warrants. However, the ticket the criminal receives will go on your driving record, because it is your information on the driver's license. It is also unlikely that the perpetrator of that fraud will actually pay the ticket, so at some point you—the person whose identity was stolen—will receive notification that your license has been revoked for failure to pay a ticket. Unless you can then prove, with witnesses, that you were not at the location in which the ticket was given at the time it was given, you may have no recourse but to pay the ticket in order to reestablish your driving privileges.

The U.S. Department of Justice defines identity theft as the following:

> *Identity theft* and *identity fraud* are terms used to refer to all types of crime in which someone wrongfully obtains and uses another person's personal data in some way that involves fraud or deception, typically for economic gain.[1]

It is important to understand that identity theft existed before access to the Internet was so ubiquitous. A person who was determined could go to county courthouses and request public records, search newspapers for personal information, and gather enough information to steal an identity. But the process was painstaking and could not be done on a mass scale; the target had to be a specific individual. The advent of the Internet has made the process of stealing a person's identity much easier. There is a wealth of personal information available online. Many states now have court records and motor-vehicle records online. In some states, a person's Social Security number is used for the driver's license number. The Intelligence Reform and Terrorism Prevention Act of 2004 prohibits states from displaying your SSN on driver's licenses or motor-vehicle registrations. The law went into effect on December 17, 2005, and applies to all licenses, registrations, and state identification cards issued after that date. So if a criminal does get a person's Social Security number, he or she cannot necessarily look up that person's driving record, perhaps get a duplicate of the person's license, find out about any court records concerning that person, and on some Web sites even check the person's credit history. Beyond those resources, many people actually post a great deal of information about themselves on social networking sites such as Facebook and MySpace. And, as we will see in just a moment, it is not a difficult task to trick people into giving up personal information. This can include credit-card numbers, account numbers, usernames, and even bank passwords. This technique for identity theft is far more common and does not require mining the Internet for personal information.

Non-Specific Identity Theft

This is the most common sort of identity theft. In this scenario, the perpetrator has no specific target in mind. Rather, he or she is trying to get as many identities as possible. It is first important to identify what sort of information an identity thief is most interested in. An identity thief seeking a wide range of identities is really seeking access to financial assets. The perpetrator may be seeking direct access to bank accounts, or enough information that he or she could open credit accounts in the victim's name. This means that this type of identity thief wants either the victim's login and passwords for their financial sites or enough personal data (such as the victim's Social Security number) to allow the perpetrator to obtain credit. This brings us to the question of how they acquire such information. There are three separate means by which identity thieves typically acquire data:

- Phishing

- Spyware

- Non computer

There are a few other obscure methods, but these three account for the bulk of identity-theft activities, so we will take time to carefully examine each of them.

Phishing

Phishing is simply the process of sending e-mails to a wide range of recipients, wherein the e-mails purport to be from some legitimate source and entice the recipient to either supply personal information or follow a link in the e-mail to a Web site to provide personal information. The most common scenario is that the e-mail will purport to be from a bank or credit-card company and inform you there is some problem with your account. You will then be asked to click on a link to log in to your account. The link will actually take you to a different Web site made to look like a legitimate financial institution. Once there, if you do log on, you will have just given your username and password to the identity thief.

Let's take a look at this from the perspective of the criminal perpetrating the crime. In other words, how would an enterprising identity thief go about setting up and executing this sort of scam? The first step is to establish a server to host the phishing Web site. Obviously, the perpetrator does not want to simply go to their Internet service provider and arrange for hosting service. This would make their eventual capture and conviction a foregone conclusion. So how do they set up a Web server that cannot be traced back to them? There are primarily two ways this is done. In the first method, the perpetrator uses a prepaid Visa card to purchase Web hosting on a commonly used hosting service, preferably one outside the country he or she will be targeting. The second method is to hack into any server anywhere that has poor security. The perpetrator can then use that server to host his or her phishing Web site. Should authorities track the phishing scheme back to the server, they will find its owners unwitting accomplices with no knowledge. This second method is actually more common than you might think; there are so many poorly secured servers that it is generally not a particularly difficult task to find one that can be compromised. This is one more reason why a greater awareness of security is critical for all people involved supporting computer networks. It is entirely possible for an unsecured (or in-adequately secured) network to be used in the commission of a crime. When a computer is being used for an attack and it has been hijacked as we just de-scribed, that computer is referred to as a *zombie*. The use of zombies in phishing, for distributing child pornography, or for launching denial-of-service attacks has become quite common.

The next step is to emulate some financial institution's Web site. This can be done by visiting the legitimate Web site for the financial institution and copying as much of the graphics and layout as possible. In many cases, one can simply right-click on an image on any Web site and save it. One can also usually right-click on the page and view the actual source-code HTML for that page. This makes it a trivial matter to effectively copy a given Web site and then, using those pilfered graphics and layouts, create a Web site that emulates the target financial site as closely as possible. The critical part is how to handle user logins. Because the perpetrator is trying to gather usernames and passwords, he or she will accept any username or password the users enter and store them. The information can be stored in a flat file, a database, or any medium the perpetrator desires. More crafty identity thieves will also gather the IP address and e-mail from the person visiting their site, the reasoning being that if this person was susceptible to phishing once, he or she may be again. So if you got information from a person in this attempt, you might attempt a second time to induce that person to give you private information. Once the user has logged on to the forged financial institution Web site, since the perpetrator cannot display actual account in-formation, the phishing Web site will instead display a message either thanking the user for confirming their login and/or stating that account information is currently unavailable and to please try again.

Now the only thing left is for the identity thief to retrieve the information. This is usually a simple matter of logging into that server and copying the information. More skillful identity thieves will do this from a common access location such as an Internet café, but there certainly are many cases of an identity thief logging into the phishing server from their own home. The bogus Web site can also be programmed to periodically send the information it has gathered to an anonymous e-mail ac-count so that the perpetrator can retrieve the data from any location.

This process happens fairly frequently. I am sure most readers have received numerous phishing e-mails trying to lure them to some Web site to enter in personal information. Hopefully, you have been shrewd enough to recognize these e-mails for what they are and to avoid them. Unfortunately, thousands of people every week do fall prey to these schemes.

Spyware

Another method of obtaining personal information is to get spyware onto a target's computer and gather information directly from the person's own keystrokes, Web-site activity, or files. This attack is becoming more prevalent. An individual spyware application can work in any number of ways to gather data. A common type of spyware is referred to as a keylogger. A *keylogger* literally logs each keystroke the user makes and puts them into a file, so everything the user types in, including Web-site addresses, usernames, and passwords, is recorded. Another type of spyware is one that takes periodic screen shots of exactly what is on the screen and saves them to a file. In both cases, the data is stored on the victim's computer temporarily and then the perpetrator must get that data off. There are several ways to do this. One would be to have spyware that periodically sends its data to a predetermined e-mail address or IP address. Another would be for the attacker to have access to the target computer and periodically log on and get the data. In the latter case, the attacker may have previously hacked into the machine and installed the spyware, and may then return later to gather the data.

Another way spyware can be used is to assist in a process called *privilege escalation*. While this is not directly related to identity theft, it is related to spyware, so let us briefly discuss it. Generally speaking, privilege escalation is any attempt to take the user account you logged onto and promote it to a higher level of access. Let's consider one simple way a person could use spyware to accomplish this. Imagine that a perpetrator is able to log on to a Windows 7 workstation as a guest account. Now, a guest account has very limited privileges and access. However, if the perpetrator loads spyware on the machine, then when any user subsequently logs on, the spyware will record their activities, including their username and password. If one of those users that logs on has higher privileges—for example, a tech-support person with administrator privileges logs on to troubleshoot some issue—then the perpetrator will have that person's logon credentials and be able to access the machine with those expanded privileges.

Delivering Spyware to the Target

While there are clearly a variety of methods for spyware to work, they all accomplish the same goal. Spyware programs can track all activity on a computer and gather information that can be retrieved by another party via a number of different methods. The real question is, how does spyware get loaded onto a target computer system in the first place? How does a perpetrator get access to a computer system to load the spyware? It is certainly possible for the perpetrator to hack into a machine or system and to load spyware in that manner. However, that method is very time consuming, requires a high level of technical skill, and must be done one system at a time. For a would-be identity thief, going after one computer at a time is simply not effective. The most common method to get spyware onto a target machine is via a Trojan horse. A *Trojan horse* is a program that appears to have some benign use but in reality is delivering a harmful pay-load such as a virus, worm, or spyware.

It is also possible that, when you visit a certain Web site, spyware may download in the background while you are simply perusing the site. Of course, if an employer (or parent) is installing the spyware, it can then be installed non-covertly in the same way that a person would install any other application. We will discuss legal uses of spyware in more detail momentarily. A common way to get spyware on your machine is simply to send an e-mail that prompts the user to open the attachment. If the user does so, they will install a spyware utility on their own machine. Figure 5.1 shows an e-mail of this type that one of the authors of this book received while writing the book.

Notice that these e-mails are identical to the types used to get a virus onto a victim's computer. In both cases, the goal is to create an e-mail that has a compelling message that encourages the recipient to open the e-mail and therefore install the software on their computer.

Legal Uses of Spyware

As we mentioned previously, there are some perfectly legal uses for spyware. The law allows for employers to monitor employer-provided computers in order to

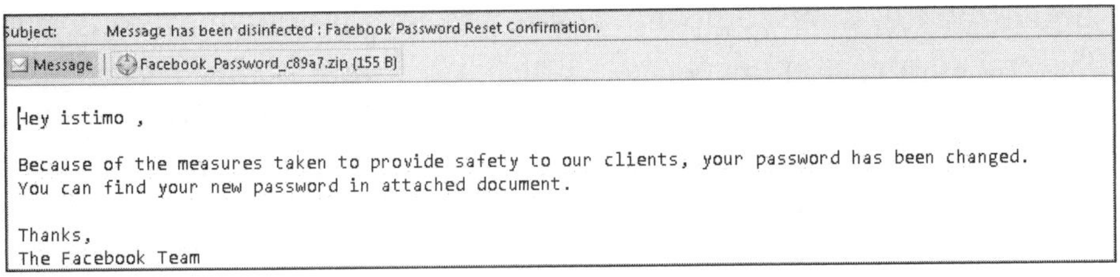

```
Subject:      Message has been disinfected : Facebook Password Reset Confirmation.

Message   | Facebook_Password_c89a7.zip (155 B)

Hey istimo ,

Because of the measures taken to provide safety to our clients, your password has been changed.
You can find your new password in attached document.

Thanks,
The Facebook Team
```

Figure 5.1
Spyware/virus e-mail.

manage productivity. Some employers have embraced such spyware as a means of monitoring employee use of company technology. Many companies have elected to monitor phone, e-mail, or Web traffic within the organization. Keep in mind that the computer, network, and phone systems are the property of the company or organization, not of the employee. This is why courts have consistently upheld the employer's right to monitor these systems. In some cases, such monitoring is considered a necessary portion of network security. Via monitoring, the company can ensure that employees are not inadvertently downloading a virus, sending out corporate secrets, or engaging in any other activity that might compromise security. These technologies are supposedly only used for work purposes; therefore, company monitoring would not constitute any invasion of privacy. While courts have upheld this monitoring as a company's right, it is critical to consult an attorney before initiating this level of employee monitoring as well as to consider the potential negative impact on employee morale.

It is also perfectly legal for parents to monitor their minor children's Internet activities. The goal is usually a laudable one, that of protecting their children from online predators. Yet, as with employees in a company, the practice may elicit a strong negative reaction from the parties being spied upon—namely, their children. Parents have to weigh the risk to their children versus what might be viewed as a breach of trust.

Obtaining Spyware Software

Because these utilities have legal purposes, a number of companies create and actively market spyware applications. You might be surprised to learn that you can obtain many spyware products for free, or at very low cost, on the Internet. You can check the Counter Exploitation Web site (http://www.cexx.org) for a lengthy list of known spyware products available on the Internet as well as information about methods one can use to remove them. The Spyware Guide Web site (http://www.spywareguide.com/) lists spyware that you can get right off the Internet should you feel some compelling reason to spy on someone's computer activities. Several keylogger applications are also listed on this site. These applications include well-known keyloggers such as Absolute Key Logger, Tiny Key Logger, and TypeO. Most can be downloaded for free or for a nominal charge. A short list of commercial spyware products is given here:

- SpectorSoft (http://www.spectorsoft.com/)

- Web Watcher (http://www.webwatchernow.com)

- Kid Safe Gaurdian (http://www.kidsafeguardian.com/)

- Soft Activity (http://www.softactivity.com/)

- Fast Tracker (http://www.fatline.com)

- IMonitor Soft (http://www.imonitorsoft.com/)

While monitoring a minor child on the Internet or an employee's work computer is legal, it is important to realize that many people attempt to utilize these types of programs for illegal purposes. For example, it is probably not legal for you to monitor the Internet activity of your spouse (the specific situation and jurisdiction will have some variation). It is also absolutely not legal for you to monitor any adult such as a friend, girlfriend, etc. Many people do this because they believe that person may be in some way betraying their trust, such as via infidelity, but this does not make placing spyware on their computer legal.

Non-Computer

While this book is about computer crime, it is important to realize that the line between traditional "real world" crime and cyber crime is becoming ever more blurred. As we have seen with cyber stalking, a crime in one arena is often tied to a crime in another. With identity theft, the goal is to get private identifying information such as credit-card numbers, driver's license numbers, and Social Security numbers. One way to do this is when handling credit cards or driver's licenses. A small hand-held scanner (also known as a *wedge*) can be purchased for about $100. Software to interpret the magnetic stripe is also very easy to write. One of the authors of this book recently wrote an application for a medical billing software company that would read magnetic stripes on insurance cards in order to check in patients, so we can attest to how simple it is to do. Such technology has many legitimate uses, but it can certainly be perverted for criminal purposes. Once one has such a device, all one needs to do is find someone who routinely handles credit cards to scan in the card at the same time they run the purchase. This has already been done via waiters and retail clerks. In those cases, the perpetrators carry a small hand-held device in their pockets and, while processing the customer's purchase, swipe the card and thus store the information. In a very short time, the criminals have a wealth of personal data to use in identity theft.

There is also a new technology that identity thieves can take advantage of: the contactless credit card. The data on these cards is stored not only on the magnetic stripe but also on a tiny microchip embedded in the plastic of the card. The data from the microchip is transmitted via radio frequency identification (RFID) technology. So instead of having to physically swipe the card's magnetic stripe in the card reader, these contactless cards need only to be waved in front of a specially equipped RFID card reading device. In fact, the card doesn't necessarily have to leave the wallet. As soon as the card comes within four inches of the reader, the antenna attached to the microchip transmits the data to the point-of-sale (POS) terminal and the transaction is complete. Identity thieves now have portable devices that one can carry and simply be next to the victim to obtain the information from the credit card.

From the criminal's point of view, this sort of identity theft is a bit more risky. It involves a person in direct contact with the victims. However, it is also a method that is guaranteed to yield significant results in a very brief period of time. From an investigative point of view, these sorts of crimes are easier to investigate than other methods of identity theft. They will usually involve a pattern of identity-theft incidents in a limited geographical area. A simple scan of recent legitimate purchases by the victims should reveal a common location they all shopped at.

Specific Target Identity Theft

Although it is far less common, there are cases where the perpetrator is going after the identity of a specific individual. While many of the methods we have just discussed can be used for this purpose, most are not suited for this. Those methods are better suited for attempting to gather a large volume of information from a large pool of victims. However, when a specific target is the goal, there are many other options. Obviously, spyware is an exception; it is well suited for identity theft whether the target is a specific individual or not. When a specific individual is the target, though, an Internet search can often be the best place to start. It is amazing what one can find on the Internet.

A first place to start in investigating a target is to ascertain physical address, phone number, and employer. There are a number of absolutely free services on the Web that allow you to perform this sort of search. Some are better than others, and obviously the more common the name you are searching for the harder it will be to find the right one. If you do a search for John Smith in California, you might have a tough time sorting through the results you get. Yahoo! People Search is one such service that is remarkably easy to use. When you go to http://www.yahoo.com, you see a number of options on the page. One option is People Search, as shown in

Figure 5.2. Note that you can look someone up by name and geographical location, or you can simply do a reverse phone number lookup. By entering a person's name, in this case one of the authors of this book, you can see quite a few options are presented. In this case, we entered just the last name and state (Easttom, Texas). You can see the results in Figure 5.3.

Figure 5.2
Yahoo! People Search.

Chuck Easttom	WILLOW CREEK TRL MCKINNEY, TX 75071	214-733-8850
Chuck Easttom	WILLOW CREEK TRL MCKINNEY, TX 75071	972-733-8850
John Easttom	N MCDONALD ST MCKINNEY, TX 75071	972-542-4279
Misty Easttom	WILLOW CREEK TRL MCKINNEY, TX 75071	214-733-8850
Misty Easttom	WILLOW CREEK TRL MCKINNEY, TX 75071	972-733-8850

Figure 5.3
Yahoo! People Search results.

You can see that a few names were found by the search. Clicking on the first name yielded the results shown in Figure 5.4. You can see the address, phone number, even a map to the home address. All of this information is available with just a few seconds' effort on the Internet.

Note

You might be wondering whose information we are publishing in this book: It is information from one of the authors. Some readers might wonder why we would be willing to put our own home address and phone number in a published book. To begin with, anyone reading this chapter will gain the requisite skills and could easily do their own search and find that information should they be so inclined. Furthermore, being an author and frequent guest speaker makes it rather difficult to hide one's identity; this author is quite easy to find. Finally, to do a demonstration, we needed a name to run, and for liability reasons we could not have used someone else's name. This is information that is publicly available in a phone book. However, should readers wish to contact this author, they are strongly encouraged to do so via his Web site (http://www.chuckeasttom.com) and e-mail address (chuck@chuckeasttom.com) rather than via phone. He will try to answer e-mails, but frequently does not even answer his phone. And we are certainly not encouraging anyone to make a surprise visit to his home!

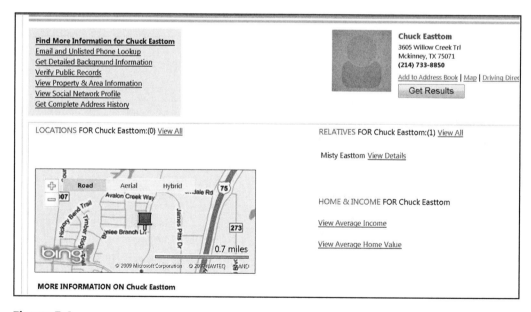

Figure 5.4
Search results refined.

The search demonstrated here is just one option for finding basic personal information. There are several others:

- http://www.smartpages.com
- http://www.peoplefind.com/
- http://www.bigfoot.com/
- http://www.whowhere.com
- http://www.ussearch.com
- http://www.switchboard.com
- http://www.anywho.com/

Obviously, obtaining basic geographic and phone information on a given person is not particularly difficult, but it is not enough to perpetrate identity theft. However, a person can use that data to look further. With just that basic information and a small fee (usually less than $40), a person can look up driving history, criminal history, and in some cases even driver's-license numbers of an individual. A few of those sites are as follows:

- http://www.backgroundchecks.com
- http://www.easybackgroundchecks.com/
- http://onlinepublicrecordssearch.com

In addition, many states now have court records online. If the individual has ever been involved in a civil suit, criminal case, or even a traffic violation, one can usually find those records online. All you need is their complete name and in some cases address, which we have already shown you how to find. Some readers may be surprised by this, but such records are public information. Prior to the Internet, one would have to go to a county clerk's office and request any records in person. It was a long and tedious process. Now, for a small fee, in about 10 minutes one can have access to all public records for an individual. This can be vital when checking out a potential new employee, your child's new soccer coach, or some other legitimate use. But it can also be a valuable tool for an identity thief who may only have part of the information they need. These search tools can give them the rest of the information to successfully steal your identity.

Fraud Techniques

Fraud is certainly not new and did not begin with the Internet. But like identity theft, fraud is much easier to perpetrate on the Internet. Widespread access to the Internet has given criminals more access to victims and a much wider area within which to perpetrate crimes. The Securities and Exchange Commission lists several types of Internet fraud on their Web site.[2] In this section, we will examine the most commonly encountered fraud schemes and discuss the methods used to perpetrate these crimes. This sort of crime is probably the easiest for experienced law-enforcement officers to understand because fraud on the Internet works in much the same way as it does in the real world, with just a few new techniques.

Auction Frauds

Auctions are one area where the Internet has vastly expanded opportunities for criminals. Prior to the advent of the Internet and online auctions, one had to bid for an item in person. If you won the auction, you paid for the item on the spot and took it with you immediately. Online auctions have changed that process significantly. Now you are bidding on an item you don't actually see, and you have to wait for it to be delivered to you. Online auctions such as eBay can be a wonderful way to find merchandise at very good prices. I routinely use such auctions to purchase goods. However, any auction site can be fraught with peril. Many questions arise, such as, will you actually get the merchandise you ordered, and in good condition? There are really three types of online fraud:

- Failure to send the merchandise

- Sending something of lesser value than advertised

- Failure to disclose all relevant information about a product or terms of the sale

Failure to deliver the merchandise is the most clear-cut example of fraud, and it is very simple to perpetrate. Once the victim has paid for an item, the perpetrator simply does not send the item and keeps the victim's money. In organized fraud, the seller will simultaneously advertise several items for sale, collect money on all the auctions, and then not send any of the items. If the perpetrator has planned the fraud well, the entire process will be done with a fake identification and an anonymous e-mail service. The person then walks away with the proceeds of the scam.

An interesting permutation of this type of fraud is to couple auction fraud with identity theft. The process is to first steal some person's identity, and then set up auctions using the stolen identity. In this method, the perpetrator is protecting himself from investigation. If an investigation into the fraud ensues, it will trace back to an unwitting third party.

The second category of fraud—delivering an item of lesser value than the one advertised—can be a gray area for law enforcement. For example, suppose the seller advertises a signed first-edition Stephen King novel but ships a signed later edition that is in poor condition. This could be deliberate fraud, or it could be simply a case of an overzealous seller who oversold the product. It could even be a simple, honest mistake. From an investigative point of view, you want to look for a pattern of behavior to help you determine whether this is simply a mistake or a case of fraud. Anyone could be mistaken or, in their exuberance, exaggerate a bit. However, if a person has a pattern of sending items that are of lesser value than advertised, then deliberate fraud is far more likely.

This problem of sending an item of lesser value is very closely related to the problem of failure to disclose all relevant facts about the item. For example, a book might be an authentic first printing and be autographed, but it is in such poor physical condition as to render it worthless. This fact may or may not be mentioned in advance by the seller. Failure to be forthcoming with all the relevant facts about a particular item might be the result of outright fraud or simply the seller's ignorance. But the fact remains that online auctions make it much easier to commit a fraud either by failure to ship or failing to send the item the bidder thought they were buying. This is one area where the Internet has made a crime very easy to perpetrate that was very difficult before.

The Federal Trade Commission (FTC) also lists three other areas of bidding fraud that are growing in popularity on the Internet. From the FTC Web site[3]:

- Shill bidding, when fraudulent sellers (or their "shills") bid on the seller's items to drive up the price.

- Bid shielding, when fraudulent buyers submit very high bids to discourage other bidders from competing for the same item. The fake buyers then retract their bids, so that people they know can get the item at a lower price.

- Bid siphoning, when con artists lure bidders off legitimate auction sites by offering to sell the "same" item at a lower price. Their intent is to trick consumers into sending money without proffering the item. By going off-site, buyers lose any protections the original site may provide, such as insurance, feedback forms, or guarantees.

Shill Bidding

Shill bidding has become the most common of the three types of auction fraud listed by the FTC. One reason for that is that it is very easy to perform. The tactic is simple: If the perpetrator wishes to sell an item on an online auction site but wants to guarantee a high price, then shill bidding can be employed. What the perpetrator does is establish several fake buyer accounts and use those to bid on their own item. This way, they artificially inflate the going price and create the illusion that the item is in high demand. This can significantly increase the price of the item. Now, isolated incidents of this are unlikely to come to the attention of law enforcement. It is often the case that the victims of shill bidding are not even aware a fraud has occurred. From an investigation point of view, the only way to confirm suspected shill bidding is to confirm the identities of all bidders. If some of those trace back to the actual seller, then you have shill bidding occurring. Of course, it is possible for more than one person to conspire together, and in that case the shill bidders would be separate individuals from the seller. Such a conspiracy would usually be ongoing and involve several auctions over a period of time. In this case, the investigation process would require some data mining. You would have to be able to show that the same bidders routinely bid on the same seller's items, drove up the price, then did not get the winning bid. This still would be circumstantial. To confirm a conspiracy to defraud, you would have to also show that the individuals had some connection to each other. One piece of evidence would be situations in which one of the shill bidders actually won an auction but never paid for it, and the seller never complained to the auction site. This would be a clear sign that they were colluding on a shill-bidding scheme, and the shill bidder accidentally won the product.

Bid Shielding

Bid shielding will rarely come to the attention of law enforcement; it is more a matter for the auction sites themselves. Ultimately, it is simply a case of a bidder wanting to scare off competing bids. The only "harm" done to the victims is that they don't win the item they were bidding on. What happens is that a person makes a low bid for an item and then either an accomplice or the same person using a different account bids outrageously high on the item. That high bid will discourage others from bidding. But when the auction is over and the winning high bid backs out of the purchase, the next highest bid wins. This way, the person guarantees that their low bid wins the auction.

This is certainly fraud, and it is common on Internet auction sites, so it is definitely a computer crime. However, it is difficult to investigate. First, it often goes undetected; usually the victim, in this case the person selling an item, doesn't realize this has occurred unless they routinely sell items and fall victim several times. Second, it can be difficult to prove there was collusion between the winning bidder and the high bidder who backed out of the purchase. It is only detectible if the two perpetrators repeat the same scam together multiple times. Finally, it is somewhat difficult to prosecute since the item was not stolen, it was paid for—the damage was simply that the seller got a lower price than they might have gotten without the scam. We are certainly not suggesting this is acceptable behavior; it is simply that it is difficult for law enforcement to investigate.

Bid Siphoning

Bid siphoning was at one time less common, but it is growing in popularity. In this scheme, the perpetrator places a legitimate item up for bid on an auction site. But then, in the ad for that item, he or she provides links to sites that are not part of the auction site. The unwary buyer who follows those links might find himself on an alternative site that is a "setup" to perpetrate some sort of fraud. However, this could be simply a means to drive traffic toward the alternative site, and no fraud is involved or intended. This is another situation that will usually fall outside the purview of law enforcement.

All of these auction schemes share the goal of subverting the legitimate and fair auction process. The normal auction process is an ideal blend of capitalism and democracy: Everyone has an equal chance to obtain the product in question if he or she is willing to outbid other shoppers. The buyers themselves set the price of the product based on the value they perceive the product to have. In my opinion, auctions are an excellent vehicle for commerce. However, unscrupulous individuals will always attempt to subvert any process to serve their own goals.

Investment Offers

Fraudulent investment offers have become a very pervasive problem. Investment offers are nothing new and some are legitimate. Even some major brokerage houses make a significant portion of their income by *cold calling,* the process of simply calling people and trying to get them to invest in a specific stock. While it can be annoying, this is a legal and legitimate way to sell stocks. However, it has also been a vehicle to perpetrate stock fraud. The Internet has allowed investment offers—both genuine offers and fraudulent—to be more easily disseminated to the general public. Most readers are probably familiar with investment offers flooding their inbox on a daily basis. Some of these e-mail notifications entice you to become directly involved with a particular investment plan while other e-mails offer free, seemingly unbiased information from investors (unfortunately, much of this advice is not as unbiased as it might appear to be). While legitimate online newsletters can help investors gather valuable information, keep in mind that some online newsletters are fraudulent.

Common Investment Fraud Schemes

Investment fraud comes in many forms. One of the more common schemes involves sending out an e-mail that suggests that you can make an outrageous sum of money with a minimal investment. Perhaps the most famous of these schemes has been the Nigerian Fraud. In that specific scenario, an e-mail is sent to a number of random e-mail addresses. The goal is to send the offer to a large volume of e-mail addresses so that even if only a small percentage of recipients respond, there will still be a significant number of targets for the perpetrator. Each e-mail contains a message purporting to be from a relative of some deceased Nigerian doctor or government official. The deceased person will be someone the victim would associate with significant social standing, thus increasing the likelihood that the offer would be viewed more favorably. That part of the investment fraud is common to all confidence schemes: The perpetrator must first gain the confidence of the victim. This is why these e-mails always claim to be in relation to some prominent member of a community, such as a doctor.

The general outline of these schemes is very similar. A person has a sum of money he wishes to transfer out of his country, and for security reasons he cannot use normal channels; he would like to use your bank account to "park" the funds temporarily. If you will allow him access to your account, you will receive a very large fee. If the intended victim does agree to this arrangement, they will receive, via normal mail, a variety of very official-looking documents, enough to convince most casual observers that the arrangement is legitimate. The victim will then be asked to advance some money to cover items such as taxes and wire fees. Should the recipient actually send any money, then the perpetrators have succeeded and that money is lost.

This scheme, like many frauds, depends on the inherent greed of the victim. It would seem that any rational person would ask why someone with large sums of money would trust a total stranger. If they really did deposit $10 million in my account, what would prevent me from stealing it? Why would they trust me? The fact is that they would not. These cases can be extremely hard to investigate because they are often perpetrated from anonymous e-mail accounts and rented mailboxes, and not infrequently they are actually conducted from overseas.

Investment Advice

The previous schemes we have discuss involved outright and clear-cut fraud. Unfortunately, not all fraud is so blatant. Some companies pay the people who write online newsletters to recommend their stocks. While this activity isn't actually illegal, U.S. federal securities laws do require the newsletters to disclose that they were paid to proffer this advice. Such laws are in place because when the writers are recommending any product, their opinion might be swayed by the fact that compensation is being provided to them for that opinion. Many online investment newsletters do not disclose that they are actually being paid to recommend certain stocks, however. This situation means that the "unbiased" stock advice you are getting could actually be quite biased. Rather than getting the advice of an unbiased expert, you may actually be getting a paid advertisement. This pitfall is one of the most common traps of online investment advice, more common than the blatant frauds. This sort of issue is not a matter for local or state law enforcement but rather falls under the purview of the Securities and Exchange Commission or the Federal Trade Commission.

Sometimes, these online stock bulletins can be part of a wider scheme, often called a *pump and dump*. A classic pump and dump is rather simple. The perpetrator selects a stock that is virtually worthless and then purchases large amounts of the stock. The perpetrator can then use a variety of techniques to artificially inflate the stock price. Sometimes cold calling is used, but in recent years spam e-mail trying to persuade people to buy the stock has become more common. It is also possible to plant fake rumors on the Internet claiming the company in question is about to have some breakthrough or land some major contract. All the various techniques have one goal: to artificially inflate the price of the stock beyond what it realistically should be.

Hacking Techniques

Many computer crimes involve a skilled computer hacker compromising the security of the target system. The important question for the investigator is, how do they do it? In this section, we will seek to familiarize the reader with basic hacking techniques. Our goal is not to make you a hacker or to go in-depth into the world of hacking. It would take several volumes to adequately cover the full gamut of techniques available to the hacker. However, we can give you a general familiarity with the most commonly used techniques. Knowing how hackers accomplish their goals can be essential in investigating computer-related crimes.

Footprinting

The first step for a serious hacker is much like the first step for a serious burglar: It is to "case" the target. Essentially, what the perpetrator does is very much the same thing a skilled burglar would do prior to attempting to break into a target building. In computer-hacking terms, this is called *footprinting*. The perpetrator must spend time learning about the system he or she wishes to break into. A skilled burglar will study a target to learn about its alarm systems, security, hours of operations, and so on. All the time he or she is really seeking some flaw that can be exploited in order to gain entrance. The same is true of the hacker. He or she needs to learn all he or she can about the target system in order to find some flaw that can be exploited in order to gain entrance. This involves a number of techniques.

To illustrate the process of footprinting, let us walk through an imaginary scenario. Suppose that you are a perpetrator who intends to hack into the network used at city hall (including the police station) for the fictitious city of Metropolis. We will walk you through the steps a skillful hacker would take to learn about the system prior to attempting to hack the system. This should help you to understand exactly how hackers conduct operations in the real world. In this scenario, I will take on the role of the hacker, showing you the exact steps I would take. We will be providing mostly broad outlines without exact detail. The goal is to give the reader a good understanding of the process, not a step-by-step guide. It should also be noted that these are the first steps often taken in penetration testing.

The first step will be rather low tech: I will search city Web sites and local news stations. The goal of the search is to find any information at all related to the technical infrastructure and employees of the city. I am looking for any news stories that reference equipment or software the city has purchased. For example, a news article discussing the city moving to Windows Server 2008 might be of interest to me. Or perhaps an article stating that the city has awarded a network contract to a given vendor. I am also looking for information on IT employees. I will use this information in one of three ways:

- When I know the hardware and operating system the city is using, I can focus my research on known flaws in that system. For example, if I search for "known flaws in routers" of a given model, I am likely to find specific Web page articles detailing known flaws in that model router. I can then use this information to plan my eventual attack.

- When I know the names of technical employees, I can then search widely known bulletin boards for any questions these people might have asked. For example, if the network administrator's name is John Doe, I will search computer boards for his name. I may find a question such as Mr. Doe asking how to properly configure a particular type of firewall. This information tells me that the city is using that type of firewall, and that Mr. Doe is not very skilled in it. This gives me a valuable target to attack.

- Finally, I might use this information for social engineering. Social engineering is the process of literally trying to talk someone out of valuable information. For example, if I know the IT manager's name is Jane Smith, I could search social networks like MySpace and Facebook to get details about Ms. Smith. I might then call a dispatcher in the police department and pretend to be a new tech-support guy working for Ms. Smith. I would drop her name and some real facts about her (perhaps that her daughter just won a state science fair) that I got from social-networking sites. This would make me sound believable to the dispatcher. Then I would claim that I was supposed to update the dispatcher's computer but had lost her password, could she please give it to me? Now depending on the sales skills of the hacker attempting this, it can be very fruitful. If I am successful and get the dispatcher's password, I would simply log on as that dispatcher and put some spyware (such as a keylogger) onto the system so that I could collect passwords of other people (perhaps high-ranking police officers). At that point, I would completely own the network without having done anything particularly technical.

Let's go forward assuming the social-engineering scenario did not work. Next, I am going to need to gather information about the target system. It is often easiest to intrude through a Web site, since by definition those need to have a public interface. I will also be gathering information on anything else I can. Here are the specific steps I would take:

1. I would use a network tool like WhoIs or a nice Web interface for WhoIs (http://cqcounter.com/whois/) to trace the Web domain for the city and all relevant offices (Police, Sanitation, etc.) as well as e-mail (the e-mail server might not be the same). I can get this information from e-mail addresses on the city Web site. What I will get from this is:

   a. The IP address for the Web server and e-mail servers.

   b. The physical address, which will tell me if the city hosts its own e-mail and Web servers or uses a hosting company. I will need these IP address in just a bit.

2. My next step will be to run the Web domain through a tool such as netcraft.com. This will give me details about the Web server, such as what operating system it is running and how long it has been since it was rebooted.

3. Using the IP address I found earlier, I will do what is called a *port scan.* You can find a lot of free port scanners on the Internet. A port scan will tell me what ports are open at that IP address and of course what ports are open on the firewall between me and that IP address. This is very valuable information. For example, if port 110 is open, then that machine accepts POP3 traffic and could be an e-mail server. If ports 137, 138, and 139 are open, then this IP is accepting NetBIOS traffic, which makes it a Windows server. That means I can search for known flaws in Windows. Table 5.1 lists many of the most often used ports. Figure 5.5 shows the output of one free port scanner. As you can see, it is relatively easy to determine what ports are open and what ports are closed.

4. Now I might use the Web site www.archive.org to see past incarnations of the city's Web site. This can give me valuable information such as personnel changes that may have occurred or announcements about changes to the IT infrastructure.

Table 5.1 Well-Known Port Numbers

Port Number	Description
1	TCP Port Service Multiplexer (TCPMUX)
5	Remote Job Entry (RJE)
7	ECHO
18	Message Send Protocol (MSP)
20	FTP—Data
21	FTP—Control
22	SSH Remote Login Protocol
23	Telnet (allows remote administration)
25	SMTP (Simple Mail Transfer Protocol—send e-mail)
29	MSG ICP
37	Time
42	Host Name Server
43	WhoIs
49	Login Host Protocol (Login)
53	Domain Name System (DNS)
69	Trivial File Transfer Protocol (TFTP)
70	Gopher Services
79	Finger
80	HTTP (Web pages)
103	X.400 Standard
108	SNA Gateway Access Server
109	POP2
110	POP3
115	Simple File Transfer Protocol (SFTP)
118	SQL Services
119	Newsgroup (NNTP)
137	NetBIOS Name Service
139	NetBIOS Datagram Service
143	Interim Mail Access Protocol (IMAP)
150	NetBIOS Session Service
156	SQL Server
161	SNMP
179	Border Gateway Protocol (BGP)
190	Gateway Access Control Protocol (GACP)
194	Internet Relay Chat (IRC)

Port Number	Description
197	Directory Location Service (DLS)
389	Lightweight Directory Access Protocol (LDAP)
396	Novell Netware over IP
443	HTTPS (HTTP secured by SSL encryption)

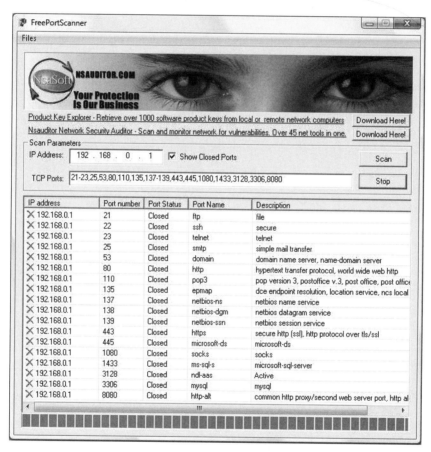

Figure 5.5
Port scanning.

5. Next, I will use a network-analysis tool such as Microsoft Baseline Security Analyzer, a free download from the Web (you can also do a search on "network vulnerability test" and find a lot of free tools). This free tool (and many others) is designed to help network administrators assess their systems. This

tool is quite easy to use, so let's look at it. The first screen lets you choose whether to scan a single computer or several, as you can see in Figure 5.6. Then you enter the IP address of the computer you wish to scan. In this example we will use an IP of a machine on a lab network (see Figure 5.7). In Figure 5.8 you can see the output of this tool. As you can see, this is a very easy tool to use and it can provide a wealth of information. While this information is designed for network administrators to monitor the security of their networks, it is also a valuable tool to a hacker.

The culmination of all these steps is that I would have a wealth of information regarding the target network. This is how real hackers begin. The obvious countermeasure is intrusion-detection systems that alert network administrators when activities like port scanning are occurring. One should also be quite careful of what information is made available to the public.

These are just some of the tools and techniques a resourceful hacker can use to learn all the vulnerabilities of a target network before attempting to break in. Smart hackers take their time to really learn a target system before intruding on it.

Password Cracking

An obvious way into a system is to crack the password of a legitimate user; one can then simply log in as that user. There are essentially two very common ways to crack a password.

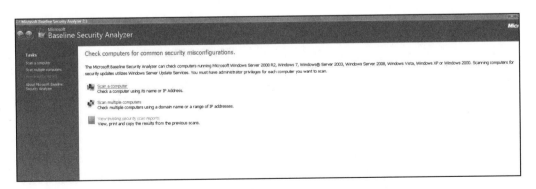

Figure 5.6
Screen one of Microsoft Baseline Security Analyzer.

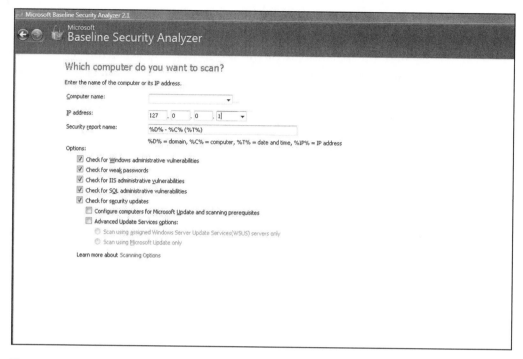

Figure 5.7
Screen two of Microsoft Baseline Security Analyzer.

Brute-Force Attack

A *brute-force attack* is literally when the software tool you are using simply tries every single permutation of letters, numbers, and symbols possible to crack the password. This will often show up in server logs as a number of failed login attempts in a short period of time.

Dictionary Attack

A simple *dictionary attack* is probably the fastest way to crack most passwords. A dictionary file is just another name for a plain text file that contains commonly used passwords. It could also be passwords specifically related to a target. For example, if the person whose password you wish to crack is a huge Pittsburgh Steelers fan, you might load a text file with a number of terms related to the Steelers. Then this file will be loaded into a cracking application (such as L0phtCrack, Brutus, etc.) and run against user accounts located by the application. Because the majority of passwords are usually simplistic, running a dictionary attack is often successful at cracking passwords. Like a brute-force attack,

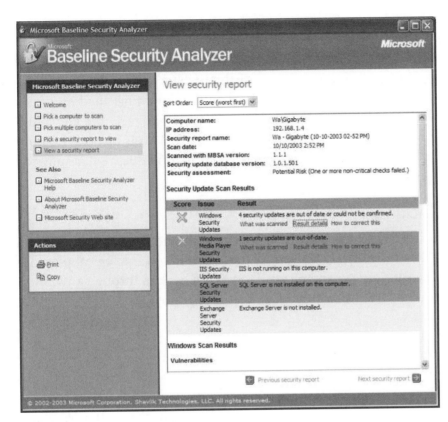

Figure 5.8
Microsoft Baseline Security Analyzer output.

this will often show up in server logs as a number of failed login attempts in a short period of time.

There are certainly other methods for cracking a password, but these two are by far the most common. They are also very easy to employ. One can do a Web search for "password cracker" and find a plethora of free tools that will assist the hacker in this endeavor.

Let's consider one popular (among the hacking community) method for hacking a Windows password. This particular method depends on the perpetrator being familiar with how Windows works. In Windows, the passwords are stored in a hash (i.e., mathematically scrambled) format on the hard drive. If one could simply put a brute-force cracker on that hash file, one would eventually get the usernames and passwords. Most Windows machines have a password lockout feature, however. After a certain number of failed login attempts, usually three, the account is locked out. The way around this is to realize that the password lockout is a feature of the Windows operating system. To circumvent that operating system, one uses a Linux boot CD to boot the computer into Linux and then puts the password cracker to work on the hashed password file. There is even a tool one can get on the Internet called OphCrack that has the Linux boot material and the password cracker. You simply burn OphCrack to a CD, put it into any Windows computer, and reboot from the CD. This is just one example of how one might crack a Windows password. This method does require physical access to the computer, however.

Web-Site Hacking

Web pages are, by definition, open to public access, and they also get a lot of traffic. This makes them the easiest target for hacking and the logical place for any intruder to start. There are many ways to try and hack in through a Web site, but we will examine just a few of the most commonly used.

SQL Injection

SQL is an acronym for Structured Query Language. It is the language used by all relational databases. If a target Web site communicates with any database, it is using SQL to do so. Clever hackers use this fact and attempt to exploit it to gain access to the system. *SQL injection* is a process whereby hackers enter SQL code directly into Web forms such as login fields or an address bar in the browser. The goal is to trick the Web page into submitting that SQL code to the database, thus executing that code. To make this work, the hacker must have an in-depth understanding of SQL. This is an effective attack, and it can also be quite devastating. Let's look at an example. Perhaps the hacker wishes to log on to a Web site. If the Web site is not very well written, then the hacker can use a feature of SQL to force the site to log him in. Here is a simple SQL statement that is often found in login screens to verify the login:

```
SELECT * FROM USERS WHERE USERNAME = 'usernameentered' AND PASSWORD =
'passwordentered'
```

The words `usernameentered` and `passwordentered` are literally what the user entered on the form. So if in the password box the hacker types `password` or `1=1`, then the SQL statement will become `SELECT * FROM USERS WHERE USERNAME = 'usernameentered' AND PASSWORD = 'passwordentered' or 1 = 1`.

In other words, "go get a user account and log me in if there is an account that matches the username and password I entered, **or if 1=1.**" It does not require mathematical skill to know that yes, indeed, 1 does equal 1 all the time. There are many permutations of the SQL injection attack; simply using a search engine to find "sql injection" will reveal many of these. And, of course, there are ways to code a Web site so this won't work. Unfortunately, many programmers don't use those methods and this trick will work with all too many logins. This is just one example of how a hacker might exploit a system. The only way to track this down in an investigation would be if the site records all logins, and thus you will see it in the log. However, sites vulnerable to this attack often don't implement extensive tracking, so it is likely to look as if a legitimate user logged in.

Cross-Site Scripting

Cross-site scripting, also known as *XSS,* is another popular technique that hackers commonly use against Web sites. This type of attack is harder to prevent than SQL injections and is becoming increasingly popular. Many well-known sites have been victims of XSS, including Google, MySpace, and even Microsoft.

XSS functions by embedding JavaScript into hyperlinks to manipulate a Web site. This gives an intruder the power to take control of individual sessions, Website advertisements, and personal information. A worst-case scenario involves a hacker gaining access to account details and taking over the entire Web site.

Session Hijacking

Session hijacking is the act of taking control of a user session after successfully obtaining or generating an authentication session ID. This type of attack requires a relatively high degree of skill and is therefore less common. Session hijacking involves an attacker literally taking over a particular session. A *session* is a valid communication established between a client and a server. When you log in to your LAN, you have established a session. These can be hijacked because every session is identified by a session ID. If you can get that ID, you can take over the session.

There are three primary techniques for hijacking sessions:

- Brute force: The attacker tries multiple IDs until one is successful.

- Calculate: In many cases, IDs are generated in a non-random manner and can be calculated.

- Steal: Using different types of techniques, the attacker can acquire the session ID.

Man-in-the-Middle Attack

The *man-in-the-middle attack* intercepts a communication session between two systems. For example, in an http transaction, the man-in-the-middle attack attempts to hijack the TCP connection between client and server. Using different techniques, the attacker splits the original TCP connection into two new connections: one between the client and the attacker and the other between the attacker and the server. Once the TCP connection is intercepted, the attacker acts as a proxy and is able to read, insert, and modify the data in the intercepted communication. Like the session-hijacking attack, this is an advanced technique that requires a high degree of skill on the part of the hacker.

Tools of the Trade

We have already seen port scanners and security analyzers used as hacking tools. We have also seen informative Web sites such as netcraft.com and archive.org being used. There are several other tools that most hackers will use.

Sniffers

A *sniffer* is a program and/or device that monitors all information passing through a computer network. It sniffs the data passing through the network off the wire and determines where the data is going, where it's coming from, and what it is. In addition to these basic functions, sniffers might have extra features that enable them to filter a certain type of data, capture passwords, and more. Some sniffers (for example, the FBI's controversial mass-monitoring tool Carnivore) can even rebuild files sent across a network, such as an e-mail or Web page. One common (and free) packet sniffer is the tool WireShark, shown in Figure 5.9.

Any packet sniffer will provide details about the packets it intercepts. More importantly, it does not prevent the packet from going through to its destination; it merely copies the content, thereby making it particularly hard to detect.

Password Crackers

A *password cracker* is a tool that attempts to automate the process of breaking passwords. It might use a dictionary attack, a brute-force attack, or a

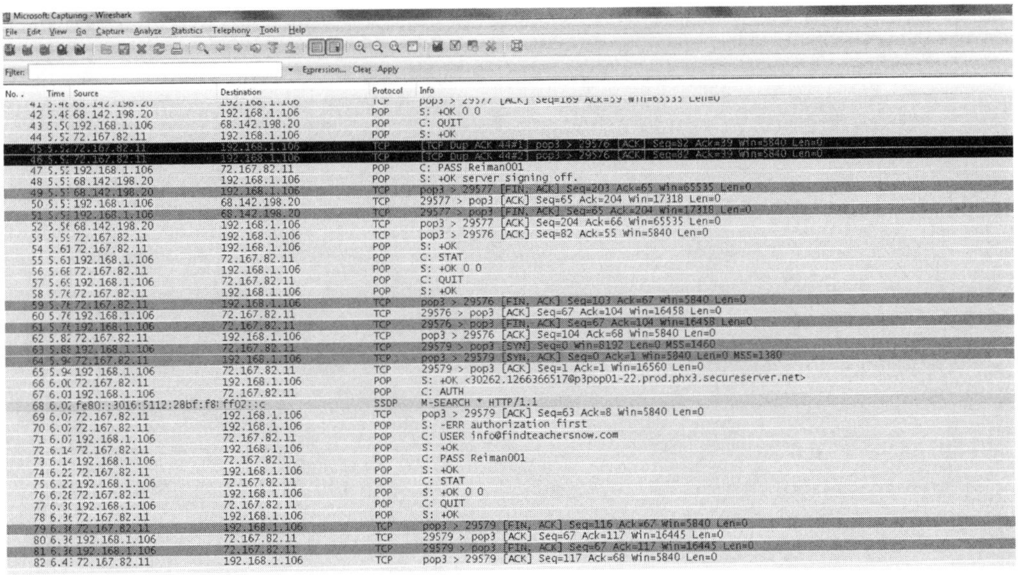

Figure 5.9
WireShark packet sniffer.

combination of both. Regardless of the methodology employed, it will certainly make cracking passwords much easier for the hacker. Figure 5.10 is a screen shot from a popular password cracking tool.

These are just a few examples of the many tools available for hackers to use. There is a wide array of utilities either designed specifically for hacking or modified for that purpose. Many are free of charge and can be readily downloaded from the Internet. Anyone who intends to investigate computer crimes should be familiar with these utilities.

Conclusion

In this chapter, we have taken a look into the world of computer crime from the perspective of the criminal. We have explored various techniques, including hacking techniques. It is important to realize that this chapter is just a brief introduction to this topic, and we have only looked at a sampling of the more common techniques. Entire books have been written on hacking techniques. But it is important that you be aware of the types of techniques a criminal might use in the commission of a computer crime. After reading this chapter you should be familiar with common techniques employed by cyber criminals and thus better able to investigate such crimes.

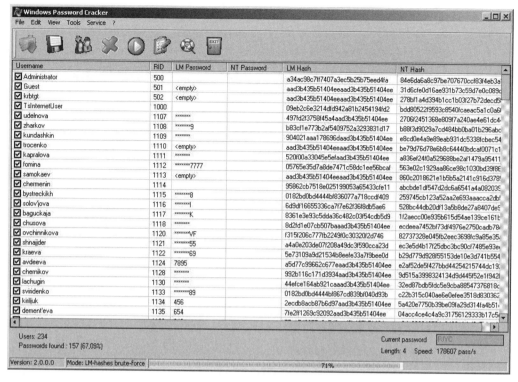

Figure 5.10
Password cracking.

Endnotes

[1] The U.S. Department of Justice Identity Theft Web page. Accessed October 2009. http://www.usdoj.gov/criminal/fraud/idtheft.html

[2] The U.S. Securities and Exchange Commission. "Internet Fraud: How to Avoid Internet Investment Scams." Accessed September 2009. http://www.sec.gov/investor/pubs/cyberfraud.htm

[3] The U.S. Federal Trade Commission. Accessed October 2009. http://www.ftc.gov/bcp/conline/pubs/online/auctions.htm

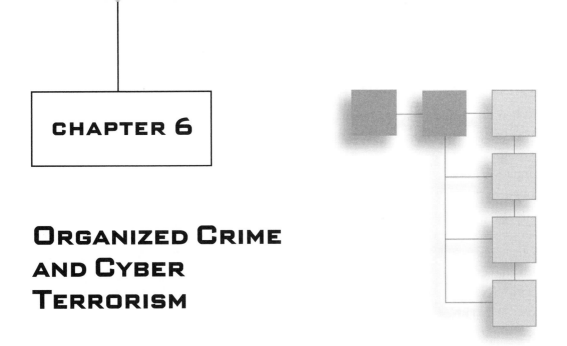

CHAPTER 6

Organized Crime and Cyber Terrorism

Introduction

In this chapter, we will be looking at two growing areas of concern. The first is the involvement of organized crime in cyber crime. Organized crime groups, including the Italian mafia, Russian mafia, and others, have been increasingly involved in a variety of computer crimes. We will also look at the growing threats of cyber terrorism and cyber espionage. Both organized crime and terrorism are real threats and should be concerns for anyone involved in investigating or fighting computer crime.

As you will see in this chapter, the involvement of organized crime in the cyber world is already quite extensive. It would be difficult to find a network-security professional who did not agree that organized crime is a significant and growing threat on the Internet. However, some in the industry believe that fears of cyber terrorism are exaggerated, and it is true that as of this writing, no major cyber terrorist attack has occurred. However, it is our contention that as society grows ever more dependent on computer systems, these systems will become a more attractive target for terrorists. It is also a fact, as we will show, that minor incidents of cyber terrorism and espionage have already occurred. The growing dependence on computer systems and the fact that minor attacks have already occurred makes a significant cyber attack more likely, in our opinion.

Organized Crime on the Internet

When one contemplates computer crime, the image is often of a nerdy guy sitting with a computer in some room listening to loud music and ingesting prodigious amounts of caffeinated beverages. And this certainly can be the case in many situations. However, there has been a steady increase in the involvement of organized-crime groups in computer crime. These groups are involved in identity theft, prostitution, trafficking in stolen goods, and other illegal activities. In previous chapters, we have touched briefly on this issue, citing specific cases where organized crime has been involved in cyber crime. In this section, we will elaborate on the specifics of how this works. There are two primary areas to be concerned with. The first is when an organized-crime group utilizes computer resources to conduct traditional crimes. In these cases, the computer systems are used to augment a criminal enterprise. While the computer systems in these cases are secondary to the actual crime, they can be an invaluable investigative tool. The second area we will examine are cases in which the crime itself is a computer crime, such as identity theft, that is being perpetrated by an organized group.

Before we delve into the types of crimes organized groups are becoming involved in, we must define what we mean by organized crime. *Organized crime* is any group that uses planning and group interaction in the furtherance of a criminal enterprise. As we have seen earlier in this book, there are groups of cyber criminals who operate together in criminal endeavors such as stealing identities and trafficking in stolen credit-card numbers. But in addition to these organized groups of cyber bandits, there is also the fact that traditional organized-crime groups are becoming increasingly involved in online crime. There have been cases of Italian mafia families such as the Bonannos of New York City, the Russian mafia, and Irish groups all involved in cyber-crime activity. Then we have the phenomenon of new groups of cyber criminals organizing themselves in a manner similar to traditional mafia families. The line between traditional organized crime and cyber crime has become blurred. This is also another example of the fact that cyber crime and real-world crime are becoming increasingly intertwined. It is critical that any person involved in investigating such crimes be aware of this interconnectivity.

Traditional Crime Augmented with Computer Systems

There are many instances wherein the computer or the network is not the primary vehicle for a given crime, but rather is used to augment the criminal activity. Take, for example, prostitution: The challenge for the criminal is to actively seek out customers for the illegal service. The Internet has made this task easier. Exotic ads on Web sites such as Craigslist allow prostitutes and pimps to advertise prostitution to a wide range of potential customers. As early as 2006, Seattle prostitution stings were showing as many as three quarters of the customers arrested had responded to erotic ads on Craigslist[1]. This is by no means isolated. Just a few of the other incidents of Craigslist being used to facilitate prostitution include:

- Newport Beach[2]

- Chicago[3]

- New York[4]

These are just a sampling of the cases regarding online facilitation of prostitution. One would be hard put to find a major city that had not experienced this phenomenon. It should be noted that while Craigslist has been in the media a great deal, erotic ads are not exclusive to Craigslist. Any online medium that allows unfettered communications will probably, at some point, become a vehicle for some criminal enterprise. Fortunately for law enforcement, these online advertisements are a double-edged sword. Many law-enforcement agencies have already implemented sting operations centered around online prostitution ads. The law-enforcement agency posts their own ad, setting up an actual meeting place to arrest the customers seeking prostitutes. This shows clearly that the Internet is a medium that not only criminals can use, but law enforcement as well.

While online facilitation of prostitution has garnered a great deal of media attention, online trafficking in stolen goods is also a growing concern. When a thief steals an item, the next step is to convert that item into cash. Traditionally, thieves had to attempt to sell the item in their own general region, and often it is the movement of the stolen goods that helps lead to the capture of the thieves. This is particularly true in cases of organized theft rings. These groups need to repeatedly move stolen goods, thus making it possible to catch them in the act. Online trafficking, however, allows an individual or group in one location to sell their stolen goods across a diverse market space, making it difficult to track the merchandise back to the thief. eBay has been a frequent avenue for thieves to sell stolen goods. Online sales venues allow a thief—particularly one who is part of an organized effort to steal and sell items—to access diverse markets. For example, if someone steals 20 high-definition televisions, trying to sell all of those in one's own locality is likely to arouse suspicion. However, selling one television in 20 different states is likely to go unnoticed. From a law-enforcement point of view, the investigation of organized theft rings should always include searches of major online auction sites for stolen merchandise. It can still be quite difficult to track the movement of stolen goods.

We have looked at a few ways organized crime can become involved in cyber crime. These examples were general overviews, so let's examine a few real-world cases. The first case we will examine is the case of Lee Klein, who compromised the Lexis-Nexis system and may have stolen personal data of up to 13,000 users[5]. In this case, Mr. Klein allegedly worked for Thomas Fiore, a Bonanno mafia family associate. Mr. Klein supplied Mr. Fiore with business names, addresses, and even account numbers to facilitate the manufacture and negotiation of counterfeit checks. Mr. Fiore then had the counterfeit checks produced and cashed, generating stolen money for the Bonanno crime family. The Bonanno crime family has also been implicated in the sale of information such as Social Security numbers and credit-card numbers.

Perhaps the traditional crime organization that has been most active in cyber crime is the Russian mafia[6]. Groups based in the former Soviet Union have been repeatedly implicated in significant computer breaches. The targets are frequently high-value economic targets including banks. In many cases, these Russian hacking rings include or are run by former KGB agents. This gives them a criminal sophistication not found in most cyber-crime rings. It also gives them a propensity and capability for violence that is not usually associated with cyber crime. The Russian mafia has also been utilizing cyber extortion as a favored technique. In a cyber-extortion scheme, the hackers infiltrate a system and steal valuable data, and then threaten the victim with exposure of that data if the perpetrators' demands are not met. The Russian mafia is also involved in identity theft on a very large scale.

The point of these stories is to illustrate a trend: Organized criminal groups, including the Italian mafia, Russian mafia, and others, are taking their traditional criminal enterprises and expanding them into cyber space. No longer are computer crimes the sole purview of disgruntled and highly intelligent "geeks." Now it is often the case that the geek is working for organized crime. This presents additional challenges as well as opportunities for law enforcement. Obviously, the involvement of organized crime makes investigations more complicated and can make involved individuals less likely to cooperate. However, this also provides one more avenue for law enforcement to utilize in the investigation of organized crime. Any organized-crime task force would be remiss not to utilize the Internet as another tool in their investigations.

From an investigative point of view, when computer systems are used to facilitate traditional crimes, investigators must have a cyber investigation running parallel with the traditional investigation. This gives two different opportunities to gather information. It is also the case that law-enforcement agencies have successfully used the Internet as part of various sting operations. Sting operations designed to catch the customers of prostitutes and to capture online pedophiles have become somewhat common. It is important to view the Internet component of a crime as an additional opportunity to gather evidence rather than an additional complication to one's investigation.

Computer Crimes Executed by Organized Groups

Another phenomenon that has developed is the emergence of purely cyber-based crime gangs. These groups are the traditional hackers most people envision, but they work in unison to perform computer crimes. In 2005, federal agents conducted a sting operation in order to arrest members of a group known as "ShadowCrew."[7] This gang was a group of hackers working together to conduct a variety of computer crimes, including identity theft. This phenomenon is international in scope. Korean authorities have also arrested gangs of online criminals[8]. The most common crime for cyber gangs is identity theft, but they also involve themselves in other illegal activities. Increasingly, hackers are organizing into criminal gangs that pool their resources and skills in order to execute crimes. There are three major types of crimes these groups perpetrate:

- Identity theft

- Stolen intellectual property

- Extortion

When organized gangs become involved in identity theft, they usually do so on a grand scale, stealing thousands of identities. Often, these groups will then sell the information rather than use it themselves. For example, a hacker gang might steal credit-card numbers and names and then sell that information to anyone who may wish to use those credit cards. Or they might sell an entire identity, including, Social Security number, driver's license number, and more. There is a growing online black market for such information. This is often a point at which the online cyber gangs work in conjunction with traditional organized crime. For example, an online cyber gang might steal 10,000 credit card numbers and then sell that information to the mafia, who might then produce credit cards with the stolen names and numbers and sell those cards to individuals.

Stolen intellectual property is a very broad category, and while this could include things such as trade secrets and confidential information, the market for such items is relatively small, making up a small portion of the total of stolen intellectual property. Much more common is the trafficking of pirated software, video, and music. There has been a great deal of media attention surrounding pirated music downloads. However, pirated software is actually an older and very widespread problem. As you may recall from our discussion in Chapter 2, "A History of Computer Crime in America," the first virus found in the wild was propagated via pirated software.

It is actually quite easy to find pirated software on the Internet. There are a number of Web sites located in various countries that sell copyright-protected software far below the normal price, often as little as 10 percent of the normal retail price. In most cases, these people have cracked a legitimate version of the software and are now selling illegal copies online. This is a growing problem, and one need only search for something such as "buy cheap Windows 7" to find examples. Figure 6.1 shows an example of this. It is a screen shot from one of these Web sites.

The problem of illegal copies of software being sold is growing, and frankly the issue lies primarily with the purchasers of such software. Many people simply do not see the harm in buying these products. It is still difficult for consumers to view intellectual property the same way they do traditional property. Many people who would be appalled at even the suggestion that they might steal have no problem at all copying their neighbors' software or downloading pirated music. The market for stolen intellectual property is so large, and the profits so easy to generate, that it is safe to assume this problem will continue to grow in the coming years.

In many cases, the traffickers in stolen software will set up a Web site offshore in a country unlikely to expend much effort investigating the crime. In many cases, these operations are small enough that they go unnoticed by both law

Figure 6.1
Stolen software for sale.

enforcement and the software vendors whose property they are stealing. And in the event that an investigation begins, the financial transactions will often be traced to some offshore account in a country with loose banking laws. The result is that this can be a difficult crime to investigate. It will also usually come under the jurisdiction of a federal law-enforcement agency, not a local one.

Extortion is another growing cyber crime. One common cyber extortion scheme is for the perpetrator to steal proprietary data and threaten to release it if their demands are not met. Or the criminals might breach a network and threaten to publish how it was done, thus allowing every hacker easy access to the target system. It is difficult to gauge just how common this crime is. The victims who pay the extortion obviously do not report the crime to the police. But enough cases have emerged in which the victims have not paid, but rather reported the incident to law enforcement, that we can safely conclude that this particular crime is become disturbingly common. This crime is usually performed by an organized group rather than an individual. The complexity of the crime makes it more suited to a group.

These cyber gangs are a growing problem. In many ways, they may be the most significant threat on the Internet, the reason being that they tend to be groups of very skilled computer criminals working in concert. This concerted effort increases the capabilities of these groups well beyond that of any individual computer criminal. Investigating online cyber gangs will require significant efforts on the part of law enforcement and will frankly require a very high level of skill on the part of the investigators. The nature of organized computer crime, like traditional organized crime, often crosses jurisdictional boundaries. Investigations are likely to involve local, state, and federal law-enforcement agencies. Coordination and cooperation in the investigation are key to solving these cases.

Cyber Terrorism

As computer crime becomes more common, we see the lines between traditional crime and cyber crime blur. The same thing is beginning to occur with cyber terrorism. The past few years have made most people very aware of the potential for terrorist attacks, and most people assume that such an attack will be in the form of a bomb, a hijacking, releasing a biological agent, or other means. But most people have not given much thought to the possibility of cyber terrorism. *Cyber terrorism* is simply the use of computer systems and the Internet connectivity between them to launch a terrorist attack. It is a fact that in time, someone or some group will use computer methods to launch a military or terrorist attack against some target. In fact, on a smaller scale, this has already occurred. Before we delve into that we have to explore exactly what is meant by "cyber terrorism." According to the FBI, "cyber terrorism is the premeditated, politically motivated attack against information, computer systems, computer programs, and data which result in violence against noncombatant targets by sub national groups or clandestine agents."[9] Cyber terrorism is simply the use of computer systems to conduct a terrorist attack. Clearly, the loss of life due to a cyber attack would be much less than that of a bombing. In fact, it is highly likely that there would be no loss of life at all. However, significant economic damage, disruptions in communications, disruptions in supply lines, and general degradation of the national infrastructure are all quite possible via the Internet. It is also possible that attacks on certain systems such as the power grid or air-traffic–control systems could lead to a loss of life.

Economic Attacks

We have already seen in previous chapters that significant economic damage can occur from cyber crimes, and it is true that economic damage is far more likely from a cyber attack than is loss of life, so let us begin by examining this aspect of cyber terrorism. There are a variety of ways that a cyber attack can cause economic damage. The simple destruction of data often has a direct negative economic impact on a company. Companies invest a great deal of resources into gathering and analyzing data for various purposes. The destruction of that data can cause significant economic damage to the target company. It is also the case that publicized network-security breaches can have a negative impact on the stock price of a company. Any breach of security on a company network can cause economic damages in several ways: by destroying data, by negative PR, in the cost to repair the breach, and finally through the actual value of the data itself.

In addition to the economic damage that could be caused by an act of cyber terrorism, there is the damage caused simply by the possibility of a security breach, whether it is connected to terrorism or not. The mere fact that companies now need to purchase antivirus software, purchase intrusion-detection software, and hire computer-security professionals means that non-terroristic computer crime has already caused economic damage to companies and governments around the world. However, the general damage caused by random virus outbreaks, hacking attacks, and online fraud is not the type of economic damage we are discussing. In this chapter, we are discussing a concerted and deliberate attack against a particular target or targets for the exclusive purpose of causing direct damage.

Let us consider a possible economically based cyber-terrorist scenario. Let's consider a fictitious terrorist group we will call ASU (U.S.A. backwards). This group has decided to launch a cyber attack against the United States. They intend for this to be a major attack that causes widespread economic damage. How might they conduct such an attack? Using a team of hackers they could select several targets for simultaneous attack. To make this scenario more plausible, we will ignore highly secure targets such as the air-traffic–control system, nuclear-control systems, and so on. This group is going to select three economic targets, and they have decided to have all three attacks occur simultaneously on January 1.

The first target will be power grids/plants. It is an unfortunate fact that many of our power plants have outdated network infrastructure and in many cases some glaring security flaws. In our scenario, the ASU would seek to infiltrate the power grid in a major metropolitan area. Once they gain access they would not immediately take any action, but simply wait and prepare for January 1. They could use existing flaws in security, Trojan horses, or spyware to gain access to the power grid of the target city. There have been breaches in security grids in the past few years, making such an attack very plausible.

The second target would be logistical systems for major distributors of fuel. This would be the companies who distribute gasoline, propane, and related fuels. The goal would be to reroute fuel shipments to incorrect destinations, which would lead to a glut of fuel in some regions and a shortage in others. This rerouting would be set to start just prior to January 1 (it would take a few days for the situation to become apparent). The attackers would only need to be able to gain access to routing and logistical systems of private companies. These are not usually highly secured systems and such a breach would be within the capabilities of many hackers.

The third target would be a financial system, such as a major banking system. There have been breaches of banks in which money was stolen, but in this case money would be randomly transferred between accounts. This would occur on December 31. Again, breaching bank systems is difficult but it has been done before, so it is not at all implausible.

So what would occur is that on New Year's Eve, some accounts would suddenly have excess funds and others would be wiped out. This would be pervasive throughout at least one major bank, possibly multiple banks. The next day, when the situation becomes obvious and the bank begins corrective action, there would be widespread blackouts (preferably in the same area that the banks in question have their IT headquarters). And in the following days, fuel shortages would occur in this area as well as many others. Now, consider for just a moment how much economic damage this would cause. Also consider what would happen in a metropolitan area with widespread power outages, fuel shortages, and large groups of individuals whose bank accounts are wiped out and have no access to funds, while other individuals suddenly find an excess of funds in their accounts. This would likely lead to panic, and might even lead to physical damage occurring in the form of looting.

While such a concerted attack has not yet occurred, it is certainly not implausible. Every type of system mentioned in this scenario has at some point been breached. Up to now, though, it has not been part of a larger concerted attack. It seems naïve to assume that no such attack will ever occur. All that is required is a small team of people with a moderate to high level of hacking expertise who choose to execute a coordinated attack. In past decades, nuclear scientists were sought after by various nations and terrorist groups. More recently, experts in biological weapons have been sought by these same groups. In time, they will see the possibilities and seek out computer security/hacking experts. Given that there are literally thousands of people with the requisite skills, it seems unlikely that a motivated organization could not find a few dozen people willing to commit these acts, whether for monetary gain, personal reasons, or ideological motivations.

It should also be noted that this scenario we just examined is a relatively minor one. As we mentioned earlier in this chapter, there now exist organized, highly skilled, online cyber gangs. It seems only a matter of time before one of these gangs turns its attention to cyber terrorism, either due to ideological issues that motivate them to commit terroristic acts or simply through greed. It would seem logical to assume that at some point, traditional terrorist groups will attempt to utilize such a cyber gang for their own purposes.

Even more disconcerting than an economic target would be a cyber attack executed directly on defense systems. When computer security and national defense are mentioned together, the obvious thought that comes to mind is the possibility of some hacker breaking into ultra-secure systems at the Department of Defense, Central Intelligence Agency, or National Security Agency, or perhaps even systems related to nuclear weapons. Our military is more dependent on information systems now than ever before. Many military operations depend on unmanned drones and satellite communications. However, such an intrusion into one of the most secure systems in the world is very unlikely. It is not impossible, but it is very unlikely. The most likely outcome of such an attack would be that the attacker is promptly captured. Such systems are extremely secure and intruding upon them is not as easy as some movies might suggest. However, there are a number of scenarios in which breaking into less-secure systems can cause significant disruption to our national defense. Let us look at one such scenario.

Consider for a moment less-sensitive military systems. By definition, a less-sensitive system would be less secure and therefore an easier target, such as systems that are responsible for basic logistical operations (food, mail, fuel, etc.). Now suppose that a terrorist cracks one or more of these systems. He notices that cargo planes are being routed to a base that is used to transport troops to and from missions (both training and real missions). This same terrorist also notices that a larger-than-normal amount of ammunition and food supplies—enough for 5,000 troops for two weeks—is simultaneously being routed to that same base. Then on yet another low-security system our cyber spy notes that a given unit—for example two brigades of the 82nd airborne division—have had all leave cancelled. It is now obvious that these troops are preparing to deploy. The fact that a deployment is going to occur, the size of the deployment, and the approximate time of that deployment have all been deduced without ever even attempting to break into a high-security system.

Now assume our hacker would like to disrupt this operation. He does nothing to change the routing of the members of the brigades or the transport planes because such activity would be obvious and quickly discovered. Instead, he alters the records for the shipment of supplies so that the supplies are delivered two days late and to the wrong location. He has succeeded in undermining the mission of these troops by interfering with logistics, and he has done so without even attempting to break into highly secured systems.

These are just two scenarios in which compromising low-security/low-priority systems can lead to significant military problems. This should further illustrate the serious need for high security on all systems. There clearly are no truly low-priority security systems. Any breach on any system can be used to cause serious damage.

It would also be likely that any act of cyber terrorism targeting a military target, such as we have just outlined, would be coupled with a real-world terrorist attack. For example, immediately following the disruption of supplies, a car bomb could be exploded. The culmination of undermining supplies coupled with an actual physical attack can have a significant impact on both morale and operational capacity.

It must also be noted that any number of systems would make attractive targets. As we have already mentioned, systems such as those that launch missiles or air-traffic–control systems are very secure. In most cases, they are not even connected in any way to the Internet, not even via intermediate systems. Compromising those systems is very near impossible. However, other systems are not so secure. Logistical systems, personnel records, and communications systems all provide attractive targets. And as we will examine later in this chapter, they also provide targets for cyber espionage.

Both of the scenarios outlined here involve specific targets with specific strategies. However, once a specific target is attacked, defenses can be readied for it. What may be more threatening is a general and unfocused attack with no specific target. The purpose of any terrorist attack is to promote fear and unrest, and a general attack on multiple targets could certainly accomplish that. Consider the various virus attacks of late 2003 and early 2004. With the exception of My-Doom, which was clearly aimed at the Santa Cruz Organization (SCO), these attacks were not directed at a specific target. However, the sheer volume of virus attacks and network traffic did cause significant economic damage. IT personnel across the globe had to drop their normal projects to work to clean infected systems and to shore up the defenses of systems.

The scenarios we have discussed here are hypothetical. As of this writing, they have not occurred. When this author suggested similar possibilities in a previous book, written in 2005, some critics said it was simple fear mongering and that a cyber terrorist threat was unlikely. However, not only is this not an implausible scenario, but there have already been some incidents of cyber terrorism.

When speaking to the Special Oversight Panel on Terrorism Committee on Armed Services in the U.S. House of Representatives[10] in 2002, FBI agent Ronald L. Dick spoke at length about the threat to our national infrastructure via terrorism. Clearly, the FBI is beginning to take cyber terrorism as a real threat.

As you learned in Chapter 2, as early as 1996, a computer hacker associated with a white-supremacist group temporarily disabled a Massachusetts ISP and damaged part of the ISP's record-keeping system. The ISP had attempted to stop the hacker from sending out worldwide racist messages under the ISP's name. The hacker signed off with the threat, "You have yet to see true electronic terrorism. This is a promise." Now, this is a relatively mild incident, but it does show people using hacking techniques for ideological goals. This early incident was a nascent example of cyber terrorism. Then, in 1998, Tamil guerrillas spammed Sri Lankan embassies with 800 e-mails a day over a two-week period. The messages read, "We are the Internet Black Tigers and we're doing this to disrupt your communications." Intelligence authorities characterized it as the first known attack by terrorists against a country's computer systems. Again, this was a very mild attack, but it was also several years ago. It does show someone utilizing the Internet to conduct an attack against a target.

In 2008 and 2009, there were several reports of attacks on various systems tracing back to South Korea or China. Given that both nations are totalitarian regimes with very strict control on their populace, it is difficult to believe that the governments of those countries were not at least aware of those attacks, and many people (including this author) suspect that these governments were actually behind the attacks. When governments use or support cyber attacks, cyber warfare has become a reality.

In May 2007, government offices of Estonia were subjected to a mass denial-of-service attack in response to a Russian WWII memorial being removed. This politically motivated attack is an example of cyber terrorism, as it caused disruption in the Estonian government.

In November of 2006, the Secretary of the Air Force announced the creation of the Air Force Cyber Command. This command's primary function is to monitor and defend American interest in cyberspace. The AFCC will draw upon the personnel resources of the 67th Network Warfare Wing as well as other resources. Clearly the United States Air Force takes the threat of cyber terrorism and cyber warfare seriously and has created an entire command to counter that threat.

In July 2009, there were a variety of cyber attacks on government Web sites such as the Pentagon and the White House in the United States as well as government agencies in South Korea. These attacks coincided with increased tensions with North Korea. It would be naïve to not classify these attacks as cyber terrorism.

The attacks we have mentioned thus far were relatively minor, and much less damaging than the hypothetical scenarios we discussed earlier. But clearly, the use of Internet-based attacks is becoming an augmentation of traditional conflicts. Given our growing dependence on computer systems, it is hard to believe that a more serious attack will not be attempted. It does not take a great deal of imagination to consider the severe damage that could be caused by the concerted efforts of a team of cyber terrorists or a group of cyber terrorist cells working in much the same way as traditional terrorists, each cell conducting attacks with no knowledge of the other. The combined effect could be a significant disruption in communications and supply transport (both civilian and military), as well as economic havoc. Some readers may still feel this is merely sensational, but the evidence seems to indicate otherwise.

If any reader still has doubts about the reality of computer terrorism and even computer warfare, then consider the situation with the United States predator drones. While writing this book, one of the authors happened to be watching CNN and a pertinent story aired. On December 17th, 2009, the story on CNN was that insurgents in Afghanistan had been able to hack into predator drones and to view the video feeds from them. So far, no one has been able to take control of such a drone, but they have been able to tap into the video feed. What makes this story even more intriguing is the fact that it is reported that the perpetrators used inexpensive utilities downloaded from the Internet. This story should definitely illustrate that computer hacking is now a very real element in warfare, and it seems clear that in the future we will see more incidents like this.

Information Warfare

A topic closely related to cyber terrorism and cyber warfare is information warfare. Information warfare has been around for almost as long as warfare itself. Information warfare certainly predates the advent of the modern computer, and in fact may be as old as conventional warfare. *Information warfare* is the attempt to manipulate the flow of information in order to alter the outcome of a conflict or a political struggle. This can mean attempting to spread disinformation in an attempt to mislead the enemy or to spread propaganda in order to undermine the enemy's morale. Such activities have been a part of political conflict and open warfare for many years. The Internet, however, has made such activities much easier.

Many people utilize the Internet as either a primary or secondary news source. This fact allows virtually anyone to spread information or disinformation on the Internet. This ease of dissemination makes information warfare on the Internet an attractive proposition. And anyone with even a passing familiarity with the Internet can attest to the proliferation of disinformation.

The first way in which the Internet is used in information warfare is in the realm of propaganda. Every stakeholder in any situation has their own interpretation of events and news. It is very difficult to find a truly unbiased opinion on any topic of controversy; this becomes evident in any conflict. Each side tries very hard to portray its cause in the best possible light and the opposing cause in the worst possible light. This begins with the simple choice of what words to use. For example, in the controversy over abortion, no one labels themselves as pro abortion or anti abortion. They label themselves pro choice and pro life. Conversely, their ideological adversaries label them as anti life or anti choice. The Internet allows anyone to take this to a new level. Rather than simply put a spin on facts and use terms with different connotations, the parties can literally make up complete falsehoods. By the time those falsehoods are exposed, it is too late. Enough people remember the ''facts'' but not where they heard the story.

There are entire Web sites devoted to debunking the urban legends that circulate on the Internet. Two well known sites are http://www.Snopes.com and http://www.TruthorFiction.com. However, this does not prevent false stories from being repeated. I am sure most readers have at one time or another received an e-mail retelling a particular story and later found out the story was fake. However, the goal of people who disseminate such fictions is to influence as many people as they can. If they can get enough stories out, they can change the way some people view a given topic. This is also the case for both criminal organizations and terrorists. As we mentioned earlier in this book, all the major motorcycle gangs have Web sites. In many cases, those Web sites serve to paint a positive image of the motorcycle gang. This is propaganda. Al Qaeda has been working to create more Web sites espousing their views. They have been particularly interested in English Web sites in an effort to sway moderate western Muslims to the extremism of Al Qaeda.

From an investigative point of view, these propaganda tools can also be a valuable resource. In order to tell their story, the organization in question must reveal some information. For example, motorcycle-gang Web sites provide photos of gang members, names of gang members, and information about public gatherings. This can be a great asset to law enforcement attempting to gather background information. The Internet can also be a communication venue for criminals and terrorist groups. Major Nidal Hasan, who has been accused of murdering 13 people at Ft. Hood, reportedly was in online communications with an extremist cleric tied to the 9/11 World Trade Center attacks, and made Internet postings on bulletin boards that indicated sympathy with terrorists. Investigators and intelligence officials must consider Internet communications as potential intelligence resources. Obviously, there are legal issues, and one cannot simply monitor all communications. Law-enforcement officials should consider the monitoring of Internet communications such as e-mail in the same light as they do monitoring phone conversations. However, public postings to bulletin boards and Web sites are, by definition, public. Anyone can observe and track such postings.

It should also be noted that the Internet provides an excellent place to conduct a disinformation campaign, and that can work for either party in a conflict. Law-enforcement agencies have successfully used fake Web sites, fake Craigslist ads, and other techniques to help capture criminals. It is also possible to utilize the Internet to feed misinformation to criminals and terrorists. To some extent, the sting operations used to catch the patrons of prostitutes are examples of misinformation being used in law enforcement. The intelligence community has even broader capacity to utilize disinformation. While writing this chapter, there was a case of five young men from the United States utilizing YouTube to attempt to connect with terrorist groups. Law-enforcement and intelligence officials can use the Internet not only for sting operations but to leak disinformation to these same groups.

Cyber Espionage

Closely related to cyber terrorism and information warfare is the topic of espionage, and in particular cyber espionage. When you hear the word *espionage,* you may well have an image of a glamorous debonair spy who dresses impeccably and drinks martinis, shaken not stirred, and travels to glamorous locations with equally glamorous travel companions. But espionage is about information, and it is usually best done without fanfare. Anonymity is the professional spy's best friend. And since so much information is stored on computers, an obvious target for any espionage operation would be computer systems. While such things are not generally publicly acknowledged, most experts agree that various intelligence agencies probably engage in cyber spying operations. In fact, one might say that for an intelligence agency to omit such a valuable resource would be negligent.

However, it is also important to realize that espionage is not only utilized by governments, intelligence agencies, and nefarious international organizations such as Al Queda. While those entities do indeed engage in espionage, they are certainly not the only organizations that do so. The aforementioned organizations' desire to acquire information for political and military goals is likely not surprising, but it may shock some readers to learn that corporate espionage is a major problem.

Now, it is not the case that major companies have corporate spies on the payroll—at least there have been no cases of that occurring that we know of. However, it is generally believed by security experts that many companies have purchased information from freelance individuals without asking where that information came from. It can be very difficult to ascertain how widespread this might be. Companies that perpetrate corporate espionage don't share the fact that they do it, for obvious reasons, and the companies that are victims of such espionage often don't wish to reveal that fact, either. Revealing that their security was compromised could have a negative impact on their stock value. It is also possible, in certain cases, that such a breach of security might make the company vulnerable to liability claims from customers whose data may have been compromised. For these reasons, companies often are hesitant to disclose any industrial-espionage activities whether they are the perpetrator or the victim.

Now, some readers might think that cyber espionage is a rare occurrence and that we are being overly sensational about the topic in this book. However, in 2008, the SANS Institute ranked cyber espionage as the third greatest threat on the Internet[11]. Most security experts agree that this activity occurs far more often than is reported, and they also agree it will continue to grow in frequency and severity. The SANS Institute also expects cyber espionage to be a growing factor in international relations as well as in industrial espionage.

Industrial espionage is the use of spying techniques to find out key information that is of economic value. By now, it should be apparent to the reader that in many cases, data is the most valuable asset any organization has. Such data might include a list of a competitor's clients, research data on a new product, or any information that might give the spying organization an economic advantage. While the rationale for corporate espionage is different from military espionage, corporate techniques are often the same as those methods employed by intelligence agencies and can include electronic monitoring, photocopying files, or compromising a member of the target organization. In many cases, spyware— the same software used to help perpetrate identity theft—can be the primary tool in corporate espionage. There have been incidents of former intelligence agents working in corporate espionage. When such individuals bring their skills and training to the world of corporate espionage, the situation becomes much more difficult for computer-security experts.

While various computer experts and government agencies attempt to estimate the impact and spread of corporate espionage, its very nature makes accurate estimates impossible. Not only do the perpetrators not wish to disclose their crimes, but often the victims won't either. But the fact is that most incidents of an information breach in a company trace back to employees, and disgruntled employees are often the source of sensitive information being leaked. The question becomes just how valuable is that information? While one can look at that question from a number of angles, it can really be simplified into two criteria. The first criterion is, what it would cost to produce that information? For example, a market-research study's worth can first be considered by how much it would cost to duplicate that research. The second factor is how much economic advantage that information gives to a competitor. You can think of this economic value of information as a simple equation:

$$VI \text{ (value of information)} = C \text{ (cost to produce)} + VG \text{ (value gained)}$$

While some people are not yet fully cognizant of the concept, data does indeed represent a valuable asset. In many cases, it is the most important asset a company has. When we speak of the "information age" or our "information-based economy," it is important to realize that these are not just buzzwords. Information is a real commodity. It is as much an economic asset as any other item in a company's possession. In fact, it is often the case that the data residing on a company's computer is worth far more than the hardware and software of the computer system itself. It is certainly the case that the data is much more difficult to replace than the computer hardware and software.

To help you truly appreciate the concept of information as commodity, consider the process of earning a college degree. You spend four years sitting in various classrooms. You pay a significant amount of money for the privilege of sitting in a room and listening to someone speak at length about some topic. At the end of the four years, the only tangible product you receive is a single piece of paper. Surely you can get a piece of paper for far less cost and with much less effort. What you actually paid for was the information you received. The same is true of the value of many professions. Doctors, attorneys, engineers, consultants, managers, and so forth all are consulted for their expert information. Information itself is now a valuable commodity, thus the term "information age."

The data stored in computer systems has a high value for two reasons. First, there is a lot of time and effort that goes into creating and analyzing the data. If you spend six months with a team of five people gathering and analyzing information, then that information is worth an amount equal to at least the salaries and benefits of six people. Second, data often has intrinsic value, apart from the time and effort spent acquiring and analyzing the data. If the facts are about a proprietary process, invention, process, or algorithm, its value is obvious. However, any data that might provide a competitive edge is inherently valuable. Even a customer contact list has a certain inherent value. For example, insurance companies frequently employ teams of statisticians and actuaries using the latest technology to try to predict the risks associated with any given group of potential insureds. The resulting statistical information might be very valuable to a competing insurance company.

Corporate espionage is neither new nor restricted to technology companies. In 1993, General Motors (GM) and one if its partners began to investigate a former executive, Inaki Lopez[12]. GM alleged that Lopez and seven other former GM employees had transferred GM proprietary information to Volkswagen (VW) in Germany via GM's own network. The information allegedly stolen included component price data, proprietary construction plans, internal cost calculations, and a purchasing list.

Another case occurred in August 2003. Oleg Zezev, a 29-year-old PC technician from Kazakhstan, broke into the Bloomberg Inc.[13] computer system and used the alias "Alex" to blackmail the firm. Zezev illegally obtained personal data about Michael Bloomberg, the founder and CEO of Bloomberg L.P., including Bloomberg's personal e-mail and credit-card information. The hacker then used that information to blackmail the firm.

After deliberating for less than six hours, the jury in the U.S. District Court in Manhattan found the perpetrator guilty of all four charges: conspiracy, attempted extortion, sending threatening electronic messages, and computer intrusion. This case is fascinating because it clearly shows that cyber espionage and cyber extortion are real problems.

CIO Magazine[14] examined the issue of government-based cyber espionage in a 2009 article. Their article discusses the possibility that the Chinese government was behind a widespread infiltration of more than 1,200 computers owned by more than 100 countries with the express purpose of spying on the activities of those countries. The same article mentions that in 2007, the British government accused China of hacking into the systems of various British banks.

Finally, a more recent and more disturbing incident: While this author was writing this book, just a week before Christmas 2009, the story broke that hackers had stolen secret defense plans of the United States and South Korea[15]. The information stolen included a summary of plans for military operations by South Korea and U. S. troops in case of war with North Korea. Authorities speculated that North Korea was responsible, although the attacks traced back to a Chinese IP address. This case clearly shows that cyber espionage is not only being executed by various entities, including governments, but that it has been quite effective. Cyber espionage and counter espionage are now critical elements in national defense.

We could examine dozens more cases like this, but at this point I think most readers can appreciate the real danger presented by cyber espionage. It seems likely that such cases will become more frequent, rather than less so. It should be clear that these problems are real and are growing.

From an investigative point of view, cyber espionage, whether it is corporate espionage or government-backed espionage, must be investigated by following the information. The information that is compromised can immediately provide clues about who would want that information. This provides investigators with immediate suspects. Coupling that information with good computer forensics can actually help make these cases a bit easier to investigate.

Conclusion

Hopefully, after reading this chapter, you have an appreciation for the sophisticated criminal activities now being perpetrated via computer systems. Organized crime, terrorists, and spies are utilizing global computer networks to perpetrate their activities. It is likely that anyone involved in investigating computer crime could at some point become involved with investigating a crime involving one of these types of activities. It should also be clear to the reader that the Internet can be a valuable intelligence-gathering tool for both law enforcement and intelligence agencies.

It seems likely that in the future, we will see cyber espionage, disinformation campaigns, and cyber warfare as part of any conflict strategy. It is important that law enforcement, military commanders, and intelligence professionals pay very close attention to this growing problem and be prepared.

Endnotes

[1] *The Seattle Times.* "Prostitution Sting Leads to 104 Arrests." 2006. http://seattletimes.nwsource.com/html/localnews/2003432936_craigslist16m.html

[2] *The Orange County Register.* "Woman Denies Running Online Prostitution Ring." 2007. http://www.ocregister.com/news/craigslist-135698-prostitution-ads.html

[3] CBS Chicago Channel 2. "Sheriff's Police Go After Craigslist Prostitution." 2008. http://cbs2chicago.com/local/craigslist.prostitution.sting.2.747638.html

[4] Canada.com. "Craigslist Faces Prostitution Controversy in NY." 2009. http://www.canada.com/health/Craigslist+faces+prostitution+controversy/1616166/story.html

[5] Information Security Resources. "Lexis Nexis Warns 32K of Breach." http://information-security-resources.com/tag/lexisnexis/

[6] Identity Theft Labs. "Russian Mafia Steals 500,000 Bank and Credit Accounts." http://www.identitytheftlabs.com/identity-theft/russian-mafia-steals-500000-bank-and-credit-accounts/

[7] *Business Week.* "Hacker Hunters: An Elite Force Takes On the Dark Side of Computing." 2005. http://www.businessweek.com/magazine/content/05_22/b3935001_mz001.htm

[8] Kotaku. "Hacker Gang Swipes Usernames, Passwords." http://kotaku.com/112234/hacker-gang-swipes-usernames-passwords

[9] Federal Bureau of Investigation. "Cyber Terrorism and Critical Infrastructure Protection." 2002. http://www.fbi.gov/congress/congress02/nipc072402.htm

[10] Federal Bureau of Investigation. "Cyber Terrorism and Critical Infrastructure Protection." 2002. http://www.fbi.gov/congress/congress02/nipc072402.htm

[11] *Network World.* "Cyber Espionage Seen as Growing Threat to Business, Government." 2008. http://www.networkworld.com/news/2008/011708-cyberespionage.html

[12] CNN. "GM vs. Lopez: Much Ado About Nothing." 1993. http://money.cnn.com/magazines/fortune/fortune_archive/1993/06/28/78038/index.htm

[13] U.S. Department of Justice. "Kazakhstan Hacker Sentenced to Four Years Prison for Breaking into Bloomberg Systems and Attempting Extortion." http://www.cybercrime.gov/zezevSent.htm

[14] *CIO Magazine.* "Cyber Espionage from State Governments? Don't Be Surprised." 2009. http://www.cio.com/article/487942/Cyber_Espionage_From_State_Governments_Don_t_Be_Surprised

[15] Yahoo! News. "Hackers Steal Military Secrets." http://news.yahoo.com/s/ap/20091218/ap_on_re_as/as_koreas_cyberattack

PART 2

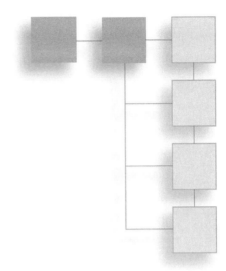

COMPUTER
FORENSICS

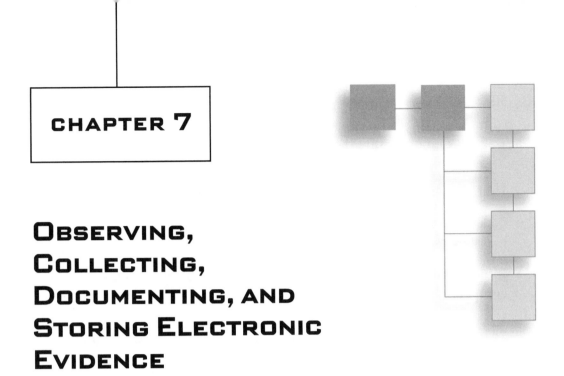

CHAPTER 7

Observing, Collecting, Documenting, and Storing Electronic Evidence

Introduction

In the preceding chapters, we introduced you to the broad spectrum of computer crime. We discussed the history of computer crime, the techniques used to commit such crimes, as well as pertinent laws. By this point, you should be familiar with the various types of crimes committed, the techniques used by criminals, and the various relevant laws. Now you have the foundation necessary to move forward and learn about the actual investigative process. An investigator will often be a member of a law-enforcement agency, but this won't always be the case. He or she could also be a corporate network-security professional doing the initial investigation prior to law enforcement getting involved. The investigator could also be an individual involved in investigation for a civil matter. Whatever the status of the investigator, if the investigation is going to withstand the scrutiny of opposing counsel, it must follow the same rigorous steps as those used by law enforcement.

In this chapter, we will outline steps for the investigator to follow when initiating any investigation. Please remember that these steps are general guidelines, and you must follow your agency policies and state laws when conducting an investigation. These same steps are most likely implemented in your agency's guidelines, but your agency might have a specific approach to each step, so it is

227

critical that you be very familiar with your agency's investigative policies. If you are not a law-enforcement officer, you will want to familiarize yourself with the procedures used by your local law enforcement and to follow those same procedures. If you cannot acquire the procedures used by your local law-enforcement agency, you can find some federal guidelines at the following sources:

- United States Secret Service (http://www.secretservice.gov/ectf.shtml)

- Federal Bureau of Investigation (http://www.cert.org/tech_tips/FBI_ investigates_crime.html)

- FBI Computer Forensics (http://www.fbi.gov/hq/lab/fsc/backissu/oct2000/ computer.htm)

It is also important to keep in mind that a few jurisdictions have passed laws requiring that the investigator must be either a law-enforcement officer or a licensed private investigator in order to extract evidence. This is a controversial law given that normally, private-investigator training and licensing does not include computer-forensics training. You should learn specifics in your state, but this prohibition generally does not preclude a computer-forensics expert from analyzing the evidence, only from doing the actual seizing and collecting of evidence. It might be appropriate for a computer-forensics expert to work in conjunction with a licensed private investigator. In most jurisdictions, this would not apply to a company's internal computer-security specialists gathering evidence from the company's own computers. Michigan and Texas currently require a private investigator's license to gather computer-forensic evidence. If you are not a law-enforcement officer, then be certain to check your state's laws on this issue.

Some searches may require you to have a search warrant dictating what you can search for at the scene. Remember that just like any other criminal investigation, if a warrant is required and you do not have one, then the evidence will most likely not be admissible in court. There are specific cases where a warrant is not required. In traditional, non-computer crimes, a warrant is not required if the evidence is in plain sight or there is an imminent danger. Those two factors are unlikely to apply to most computer crimes. However, one exception to the requirement for a warrant that will apply is if you have the permission of the owner of the equipment. If the computer equipment's owner grants you permission to conduct a search, you do not need a warrant. In the case of the victim's computer system, such cooperation is almost always forthcoming. However, it is always a good idea to at least ask a suspect for permission to examine his or her computer system. It is not at all uncommon for a suspect to grant such permission.

If you are a small department and you do all the investigation, make sure you take your time. If you're part of a larger department, you may assign other investigators to help in the tasks. But regardless of the size of your team, remember you have to do it step by step. Any rush through the process is likely to cause significant problems when the case proceeds to trial, be that a civil or criminal trial. Regardless of the situation, it is important to realize that securing the scene and gathering the evidence follows very much the same process in computer crime as it does in traditional crimes.

Federal Guidelines

We previously listed some agencies that have clear and explicit guidelines for computer forensics. Before we delve into the basic procedures for computer forensics, we will examine these guidelines. In this section, you will see an overview of the FBI's recommendations for computer forensics. While there are other agency guidelines, such as the Secret Service guidelines, most are very close to the FBI guidelines. If you want more details, you can visit the Web sites previously listed. We won't go over every element of every federal agency's guidelines here, as that would include a great deal of duplication. But let's look at a few elements of specific agencies' guidelines that are particularly worthy of note.

FBI Forensics Guidelines

The FBI provides some valuable guidelines to individuals and businesses who are victims of a computer crime. These guidelines are very important. The first person to respond to an incident is likely to be a network administrator or support technician. Their first steps are critical in preserving the evidence. If an incident occurs, the first responder is encouraged to preserve the state of the computer at the time of the incident by making a backup copy of any logs, damaged or altered files, and of course any files left by the intruder. This last part is critical. Hackers frequently use various tools and may leave traces of their presence. Furthermore, the FBI warns that if the incident is in progress, you should activate any auditing or recording software you might have available. You want to collect as much data about the incident as you can.

Another important step is to document the specific losses suffered as a result of the attack. Losses typically include the following:

- Labor cost spent in response and recovery. (Multiply the number of participating staff by their hourly rates.)

- If equipment was damaged, the cost of that equipment.

- If data was lost or stolen, what was the value of that data? How much did it cost to obtain that data and how much will it cost to reconstruct it?

- Any lost revenue including losses due to down time, having to give customers credit due to inconvenience, or any other way in which revenue was lost.

Documenting the exact damages due to the attack is just as important as documenting the attack itself.

The FBI computer-forensic guidelines stress the importance of securing any evidence. They further stress that computer evidence can come in many forms. A few common forms are as follows:

- Hard drives

- System logs

- Portable storage (USB drives, external drives, etc.)

- Router logs

- E-mails

- Chat-room logs

- Logs from security devices such as firewalls and intrusion-detection systems

- Databases and database logs

According to the FBI guidelines, a critical early step is to create a copy of the data and to ensure that the copy is accurate. Later in this book, we will discuss tools such as EnCase that make forensic copies of data for you. However, there are general principles involved in making forensically valid copies of data, whether you use a tool or do it manually. Factors that complicate the copying of data include the size of the data set, the method used to create it, and the media on which it resides. In some cases, it may be sufficient to merely compare the size and creation dates of files listed in the copy to the original. In others, it may require the application of more technically robust and mathematically rigorous techniques such as a cyclical redundancy check (CRC) or calculating a message digest (MD).

CRC and MD are computer algorithms that produce unique mathematical representations of the data. They are calculated for both the original and the copy and then they are compared for identity. This allows the forensic examiner to scientifically verify that his forensic copy is identical to the original. Many popular forensic tools include such algorithms in their verification process.

A forensic examiner who is responsible for duplicating evidence must first determine an appropriate level of verification to weigh time constraints against large file types. The mathematical precision and discriminating power of these algorithms are usually directly proportional to the amount of time necessary to calculate them. In many cases, the tool you are using will help you in this process.

Most forensic guidelines you refer to will describe similar processes. What makes the FBI guidelines worthy of note are the two factors we have just discussed. The fact that their guidelines give advice for the first responders is critical because it will affect the entire investigation. The second factor is that the FBI guidelines give more detail about the process of verifying forensic copies than many other references do. It is important that the forensic examiner understand how copies are verified, even if he or she will use a forensic tool to accomplish this goal.

Seizing Without a Warrant

Let us begin this section by stating clearly that getting a warrant is the best way to ensure that evidence will be acceptable in court. That said, the United States Department of Justice does outline situations where a warrant will not be necessary.[1]

The Fourth Amendment of the Constitution states

> The right of the people to be secure in their persons, houses, papers, and effects, against unreasonable searches and seizures, shall not be violated, and no Warrants shall issue, but upon probable cause, supported by Oath or affirmation, and particularly describing the place to be searched, and the persons or things to be seized.

According to the Supreme Court, a "'seizure' of property occurs when there is some meaningful interference with an individual's possessory interests in that property," (United States v. Jacobsen, 466 U.S. 109, 113 [1984]), and the court has also characterized the interception of intangible communications as a seizure in the case of Berger v. New York, 388 U.S. 41, 59-60 (1967). What this means is that law enforcement need not take property in order for it to be considered seizure; merely interfering with an individual's access to his or her own property constitutes seizure. The Berger v. New York decision extends that to communications. So if law enforcement's conduct does not violate a person's "reasonable expectation of privacy," then formally it does not constitute a Fourth Amendment search and no warrant is required. Now, there have been many cases in which the issue of reasonable expectation of privacy has been argued. But to use an example that is quite clear, if we save a message in an electronic diary, we clearly have a reasonable expectation of privacy. But if we post such a message on a public bulletin board, we can have no expectation of privacy. In less-clear cases, a general guideline is that courts have held that law-enforcement officers are prohibited from accessing and viewing information stored in a computer if they would be prohibited from opening a closed container and examining its contents in the same situation.

Agents may search a place or object without a warrant or even probable cause if a person with authority has voluntarily consented to the search; this is well-established law. However, it can become a matter of debate whether consent was voluntarily given. While no single aspect of consent controls the result, the Supreme Court has identified the following important factors: the age, education, intelligence, physical condition, and mental condition of the person giving consent; whether the person was under arrest; and whether the person had been advised of his right to refuse consent. In essence, this means an adult of average intelligence and education who gives consent while in normal mental and physical condition and not under arrest can certainly be legally considered to have given consent. However, let's assume that individual is mildly retarded, has a medical condition that would affect his or her reasoning, or perhaps never graduated from primary school. Any of those factors might be considered as rendering a person unable to give consent. The key principal is to ensure that the person is capable of granting consent and understands what is being asked of him or her.

In computer-crime cases, two consent issues arise particularly often. First, when does a search exceed the scope of consent? For example, when a person agrees to the search of a location, such as their apartment, does that consent authorize the retrieval of information stored in computers at the location? Second, who is the proper party to consent to a search? Can roommates, friends, and parents legally grant consent to a search of another person's computer files? These are all critical questions that must be considered when searching a computer. In general, courts have held that the actual owner of a property can grant consent—for example, a parent of a minor child can grant consent to search the living quarters and computers. However, a roommate who shares rent can only grant consent to search living quarters and computers that are co-owned by both parties. A roommate cannot grant consent to search the private property of the other person.

These federal guidelines are important to consider when you proceed with computer forensics. Your particular jurisdiction may or may not follow these same guidelines exactly, but there will certainly be significant similarities between the federal guidelines and those in your jurisdiction.

Basic Forensics

At this point, you should be familiar with federal guidelines regarding computer forensics. Keep in mind that the forensics steps can be followed only after the crime scene is secure from any harm to you or anyone else at the scene. When we talk about securing the crime scene, we mean a number of different but related activities. Remember that securing the crime scene is really not that different with computer crimes than it is with traditional, non-computer crimes. First and foremost is preserving the officer's (or civilian investigator's) safety, the safety of the bystanders, and the victim's welfare. In some cases, the first responders may not be trained in computer forensics and might focus instead on the non-computer elements of the crime. Sometimes the first responder at the crime scene may fail to look at the overall types of crime that may have occurred. That first responder is generally more interested in direct, physical threats.

Every crime scene will be different, but the following guidelines must be established. First and foremost, the boundaries of the crime scene must be observed. There is usually an inner perimeter—the spot the crime occurred—and an extended perimeter. The inner perimeter is where the actual crime occurred, and the extended perimeter would the surrounding area where the suspect may have entered or exited the scene or left clues that need to be documented. Establishing and maintaining that boundary is critical to maintaining the chain of evidence and ensuring that you collect all the relevant evidence. As we will discuss in the next section, the precise definition of a perimeter can be quite different in a computer crime versus a traditional non-computer crime. There are three steps in the initiation of any forensic investigation, including computer forensics:

1. Secure the crime scene.

2. Remove individuals involved.

3. Document all activity.

Securing the Scene

In a traditional crime, such as a robbery or murder, the perimeter is usually marked with police tape or police barriers. The police tape itself is just a reminder to all parties of where the perimeter lies for the crime scene. It defines the area that must be secured. Securing that area includes a number of steps. First and foremost, you must remove any unnecessary individuals from the scene. The rule is simple: If someone does not absolutely have to be there, they should not be, and that includes other law-enforcement personnel. Unnecessary people at a crime scene simply present opportunities for the evidence to be compromised. Next, it is critical to mark off the area, isolate the crime scene, and stop people from entering the crime scene. Remember, the more people inside the crime scene, the more you have to explain why they were there contaminating it. Each person in the scene could leave some type of trace evidence, such as hair, clothing fiber, or other contaminants. Keep the foot traffic to a minimum by allowing only the necessary personnel into the perimeter. Those personnel are responsible for what they do in the scene and they will document it with their supplements to the initial report. There also will be police personnel keeping a log of who enters and exits the scene. If you go to trial, you will understand why the log is so important. The defense attorneys will try to show that the scene was contaminated because of the different people in the scene who were not necessary.

The process is very similar with a computer crime. You must first and foremost secure the crime scene. Obviously, securing a computer crime scene can be different from securing a traditional crime scene. The crime scene is usually the actual computers, routers, and servers related to the crime. In order to secure them, you must take them offline. You must also prevent users from accessing them. If there is a computer that is suspected of being the instrument of a crime (i.e., a tool used by the perpetrator), then it too must be secured. This is where computer crime differs from traditional crime: determining the area of the crime. The various machines may be geographically isolated from each other, but it is still just as vital that they are secured and isolated so that they can be examined. You then need to limit the number of people who have access to the crime scene and document all interactions with the crime scene (i.e., the servers, workstations, routers, logs, or other elements of the crime scene). In many cases, the systems involved may be needed for the victim's operations to continue. For example, if a company's database server has been hacked and data stolen, they will still need the server to continue conducting business. The approach then is to take the server offline temporarily, duplicate the hard drive(s) for the server, and then put the duplicate drives back into service, thereby keeping the original drive secured as evidence.

Remove Individuals Involved

In any criminal investigation, the witnesses and suspect(s) who were at the scene should be removed and placed in separate holding areas. Never leave the witnesses or suspect(s) together and unattended. Separating these parties will protect the integrity of traditional and electronic evidence that will be collected. This is also true in investigating computer crimes. Just as with any other crime scene, anyone who absolutely does not need to be at the crime scene should not be. Only those essential personnel needed for the investigation should be given access to the computer equipment involved, and every occurrence of that access must be documented.

The individuals related to the crime must be separated from the computer equipment involved. This prevents the accused from deleting evidence, and it prevents all parties from accidentally altering or destroying evidence. Remember that in any trial, civil or criminal, maintaining the chain of custody will be a critical factor. Any issues with chain of custody will allow the opposing counsel to challenge the admissibility of the evidence.

There is one more important issue: If you need help, just ask. There are many agencies that will assist you in the search for and collection of evidence, especially if you have not done it before. One can also often find non–law-enforcement consultants that can assist in computer forensics. You may find computer-science professors or other experts in computer forensics that are willing to assist.

(In Chapter 11, "Experts and Expert Reports," we discuss expert consultants and the criteria for selecting one.)

While you are conducting the forensic investigation, make sure you are adhering to every step. Keep in mind that any error in the forensics process can taint a trial. If you become involved in an investigation where you feel you need additional expertise, do not let your ego prevent you from seeking that assistance.

Document Everything

Documentation has already been mentioned, but must be stressed again. Proper documentation may be the most critical part of any forensic investigation, and any failure to properly document evidence can render it inadmissible. The first step in documenting is to observe the crime scene for electronic evidence and be aware that the scene of a computer crime may not be like other crime scenes (see Figure 7.1). You always look to see what your crime scene has to offer as evidence for the investigation. Any evidence seized must be cataloged properly. Evidence tags are usually used to mark evidence.

In our current electronic age, there are many different types of electronic devices that criminals can use to store evidence. It's not just the computer and its hard

Figure 7.1
Examine the crime scene.

drives that we might look for. Here are some examples of what you may notice while observing the scene:

- Cell phones

- PDAs

- Digital cameras

- Video cameras

- Memory cards

- USB dongles or flash drives

- Floppy disks

- Zip drives

- Hard drives (internal or external)

- DVDs

- CDs

- The list goes on . . .

Remember that electronic evidence is not just those devices used to store the information, but also printed materials, notes with passwords, pictures, videos, recordings, and much more. When you are observing the scene, never think that something is not important. For example, would the investigator note what side the mouse is on next to the computer? Why would this be important? The victim or suspect maybe left handed or right handed. The least significant item could be the most important piece of evidence for your investigation. During the observation, check and see if the computer or any other device is on; the computer usually has a fan running or a light visible. You cannot depend on the monitor to determine if the computer is on.

Remember that you must never touch anything until you start collecting the evidence. Once you have walked through and observed the scene, now it's time to record what you observed. Videotaping the entire crime scene is an optional step in documenting the evidence. If you choose to videotape the crime scene, it should be a 360-degree view of the room. The video is like a second view of the scene, and it can also be helpful for a jury to see what you saw during the investigation. The investigator should always state at the start of the video the person who is making the tape and make sure the date and time are correct. During the video, if something stands out, make a remark about it; it could be about how the connections are attached to the computer or other devices or perhaps just a description of the room. In any case, a videotape allows anyone else, including the jury, to view the room as you first saw it, and your comments are a part of that. Do be careful what you say on the video, though. You must be professional at all times. A negative comment, or worse an exclamation, on the video could cause doubts about your investigative skills. A defense attorney would notice any negative comment you make on the video and use that to question your impartiality and your investigative technique. Then you would have to explain why the comment was made to the defense attorney and the jury. This is just one more thing the defense attorney can use against your process.

After videotaping, take digital photos of the scene. The same rules apply in photographing the scene as in videotaping it: Be detailed. Remember, if your digital camera has a date and time, make sure they are set properly. There is no such thing as too much evidence on your behalf about what you observed during your investigation. After you have finished the video and digital pictures, you must document them (see Figure 7.2). With digital photos or 35mm film, we use a storyboard sheet to document the photos.

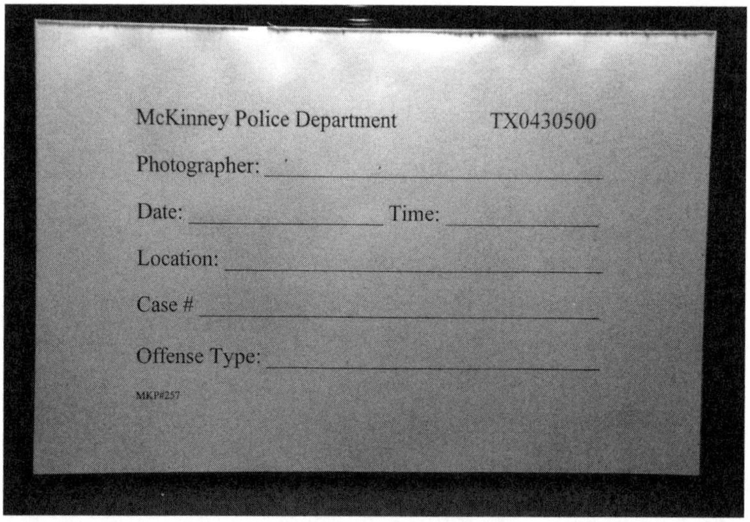

McKinney Police Department TX0430500

Photographer: ______________________

Date: ______________ Time: ____________

Location: ______________________

Case # ______________________

Offense Type: ______________________

MKP#257

Figure 7.2
Document the photos.

Some departments still use 35mm film, so if that is the case for you, make sure you document the rolls of film to be processed. Make sure to follow whatever system your department uses for documentation. Do not take shortcuts in this process. If digital photos are being used, document how and what you do with the digital photos.

Several years ago, there was a lot of controversy about digital photographic evidence being admissible in court. The concern was that the digital photos could be altered. A book written by Steven Staggs, *Crime Scene and Evidence Photographer's Guide,* is a very good guide for you or your crime-scene tech to read. In the book, Staggs provides some principal requirements to get the photos into evidence:

- Develop a SOP (standard operating procedure)

- Preserve the original digital image. This is critical. You may need to enhance images to see some detail, but that enhancement should be done to a copy, never to the original file. You should retain the original image exactly as you took it. The original file must never be written over or deleted.

- Preserve images in their original format.[2]

Documenting all items of evidence can be laborious, but it is critical. How detailed that process will be will depend on the circumstances of the particular computer crime. This may sound contradictory, but until you observe a scene, you may not fully realize what we are talking about. The documentation of collecting the evidence is very important as well—you must document exactly *how* you collected the evidence in addition to documenting the evidence itself. As mentioned earlier, you must never alter any of the devices. In other words, you should not actually do anything on the computer, router, or other device. Any action you take may change data and thus render any evidence obtained inadmissible. We will discuss this in greater detail in Chapter 8, "Collecting Evidence from Hardware." If the computer is off then it can be collected. If it is on, then it must be shut down properly first. Shutting down laptops may be different from shutting down desktop machines.

Since there are usually cables attached to the computer, you may need to colorcode them; if you have to reconnect the cables later, you will be able to do so. After you have the cables properly color coded, start documenting the devices that were attached. When the documentation is complete, then you can begin to disconnect the different devices.

When we say document, we mean you must get out a notepad and evidence cards. The different pieces of evidence must be documented, as should the location from which they were retrieved. The notepad will help you keep track of this. Each item you seize should also have an evidence card. The card will note the date, time, location (address), offense, item seized, service number, and the officer who obtained the item.

On the back of the card is where one documents who handled the evidence and when: the chain of custody (see Figure 7.3). Remember that the chain of custody is very important. Now what is chain of custody? According to SANS Institute-Score, "it is a legal term that describes the collection, transportation, and storage of evidence to prevent altercation, loss, physical damage, or destruction."[3] If you don't have adequate chain of custody documented, the defense attorney will try to make it appear that the chain of custody has been contaminated in some way, which introduces doubt about the integrity of the collection of evidence during the process. The attorney's whole objective is to put doubt in the jury's minds about the reliability of the evidence. This process should be consistent in each crime scene that you document.

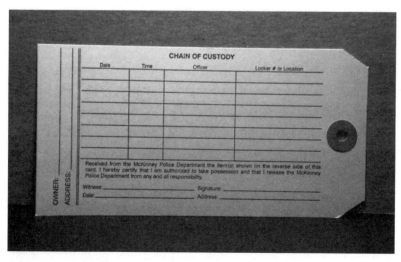

Figure 7.3
The chain of custody.

Let us give you an example of chain of custody. Let's say you are the detective collecting the electronic devices at a crime scene. You have all the devices properly marked, and they are still located in the inner perimeter of the crime scene. When you take them to your vehicle to secure them, the officer who is logging your moves in and out of the crime scene notes what you are doing. Now suppose another detective is helping you; he is also being logged going in and out with the electronic devices. Later, when you create your supplement on what you did at the crime scene, suppose you neglect to mention the other detective. Then, when you fill out the evidence cards on the chain of custody, the other detective is still not mentioned. When the defense attorney gets the log or a copy of the evidence card and sees who did what and that you did not mention the other detective, this will introduce a question about how thoroughly you performed your investigation. If a small detail was left out, then what big detail did you not mention in your supplement or show on the evidence card? Who else may have handled the devices and was not mentioned? Was the evidence contaminated in some way? The worst thing that can happen on the stand is to have your credibility questioned by the defense attorney. If the defense attorney can show this, then he has done his job: to create doubt among the jury. Remember, chain of custody is a crucial part of the investigation you do. Once the documentation process is completed on all the items, you need to place each item collected into an evidence bag that has been properly marked. Make sure you wear anti-static gloves while you collect and bag the evidence. Some items may be placed in paper bags and others may require non-static bags to keep the evidence from being damaged or altered. This applies particularly to the devices that were mentioned earlier (digital cameras, cell phones, etc.). Each item that is bagged will have an evidence card with it. The bag will also have noted on it information that matches the evidence card. This will help you keep track of each item. Once it is bagged, keep all the evidence at the scene with you until you are ready to take it to the secure area of your department. Do not let other officers or investigators place the evidence in their vehicle; they may not be aware of the elements that could cause damage to some devices, and you will not be able to keep control of the property. Remember that chain of custody is crucial.

The next step is to pack up the evidence and transport it to your department's secured area. In our department, we have lockers in which to place the evidence. If a large amount of evidence is collected, we have a room to place it in that can be secured. Our property clerk will then retrieve the evidence and properly log it into the storage area. Our evidence tags will show the chain of custody of the evidence. If you are the one who places all the evidence in the property room, then the evidence card will show that. Our property clerk knows where he can put certain items and where not to put others. If you're the investigator who places the items into the secure evidence room, just be aware of where you are placing them. For example, you would not place computers next to large boombox speakers, as the computers could be affected by the magnets in the speakers. If data is altered in any way, it may be inadmissible in court. At a minimum, any alteration will give the opposing counsel opportunity to question the entire forensic process and may seriously undermine the case.

The procedures we have mentioned have been very successful for our department. Each department may have its own guidelines to handle these processes. Just remember to follow the guidelines in a consistent manner; develop it like a habit. If you do not change the way you perform the process, the defense attorney will not be able to question your process—and if he does, you will have the answer that is needed.

The processes outlined here will help the investigator achieve his or her goal for a solid case to be presented in court. But you may ask the question, "Why is each step so important?" Our best answer would be this: If you have gone to court on any case and the opposing attorney asks you questions on how or why you performed the investigation the way you did, what would be your answer? Can you remember all that was done at the scene? As the investigator, can you tell step-by-step how you completed the process of collecting the evidence? Remember, the opposing attorney's job is to introduce doubt in the jury's mind and discredit your investigation. Let us give you an example. When you have a major crime scene (we will use a homicide in this example), the scene can be overwhelming to the investigator. Whether you have one or 10 investigators, there is going to be a plan set in motion.

One homicide that comes to mind was that of a woman who worked for a prominent builder in our city. She was showing model townhomes to prospective buyers. While she was inside a model, a man made contact with her, probably under the pretense of looking at the model home. But the truth was that he was there for another reason. The female was brutally stabbed and some personal property was taken from her. One of the authors of this book was the investigator on call that week, so when he arrived, he was in charge of the scene.

But a plan had already been implemented before he arrived. The first responders knew exactly what to be do. Supervisors were called and the command staff was notified. The scene was secured until the other investigators arrived at the scene. When the author's supervisor arrived, he assumed charge of the scene. By the time the command staff arrived, the plan was taking shape. Each investigator at the scene was given a job to do. Some were photographing the scene, others were contacting anyone who was on the property to see if they had witnessed anything, and still others were collecting the evidence at the scene. Step by step, the process was followed and the evidence was documented. Each investigator gave a detailed written supplement for the case. After compiling all the information, they had a good idea of what happened. After several months, a suspect was located, arrested, and convicted, all due to the planning that was done to get a solid case and get a conviction. Planning, documenting each step, photographing, collecting evidence, and detailed statements gave them a solid case to get the conviction. This example might be a bit long, but it really is an excellent example of how an investigation should be conducted.

As you know, not all cases will be won, but if the steps are followed, it won't be lost due to errors in your investigation and documenting and collecting the evidence. The defense attorney would not have much to challenge in this area, and taking away any questions in this area will give you the edge on him. Once you are consistent on all three steps of the investigation, then you are the winner.

While the example given is that of a homicide, the same process applies to computer-crime investigations. One of the authors of this book was involved as an expert witness in a civil case that arose from an underlying accusation of a computer crime. In that case, a former employee of a company was accused of compromising the computer system of the company by utilizing another employee's password. In this case, the first responders, as well as the investigators, all handled the situation improperly. First, the server that was alleged to have been hacked was never taken offline and isolated. Instead, they left the server online in operation and simply copied and pasted the segments of the server log they felt where relevant into an e-mail. (The company's network administrators were the first responders in this case.) This demonstrates why network administrators and technical-support personnel need to be familiar with basic forensics. A failure to secure the evidence at the beginning of an investigation can be devastating to any case.

Next, the investigators failed to secure the computer(s) of the accused perpetrator. They did not get a warrant to seize or search the accused perpetrator's computer, and in fact did not even ask the accused for permission. If the accused had used that computer to execute a crime, it is entirely likely that there was evidence of that fact on his computer. Failing to even examine that potential piece of evidence was a serious mistake. Finally, no one—not the network administrators of the company in question or the law-enforcement officers investigating the alleged crime—ever subpoenaed records from the relevant Internet service provider in order to determine who connected to what system at what time. The culmination of this botched investigation was that not only was the alleged perpetrator acquitted at his criminal trial, but he later successfully sued the accusers.

What these two cases illustrate, very dramatically, is that following forensics procedures correctly is absolutely critical in both criminal and civil cases. Failure to secure the scene and maintain the chain of evidence can ruin an investigation. The first step is to ensure that the crime scene is completely secure. Then you must make certain that all the evidence is gathered according to forensic procedures. The second case illustrates how with computer crimes, unlike other types of crimes, the first responders are often not law enforcement. It will often be a network administrator or technical-support person. Not only must law-enforcement officials conduct forensics appropriately, but computer professionals must as well. Finally, you must document everything.

Now that we have explored the three steps you must take with any crime scene, let's apply those to the second scenario we mentioned earlier. We will show you what a skilled investigator should have done in that situation. The first step is to secure the server in question. If you believe someone has compromised your server, you must secure that server. So the network administrators should have taken that server offline, copied the hard drive to a new one, and put the copy in service, keeping the original hard drive for evidence. The entire process must be documented. That documentation should detail who was involved in the process, when the process occurred, and every step taken in the process. It is also a good idea to videotape the process. Then, the hard drive would be analyzed so any data from logs or other sources could be examined for evidence. That evidence would then be documented. For example, you would document that the access log showed that the server was accessed from a given IP address at a given time. The next step would be to subpoena the suspect's Internet service provider so you could trace back the IP address that connected to the server and determine if the connection did indeed come from the perpetrator. Finally, you would absolutely need to secure access to the perpetrator's computer and to handle it the same way you did the server, carefully documenting each step.

Conclusion

In this chapter, we examined a crucial element of computer crime: the initial crime-scene investigation. We have examined the importance of properly securing the crime scene and documenting the procedures used. It cannot be overemphasized how important these steps are. As we have seen from real-world examples in this chapter, if one does not follow proper procedures, one can render a case unwinnable.

Endnotes

[1] Electronic Crime Scene Investigation. U.S. Department of Justice. Available at National Criminal Justice Reference Center. http://www.ncjrs.gov/index.html

[2] Staggs, Steven. *Crime Scene and Evidence Photographer's Guide.* Staggs Publishing. Wildomar, California.

[3] SANS (SysAdmin, Audit, Network, Security) Institution. https://www.sans.org/score/faq/law_enf_faq/chainofcustody.php

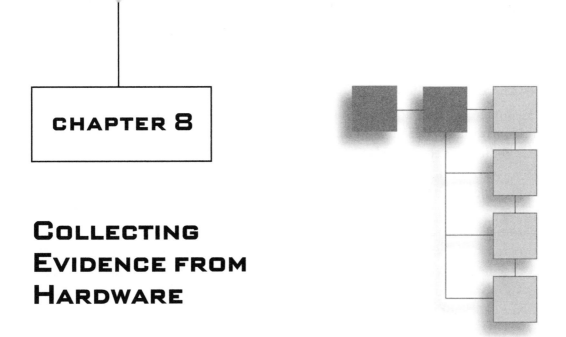

CHAPTER 8

COLLECTING EVIDENCE FROM HARDWARE

Introduction

In the previous chapter, we discussed the importance of observing, collecting and documenting, and securing and storing electronic evidence. In this chapter we will discuss how to perform a forensic examination of a hard drive and how to find and catalog the evidence from the hard drive. Keep in mind the lessons you learned in the previous chapter, particularly those about restricting unnecessary people from the scene and documenting evidence. When gathering evidence from a hard drive, you need to make sure no unnecessary personnel have access to the hard drive, and you must carefully document every step you take.

Forensic Tools

There are many tools available that one can use to gather evidence from a hard drive. The bulk of this chapter will focus on the tool used by this author and most commonly used in law enforcement. However, it is always a good idea for any investigator to be aware of his or her options when selecting forensic tools, so we will also take a quick look at a few that you should be familiar with. Just make sure that whatever tool you choose has actually been successfully used in court cases. If you use a tool that is either unproven or has been rejected by a court, it could undermine your entire case.

AccessData Forensic Toolkit

A company founded in 1987 called AccessData Corporation[1] pioneered digital investigation by presenting FTK (Forensic Toolkit) for computer forensics. It has the ability to deliver analysis, decryption, and password cracking all within an intuitive, customizable, and user-friendly interface. Two very important features of this tool are its ability to analyze the Windows Registry and its ability to crack passwords. The Windows Registry is where Windows stores all information regarding any programs installed, including viruses, worms, Trojan horses, hidden programs, and spyware. The ability to effectively and efficiently scan the Registry for evidence is critical, and the ability to break passwords for common applications is important as well. Evidence can be stored in a password-protected Adobe PDF, Excel spreadsheet, or other application. The AccessData FTK can crack passwords in more than 100 commonly used applications.

Another exciting feature of this toolkit is its distributed processing capability. Scanning an entire hard drive, searching the Registry, and performing a complete forensic analysis of a computer can be a very time-intensive task. With AccessData's Forensic Toolkit, that processing and analysis can be distributed across up to three computers. This lets all three computers process the analysis in parallel, thus significantly speeding up the forensic process.

FTK is also available for the Macintosh. Many commercial products are only available for Windows, and the open-source community usually focuses on Unix and Linux, so the Macintosh compatibility is very important. In addition, FTK has an Explicit Image Detection add-on that automatically detects pornographic images, which is very useful in cases involving allegations of child pornography.

E-fense Helix

E-fense Helix[2] boots into a customized Linux environment and includes many applications dedicated to the incident response and forensics of Linux, Unix, and Windows machines. Helix has been carefully designed to not touch the host computer in any way, therefore keeping the computer forensically sound. This is critical in any forensic tool. If, during an investigation, you or the tool you use modifies files in any way, you may render the evidence unusable.

In addition to examining hard drives, Helix can grab live volatile evidence from RAM or from USB-attached devices. This is a very important feature because whatever is in RAM will be lost when you turn off the machine. It is important to secure that evidence while the machine is still running.

The Helix product also has an enterprise edition that can run live on your network to secure and catalog evidence. This product will also monitor employee usage, and even take screen shots of various PC screens. This multi-purpose aspect of Helix may be considered an advantage to some investigators but can be deleterious to others. If you have broad-reaching security responsibilities, a multifaceted tool may be exactly what you need. However, if you are solely focused on forensics, particularly in connection with law enforcement, then a dedicated tool with a narrowly defined purpose might be more advantageous to you.

ILook

ILook[3] was created by Elliot Spencer, and was federally funded by the government until 2008. The last version was 8.0.18. This tool is a comprehensive suite of computer-forensic tools used to acquire and analyze digital media. It can support a wide variety of file systems. It is not free or open source, but rather is a commercial product.

ILook has built-in file salvage to recover deleted files. There are other ways to recover deleted files, as we will see in Chapter 9, "Collecting Evidence from the Operating System," but having that feature built into the forensic tool is advantageous. Also built into the product is a recovery tool that allows you to recover Outlook e-mails, even if they are not currently loaded into Outlook or are archived files. This tool also has a Windows Registry explorer that facilitates scanning the Registry for evidence.

EnCase

While the previously mentioned tools are all legitimate tools, EnCase[4] may be the most widely recognized law-enforcement utility for computer forensics. One of the authors of this book has had extensive training and years of practical experience with EnCase, so we will take a bit closer look at this particular forensic tool.

The current version now in use by the author is EnCase 6. His extensive training in this product began with the version of EnCase 4. Through the years, he has had real-world experience with the tool. Like many software products, EnCase often comes out with new versions with new features that do more things. As of this writing, EnCase actually has multiple separate products for various purposes, including both enterprise and mobile editions. With forensic tools, frequent updates are critical; computer software and operating systems change often, therefore the forensic tools must also evolve to accommodate those changes. In this chapter, we will cover the basics of acquiring data utilizing En-Case. This chapter certainly won't make you an expert in using EnCase, but it should give you a general working knowledge—enough to get started.

In order to properly utilize EnCase or any forensic tool, you need to have a solid understanding of computer hardware, operating systems, and general computer concepts. You should be quite comfortable with terms such as ASCII codes, bits, DOS, IDE, Fat32, NTFS, SATA, and the list goes on. The purpose of this book is not to introduce you to the basics of PCs; there are certainly plenty of books on the market that can do that. Just be aware that without an understanding of these essentials, you will have a difficult time with forensics. Appendix A, "Introduction to Computer Networks," gives a brief introduction to network concepts that some readers might find useful.

In the previous chapter, we talked about shutting down a computer and not changing any data on it. We will elaborate on this now. First, you must stop all operations on the target computer. If the computer is on a network, disconnect it—but make sure you check with the IT department to make sure that disconnecting it from the network will not damage the network first. If it does not, just unplug it from behind the suspect's computer. If the monitor is on and there is something on it, photograph the monitor. Then, in shutting down, just unplug the suspect's computer from behind the CPU. This will not affect the data on the computer. Note: In most cases, never do an automatic shut down on the computer. This will alter the timestamp in the system.

What is important is that you do not alter anything. Don't attempt to copy individual files off the computer while it is running. The forensic software we mentioned in Chapter 7, "Observing, Collecting, Documenting, and Storing Electronic Evidence," such as EnCase, will be run from a different hard drive, and you will pull the data off the suspect hard drive in that manner. Any changes you make will change file date/time stamps and might render the evidence unusable.

It is also important to identify the operating system the computer is using. Your forensic approach will be different for a Windows 7 machine than it is for a Linux, Macintosh, or even Windows Vista machine. The first step is to determine if this is a stand-alone computer or if it is networked. If the computer is on a network, disconnect the network cable from the computer first, and then you can shut down the computer. This is how you secure the scene with a computer. If it's possible, consult the IT department for the company or business that you are working for. Whenever possible, you do not want forensic activities to disrupt the business activities, so coordinating with the IT department can help alleviate that. Obviously, coordinating with the IT department is not appropriate if the IT department is suspected of criminal activity.

Preliminary Activities

Before you can actually do any forensic investigation on the suspect's computer, you must have a working knowledge of your own operating system. It is critical that a forensic examiner be skilled in basic PC, network, and operating system functions. EnCase operates in a Windows environment, and we will briefly examine some navigation processes here. But it must be stressed that if you are not reasonably familiar with Windows and PC operations, you should correct that deficiency before engaging in any forensic investigation.

Before covering any forensic work done with EnCase, we are going to review how to set up folders in Windows. You may ask, why review something that you should already know? This is the first step in EnCase when doing the forensics. Even though this is basic information, we feel it's important for you to understand. Let's start by examining how you can look at the contents of your own computer using Windows Explorer. You can start by clicking on the Start button, clicking All Programs, clicking Accessories, and then clicking Windows Explorer. (Note: You can make a desktop shortcut for Windows Explorer to make it more accessible. When you locate it in the Accessories folder, just right-click it, choose Send To, and create the shortcut.) This will bring up the Windows Explorer window, as shown in Figure 8.1.

Notice the two panes: They show you the drives, folders, and files available on your computer. (Remember panes, because EnCase uses them as well.) The left pane in Windows Explorer displays the logical volumes of your computer and allows you to navigate through folder structures with the plus and minus signs, as shown in Figure 8.2.

The contents of the various folders display in the right pane. The reason you need to know this is that when you start the forensic analysis, you need to create a folder that will contain your forensic cases. Let us show you how to do this.

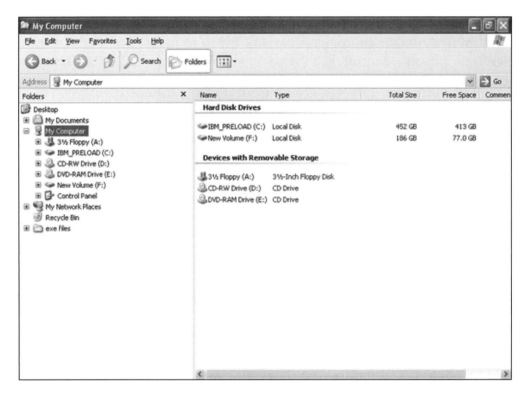

Figure 8.1
Windows Explorer.

In the left pane of Windows Explorer, click on your C drive. The right pane will display the contents of the drive. In the right pane, right-click in a blank area; a small pop-up menu will appear. Click New, and then click Folder; then name the new folder Cases, as shown in Figure 8.3.

When you create this folder, it will show up in the left pane under the C drive that is expanded (showing all the folders). In this particular folder will be all the forensic cases that you work on. Find the Cases folder in the left pane and click on it. The right pane will be empty. You now need to repeat the steps to create another folder in the right pane (inside the Cases folder) using the service number of the offense along with the suspect's last name, such as 09-33580 Lacombe. This is how we keep track of the cases we're working on. In the left pane under Cases, you will now find the subfolder 09-33580 Lacombe. Click on that case file in the left pane, and your right pane will again be empty. Now create

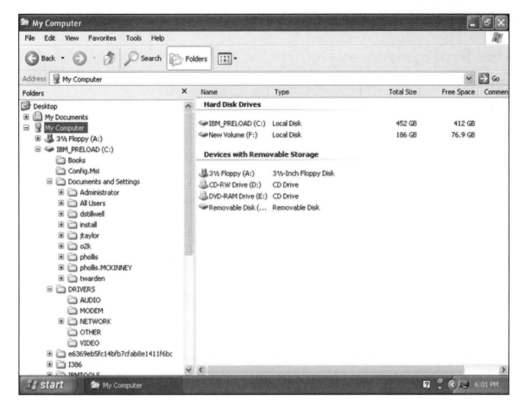

Figure 8.2
Windows Explorer folder navigation.

three new subfolders in the right pane: an export folder, a temporary folder, and an index folder, as shown in Figure 8.4.

These subfolders should all be inside the case name folder, in this example the folder named 09-33580 Lacombe. Remember: Just keep making the folders in the right pane. Every forensic case that you do will have a case name with three subfolders, and all will be under the C drive.

Working with EnCase

Well you learned a little about Windows Explorer and the contents of your computer. You also learned how to make folders for your forensic cases under the C drive in your computer. So now let us talk about the computer evidence that you are searching for. Computers can be used in an instrumental way for a variety of different crimes, including gambling, telemarketing, counterfeiting,

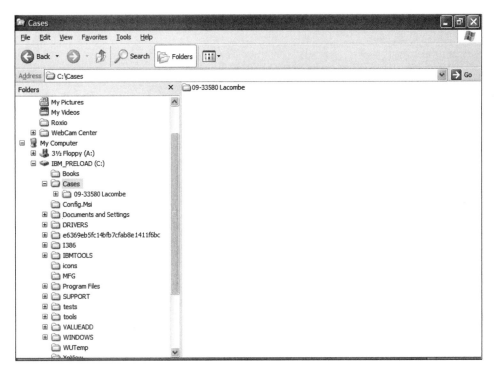

Figure 8.3
The Cases folder.

fraud, child pornography, and child exploitation (this list could go on). The computer might simply store the evidence; it may not be the evidence in and of itself. Some common types of evidence that could be found on a computer include business records, bank records, correspondence, criminal profiling, dates and times of events, and pornography (this list could go on as well). One important factor in computer forensics is that it is not just a hard drive you may be looking at, but cell phones, digital cameras, PDAs, flash drives—anything that can store data that the investigator will want to retrieve.

Now let's begin learning the essentials of EnCase. We want to stress again that this is an overview with the intent to give you a working knowledge. If you intend to use this tool in forensic investigations, more thorough training is highly recommended. The EnCase concept's whole methodology is the Evidence File, which contains the header, the checksum, and the data blocks. These all work together to provide a secure and self-checking description of the state of the computer disk at the time of analysis. When you add the Evidence File to the case,

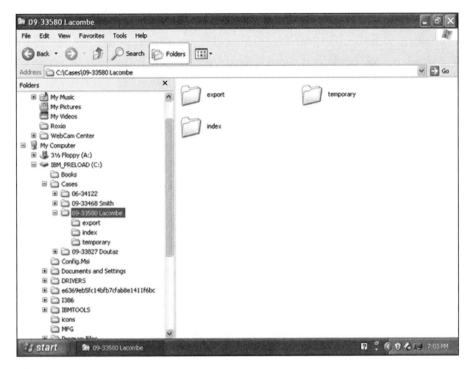

Figure 8.4
Folders.

it will begin to verify the integrity of the entire disk image. The Evidence File is an exact copy of the hard drive, and this is verified with the cyclical redundancy check (CRC). Every byte of the file is verified, making it nearly impossible to tamper with the evidence once it has been acquired. EnCase will calculate an MD5 hash when the drive is acquired. When the investigator adds the Evidence File to the case, it recalculates the hash, which will show that nothing has changed since the drive was acquired. Both of the hashes will automatically appear in the final report. These confirmations confirm the integrity of your Evidence File; this is the edge the investigator has when the Evidence File is presented in court.

EnCase offers several ways to do acquisitions on a suspect's computer. We are going to mention each of the different ways, but will not go into great detail about them. We just want you to be aware that these methods exist. One such method is with an EnCase boot disk (also called the barebones boot disk), which can be created by using both the EnCase program and from Guidance software's Web site. The boot disk is used to acquire digital media in DOS mode instead of the Windows environment. The reasoning behind using DOS mode is that it allows the investigator to do a forensically sound acquisition without taking any special precautions first. In DOS mode, you will have no data changes in acquisition as it would be in the Windows environment. In Windows is where you would have to use a write-protector device.

Another boot disk is the EnCase Network boot disk (ENBD). The ENBD has more features that allow crossover cable preview and acquisition. Another method is the LinEn boot disk. This method allows the user to acquire the contents of Linux machines with a crossover cable similar to the method in EnCase DOS. If you decide to use the LinEn boot disk, you must obtain it from a Linux distributor. The three distributors can be found at www.novell.com/linux, www.redhat.com, and http://knoppix.com. The LinEn boot disk method has to be configured due to the nature of Linux and the distributors.

Now we are going to talk about the different panes that EnCase has. EnCase is divided into four panes, as you can see in Figure 8.5.

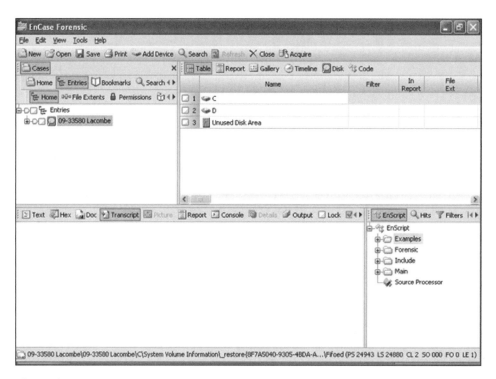

Figure 8.5
EnCase panes.

The top-left pane is the Tree pane, the top-right pane is the Table pane, the bottom-left pane is the Viewing pane, and the bottom-right pane is the Filter pane. When EnCase is open on the investigator's computer, you will see all four panes. The Tree pane is like Windows Explorer; it displays all the folders, with the plus and minus signs to expand and collapse them. The Table pane has the sub-folders and files that are contained within the folder that is currently selected in the Tree pane. The Viewing pane displays what you have selected in the Table pane. In EnCase 6, the Viewing pane will open in Report mode by default. The Viewing pane has different options that allow you to view the item you choose. This pane actually shows the first eight extents of some piece of evidence. For example, if a file has a .jpg extension (which is a picture), you could select the Picture option and then see the picture in the View pane. The picture will appear in the pane as shown in Figure 8.6.

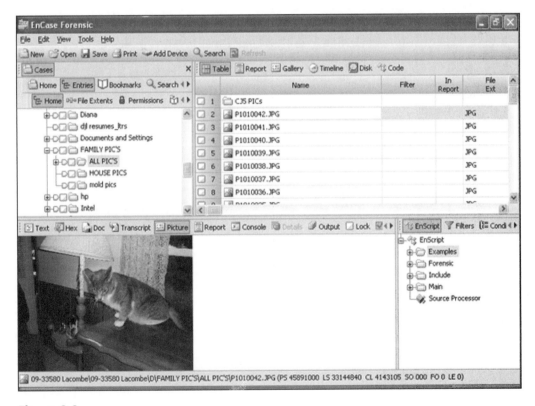

Figure 8.6
A picture file in the Viewing pane.

The Filter pane is a useful tool that can affect the data you view in the Table pane. It does not remove it from the case, but instead hides it in the Table pane. The different tools in the Filter pane (which expands with the arrows) are EnScripts, Hits, Filters, Conditions, Queries, and Text Styles (see Figure 8.7).

Some of these tools we have used and some we have not. If you are not familiar with the particular tool, please read up on it and its uses. An example would be running EnScripts; this tool is an executable file and should be treated with the same caution as any other executable file. It is recommended that you get EnScripts from Guidance Software. We have briefly described the different panes and some of their functions. There are many more functions that could be examined, but these are the essential functions for EnCase. When we show you how to actually acquire the suspect's hard drive, we will explain the procedure we use in obtaining the Evidence File.

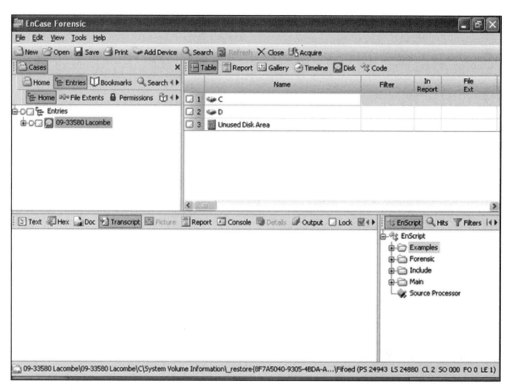

Figure 8.7
Filter pane tools.

Computer Acquisitions

We have gone over some of the features that EnCase offers. Now we will describe how we do the acquisition of the suspect's computer. In Chapter 7, we talked about the chain of custody. When we retrieve the computer from the evidence room, we sign it out, keeping the chain of custody intact. We bring the computer to the forensic lab where the forensic analysis will be done. If it's a stand-alone computer, we will remove the hard drive from the unit. Most stand-alones are easy to access; just remove the cables that are attached. Now, if it's a laptop, we must first remove the battery pack from the unit. Some laptops even have two batteries; if that is the case, both must be removed. The reason for this is that you do not want to short out any components in the laptop when removing the hard drive. Some laptops' hard drives are not easily removed. We have even had to Google to check the specs on a laptop. You should never try to remove a hard drive if you do not know how. You must remember that you are responsible for the computer that you do the forensic work on. If you don't know how to do it, ask someone. When you find the procedure to remove the hard drive, it usually just unplugs from an attached circuit board. After the hard drive is removed, we will then set up the forensic computer with the proper files. The Evidence File will be exported to the Case folder and subfolders you created earlier, which is where it will create your final report.

Remember that you do not do the forensics on the suspect's hard drive at this point. We actually remove the hard drive and acquire it with EnCase. When the hard drive is removed, you do not want to change or write any of the data during the forensic procedure. To keep from doing just that, there are two devices that we can use: a FastBloc or the FastBloc FE portable, as shown in Figure 8.8.

 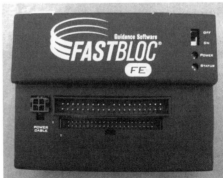

Figure 8.8
FastBloc.

Both the FastBloc and FastBloc FE are hardware write-blocking devices used for IDE hard drives or SATA hard drives. The FastBloc enables you to safely preview and acquire the suspect's hard drive in Windows to an EnCase evidence file. The FastBloc can connect directly from the forensic computer to an IDE channel on the motherboard, or you can get the portable FastBloc to use outside the forensic lab.

Another device we often use is a Tableau, shown in Figure 8.9. The Tableau Forensic SATA Bridge is a write-blocker for use with Serial ATA (SATA) hard disks. This device is used in the same way as the FastBloc; it just depends on what type of hard drive you have to acquire the information from—either IDE, as shown in Figure 8.10, or SATA as shown in Figure 8.11. The most obvious difference is the data connection.

After you have the suspect's hard drive removed, connect the suspect's hard drive with the cables to either the FastBloc or Tableau, which is connected to the forensic computer. Turn on the device you are using so that the Windows

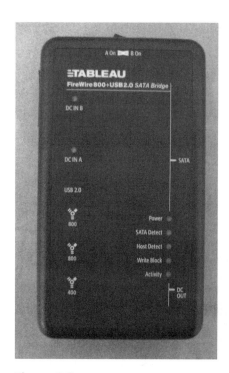

Figure 8.9
Tableau.

Figure 8.10
IDE drive.

operating system will recognize it. Windows should recognize the new hardware attached to the forensic computer, but if it does not, you will have to reboot your forensic computer with the FastBloc or Tableau left on. If you have to reboot the computer, you will also have to reopen EnCase as a new case and fill in the blanks as described below.

Open the EnCase program that you downloaded to your forensic computer. At the top of the toolbar on EnCase, click on New, which will instantiate the new case you will be working on. The Case Options dialog box will open, as shown in Figure 8.12.

Figure 8.11
SATA drive.

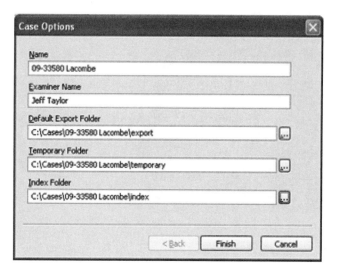

Figure 8.12
The Case Options dialog box.

First, type in the case name you are working on (the example we used earlier was 09-33580 Lacombe). The next line asks for the examiner's name, which would be the person who does the forensics. The next three boxes are the default folders: export, temporary, and index. When you click each of the boxes on the right side, a pop-up window will appear; navigate (scroll up or down) to the folders that you created earlier in Windows Explorer on your C drive. Scroll up to Computer, click the plus sign, and go to Cases. In Cases, you will find the folder named 09-33580 Lacombe. Open this folder to display the three subfolders: export, temporary, and index. For the Default Export Folder field, choose C:\Cases\09-33580 Lacombe\Export. This is the path the folder will take now. Choose C:\Cases\09-33580 Lacombe\Temporary for the Temporary field and choose C:\Cases\09-33580 Lacombe\Index for the Index Folder field. Now your Evidence File will be sent to the paths indicated later on in the procedure.

Note

If you do not follow this procedure, the export, temporary, and index files will have a path of C:Program Files\EnCase\export, etc. Your evidence will not be created for your case.

Now that you have created the case, save it by clicking on the Save button on the EnCase toolbar. After the case is saved, it's time to add the device you are obtaining. On the EnCase toolbar, click on the Add Device button. A window will appear asking which device to add, as shown in Figure 8.13.

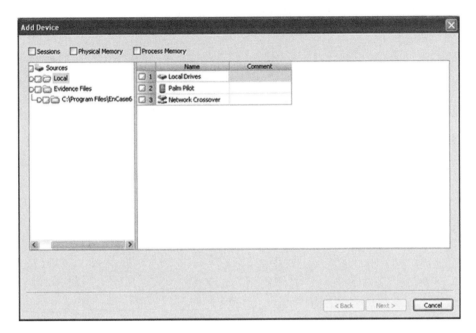

Figure 8.13
The Add Device dialog box.

The left pane will show devices with the subfolders Local and Evidence Files. The right pane will show the options Local Drives, Palm Pilot, and Network Crossover. In this procedure, select the Local Drives option in the right pane. After EnCase reads the local drives, the window shown in Figure 8.14 will appear.

This window will show all the different drives on the computer. A list will appear in the right pane displaying the names A, C, F, G, 0, 1, 2 (or whatever drives you may have). The list will have the name of the drive, access, sectors, size, process ID, write block, read file system, and parse link files. You want to determine which device is the write-block and check it. You will not check the actual letter drive, but the number below that corresponds with the letter. You can determine this by the actual size of the drive and the drive shows to be write blocked. The drive will also be surrounded in a different color, which helps you to see the write-protected drive. After you have selected the drive, the Preview Device window will appear. Click Finish, and it will be added so that the device can be previewed in EnCase.

If you find something in the preview mode that pertains to the investigation, you can acquire the drive to your Evidence File. On the EnCase toolbar, there is

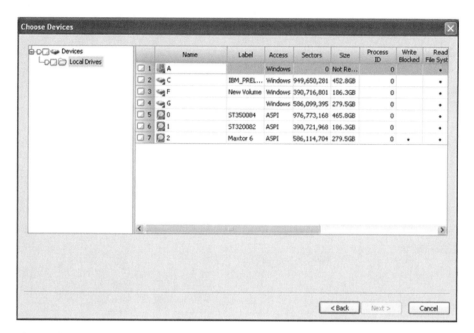

Figure 8.14
The Choose Devices window.

an Acquire button. Click the button and another window opens, as shown in Figure 8.15. The window is called the After Acquisition window. There are several options in this window. In the After Acquisition window, we select the Add to Case option. We also check Search the Hash and Signature Analysis. Then click Next to continue. A new window called Search will appear, as shown in Figure 8.16.

Since you do not have any keywords yet, you will leave that box unchecked. Check Search Entire Case, Compute Hash Value, Recompute Hash values, and Search for Email. We also check the Recover Deleted folders, as well as the additional options Verify File Signatures, Search for Internet History, and the Comprehensive Search before we continue. Now click Next; another window appears, called Options (see Figure 8.17). In the Name area, put the case, in this example 09-33580 Lacombe, which in turn will be placed in the evidence number. The notes are where we record the serial number of the suspect's hard drive, but another forensic investigator may just put some notes in this area. The file segment is 640, the start sector is 0, and the ending will be where the computer shows it to stop. The compression (the rate to acquire the files from the suspect's computer) is set to Good. The block size is 64 and the error granularity is 64.

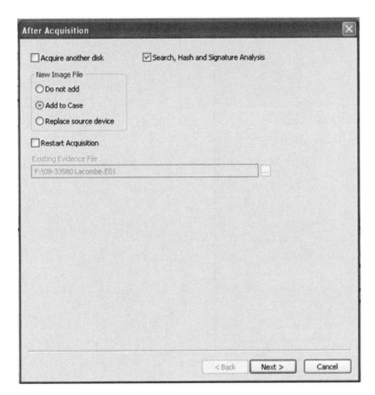

Figure 8.15
The After Acquisition window.

These areas are usually set as the default. The password is left blank. Now check the Acquisition MDS option. The output path is the location where you will be sending the data for the investigator to examine.

During our forensics, we use an ADS external hard drive storage to forward the data. The ADS allows us to use the same size hard drive as the suspect's hard drive, so the acquisition will be the same. When the ADS drive is turned on, the operating system will recognize the drive and assign it a letter. In our computer, it places the drive as F. Note that different computers may assign a different number. In this example, the output path will be F:\09-33580 Lacombe.E01, as you can see in Figure 8.17.

The data from the suspect's hard drive will be transferred to the F drive, which is where the investigator does the forensics. All you have to do is click Finish and the acquisition will start. It may take several hours to acquire the suspect's hard drive, depending on the size. When EnCase is finished, it will verify the files after

Figure 8.16
The Search window.

they are acquired. After the acquisition, you need to recover the lost files in FAT partitions. Right-click on each of the devices and then click Recover Folders. The device icon appears as a hard drive under the volume disk. Make sure this is complete. You will also need to recover folders in NTFS folders. Right-click on the volume and click on Recover Folders. The volume device appears as a disk in the Tree pane. The benefit of this is that EnCase may find folders that were deleted for maybe the wrong reason by the suspect. Lots of evidence can be found in these recovered areas. EnCase can also recover folders in hard drives that have been formatted. It can even recover the partitions in the hard drive.

When the acquisition is complete, turn off the write-blocker software and remove the suspect's hard drive. We usually replace the drive in the computer and return it to the evidence locker, at which point the suspect's computer is logged back in, once again preserving the chain of custody. Now we can actually start do some forensic work on the drive that was obtained in the ADS. Remember earlier in this chapter when we mentioned the four panes of EnCase? You will use the four panes to do the forensics on the hard drive and view the evidence in different ways.

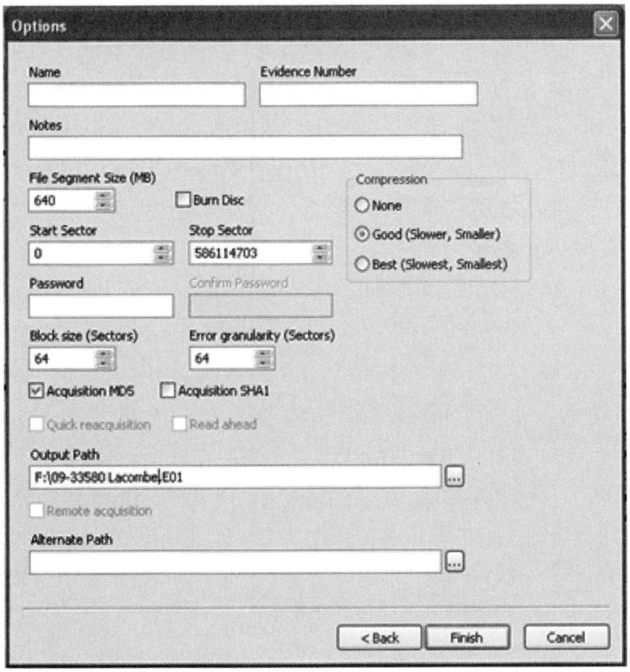

Figure 8.17
The output path of the suspect's data.

EnCase also gives the investigator the option to use external software to view files. Our forensic computer has FunDuc, XNView media, and Quick View Plus along with several media players. Some of the software is free and some has to be purchased.

EnCase will let the investigator do keyword searches within the case. You can look for words, phrases, and even hex strings. You can create a keyword list prior to the case if you know what you want to search for. An example for child pornography would be the keyword R@ygold, which is a pseudonym for the king of Internet child pornography. (This keyword is commonly used in peer-to-peer networking, where pedophiles obtain child pornography.) You can create the list by clicking View in the EnCase toolbar and choosing from the drop-down list for keywords. Another way is to click the Keyword tab. When you do, a folder will appear in the Tree pane. You can right-click in the Table pane to create the keywords. When creating a keyword, you have several options, as shown in Figure 8.18.

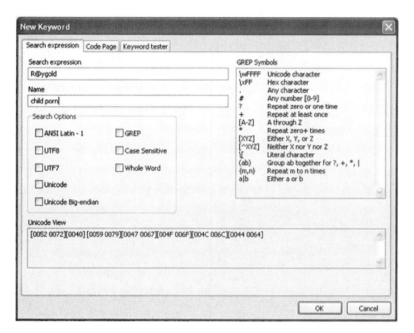

Figure 8.18
Keyword options.

We usually leave the Search Option boxes blank, since EnCase will search the entire drive no matter how big it is. When the keyword search is complete, the View pane will show the word in the text where it was used. Just click on the item in the Table pane to see it in the View pane. The keyword(s) will be highlighted. In the Table pane there are also tabs: Table, Report, Gallery, Timeline, Disk, and Code. One handy sub-tab is Gallery, shown in Figure 8.19.

You can actually view any type of photo no matter what the extension is of that file. When we say extension of a file, we are referring to files that have .jpg, .bmp, and more, such as PICT0433.jpg, shown in Figure 8.20. If you click on the picture in the Table pane, the View pane will show a bigger size of the photo.

Now, when analyzing and searching files, EnCase will do a Signature Analysis (SA), which is used to compare file headers and file extensions. The file header contains identifying information called the signature, and all the matching files have the same header. An example would be a file with the extension .png (graphic file). The signature of this file is BM8. The Signature Analysis will make sure it matches. Why would you run the SA? Sometimes, suspects will try to hide a file by changing the extension of the file; the real file may be a .jpg and the suspect

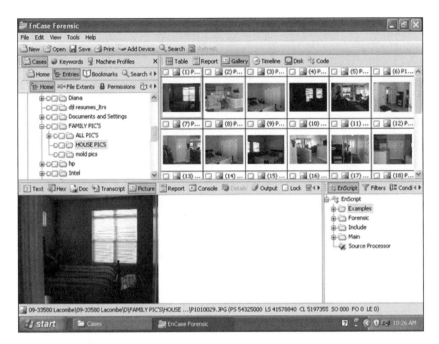

Figure 8.19
The Gallery tab.

will change it to a .doc extension. Windows associates the file extension with the corresponding applications by use of file extensions. The SA was run earlier in the After Acquisition option.

The Hash feature in EnCase creates a unique value for every file. Hashing essentially creates a digital fingerprint of a file. The odds of two files having the same hash would be 3.40282×1038. Hash analysis compares file hash values with known stored hash values, as shown in Figure 8.21. You can run the hash by selecting it in the Acquisition window before the acquisition or run it later by clicking the Search button and then, in the bottom-left corner, clicking Computer Hash and Recomputed Hash.

The Indexing feature in EnCase is used to improve the search engine. This feature is new to EnCase 6. The purpose is to enable quick access to data. You will need to be careful running this feature, as you could actually slow down the forensic computer or even have it shut down. When using this feature, do only small areas at a time.

Figure 8.20
Viewing an image file.

The EnScripts were discussed a little bit earlier in this chapter. EnCase has a number of EnScripts installed that provide a useful function for the investigator to save time and effort. You can access the EnScripts from the toolbar under View or from the Filter pane. You can also get more EnScripts through the Guidance Software portal.

EnCase will let you search for artifacts of various e-mails. In the After Acquisition options, the list was provided. You can also check artifacts in Web mail, including Netscape, Hotmail, and Yahoo!. This is done by clicking Tools in the EnCase toolbar and choosing Webmail Parser. In the window that opens, check each type of mail that you want EnCase to collect. The Tree pane will display the discovered files, which you can then view. EnCase offers a way to bookmark the evidence so that you can export it to the folders you created in Windows Explorer at a later time.

The next task in EnCase is to bookmark the files you want to keep. If you right-click on the piece of evidence (the file name) you want to bookmark in the Table

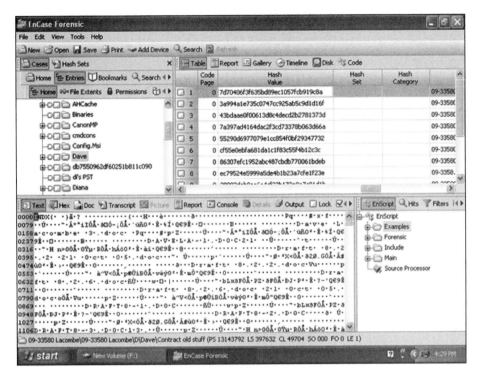

Figure 8.21
Hash analysis.

pane, the Bookmark Data window will appear. The Bookmark Data window will let the investigator create a new folder within EnCase. You can name that folder according to the data you marked (an example would be "Daves MP3"), as shown in Figure 8.22. If you have several files that are related to the file you created, just uncheck the Create New Bookmark Folder checkbox and pick the file Daves MP3. The bookmarked data will be placed there.

You can name the folder in whatever way best meets the need for the evidence. To view the bookmarks in the actual file you created, there is a Bookmarks tab just above the Tree pane. Just click on it, and the folders will appear in the Tree pane and the Table pane. The Table pane will display the list of folders you bookmarked for viewing. To view the individual bookmark, just click the folder in the Table pane and the View pane will display it. Remember that there are tabs for you to view the bookmark. The bookmark could be a photo, document, or text. The reason for bookmarking is that the evidence is placed in one area for

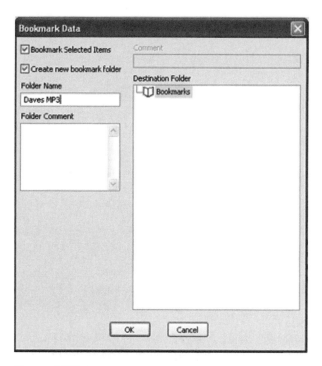

Figure 8.22
Bookmark Data window.

you to view and apply to the final report if needed. The different types of bookmarks are Highlighted Data, Notes Bookmarks, Folder Information, Notable Files, Snapshots, Log Records, and many others. Just about anything you can search for can be bookmarked. When you bookmark a piece of evidence, you can also add a note to it. Just like in Windows, you will be able to edit the bookmark for your purposes in the case.

Once you complete your notes and changes, EnCase gives you the ability to export your results in three ways. You can export in text, RTF (Rich Text Format, a document file format), or HTML format (HTML is a text and image formatting language used by Web browsers). The export type depends on the investigator and how he or she wants to present the case. We have exported in text and HTML formats to do the final report. The path will be the folders you created in Windows: export, temporary, and index. To export the bookmark, open the folder by clicking the Bookmarks button on the toolbar. This will show all the folders that you bookmarked. If you want to export more than one file, place a check on each one. You then right-click on the Table pane and choose

Export in the drop-down that appears. All the files will be sent to the path you selected.

After all the searches are done, EnCase provides the investigator with a report of the findings that were found on the suspect's computer. The report should be organized and presented in a readable format that the layperson will be able to understand. When you present the case, the courtroom, jury, and judge will be able to understand your presentation. EnCase provides several methods for generating a final report. Our favorite method is to do a summary in text and HTML explaining our findings and showing the findings we obtained in the bookmarks. We also click on the Device icon, which will display in the View pane, showing all the information about the device. We right-click in the View pane and export it in RTF format. If we have more than one device, we would do each one. This page of our report would be the first. We would then attach each file that we bookmarked in the way we wanted our presentation to be. Once the report is compiled, we would then burn it to a CD for the DA's office to review.

The information that we have provided in this chapter is just the basics. To go in detail, as we said earlier in the chapter, would result in a book on EnCase. These basic procedures will let you perform a basic forensic analysis of a hard drive and produce a final report. Other investigators may have other ways to do the analysis, but we can say that the procedure we've outlined here has been very successful for us in our county district courts. Remember that this procedure is for a stand-alone computer. Networks (workstations only) and RAID-type setups are different. We would have to ask someone to assist in these situations. We recommend if you get into this field, practice on some hard drives to get your procedure down. Keep up on all the new versions of the software and learn the different features that you can use. It will be a continuous learning experience. You will make mistakes and find that questions will need to be asked and answered. If you have to call someone with more experience, do so. There is no such thing as a dumb question in this field of work.

Conclusion

In this chapter you have learned the basics of getting evidence off of a hard drive. You should be familiar with several tools, such as ILook and Helix, and have a basic working knowledge of EnCase. It is imperative that whatever tool you choose, you study that tool thoroughly. A failure to fully understand your forensic tools could lead to serious errors that can undermine your case.

Endnotes

[1] Access Data Corp. http://www.accessdata.com/forensictoolkit.html

[2] E-fense. http://www.e-fense.com/helix/

[3] IRS-CI Electronic Crimes Program and Perlustro, LP. http://www.perlustro.com/

[4] Guidance Software Inc. http://www.guidancesoftware.com/

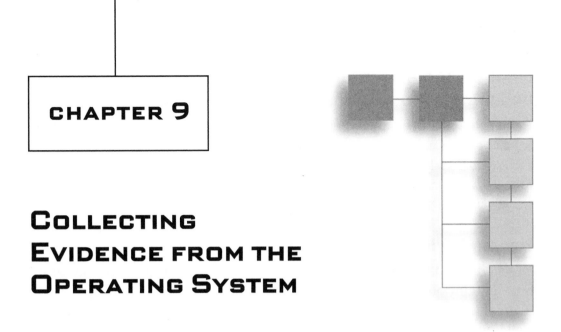

CHAPTER 9

COLLECTING EVIDENCE FROM THE OPERATING SYSTEM

Introduction

In Chapter 8, "Collecting Evidence from Hardware," you learned techniques for gathering evidence from a hard drive. You also learned basic forensic procedures and guidelines. In Chapter 7, "Observing, Collecting, Documenting, and Storing Electronic Evidence," you learned how to secure a crime scene and how to document your procedures and findings. In this chapter, we will discuss how one gathers information from the operating system and from various software on the computer. We will be looking at system logs, history, cookies, and other elements that can assist an investigator in tracking down evidence. Remember that you must still adhere to the rules set forth in Chapter 7. And also remember that it is absolutely critical that you carefully document every step you take. You will see that admonition repeated—it is the most critical aspect of a forensic examination.

Chapter 8 also focused on the EnCase tool. It is a very popular tool with law-enforcement agencies, and in many cases it might be the primary or only tool used by a particular agency. But it is important for any investigator to realize that there are other tools available, and there are even manual techniques for extracting evidence.

Finding Evidence in Browsers, Chat Logs, and Other Applications

Any application one can use to communicate on the Internet can potentially contain evidence. Web browsers, e-mail clients, and chat logs are some common places you should look for evidence. In this section, we will specifically consider browsers and chat logs. In Chapter 10, "Collecting Evidence from Other Sources," we will examine how to gather evidence from e-mail clients.

Finding Evidence in the Browser

Depending on the computer crime in question, one might find evidence in the browser. Obviously, in cases of child pornography, the browser might contain direct evidence of the specific crime. But in almost any computer-crime case, it could provide indirect evidence. For example, if a person is suspected of having cracked a password to hack into a server and steal financial data, you might find indirect evidence in that person's browser. You could find that the person had recently searched for methods of cracking passwords and perhaps downloaded some password-cracking utilities. That alone is certainly only circumstantial evidence, but it can help bolster a case, and more importantly it could provide a clearer view of exactly what occurred. Knowing what tools the person searched for could give you insight into the exact methods the perpetrator used and allow you to more accurately reconstruct what occurred. Remember that in a criminal investigation, even information that might not be directly incriminating can be helpful in understanding the crime. So with that in mind, let's see how you can get information from a browser. We will look at several different browsers.

When using Internet Explorer, one can go to the toolbar and see the entire browsing history for that user. This is shown in Figure 9.1. Obviously, many computer criminals will be savvy enough to erase their browser history. But it takes very little time to check the browser history and it might yield interesting results. Remember that even if the browsing history is only circumstantial evidence, it still might provide a valuable piece of the overall story. You can view the history in any browser. Figure 9.2 shows this in Mozilla Firefox. Most browsers have an option to allow you to view the browsing history, but they also have an option to clear that history. That is why this particular aspect of the system will often not yield results—but it is still worth checking out.

Another thing to check is the address bar. Some people do not realize that this is separate from the history. The address bar records only those Web addresses that

Figure 9.1
Internet Explorer browser history.

you type in, not Web sites you may have searched for via a search engine such as Google or Yahoo!. I have personally seen situations where someone did delete their history but forgot to clear the address bar. The address bar could be particularly incriminating in the case of child-pornography investigations. The perpetrator may claim that they "accidentally" came across child pornography due to an error in searching for some innocuous topic. However, it is difficult to use that excuse if one directly typed the exact Web address into the address bar. The address bar is shown in Figure 9.3.

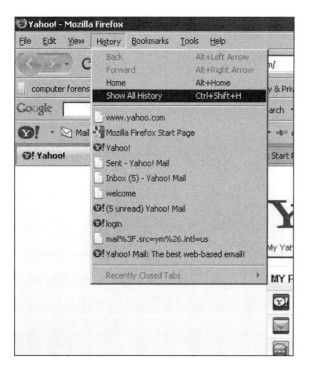

Figure 9.2
Mozilla Firefox browser history.

Figure 9.3
The browser address bar.

Another item that many people forget to clear is their forms. Most browsers will save search terms you have previously entered, which makes it easy for you to conduct that search again if you need to. If you type in a few key words in the search bar of any search engine, you may see the auto complete feature finish spelling out the term for you. If you suspect someone used this computer to find password crackers, try typing in terms like "password cracker" into the search engine.

None of these particular techniques are foolproof. They only work if the suspect has used this method to find incriminating material on the Web and has not yet deleted the evidence from his or her browser, and it is certainly a trivial task to delete such evidence. However, it takes just a little time to check, and may well yield important information. Another issue to be aware of is that many users have more than one browser. It is not uncommon for someone to have Internet Explorer and another browser such as Firefox or Opera. A clever criminal might have one browser that does not have an icon on the desktop and thus is not easy to find, and that is the browser he or she uses for illicit activities. Make sure you search for all browsers on the computer in question.

Finding Evidence in Chat Logs

Chat-room programs are frequently used for communication. We have already discussed in previous chapters the possible use of chat rooms by terrorists. It is also true that pedophiles sometimes use chat rooms to exchange information. (We will look closely at pedophiles on the Internet in Chapter 14, "Protecting Children on the Internet.") However, any criminal activity could be facilitated via chat-room discussions. Trafficking in stolen goods, prostitution, and other non-computer crimes all require communication between the involved parties. Chat rooms are an excellent way for people to communicate.

Fortunately, most chat software keeps at least a temporary log of conversations. This is true for MSN Messenger, Yahoo! Messenger, and many others. The exact path for viewing those logs will vary from product to product. However, somewhere on the drop-down menus you should find an option to view the log and an option to save that log. You should always check chat software to see if there are current logs to view or if the suspect has archived previous chats. This may provide valuable clues.

Finding Evidence in System Logs

Every operating system maintains logs that can provide a wealth of information. It is critical that you search these logs for evidence. System logs often show login attempts, failed or successful, as well as any alerts the operating system has given. The various Windows Server versions also record every reboot of the system in their logs. So let's take a look at the logs in a few operating systems and find out what we can learn from them.

Windows Logs

Let's start with Windows XP/Vista/7. In all of these versions of Windows, you can find the logs by clicking on the Start button in the lower-left corner of the desktop, then clicking Control Panel. You then click on Administrative Tools and then Event Viewer. The process of finding the logs in Windows Vista is

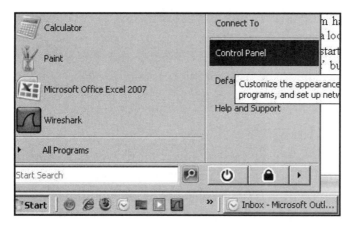

Figure 9.4
Finding the Control Panel.

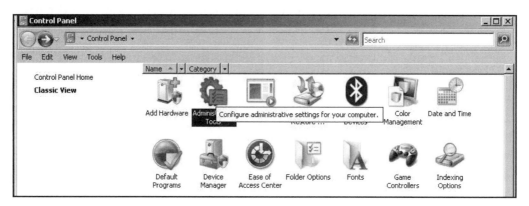

Figure 9.5
Administrative Tools.

shown in Figures 9.4 through 9.6, but the process is the same in Windows XP and in Windows 7 as well.

At this point, you should see the Event Viewer, which is shown in Figure 9.7. Now, from this screen, you can view events and logs. Let's briefly describe each type of log you might find in a Windows system. Please note that if you are dealing with a version of Windows prior to XP, then some of these logs may not be present:

- **Application log.** This log contains various events logged by applications or programs. Many applications will record their errors here in the application log. This can be useful particularly if the log is on a server that has a database

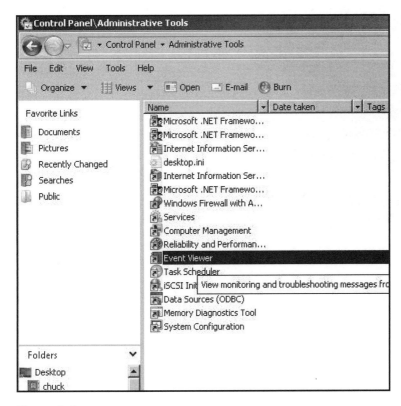

Figure 9.6
Finding the Event Viewer.

server like SQL Server installed. Examining this log can provide clues that someone has been attempting to compromise the database.

- **Security log.** The most important things you will find in the security log are successful and unsuccessful logon attempts. This log also records events related to resource use, such as creating, opening, or deleting files or other objects. Administrators can specify what events are recorded in the security log. Logon auditing can be turned off, but it never should be. Some hackers/crackers turn off the security log in order for their activities to not be recorded.

- **Setup log.** The setup log contains events related to application setup. This will show new applications installed on the machine. Obviously, most viruses and spyware won't write to the application log. However, this log can let you know if new applications have been installed that might either have a security flaw or be Trojan horses.

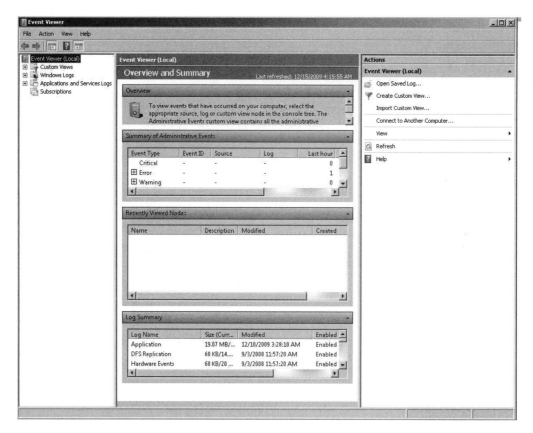

Figure 9.7
The Event Viewer.

- **System log.** The system log contains events logged by Windows system components. This includes events like driver failures. This particular log is not as interesting from a forensic perspective as the other logs are.

- **ForwardedEvents log.** The ForwardedEvents log is used to store events collected from remote computers. This log is important in a networked environment. However, the various systems must be configured to populate this log; it won't occur by default.

- **Applications and services logs.** Applications and services logs are a new category of event logs. These logs store events from a single application or component rather than events that might have systemwide impact. This can reveal problems with a specific application or Windows component. This is not as interesting from a forensic perspective as the other logs are.

The two critical logs are the security log and the system log. The most important item in the security log is the record of all login or logout attempts, whether they are successful or not. This is often the first sign of an attempt to break into a server. If you see numerous failed login attempts, or if you see account logins at odd hours, that can be an indication that illicit activity is taking place. This is one of the easiest things to check, so you should definitely not skip this.

Linux Logs

The Linux operating system also logs activities. All operating system logs can be found in the /var/log subdirectory. There are several logs you will find in this directory. A few of these may not be present in all Linux distributions, so simply look in that directory and see which logs are present:

- **/var/log/faillog:** This log file contains failed user logins. This can be very important when tracking attempts to crack into the system.

- **/var/log/kern.log:** This log file is used for messages from the operating system's kernel. This is not likely to be pertinent to most computer-crime investigations.

- **/var/log/lpr.log:** This is the printer log and can give you a record of any items that have been printed from this machine. This can be useful in corporate-espionage cases.

- **/var/log/mail.*:** This is the mail-server log and can be very useful in any computer-crime investigation. E-mails can be a component in any computer crime, and even in some non-computer crimes such as fraud.

- **/var/log/mysql.*:** This log records activities related to the MySQL database server and will usually be of less interest to a computer-crime investigation.

- **/var/log/apache2/*:** If this machine is running the Apache Web server, then this log will show related activity. This can be very useful in tracking attempts to hack into the Web server.

- **/var/log/lighttpd/*:** If this machine is running the Lighttpd Web server, then this log will show related activity. This can be very useful in tracking attempts to hack into the Web server.

- **/var/log/apport.log:** This records application crashes. Sometimes, these can reveal attempts to compromise the system or the presence of a virus or spyware.

- **/var/log/user.log:** These contain user-activity logs and can be very important to a criminal investigation.

There are several methods for viewing these logs, including several shell commands one can enter to view system logs in Linux. For example, if you wanted to view the printer log, any of the following would work, although some won't be supported by every Linux shell:

- `# tail -f /var/log/lbr.log`

- `# less /var/log/ lbr.log`

- `# more -f /var/log/ lbr.log`

- `# vi /var/log/ lbr.log`

However, using the Linux `dmesg` command is the preferred way to view logs from the shell. It works like this:

`dmesg | lpr`

Note that some logs require you to be logged on as root in order to view them.

If you are using the Gnome graphical user interface, it comes with a utility named System Log Viewer. This utility is a graphical, menu-driven viewer that can be used view all system logs. System Log Viewer comes with built-in functionality that includes a calendar, log monitor, and log statistics display. This is a very useful tool for examining Linux system logs.

You should be aware that there are techniques that can be used to either clear event logs completely or to selectively clear certain entries. There are also ways a hacker can turn logging off while they operate and then turn it back on when they leave. Fortunately, not all computer criminals are well versed in these techniques, so it is always a good idea to at least check the event logs. However, the absence of evidence in the event logs does not guarantee that no security breach occurred.

So that you are aware of these techniques, we will briefly describe a few of them:

- Clearing the log. Any user with administrative privileges can simply wipe out a log. However, this will be obvious when you see an empty event log.

- Using auditpol.exe. This is an administrative utility that exists in Windows systems. It won't show on the desktop or in the programs; you have to know it's there and go find it. Using `auditpol \ipaddress /disable` turns off logging. Then, when the criminal exits, he or she can use `auditpol\ipaddress /enable` to turn it back on.

- There are a number of utilities on the Web that can assist an attacker in this process. For example, WinZapper allows one to selectively remove certain items from event logs in Windows.

These are just a few examples of techniques hackers can use. Given that event logs can be compromised, you might wonder why you should even bother checking them. The fact is that most computer criminals are not highly skilled hackers. As we mentioned in earlier chapters, most computer criminals have learned a few tricks or downloaded some utility, and now call themselves hackers. They are in fact script kiddies. (Remember, that is a derogatory term the hacking community applies to those who try to apply some utility or technique without understanding it.) Contrary to what one sees in movies, there are not that many highly skilled hackers. There are literally tens of thousands of script kiddies, but few highly skilled hackers. In most investigations of computer crime, the perpetrator will not have the skill to cover his or her tracks. Furthermore, you must remember that even the most skilled criminals may overlook something. They may have covered some of their tracks, but it is likely they missed something. So look everywhere. We mention these particular methods for clearing the logs so that you, the investigator, will be aware of them.

Recovering Deleted Files

In any criminal enterprise, getting rid of evidence is often a concern for the perpetrators. Frequently, people will delete files they believe may be incriminating. Whether the files are child pornography, spyware, or documents, the perpetrator may delete key files. Fortunately for the investigator, it is often possible to get those files back. Files are stored on some drive, and the operating system keeps a record of all files on the machine's hard drives. Depending on which operating system the computer is running, you will have some method for retrieving deleted files.

Recovering Files from Windows

In the Windows operating system, the file records are in a table called a File Allocation Table (FAT). Incidentally, that is where the FAT and FAT32 names come from for the file systems used in Windows 3.1 and Windows 95/98. Since Windows 2000, Microsoft operating systems have used NTFS for their file system; however, NTFS still keeps a file table. When a file is deleted, it is first moved to the Recycle Bin. As an investigator, you should always check there first. If anything is in the Recycle Bin, you can simply restore it, as shown in Figure 9.8.

If the suspect has already emptied the Recycle Bin, don't worry; all is not lost. The way Windows works is that when you delete a file, it is actually just moved to a new location, the Recycle Bin. When you empty the Recycle Bin, the file is simply removed from the file allocation table—but it is still on the hard drive. Now, that part of the hard drive is now marked as "free" and in time, other files may be written over it. But it is entirely possible, particularly with recently deleted files, that the file will still be on the hard drive. Incidentally, many vendors such as McAfee make a utility that takes a file and not only deletes it and removes it from the file allocation table but then overwrites that file space with random data, then deletes the random data. This process is repeated multiple times to ensure that the original file is truly deleted. That process is often referred to as *shredding*. If the suspect has not done this, you may still be able to recover the

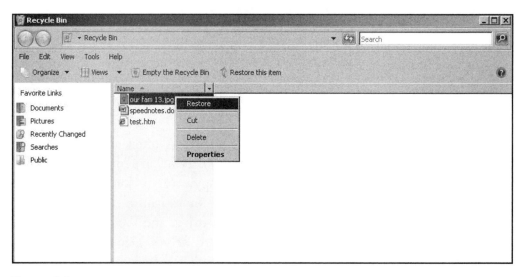

Figure 9.8
The Recycle Bin.

file, but you will need some sort of undelete utility to do so. There are a number of such utilities available on the Internet. Most are low cost and some are even free downloads. Let's look at a few of these.

UndeletePlus

UndeletePlus is available from http://www.undelete-plus.com for $29.95. What makes this tool worthy of mention is that it is very easy to use. You simply select a drive and click the Scan button, and it will list any deleted files it finds (see Figure 9.9).

DiskDigger

This product is available at http://dmitrybrant.com/diskdigger and is freeware, which makes it an attractive product. The site does accept donations, but you are

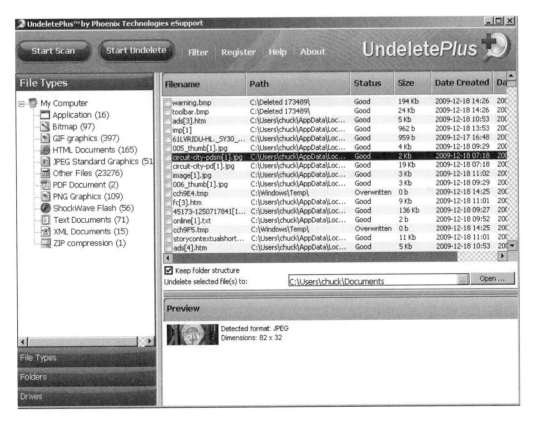

Figure 9.9
Undelete Plus.

free to download and use this product at no charge. This utility has a wizard interface that walks the user through the process. The initial screen, shown in Figure 9.10, asks the user which drive they wish to scan. Then the user is asked what type of search they want. It is possible to do a quick and less thorough search, or a deeper but slower search, as you can see in Figure 9.11. Finally, the user may select to only search for certain files. This can be very useful if you know what you are looking for. This is shown in Figure 9.12.

There are many other utilities available. Simply searching via Yahoo! or Google will yield several. But it is important to realize that the efficacy of any of these tools will depend on a number of factors. The time since the file was deleted is one such factor. The longer it has been since a file was deleted, the more likely it is that the file has been overwritten. Another issue is the frequency with which

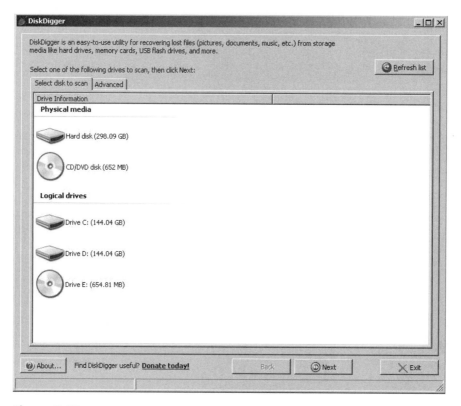

Figure 9.10
DiskDigger drive selection.

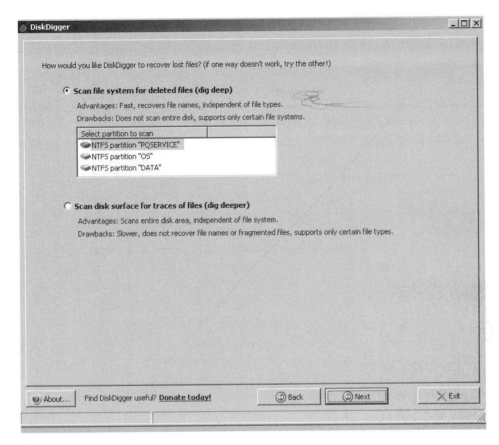

Figure 9.11
DiskDigger search level.

the hard drive is defragmented/optimized. Each time it is defragmented, there is a chance of overwriting the deleted file. But it is always a good idea to at least attempt to recover deleted files from the machine.

You should also be aware that there are manual methods for restoring deleted files in Windows. In order to restore a file, you will need to rename the file so that its initial character is different. You will also need to fix the cluster chain (directory listing, FAT, clusters). This can be done manually by using a manual disk editor. That process can be tedious, though, and is not recommended. The exact details of how to execute this procedure are beyond the scope of this book, but they are also not necessary. As we have already discussed, there are plenty of third-party tools that will assist you in this endeavor.

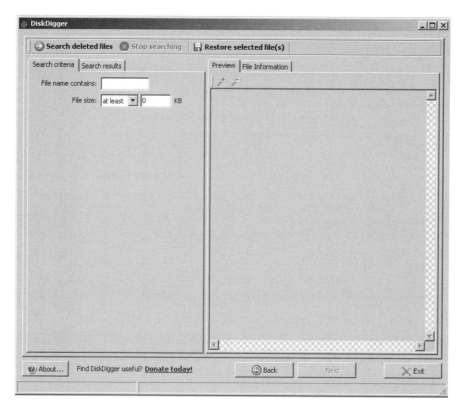

Figure 9.12
DiskDigger file search.

Recovering Files from Unix/Linux

When using Unix or a related operating system such as Linux or free BSD, when a file is deleted, the link counter is decreased. As soon as the link counter hits 0, the file is "unlinked," and thus removed. Because Linux is a multiuser and multitasking operating system, other users or processes can overwrite deleted file disk space. So you first need to take the system down to single-user mode. A file can be undeleted by using the `debugfs` tool: first changing the deletion time to 0, next increasing the link count to 1. Afterward, running `e2fsck` will enable you to map the unlinked clusters to the lost+found directory. There are many methods that will allow you to recover a deleted file. Here is one step-by-step process:

1. First, use the shell command # `wallOutput` to tell users that the system is going down in a single-user mode. This will give you the following

output: `System is going down to . . . . please save your work.`
`Press CTRL+D to send message.`

2. Once you have moved to single-user mode, there are several methods you might use. The following is a rather traditional Unix/Linux method using the `grep` command. Use the following `grep` syntax:

```
grep -b 'search-text' /dev/partition > file.txt
```

You could also use the following:

```
grep -a -B[size before] -A[size after] 'text' /dev/[your_partition] >
file.txt
```

The flags used are defined as follows:

- `-i`: Ignore case distinctions in both the PATTERN and the input files (i.e., match both uppercase and lowercase characters).

- `-a`: Process a binary file as if it were text.

- `-B`: Print number lines/size of leading context before matching lines.

- `-A`: Print number lines/size of trailing context after matching lines.

For example, to recover a text file starting with nixCraft on /dev/sda1, you can try following command:

```
# grep -i -a -B10 -A100 nixCraft' /dev/sda1 > file.txt
```

3. Next use `vi` to see file.txt. This method is only useful if the deleted file is a text file.

Just like Windows, there are utilities one can use to undelete Unix files. It is usually better to use a convenient utility than to try to manually recover files. Here are a few:

- **Midnight Commander:** http://www.datarecoverypros.com/recover-linux-midnightcommander.html

- **Disk Doctors:** http://www.diskdoctors.net; note this product also comes in versions for Windows and for Macintosh.

Whether you recover the deleted files manually or by using a utility to accomplish it, the issues will be the same. As we previously discussed, there is no guarantee that a deleted file has not been overwritten. And a savvy computer criminal will use tools such as McAfee's shredder or simply the Windows defragmenter to make recovering deleted files more difficult. But it is always a good idea to check. It is amazing how often one will find incriminating evidence in this manner.

Other Forensic Tools

In Chapter 8, you learned how to use the popular EnCase forensic tool. That is one of the most popular tools in the law-enforcement community. However, it is not an inexpensive tool, and there are other tools you should consider. In this section, we will briefly look at a few of these tools. It is not the purpose of this book to be a technical manual for every tool available, therefore we won't be going into extensive detail on these products. We'll provide just an overview so that you are aware of the options you have available to you.

The Sleuth Kit

The Sleuth Kit is a collection of command-line tools that are available as a free download. You can get them from http://www.sleuthkit.org/sleuthkit. This toolset is not as rich or as easy to use as EnCase, but it can be a good option for a budget-conscious agency. The most obvious of the utilities included is ffind.exe. It has a number of options, as shown in Figure 9.13.

As you can see, there are options to search for a given file or to search for only deleted versions of a file. This particular utility is best used when you know the specific file you are searching for; it is not a good option for a general search.

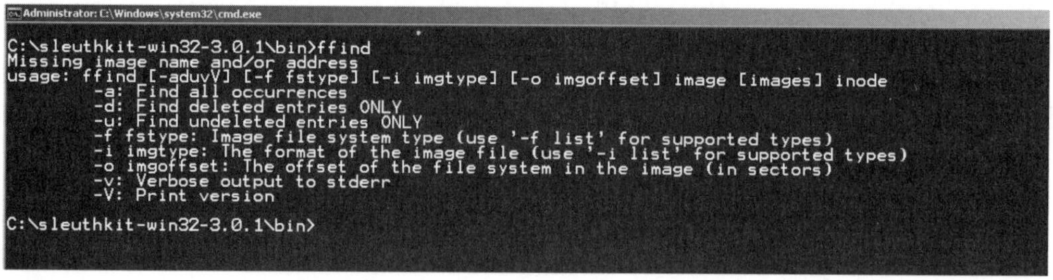

Figure 9.13
ffind.exe options.

There are a number of utilities available in Sleuth Kit, but many readers may find using command-line utilities to be cumbersome. Fortunately, a GUI has been created for Sleuth Kit called Autopsy, and it is available at http://www.sleuthkit. org/autopsy/download.php.

Disk Investigator

Disk Investigator is a free utility that comes as a graphic user interface for use with Windows. You can download it from http://www.theabsolute.net/sware/dskinv. html. It is not a full-featured product like EnCase, but it is remarkably easy to use. When you first launch the utility, it will present you with a cluster-by-cluster view of the hard drive in hexadecimal format. This is shown in Figure 9.14. Under the View menu, you can view directories or the root. The Tools menu allows you to search for a specific file or to recover deleted files.

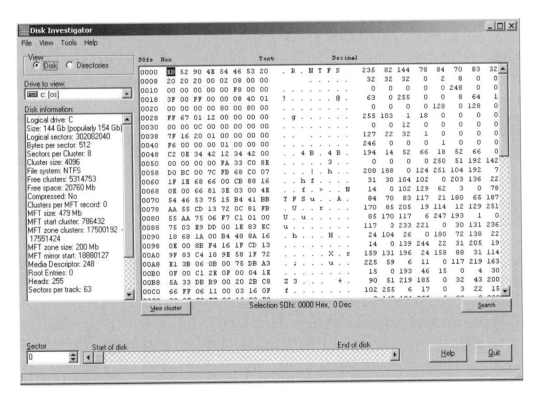

Figure 9.14
Disk Investigator.

Computer Online Forensic Evidence Extractor

This tool (also called by its acronym, COFEE) was created by Microsoft specifically for use by law enforcement. It is an online tool that is being provided free of charge to law-enforcement agencies by Microsoft. This tool is meant to be very easy to use so that with minimal training, any law-enforcement agent can utilize the tool. It is also meant to be used on live systems. This tool has the ability to do the following:

- Decrypt passwords.

- Search a computer's Internet activity.

- Analyze what is live in volatile memory.

COFEE was developed by a senior investigator on Microsoft's Internet Safety Enforcement Team, Anthony Fung. Mr. Fung is a former law-enforcement officer and has direct knowledge of the needs of law-enforcement officers.

You can learn more about COFEE at http://www.microsoft.com/industry/government/solutions/cofee/. This tool is primarily an easy-to-use wrapper around other already-existing forensic utilities. It should also be pointed out that the hacking community has already created a response to COFEE. The tool DECAF is a utility specifically created for the obstruction of COFEE. DECAF is an acronym for Detect and Eliminate Computer Assisted Forensics. DECAF provides real-time monitoring for COFEE signatures and will attempt to interfere with the operation of COFEE. For example, if COFEE is detected running on a USB device, DECAF will eject that device.

One could write an entire book just about the various forensic utilities available on the Internet. It is a good idea for any investigator to spend some time searching the Internet and experimenting with various utilities. Depending on your own skill set, technical background, and preferences, one utility might be more suitable than another. It is also recommended that once you select a tool to use, you scan the Internet for articles about that tool. Make certain that it has widespread acceptance and that there are no known issues with its use. It can also be useful to use more than one tool to search a hard drive. If multiple tools yield the same result, this might preempt any objections the opposing attorney or their expert may attempt to present at trial. And remember: Document every single step of your investigative process.

Important Locations to Check

In any operating system, there are key folders that will contain valuable information. That information could include files, images, and Internet cookies. Those locations will be different with each operating system, so we will look at each system separately.

Checking in Windows

When installing Windows, the installer can select any location it wants. However, on most machines, you will find the default locations, so it is a good idea to start looking there. Many of these areas, such as the c:\users folders, are only accessible if you are logged in as a user who has administrative privileges.

- **C:\Program Files.** This is where most programs are installed. Even if you don't see a program on the desktop or in the Start menu, it does not mean the program is not on the machine. This is a good place to look for spyware, hacking tools, and other software that might be related to a computer crime.

- **C:\Program Files (x86).** If the computer is a 64-bit operating system, this is where you will find any 32-bit programs. It is essentially the same thing as C:\Program files, only for 32-bit programs on a 64-bit machine.

- **C:\Windows.** This is where the operating system itself is stored. Checking the temporary subfolder can yield useful evidence. It is also a good idea to look for any new files in this folder, as they could be indicative of spyware or a virus.

- **C:\Windows\System32.** This subfolder contains critical system DLLs (dynamic link libraries). If you see recent additions here, it might indicate new software was installed. That new software could include chat programs, spyware, or a virus.

- **C:\Users*username*\Documents.** This is the default location for documents, and is clearly a good place to check. When you are logged onto Windows and you go to My Documents, you are going to the C:\Users*username*\Documents folder for the user currently logged in. That is why you cannot just be satisfied with checking My Documents, since you are only checking the Documents folder for the current user. You must check in

C:\Users and check the Documents, Pictures, and other folders for *each* user.

- **C:\Users*username*\\Pictures.** This is the default image folder for Windows, just as Documents is the default document folder. If there are incriminating photos on the computer, they may well be stored here.

- **C:\Users*username*\\Favorites.** This is where the Internet Explorer favorites are stored for each user. When you are logged into Windows, you only see the currently logged in user's favorites in Internet Explorer. If you go to this directory, you can see all users' favorites. This lets you find out what Web pages each user has bookmarked.

- **C:\Users*username*\\Desktop.** This will show you the desktop for each user.

- **C:\Users*username*\\Downloads.** This folder is very important from a forensic point of view. This is the default location for any programs downloaded from the Internet.

Nothing prevents a user from saving folders or documents to other locations, but these are default locations, and you will frequently find information here.

Checking in Linux

Just like Windows, Linux has some important directories that should be examined. And also like Windows, you need to be logged on as a user with administrative privileges to view some of these. In Linux, indeed in all Unix-like systems, the administrator account is called *root*.

- **/home.** This directory contains the various home directories for each user. It is analogous to C:\Users in Windows. You definitely want to check this out, and look in each user's subdirectory.

- **/root.** This is the home directory for the root user. Since this is the administrator account, you will want to look at this very carefully. Hackers always aspire to hack the root account on any Unix-like system.

- **/var.** This directory contains administrative items such as logs, so it is critical that you examine this directory thoroughly.

- **/temp.** This contains temporary files. You will want to look through this as well.

- **/etc.** This contains configuration files. When you are investigating an intrusion, keep in mind that it is often the case that the perpetrator has changed configuration files. So comparing the configuration files on the suspect computer with backed-up versions can be useful. If the owner of the system keeps backups of these files, you can use a command-line utility such as file compare to see if any changes have been made. We will be discussing these operating-system utilities in the next section of this chapter.

Operating-System Utilities

Within each operating system are certain utilities that can help you in your forensic endeavors. Some we will talk about in other chapters because they are more related to the specific material in those chapters. However, there are some general utilities that might help you that we can discuss now. We will also denote what operating system these are for. All of these are run from a command line (Windows) or shell (Linux).

The first utility we will look at is netstat. This utility works in Linux or Windows. It is short for "network status," and lets you know any live connections on the machine. If someone is currently accessing the computer or if the computer is accessing some remote resource, it will show in netstat. You can see netstat in action in Figure 9.15.

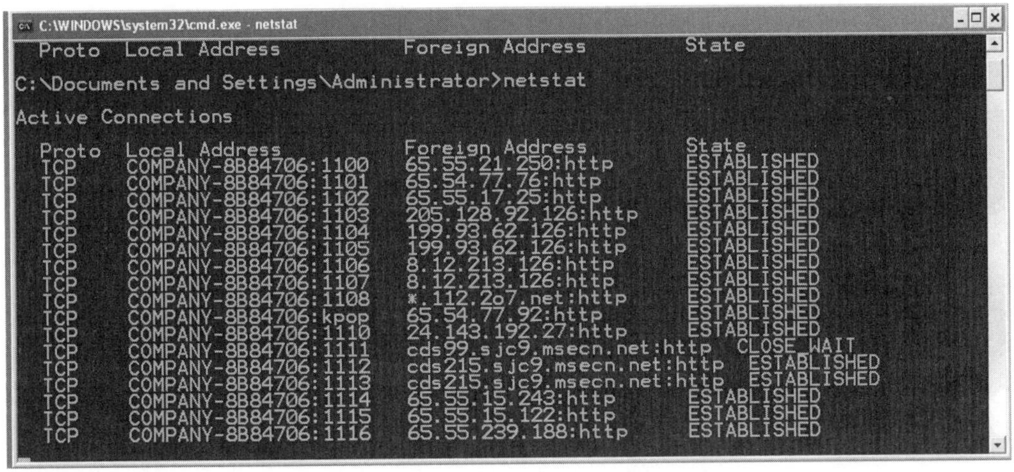

Figure 9.15
Netstat.

You get to the command line to run this by choosing Start, Run, and then typing cmd, if it is Windows XP, or by choosing Start and typing cmd into the search box if it is Windows Vista or Windows 7. Another command you can run from the command line is fc, which stands for file compare. For example, if you have a configuration file that you believe has been altered and you have a previous copy you know to be good, you can use fc to compare the two; it will output only the differences. You can see an example of two text files compared with fc in Figure 9.16. The same thing can be done in Linux with the cmp command from any Linux shell.

A very useful command in forensic examination is recover. This command will attempt to recover the readable portions of a corrupt file. You can see the recover utility in Figure 9.17. There is a similar utility in Linux called ddrescue.

A useful command available in Linux, but not Windows, is ps. This gives you a list of all running processes. If any virus or spyware is running in the background, you will see it in the process list. The ps command is shown in Figure 9.18.

These are just a few utilities you might find useful in your forensic examinations. It is always recommended that you learn as much as you can about the

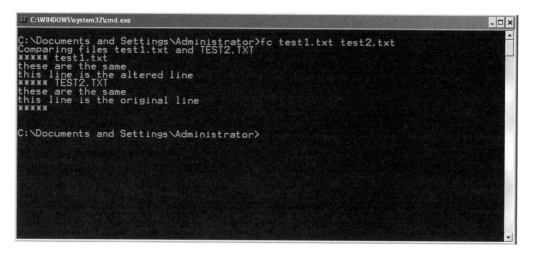

Figure 9.16
fc.

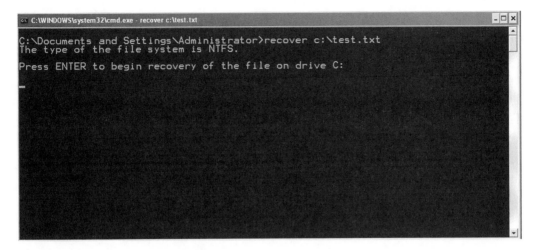

Figure 9.17
recover.

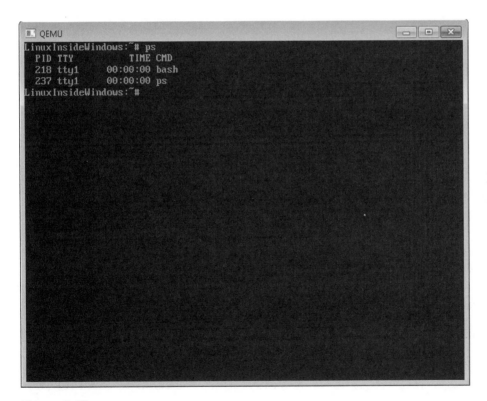

Figure 9.18
ps.

operating systems you will be working with so that you have a wide repertoire of operating-system–specific utilities at your disposal.

Conclusion

The operating system can be a treasure trove of evidence and information. The system logs, the browser, and even deleted files can all provide valuable information. It is critical that you scan these resources for whatever evidence might be available. However, also be aware that you must document every step in the process. If you use some utility to recover deleted files, you must document what utility you used and exactly what steps you took.

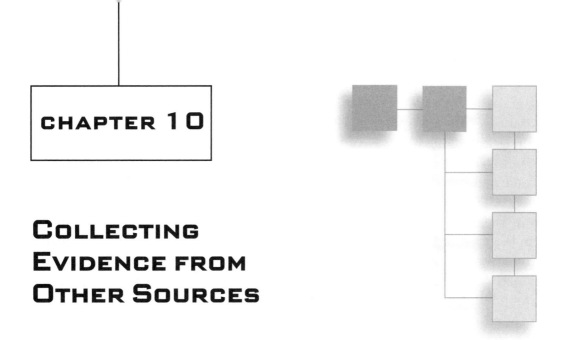

CHAPTER 10

COLLECTING EVIDENCE FROM OTHER SOURCES

Introduction

In the past few chapters, we have looked at several different sources for evidence, including the hard drive and the operating system. We have also explored techniques for gathering evidence from a computer's browser and even using utilities available in the operating system to look for evidence. However, the evidence you're looking for might not always be found in those locations—or, for that matter, even be on a computer, or at least not on a computer you have access to. For example, evidence might be on an e-mail server in a remote location, or you may need to track down the perpetrator's computer. It is also possible that routers and other devices might contain evidence. It is important that your investigative skills include the ability to effectively gather evidence from these sources as well. In this chapter, we will explore these additional venues for evidence gathering.

Tracing IP Addresses

Sometimes you will have data that you need to track to its source. There are several crimes that would require this sort of activity—for example, if the victim receives threatening e-mails or perhaps you wish to trace back the source of a security break-in. It is also true that in most child-pornography cases, it will be important to trace the images back to a specific location. In this section, we will discuss what IP addresses are, how they work, and how they are tracked.

Let us begin by discussing what an IP address is. Some readers may already be familiar with IP addresses, but if you are not, it is critical that you get a general overview before we proceed. IP stands for *Internet protocol.* An IP address is a numerical address that identifies a node on a network. A *node* is any device connected to a network. A node can be a personal computer, a server, a router, or some networked device such as a printer. IP addresses consist of four numbers between 0 and 255; an example would be 212.44.33.144. There is a good reason why the number must be between 0 and 255. While humans are most comfortable with base 10 numbers, computers work best with base 2 numbers (binary). In binary numbers, eight bits can hold at most the equivalent of 255 in base 10. You can test this with the Windows calculator. Open up the Windows calculator (found under Start > Programs > Accessories) and use the View menu to switch to Scientific mode. Click the Binary option and then type in eight 1s. Now click the decimal option and you will see that eight 1s in binary is equivalent to 255 in decimal. This is why an IP address number must be between 0 and 255. Each number is a byte, and the largest binary number that can be stored in a single byte is eight 1s, which is equivalent to 255 in base 10.

N o t e

This is the IP version 4.0 format. There are also IP version 6 addresses, but they are not widely used. You will almost always encounter version 4.0 addresses.

That IP address uniquely identifies a given node. It works much like a street address: A portion identifies what network the node is on, and the rest identifies what node on the network you are trying to reach. However, there is a problem with IP addresses. That problem is that humans don't work well with numbers; we work better with names. We prefer addresses like http://www.chuckeasttom.com to numbers. There is a solution for this dilemma. When you type http://www.chuckeasttom.com into your browser, a service called Domain Name Service (DNS) checks with your ISP or employer's DNS server to find out what IP address is associated with http://www.chuckeasttom.com. The user-friendly words you type in are referred to as a *uniform resource locator,* or *URL.* Computers only understand IP addresses, not URLs, and humans deal much better with meaningful names rather than long strings of numbers. You can find more details on IP addresses in Appendix A, "Introduction to Computer Networks," but this is enough information for you to be able to understand this chapter.

When any sort of communication is established, there is a destination IP address and a source IP address. You can think of the source IP address as a return address, just like what is used when mailing a letter. Now, if you are investigating communication coming from a source that you believe is committing a crime, the first step you want to take is to track down that source—that IP address should trace back to some physical address. There are many ways to trace an IP back to its source. The first is a built-in command-line tool called `tracert` (in Linux/Unix it is `traceroute`). First you open a command window; in Windows, you go to Start and then type `cmd` into the Start Search textbox. If you are using Linux, open any shell, type in `tracert`, and then the IP address or URL you want to trace. You will see something very much like what is shown in Figure 10.1.

What this is showing you is all the intermediate hops between the machine you are on and the final destination—the last entry is the final destination. Now that you know the final destination IP address, you can find out information about it using a database such as Whois. A number of Web sites offer a user-friendly interface to a database that contains information on who has registered a given Web site or domain. A few such Web sites are listed here:

- http://www.whois.net

- http://www.networksolutions.com/whois/index.jsp

- http://www.who.is

```
Administrator: C:\Windows\system32\cmd.exe
Microsoft Windows [Version 6.0.6001]
Copyright (c) 2006 Microsoft Corporation.  All rights reserved.

C:\Users\chuck>tracert www.ChuckEasttom.com

Tracing route to sbs-p6p.asbs.yahoodns.net [98.136.92.77]
over a maximum of 30 hops:

  1    <1 ms    <1 ms    <1 ms   192.168.1.1
  2     *         *         *     Request timed out.
  3    17 ms    30 ms    17 ms   24.164.211.145
  4    16 ms    19 ms    17 ms   24.164.209.116
  5    19 ms    11 ms     8 ms   gig5-0-0.dllatxchn-rtr5.tx.rr.com [70.125.217.10
  6    35 ms    25 ms    22 ms   gig2-0-2.hstntxl3-rtr1.texas.rr.com [72.179.205.
  7    23 ms    22 ms    15 ms   xe-9-1-0.bar1.Houston1.Level3.net [4.79.88.25]
  8    32 ms    19 ms    21 ms   ae-0-11.bar2.Houston1.Level3.net [4.69.137.134]
  9    35 ms    35 ms    37 ms   ae-7-7.ebr1.Atlanta2.Level3.net [4.69.137.142]
 10    32 ms    35 ms    48 ms   ae-73-70.ebr3.Atlanta2.Level3.net [4.69.138.20]
 11    50 ms    51 ms    53 ms   ae-2.ebr1.Washington1.Level3.net [4.69.132.86]
 12    56 ms    53 ms    56 ms   ae-61-61.csw1.Washington1.Level3.net [4.69.134.1
 13    48 ms    47 ms    45 ms   ae-11-69.car1.Washington1.Level3.net [4.68.17.3]
 14    55 ms    56 ms    57 ms   4.79.228.2
 15    59 ms    65 ms    65 ms   xe-7-0-0.msr2.ac2.yahoo.com [216.115.108.129]
 16    56 ms    60 ms    63 ms   te-9-1.bas-b1.ac4.yahoo.com [76.13.0.207]
 17    71 ms    65 ms    62 ms   p6p2.geo.ac4.yahoo.com [98.136.92.77]

Trace complete.

C:\Users\chuck>
```

Figure 10.1
`tracert`.

- http://www.internic.net/whois.html

- http://cqcounter.com/whois/

Notice that you can also enter a URL into these Web sites. Let's see what the last one, http://cqcounter.com/whois/, can tell us about http://www.chuckeasttom.com. Figure 10.2 shows the results.

As you can see, we are shown when the domain was registered (24 July 2001), who is hosting the Web site (Yahoo!), and other details. The hosting company alone can be invaluable information if you need to serve a subpoena for more detailed activity records.

Other Whois Web sites may provide even more details. For example, when we run the URL http://www.chuckeasttom.com through Network Solutions' Whois tool (http://www.networksolutions.com/whois/index.jsp), we can see the additional information shown in Figure 10.3.

You can see in Figure 10.3 that we now know the administrative contact's name, address, and phone number. This can be invaluable information both to hackers and to law enforcement. For law enforcement, it gives you a specific person to contact. In many cases, if the crime is being perpetrated by a third-party ISP, then this information will tell you where to serve subpoenas. If the crime is being

CHUCKEASTTOM.COM - Domain Information new	
Domain	CHUCKEASTTOM.COM [Site Info Traceroute RBL/DNSBL lookup]
Registrar	MELBOURNE IT, LTD. D/B/A INTERNET NAMES WORLDWIDE
Registrar URL	http://www.melbourneit.com
Whois server	whois.melbourneit.com
Created	24-Jul-2001
Updated	16-Aug-2009
Expires	24-Jul-2011
Time Left	569 days 20 hours 56 minutes
Status	ok
DNS servers	NS8.SAN.YAHOO.COM 66.218.71.205 NS9.SAN.YAHOO.COM 66.196.84.168

Figure 10.2
Whois search.

```
Domain Name......... chuckeasttom.com
   Creation Date........ 2001-07-24
   Registration Date.... 2001-07-24
   Expiry Date.......... 2011-07-24
   Organisation Name.... Chuck Easttom
   Organisation Address. 1845 W. Walntu Unit C
   Organisation Address.
   Organisation Address. Garland
   Organisation Address. 75042
   Organisation Address. TX
   Organisation Address. UNITED STATES

Admin Name........... Chuck Easttom
   Admin Address....... 1845 W. Walntu Unit C
   Admin Address.......
   Admin Address....... Garland
   Admin Address....... 75042
   Admin Address....... TX
   Admin Address....... UNITED STATES
   Admin Email......... admin@chuckeasttom.com
   Admin Phone......... 972-494-1747
```

Figure 10.3
Network Solutions Whois search.

conducted from a server the perpetrator is hosting themselves, this information might help you determine their physical location. Hackers also use this information to assist themselves in social-engineering exploits. Knowing key administrators' names and contact information allows them to be more effective in trying to pose as an employee of the target company.

As you can see, tracing back an IP address is fairly easy and can be quite informative. However, there are very inexpensive tools that make the process even more informative and even easier to do. One such tool is Visual Route (http://www.VisualRoute.com). They have a very inexpensive program you can buy that will trace IP addresses and URLs. (There is also a live demo you can run online and a "lite" version of the product you can download for free.) In Figure 10.4, you can see the detailed information that Visual Route provides you about each hop between your location and the final destination.

Visual Route also provides a full-color map showing each hop between your computer and the destination, thus giving you clear information as to where the network traffic is going.

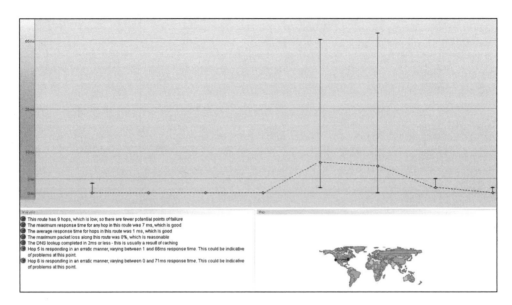

This route has 9 hops, which is low, so there are fewer potential points of failure
The maximum response time for any hop in this route was 7 ms, which is good
The average response time for hops in this route was 1 ms, which is good
The maximum packet loss along this route was 0%, which is reasonable
The DNS lookup completed in 2ms or less - this is usually a result of caching
Hop 5 is responding in an erratic manner, varying between 1 and 66ms response time. This could be indicative of problems at this point.
Hop 6 is responding in an erratic manner, varying between 0 and 71ms response time. This could be indicative of problems at this point.

Figure 10.4
Visual Route search.

Any of these methods can help you find out information about the source IP address. It is important to keep in mind, though, that it is possible that the packets reaching you have been *spoofed,* which means altered to make the source IP address seem different than it actually is. However, in many, cases you will be able to find the real source IP address. As we have stated in previous chapters, the number of highly skilled hackers is actually quite small. Most perpetrators of computer crime are actually of low to moderate skill and will leave some aspect of their crime vulnerable to forensic examination. And in many cases, such as cyber-stalking cases, the perpetrator may indeed be a computer novice and take no steps at all to cover their tracks.

Of more concern than spoofing IPs is the issue of e-mail *anonymizers.* There are a number of Web sites that will allow one to send e-mail and put in any source e-mail address they want. With some of these, you can still track the IP address of the e-mail server, but that will usually not be of much help. Those services usually do not keep any records of visitors to their sites, and it is likely they will have no record of who actually sent the e-mail. A few such anonymizers are listed here:

- http://www.anonymizer.com/
- http://anonymize.net/

- http://www.publicproxyservers.com/

- http://www.ultimate-anonymity.com/

- http://www.mutemail.com/

But just like with other items, such as the event logs mentioned in Chapter 9, "Collecting Evidence from the Operating System," even though it is possible that a clever criminal may have erased his or her tracks, you must still check for forensic evidence. It is always possible the perpetrator was unskilled and did not cover his or her tracks. It is also true that every human being, no matter how clever, eventually makes mistakes.

Gathering E-mail Evidence

There are two different ways in which you can gather evidence from e-mail. The first is to track down the origin of an e-mail that has been received. The second is to gather e-mail from an e-mail server. Let's look at tracking down e-mail origins first. This can be an important and common task in many computer-crime investigations. When dealing with cyber stalking, viruses, or child pornography, there will often be e-mails related to the crime, and tracing them is a very important part of your investigation.

The first place to look is in the e-mail header. All e-mails have a very informative header. The specific e-mail client you are using will determine how you get to that header. If you are using Yahoo! E-mail's Web interface, for example, then in the individual e-mail at the bottom-right corner you will see an option labeled Full Headers (see Figure 10.5). When you click on that, the e-mail will display its full header information, as shown in Figure 10.6. There is a lot of useful information in that image. The return path tells you where your e-mail will go if you hit Reply. The originating IP is very important; it tells you the IP address that e-mail came from. Most likely that will be the IP address of the e-mail server the person is using, not their individual machine. But you can use the

Figure 10.5
Find Yahoo! E-mail full headers.

ımazon.com Author Central Team Wed Dec 16 02:17:03 2009

X-Apparently-To:	chuckeasttom@yahoo.com via 206.190.48.191; Tue, 15 Dec 2009 18:17:09 -0800
Return-Path:	<20091216021703f0099751069046bfa5eaa966e3b48697@bounces.amazon.com>
X-YMailISG:	s6zas7sWLDuS2kDU9iAL1VpupHZ4KVrj1cdgEupzMKO.MrIXY67vKqIzvUPVOPigkLI5troH.hSSkKAGCHYD2YnNHSgLÇ
X-Originating-IP:	[207.171.164.35]
Authentication-Results:	mta1098.mail.re4.yahoo.com from=amazon.com; domainkeys=pass (ok); from=amazon.com; dkim=neutral (no s
Received:	from 127.0.0.1 (EHLO mm-notify-out-1101.amazon.com) (207.171.164.35) by mta1098.mail.re4.yahoo.com with
DomainKey-Signature:	s=rte02; d=amazon.com; c=nofws; q=dns; h=Date:From:To:Message-ID:Subject:MIME-Version: Content-Type:C
Date:	Wed, 16 Dec 2009 02:17:03 +0000 (UTC)
From:	"Amazon.com Author Central Team" <ac-no-reply@amazon.com>
To:	"chuckeasttom@yahoo.com" <chuckeasttom@yahoo.com>
Message-ID:	<1882985069.21977901260929823826.JavaMail.correios@na-mm-relay.amazon.com>
Subject:	Amazon.com Author Central Update - December 15, 2009
MIME-Version:	1.0
Content-Type:	text/plain; charset=UTF-8
ıtent-Transfer-Encoding:	quoted-printable
-AMAZON-CLIENT-HOST:	cscentral-batchportal-processor-na-6002.iad6.amazon.com
Bounces-to:	20091216021703f0099751069046bfa5eaa966e3b48697@bounces.amazon.com
ıZON-CLIENT-SENDTIME:	Wed Dec 16 02:17:03 UTC 2009
ıZON-MAIL-RELAY-TYPE:	notification
-AMAZON-RTE-VERSION:	2.0
Content-Length:	3178

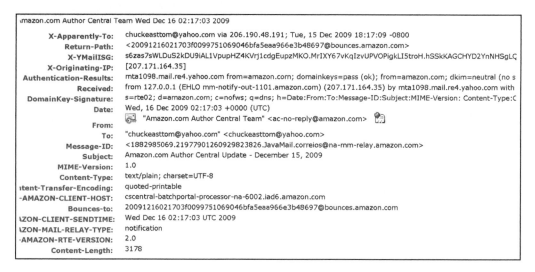

Figure 10.6
View Yahoo! E-mail full headers.

aforementioned Whois searches to trace down this IP address just like we did previously in this chapter. Visual Route, which we mentioned earlier, also makes a product called eMailTrackerPro, which provides similar functionality for e-mail. That product plugs into Outlook, as shown in Figure 10.7. When you have any e-mail highlighted, you can click on the eMailTrackerPro button and a trace will be executed, as shown in Figure 10.8.

As we have already seen, you can manually track down an IP address, but tools such as eMailTrackerPro make the tracing process much more convenient and provide a rich set of data about the e-mail being tracked.

While you should always attempt to track down e-mails related to a crime or civil dispute, this avenue of investigation will not always be fruitful. It does not take a great deal of effort for a person to set up an anonymous Hotmail, Google, or Yahoo! e-mail account. Such accounts will be difficult to trace to an individual person. Now, if you can trace back to the originating IP, you then have the

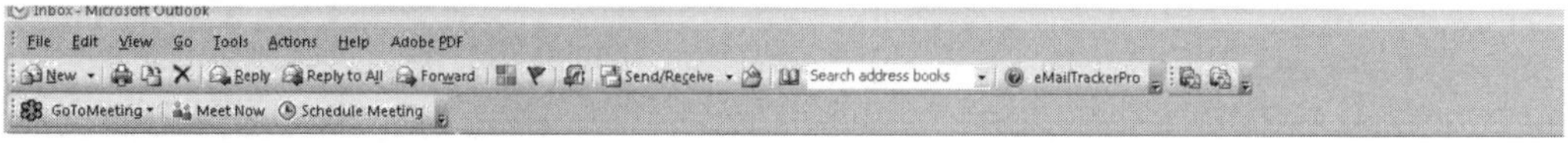

Figure 10.7
eMailTrackerPro in Outlook.

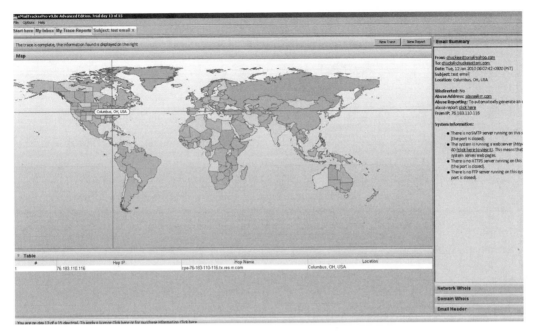

Figure 10.8
eMailTrackerPro trace.

option of getting a subpoena for that service provider so that they can tell you what specific machine/IP address was used to send that e-mail.

It is also important that you not simply rely on the e-mails you see in the e-mail client. Most e-mail clients allow a person to save e-mails to a file. This is usually for the purposes of archiving old e-mail. However, it is entirely possible that a suspect may have e-mails you don't see in his or her e-mail client. Consider Outlook as an example. E-mail in Outlook is stored in files with a .pst extension. If you find such files on the computer, you can open them in Outlook by simply choosing File > Open > Outlook Data file, as shown in Figure 10.9. And at the end of your other personal files in Outlook, you will now see the new folder shown in Figure 10.10. You can see that there is now an entirely new set of personal folders that you can examine. This will include an Inbox, Sent folder, Deleted folder, and any subfolders. It is important to search the hard drive for any .pst files and examine them. A clever perpetrator may keep a separate .pst file that they use for their illicit activities. The example we just viewed is in Outlook, so you will have to do a bit of research on the specific e-mail client that you find on the suspect's computer. Most e-mail clients, including Outlook and Eudora,

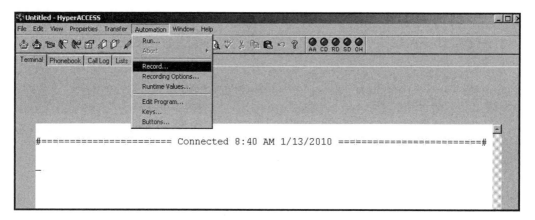

Figure 10.9
Opening a .pst file.

Figure 10.10
Viewing e-mails.

allow for the backup of e-mails to a file, as well as the ability to open and read those files in the client.

You may also need to gather evidence from e-mail servers. A person may delete e-mails from their machine, but in many cases those e-mails are still kept on the e-mail server of the sending or receiving party. The first thing to be aware of is the time-sensitive nature of such evidence. Most companies have a rotation policy wherein e-mails on the server are periodically cleared out. If they did not do this, eventually their e-mail server's hard drive would be full of e-mails.

Obtaining e-mails directly from a server will often mean serving a subpoena on a third party, such as an Internet service provider. In these cases, the first step will be to define the scope of the subpoena. You cannot simply get every e-mail on a server, as most of the e-mail will be unrelated to your case. Not only would this violate those individuals' privacy but it would create a greater workload for you. The real issue with third-party e-mail servers is chain of custody. The best approach is for the investigator (you) to retrieve the e-mails personally and carefully document your steps in retrieving the data. However, this will not always be possible. In cases where you must rely on the third party's staff to retrieve the e-mail, make certain you discuss with them how you want the data to be handled and retrieved, and get an affidavit from them attesting to when and how the e-mails were retrieved and that none were altered during that process. You cannot simply assume that someone else's staff will know how to handle evidence and will do so properly.

Gathering Evidence from Routers

At some point, all Internet communications go through routers; in the case of an attack on an organization's network, that attack had to go through the company's routers. Therefore, it is prudent to consider examining routers for evidence. It is impossible to cover every router model from every manufacturer here, but Cisco routers are the most widely used. You will also find that some other router brands function exactly like a Cisco router. For this reason, we will focus on general principles of gathering data from a Cisco router in this chapter. The first issue is to differentiate between volatile data you want to obtain and non-volatile data. *Volatile data* is data that is not stored permanently and will be lost when you power down the device. In Cisco routers, non-volatile RAM (NVRAM) is the stored configuration of the router. However, the current running configuration is that volatile data is kept in random access memory (RAM).

To retrieve data from RAM (volatile) and NVRAM (non-volatile), you first must establish a connection to the router. The best method is to simply connect a cable to one of the RJ 45 jacks on the router. If direct connection is not possible, then you can remotely access the router. If you are remotely accessing the router make sure you use SSH (Secure Shell); it is encrypted. Since Chapter 7, "Observing, Collecting, Documenting, and Storing Electronic Evidence," we have been emphasizing the need to document what you do. That will be easier in this situation: Just make sure you log the entire session with Hyper Terminal. Hyper Terminal is a popular tool for remotely connecting to a system and is available for many operating systems, including Windows 7. You can get Hyper Terminal at http://www.hilgraeve.com/. There is a free trial version available. Hyper Terminal will allow you to use SSH to secure your connections. When using Hyper Terminal you can choose to record your session by selecting Automation and Record, as shown in Figure 10.11.

Cisco routers have multiple modes, such as login prompt, enable, initial setup, configuration, and interface. The two primary modes are user mode and enable (privilege) mode. To gain access to privilege mode, the password must be known by the analyst. It should be noted that another way hackers attempt to intrude on a system is to try to remotely log in to the router/gateway using a tool like Hyper Terminal. It is always best to configure routers to require a password, and if it is feasible, only allow direct connections, not remote connections.

When you connect to the router you will want to record the time. Recording the time will be critical later when you are cross-referencing data during an incident. You can use the shell command `show clock` to show a clock and record times. There are other router commands you can enter at the command line that will probably help you:

▪ `show version` provides a significant amount of hardware and software information about the router. It will display the platform, operating-system

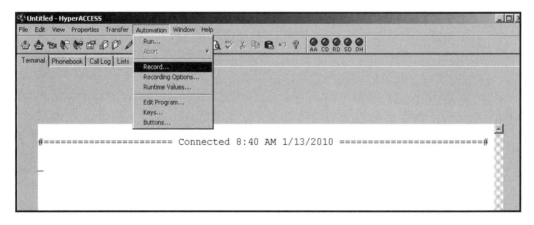

Figure 10.11
Hyper Terminal recording.

version, system image file, any interfaces, how much RAM the router has, and how many network and voice interfaces there are.

- The `show running-config` command will get you the currently executing configuration.

- The `show startup-config` command will get you the system's startup configurations. Differences between `startup-config` and `running-config` can be indicative of a hacker having altered the system.

- The `show ip route` command will show the routing table. Manipulating that routing table is one primary reason hacker's infiltrate routers.

These are just a few of the more important router commands that can give you valuable information. Now, if you are not at all familiar with Cisco routers, this may seem a bit confusing to you. Obviously, if you have no experience at all with routers, it is best to get someone who does have experience to extract the evidence from the router for you. This illustrates two valuable points. The first is that to be a successful computer-crime investigator requires a breadth of skills. You need to be proficient in operating systems, network operations, and routers. You should always be adding to your skill set and expanding your knowledge. The second point is that no matter how much you know, you will encounter areas outside your expertise. This may necessitate bringing in an expert consultant to assist with those issues. The issue of expert consultants is addressed in Chapter 11, "Expert and Expert Reports."

Gathering Evidence from a Cell Phone

In our modern times, cell phones are ubiquitous, and as common as they are, it should be no surprise that cell phones can play a role in some computer crimes. As we discussed in previous chapters, there are even some crimes that are primarily executed via cell phones. Sending pornographic images via cell phone is one such crime. It is often a good idea to secure data from a suspect's cell phone in any criminal investigation. Some of the kinds of data that may be retrieved and examined during a cell-phone forensic investigation include the following:

- Photos

- Videos

- Text messages or SMS messages

- Call times, dialed and received calls, and call durations

- Contact names and phone numbers

Obviously, photos, videos, and text messages could contain evidence of a crime. However, contact information can be valuable as well. We have already seen in the first few chapters of this book that criminals frequently work in concert. A contact list can help you track down other perpetrators.

While it is beyond the scope of this book to deal with the details of every model of cell phone, there are a few general forensic rules to be aware of:

- Always document the cell phone make, model, and any details regarding its condition.

- Photograph the initial screen of the phone.

- The SIM card will be the location of most of what you need to find.

- It is important to note that there are many software packages one can use to get information from a SIM card, such as the following:

  - **Data Doctor.** This product sells for $169. It recovers all inbox and outbox data, recovers all contact data, and boasts an easy-to-use interface. Most importantly, it has a free trial version. It is available from http://www.simrestore.com/.

  - **Sim Card Data Retrieval Utility.** This product is available from http://shareme.com/details/sim-card-data-retrieval-utility.html for $65. It retrieves inbox and sent message data as well as contact data. It runs on various Windows versions but has not yet been tested with Windows 7 as of this writing.

  - **Device Seizure.** This is available from Paraben Software (http://www.paraben.com/) for $1,095. Paraben makes a number of forensics products.

The choice of tools is important. You want to make sure you use a tool that is reliable and that you are comfortable with. But more important than the specific tool you use is the documentation of your process. By now, you may have noted that in all of the chapters since Chapter 7, we have continually reiterated the issue of documentation. That is because it is the most critical element of your forensic analysis, and the area where most mistakes occur.

Gathering Evidence from Firewalls

Any attack that originates from outside the network must traverse the firewall. Usually, an attempt to breach the firewall is precipitated by scanning and port sniffing, and then the attempt will be made to breach security. Most firewalls log activities, and by checking the firewall logs one can gain valuable evidence.

Firewalls usually log events that can be categorized into three broad categories: critical system issues, administrative actions, and network connections. Critical system issues include hardware failures. Administrative actions include adding users, changing permissions, and related tasks. Network-connection logs are literally logs of all successful and unsuccessful connection attempts.

Each of these types of logs can provide valuable information. Obviously, connection attempts will be the prelude to any attack, and in fact may be part of the attack. Administrative actions can also be part of an attack; an intruder will often want to perform administrative tasks either to create a back door whereby he or she can re-enter the system or perhaps to gain access to some resource on the network. And of course a failure of any device could be the result of some computer crime having been perpetrated. All of these items must be searched for in the firewall logs.

Gathering Evidence from Intrusion-Detection Systems

Intrusion-detection systems are applications that monitor either an individual server or a firewall—or the entire network—for signs of an impending attack. For example, an intrusion-detection system will note when someone is conducting port sniffing or packet scanning on the network and alert the network administrator. Of course, not all networks employ an intrusion-detection system, but if the network you are examining does, then you must check that system's logs. Just like firewalls, intrusion-detection systems have logs. Those logs record any events that occur. Any network-security breach will leave signs in the logs of the intrusion-detection system.

Conclusion

You can get information from e-mail clients, routers, cell phones, and any device that can store data. These sources of information can be a treasure trove of evidence and information. However, also be aware that you must document every step in the process. If you use a utility to recover deleted files, you must document what utility you used and exactly what steps you took. Also, don't limit your forensic investigation to computers. You should view routers and cell phones as also containing potentially important evidence. Any device that a perpetrator can use to transmit data, or a victim can be connected to, could potentially contain evidence.

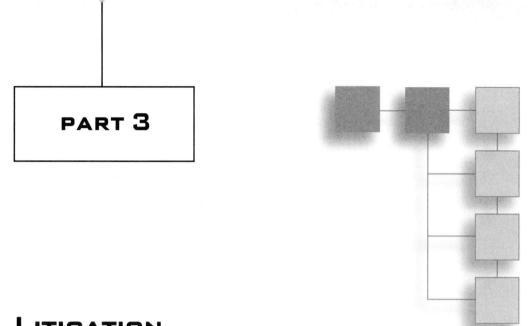

PART 3

LITIGATION

CHAPTER 11

EXPERTS AND EXPERT REPORTS

Introduction

Expert consultants are often a part of both criminal and civil investigations. There are several reasons why you may need an expert to assist you. The first would be a scenario in which you are dealing with some technology you are unfamiliar with. For example, you might be well trained in forensics and skilled with the Windows operating system, but if a case involves Unix or Linux, you might wish to consult with someone who has expertise in those operating systems. Another scenario in which you might want assistance from an outside expert is when a case has specific technical complexities that are beyond your skill level. As we stated in an earlier chapter, don't let your ego stop you from asking for help. Finally, it is common practice to get an outside expert to testify at any trial. This is common in both civil and criminal cases.

In this chapter, we will examine the use of outside experts either as consultants or as testifying witnesses. We will look at how you select such individuals and how to work with them. It is critical, however, that before you bring in outside expertise, you must get approval from your supervisors. This is particularly important if you are in law enforcement.

Selecting an Expert

Sometimes, a company or even a law-enforcement agency may need an outside consultant or an expert for testimony at a trial. It is important to know what to look for in such a person; selecting the wrong consultant or expert can ruin a case. There are a few items you should always look for in an expert:

- Clean background check

- Well trained

- Experienced

- No conflicts of interest

We will discuss the facets of each of these in the rest of this chapter. If you are seeking a testifying expert, then it is also important that the individual have some notoriety in the industry. This can come from published academic papers, published books, serving on standards-setting committees, or other activities that clearly indicate a high level of expertise in the industry. Remember that the opposing side in any trial, be it criminal or civil, will try to attack your expert witness's credibility. It is important that the expert's professional qualifications be such that a jury will clearly accept his or her expertise.

Clean Background Check

It is absolutely critical that anyone working with computer-crime investigations have a thorough background check. That may seem to be obvious, but there are plenty of companies that don't do any background checks on their employees. When you are dealing with actual law-enforcement officials, this point is already covered; those individuals already have had background investigations or they would not be in law enforcement. However, when dealing with civilian experts or consultants, it is critical that you run a background check. So what issues would disqualify an individual from being an expert? Of course, you cannot have a consultant or expert who has a past issue with computer-security violations or a felony conviction. However, particularly with experts who will serve as testifying expert witnesses at trial, even minor misdemeanor issues should be a concern. It is probably best to make sure that any civilian consultant passes the same background check given to law enforcement and is held to the same standard.

You may think that anyone working in information security has had a background check. Unfortunately, this is not always the case. Sometimes, companies either do no background check or only a cursory one. One of the authors of this book encountered an Internet service provider whose technical-support manager had twice been in federal prison, and on both occasions identity theft was one of his offenses. This simply is not acceptable for anyone working with computer security. You cannot simply assume that someone in a professional position necessarily has a clean background; you must make sure of it.

Well Trained

Obviously, in order to be an expert in any field, one must be well trained and have adequate experience. But what do we mean by well trained? Normally, this can be a combination of academic degrees along with specific industry training/ certifications, and possibly corporate or organizational training. Depending on your needs, one may be more important than the other.

Academic Training and Programs

If one is going to serve as a testifying expert, it is best to have a graduate degree. In many cases, expert testimony comes from those with a doctorate degree, but many people with a master's degree and several years of experience have served as expert witnesses. For a consultant, you want at least a bachelor's degree in some related field such as computer science, computer information systems, computer engineering, or a related field. These academic programs ensure that the individual has a thorough baseline understanding of computer systems, operating systems, networks, programming, and related topics. How much formal education is needed will vary depending on the individual situation and that person's other qualifications. For example, a person with a bachelor's degree but multiple industry certifications and 10 years of experience might be just as qualified as someone with a master's degree and only two years of experience. Ultimately, it is a judgment call on your part, but you should require some formal education. This is not a field where being self taught is preferred.

The nature of the academic training is also important. Obviously, you won't always be able to find an expert with a doctorate from a prestigious institution such as Harvard, Princeton, or MIT. However, you do need to make certain the institution the expert's degrees are from is regionally accredited. This may sound like an unnecessary statement, but degree fraud is a significant problem. People do go to diploma mills and unaccredited, substandard schools just to get some title such as "Dr." While most diploma mills are online, this does not mean that online education is inadequate, merely that you need to check to ensure any program has regional accreditation. In our modern times, most universities offer some programs online, and entire degrees from legitimate universities can be accomplished online.

Academic Credibility

Academic standing may not be critical if what you are seeking is just a consultant to assist with investigation. In such cases, their technical skill is what is most important. However, if you are seeking an expert witness to testify at a trial, their credibility in the academic and scientific community is critical. Juries will often weigh the credentials of an expert when evaluating his or her testimony. It is also frequently the case that both sides in a trial have retained experts to support their viewpoint. In those cases, it may be difficult for a jury to decide which expert to believe. Aside from their personality and the delivery of their testimony, the experts' credentials may be the only factor the jury has to use in deciding which expert to believe. How do you know if a particular individual has that credibility? To a layperson, simply having an advanced degree would seem to be evidence enough, but that is not the case. One needs to have contributed meaningfully to that particular academic discipline. That can mean any number of things. It is often evidenced by particular awards such as endowed chairs at universities. It can be evidenced by the publication of both research papers and books.

It is usually a good idea to do an amazon.com search on any potential expert to find books they may have authored or co-authored. Of course, one can certainly be an expert in one's field and have simply never taken the time to write a book; a lack of published work does not mean one doesn't have expertise. It does not even mean one has not published important research. Another tool you can use is the Google Scholar search. This will give you research papers that person may have published, as well as papers that have referenced that person's work. A good indicator of expertise is how often other experts refer to someone's work. If you find that no other researchers reference a person's work, this is a strong sign that the person's work is not considered credible or noteworthy by his or her professional peers. However, even if an expert has not published books or research papers, he or she may still be a qualified expert.

As with all the various aspects we recommend you examine, academic standing is simply one attribute. Remember, we are looking at the total background of the expert. Obviously, a perfect expert witness would be one with a doctorate degree, multiple certifications, multiple publications, at least 10 years of practical experience, numerous awards, and a background in teaching. However, you will most often find experts with some combination of these attributes, but not all of them. It is also worth pointing out that normally the more qualified the expert is, the higher rate he or she charges.

Certifications

Industry certifications are a significant part of the computer industry. Microsoft Certified Software Engineers, Red Hat Certified Engineers, Certified Java Programmers—all are part of the IT profession. And the same is true with the security profession. There are a number of certifications relevant to IT security and forensics that might be of interest to you when selecting a consultant or expert witness. However, people's attitudes toward certifications vary a great deal. Some people will tell you that they would never hire a person who was not certified; other people may claim certifications are worthless. This stems from a lack of understanding of what a certification is. Passing a certification test means that the individual has achieved the minimum level of competency in the area that exam tests, nothing more and nothing less. To use an analogy, having an M.D. does not make the person a brilliant surgeon; it simply means the person met the minimal requirements to be a physician. So never take certifications by themselves as indications of high skill level. But certifications can indicate a minimum skill level. Of course, the same can be said of academic degrees. The ideal situation is when certifications are coupled with degrees and experience; together, they make a powerful statement about the person's qualifications. However, since certifications play an important role in the computer industry, it is important that you understand the major certifications, what they mean, and which ones are more accepted within the computer community itself. Let's look at the most prominent relevant certifications.

Security+

This certification is administered by the Computer Technology Industry Association (CompTIA), famous for A+, Network +, and Linux + certifications. The test itself covers security concepts. It is not a hands-on test, but rather a test of general security knowledge. It is also not a computer-forensics test, but rather a computer-security test. By itself, this certification may not be adequate training because it only tests the person's knowledge of security concepts. It does not test knowledge of general networking, penetration testing, or other concepts related to security. However, when coupled with other certifications, experience, or academic degrees, it can clearly show that the holder has a solid basic understanding of security, including common attacks, countermeasures, policies, and procedures. In general, this is a good certification to indicate breadth of security knowledge, but should be coupled with some other indications of skill and training.

While Security+ is the CompTIA certification most relevant to computer crime and investigations, there are a few other CompTIA certifications that have some relevance:

- **A+.** This is a general PC technician test. It shows the holder has a general working knowledge of PC hardware, operating systems, and networking.

- **Network+.** This is a general network-administration test. It shows the holder has a good working knowledge of computer networks at a level that would allow him or her to function as a network administrator.

- **Linux+.** This test covers a broad range of Linux operating-system topics including administration of a Linux system. It shows that the holder has a good working knowledge of Linux.

CIW Security Analyst

This exam is quite similar in content to the Security+ exam; it asks general security-knowledge questions. Its content is a bit more broad and inclusive than that of Security+, and it does not delve into hands-on security knowledge. However, it has one very significant advantage over Security+: Before you can take this exam, you must first pass the CIW Security Professional exam and the CIW Foundations exam, as well as one of the following:

- Microsoft Certified Systems Administrator (MCSA)

- Microsoft Certified Systems Engineer (MCSE)

- Certified Novell Engineer (CNE)

- Cisco Certified Network Professional (CCNP)

- Cisco Certified Network Associate (CCNA)

- Cisco Certified Internetwork Expert (CCIE)

- Linux Professional Institute (LPI) Level 2

This means that in addition to basic security knowledge, the holder of this certification has had at least two other CIW certifications as well as at least one major network certification. This combination of certifications is a likely indicator of competence in network security. You can find out more about this exam at http://www.ciwcertified.com/.

MCSE Security Specialization

Microsoft Certified Systems Engineer (MCSE) is the premier Microsoft certification. It consists of seven separate tests covering networking and Microsoft operating systems. Microsoft Windows is a very widely used operating system, and Microsoft-based networks abound. It will not be uncommon for computer crimes you will investigate to, at some point, involve a Microsoft system. Therefore, knowledge of Microsoft will likely be very useful. Microsoft has added a specialized track within the MCSE specifically for those people interested in security. In addition to the basic fundamentals of the MCSE, the security specialization requires three security-specific certification tests. That means that the individual who has the MCSE with the security specialization has passed seven tests about Microsoft technologies, three of which are specific to securing those systems.

MCSE security, or frankly any certification in Microsoft systems, can be quite useful in computer-crime investigations. Remember: A thorough knowledge of the systems used by the victim or the perpetrator can be crucial in investigating computer crime. There are some other Microsoft certifications that are also of value:

- **Microsoft Master Certifications.** The Microsoft Master series is a new addition to the repertoire of Microsoft certifications. These certifications require the holder to first have an existing certification, like MCSE, and anywhere from two to five years of hands-on experience, as well as to pass one or more additional tests. The addition of hands-on experience requirements is becoming more common in IT certifications in general. The CISSP and CEH, which we will discuss in a moment, have always had a hands-on experience component.

- **Microsoft Certified Systems Administrator.** This certification is awarded after passing four certification tests covering various aspects of Microsoft networks. It demonstrates a solid working knowledge of Microsoft network administration.

- **Microsoft Certified Systems Engineer.** This certification is awarded after passing seven certification tests covering various aspects of Microsoft networks. It demonstrates a deep understanding of Microsoft networks.

- **Microsoft Certified Technology Specialist.** This certification requires one or two tests that cover a specific Microsoft technology and demonstrates a mastery of that specific technology.

CISSP

The Certified Information Systems Security Professional designation is the one of the most widely recognized and prized computer-security certifications. This designation is simply the most sought-after security certification. The reason is the rigorous standards involved. The requirements are as follows:

- Pass a grueling exam that takes several hours.

- Have at least four years of security experience or three years of experience and a bachelor's degree. This experience must be certified by either another CISSP or by an officer in your corporation. This may be the most important part of this certification. One must have real-world experience as well as pass the test.

- After passing the test, the CISSP holder must meet certain continuing-education requirements every 36 months in order to retain his or her certification. This is also an element of the CISSP that differentiates it from other certification exams. It ensures that the person holding the CISSP is keeping his or her knowledge current.

- A certain percentage of those who pass the exam are randomly selected for an audit and investigation of their background. This aspect alone makes the CISSP valuable. It ensures that CISSP holders have legitimate experience.

With the CISSP, the test itself is not what makes the certification meaningful. It is the requirement for verifiable work experience as well as ongoing continuing education that makes it stand out. Due to those additional elements, the CISSP should definitely be considered a valuable credential in a computer-security expert or consultant.

Certified Ethical Hacker

This particular certification has not gained as much recognition in the IT industry as some of the others. However, it is an excellent certification for computer-crime investigations. This particular certification covers methods for compromising system security and gaining access to those systems. The test literally covers hacking skills. People holding this certification have proven they have the requisite skills needed to compromise the security of a system. In other words, they know hacking as well as most computer criminals. This test also requires the person to have two years of verifiable security experience prior to taking the exam or to have attended an EC Council–sponsored training course. This certification would clearly indicate the holder has a very good understanding of hacking techniques. This could be an invaluable skill for computer-crime investigations.

Forensic Certifications

Just as there are a number of security certifications, there are also a number of computer-forensic certifications available, including the following:

- **The Cyber Security Institute's Cyber Security Forensic Analyst (CSFA).** This certification is very intriguing, as they require a background check before allowing you to take the test. This fact makes this certification quite valuable. This test also requires the test taker to actually conduct forensics steps within a time frame; it is not simply a written multiple-choice test, as are most IT certification tests.

- **SANS Institute GIAC Certified Forensics Analyst.** This certification involves 150 questions that must be completed within four hours. The certification must be renewed every four years to ensure the certificate holder has kept current.

- **The International Society of Forensic Examiners Certified Computer Examiner.** This certification requires that the test taker either attend their training session or be able to show a minimum of 18 months of verifiable forensic work experience.

- **Computer Hacking Forensic Investigator.** This test was created by the same people who created the Certified Ethical Hacker exam. Like the Certified Ethical Hacker test, one must either attend the EC Council's training course or show real-world experience in the field.

It should be noted that certification in the field of computer forensics is relatively new. You will probably encounter qualified professionals who don't hold one of these certifications. That should not necessarily dissuade you from using their expertise. Remember, certifications are just one element of an expert's qualifications. Just as such a certification by itself is not adequate evidence of expertise, the absence of a particular certification is not evidence of a lack of expertise.

Experience

Training and education are important, but frankly, experience is king. It is certainly valuable to have obtained training, but it is just as important to have actual experience. When you are seeking a computer-crime expert or consultant, you need someone who has real-world, hands-on experience. Now, you may or may not need someone who has investigated computer crimes. That may sound like an odd statement, and obviously you would prefer someone with experience investigating computer crimes. However, someone with a strong understanding of investigation and forensics and who has extensive experience in computer systems and networks can be a useful asset; that knowledge of operating systems and networks can be as important, if not more important, than investigative experience. Of course, the ideal candidate will have both skill sets. But in no case should you use someone who has only academic training and has never functioned as a network administrator, security administrator, or network consultant, or in a related job.

The obvious counter argument to this is that for everything there must be a first time. Even the most experienced professional had to have his or her first investigation. Ideally, however, that first investigation was assisting someone with more experience. You certainly do not want your case to be someone's first real-world attempt. If you are going to utilize an expert, it is important that that person have experience, not just extensive training. And the more experience he or she has, the better.

No Conflicts of Interest

It is absolutely critical that your expert have no conflicts of interest. When law firms are considering experts to use in a case, one of the first things they check for is a conflict of interest. This means the expert witness should have no prior business or personal relationship with any of the principal parties in the case. In civil litigation, this means the expert should have no prior relationship with the plaintiff or the defendant. In a criminal case, it usually just means the defendant, since the plaintiff is the state. What exactly constitutes a prior relationship? In most cases, this means no substantive contact—that the two parties do not know each other on a personal level or have business contact. Some attorneys are even more strict and require that the expert has never even met the involved parties and has no direct communication with them outside of courtrooms and depositions. Remember that, for better or worse, our legal system is adversarial. If there is any way the opposing counsel can construe your expert as being biased, they will do so. For this reason, it is best to avoid even the appearance of any relationship with any relevant parties.

Conflict of interest goes beyond direct relationships between the parties. It literally means that the expert has some interest in the outcome of the case. Ideally, an expert's only interest should be in the truth. He or she should have no personal motive in seeing the case decided in favor of one party or the other. For example, an expert witness for the prosecution in a case involving child pornography might be considered to have a conflict of interest if someone close to him or her has been a victim of child pornography. Or an expert for the defense might be considered to have a conflict of interest if that expert is a member of the same fraternity, church, or social group as the defendant. Remember: The appearance of a conflict of interest can be enough to change the outcome of a trial. You must therefore carefully screen potential expert witnesses for conflicts of interest.

Personality Issues in an Expert

We have discussed the technical specifics to look for in an expert, but what about issues not found on a resumé that might make a good (or bad) expert? These issues are important in any expert, but are most important in a testifying expert witness. First and foremost, can the expert teach? You are looking for an expert to analyze some evidence and explain it to you, other law-enforcement officers, and perhaps a jury. It is not enough that your consultant be an expert in the field, he or she must be able to effectively explain what his or her findings mean to laypeople. You want to avoid experts who are unable to communicate their ideas to others. Related to that is their ability to speak in front of groups. If he or she is to testify in court, it is critical that the expert be comfortable speaking to groups. This is why lawyers often use professors as expert witnesses; they are comfortable teaching and speaking in front of groups.

Next, you want to find someone who will keep calm. If this becomes a testifying situation or a deposition situation, the opposing attorney will try to make your expert feel uncomfortable. The opposing counsel may try to turn your expert's words on him or her, or ask questions designed to rattle the expert. It is also not uncommon for the opposing attorney to question the credibility of your expert. If your expert is easily irritated, gets defensive, or becomes agitated, this can severely damage your case.

In addition to traits you are looking for in an expert, there are traits you want to avoid. Obviously, you want to avoid any character traits that are in opposition to the desired traits we have discussed. You don't want an expert who is a poor communicator, overly shy, or arrogant. Arrogance is an issue that comes up from time to time. Clearly, someone with a high degree of expertise is proud of his or her accomplishments and confident in his or her professional skills, and that is a desired trait. An expert who lacks confidence, particularly when testifying, is a liability. However, arrogance can also be a liability for two reasons. The most obvious reason is that if one is perceived as arrogant by a jury, they may be less likely to accept that expert's opinions. But beyond that, arrogance can blind one to pertinent facts. An arrogant person may have difficulty taking suggestions from others or admitting when he or she is wrong. So for these reasons you want to avoid using experts who are arrogant.

Another important trait to avoid is the professional witness. Many experts do testify frequently, and that is acceptable, but is testifying the person's sole or primary income? An opposing attorney will portray that expert as an "opinion for hire" and imply that the expert will say anything for a fee, whether that is accurate or not. Normally, you want an expert who has some other endeavors such as teaching, a consulting practice, research, or writing, and who simply spends part of his or her time as an expert witness. This not only defeats the allegation that he or she is a witness for hire, but it makes it more likely that he or she is up to date on the latest trends in his or her field. Being active in a given field is crucial for keeping up on the developments in that subject.

Another issue to be aware of with experts is their history of testimony and expert reports. Have they previously testified to or made a public opinion that could reasonably be construed as contrary to the opinion they will be taking for you? For example, if an expert previously wrote an article stating that online sting operations to catch pedophiles are inherently unreliable, you cannot now use that person to testify for you in support of evidence gathered in an online sting. Now, this may seem obvious, and you may think that no expert would want to testify contrary to an opinion he or she previously espoused. However, it is an unfortunate fact that there are a few experts who indeed will say anything for a fee. So you (or the attorney handling the case) need to expressly inquire about this issue. It is important to note that the number of experts willing to say things they don't believe for a fee is far lower than some elements in the public believe. This is particularly true in technical subjects, where the elements of the case are relatively concrete and less open to interpretation. The majority of experts will simply turn down a case if they don't agree with the conclusions that the client (in this case, you) want them to support.

Related to past public opinions and testimony is the issue of honesty. Contrary to what you may have seen on television and movies, the vast majority of experts will not prevaricate in testimony or in their reports. Obviously, some issues are open to interpretation, even in technical disciplines. And some experts are more willing than others to make a more creative interpretation of the evidence. However, stating an outright falsehood, either through intentional lying or just being in error on the facts, is usually the end of an expert witness's ability to function in court cases.

Hiring and Paying Experts

Depending on the qualifications and the field the expert is in, expert consultants often charge from $150 to $300 per hour, and some renowned experts charge even more. So it is not an inexpensive proposition to have an expert witness work on your case. Usually, the attorney handling the case will determine if an expert witness is required, and if so will hire one.

Normally, experts bill for their time on a monthly basis and are paid by the client who hired them. It is not at all unusual to establish a budget with the expert so that costs are predictable and can be budgeted for.

There are organizations that specialize in screening experts and matching them with law firms. The National Expert Witness Network (http://www.newnexperts. com/) and The Round Table Group (http://www.roundtablegroup.com/) are two such organizations. These groups screen expert witnesses. They have often worked with that expert before and know his or her capabilities. However, these groups usually charge an hourly fee that is added onto the expert's own hourly rate.

There are also Web sites where experts list their profiles for a fee. These sites allow people to search the profiles, often at no charge. This is certainly a more affordable route, although these Web sites tend not to verify anything in the expert's profile, nor do they assist in finding the right expert. They simply list profiles that you search; you are then responsible for verifying the expert's background. Such Web sites include Juris Pro (http://www.jurispro.com/) and Expert Witness (http://www.expertwitness.com/).

Volunteer Experts

It sometimes happens that a civilian expert might volunteer to assist with a law-enforcement agency. This might sound like an oddity to some readers and a boon to others. Some people immediately assume anyone volunteering to help law enforcement must be a frustrated would-be officer and reject them without seriously considering their offer. Others might feel like free help is a wonderful thing, given the strained budgets of most law-enforcement agencies, and immediately embrace such an offer without clearly considering it. Either extreme view is in error. Let's examine the criteria you should consider in evaluating an offer of volunteer help.

First, you should not reject such an offer out of hand. While law-enforcement agencies do get offers of help from psychics, people claiming to have information, and frustrated would-be officers, this is less likely to be the case with a computer-forensics expert. If this person is actually an expert, it is likely that he or she has a professional occupation, a high level of education, and is mentally stable. Obviously, you would need to check his or her background before accepting his or her offer. Not only do you want to verify the person's expertise, you want ensure that he or she doesn't have a criminal past and thus an ulterior motive for working with police. Some readers might be wondering why someone with valuable expertise might volunteer his or her time. There are many valid reasons, some altruistic and some less so.

Altruistic reasons would include a simple desire to be an asset to his or her community. Many people feel a duty to aid their community in whatever way they are best suited. An expert in computer science may feel that assisting law enforcement with investigating computer crimes is the best way he or she can give back to the community. Another reason might frankly be guilt. A computer expert who has been very financially successful might feel a certain amount of guilt over his or her financial success, and want to assuage that guilt by volunteering. It is also possible that the computer expert might find working with law enforcement to be more glamorous than his or her usual projects. That is an acceptable reason to volunteer, provided it is within reason.

There are also less altruistic, but still valid reasons an expert might volunteer with law enforcement. If one routinely works as a paid expert witness, any work with law enforcement can improve one's credentials and help to land new paying expert-witness projects. Again this is a valid reason, provided it is within certain limits. For example, if the expert wants to mention on his or her curriculum vitae "volunteers with X law-enforcement agency on computer-crime cases," that is reasonable. If he or she wants to give specifics about what cases, details, or procedures, or in any way act in a manner that could reasonably be deemed as exploiting the law-enforcement agency for marketing purposes, then that expert's offer to volunteer should be rejected.

If an expert is willing to volunteer with a law-enforcement agency, you have verified his or her expertise, and his or her background check is clear, the only issue left is his or her motivation. Provided it is a reasonable motivation, then it is often a good idea to accept his or her offer. Most-law enforcement agencies are under budgeted and most law-enforcement agents are overworked. Having even occasional assistance with a case can be a benefit.

Expert Reports

Whether you are using an expert as a consultant or as a testifying witness, at some point that expert will need to provide a report of his or her findings. Now, an informal report for internal use may seem to be less rigorous, but it is usually best to prepare any report as if it were going to be used in court proceedings. For that reason, we will examine the requirements of an expert report for court.

Expert reports generally start with the expert's qualifications. This should be a complete curriculum vitae detailing education, work history, and publications. Particular attention should be paid to elements of the expert's history that are directly related to the case at hand. Then the report should move on to the actual topic at hand.

An expert report is a very thorough document. It must first detail exactly what analysis was used. How did the expert conduct his or her examination and analysis? In the case of computer forensics, the expert report should detail what tools the expert used, what the results were, and the conditions of the tests conducted.

Also, any claim an expert makes in a report should be supported by extrinsic reputable sources. This is sometimes overlooked by experts because they themselves are sources that are used, or because the claim being made seems obvious to them. For example, if an expert report needs to detail how domain name service works to describe a DNS poisoning attack, then there should be references to recognized authoritative works regarding the details of domain name service. The reason for this is that at trial, a creative attorney can often extract nontraditional meanings from even commonly understood terms. And a change in the meaning of a word changes the entire case. In fact, in patent-infringement cases, one of the early steps is called a Markman hearing, and it is expressly for defining terms that might be in dispute between the two parties. One of the authors of this book has personally seen simple terms like *network* and *process* argued vehemently in cases. If your expert's only support for his chosen definition is his own opinion, that is not as strong as coupling his opinion with one or more widely recognized resources. This leads to another element an expert report must have: definitions of terms. Any term that is technical or scientific in nature and for which there is any possibility of the opposing attorneys/experts disagreeing with or misinterpreting should be defined in the expert report.

The next issue with an expert report is its completeness. The report must cover every item the expert wishes to opine on, and in detail. Nothing can be assumed. In some jurisdictions, if an item is not in the expert report, then the expert is not allowed to discuss it during testimony. Whether or not that is the case in your jurisdiction, it is imperative that the expert report that is submitted be very thorough and complete. And of course, it must be error free. Even the smallest error can give opposing counsel an opportunity to impugn the accuracy of the entire report and the expert's entire testimony. This is a document that should be carefully proofread by the expert and by the attorney retaining the expert.

As you can see, an expert report can quickly become a rather long document. Even small cases often involve expert reports that are in excess of 30 pages. In more complex cases, expert reports that are 100 or more pages long are not unusual. However, this is not meant to indicate that one should be unnecessarily verbose in a report. Quite the contrary. Be as concise and clear as possible. However, the necessity of explaining all the testing and analysis done and defining terms is likely to increase the size of the report.

Conclusion

In this chapter, we looked at the qualifications of an expert consultant or witness. You should now have a good idea of what to seek in any expert: the combination of experience, training, and academic credentials that make up a credible expert. It is also important that your expert witness be likable to a jury, be able to clearly communicate ideas, and not have the image of a "testimony for hire." We also examined the essentials of an expert report. With the information in this chapter, you should be able to select an appropriate expert should you require one. You also know what to look for, and what to look out for, in any expert who might want to volunteer with your law-enforcement agency.

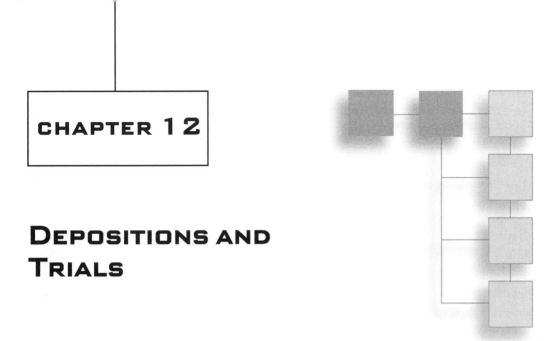

CHAPTER 12

DEPOSITIONS AND TRIALS

Introduction

In the preceding chapters, we have examined the various laws, types of crimes, and investigative methods. By this point, you should have a very solid understanding of computer crime, related laws, and the basics of conducting a computer-forensic investigation. In Chapter 11, "Experts and Expert Reports," we gave you an overview of how to select an expert consultant. In this chapter, we will explore what happens after the investigation, when a matter proceeds to trial. Now, both sides have an opportunity to examine the other side's evidence, prepare for trial, and ultimately conduct a trial. Just as a misstep during the investigation can irrevocably damage your case, so too can a misstep during the pretrial and trial phases. Obviously, an attorney will be assisting you in preparing for trial and you should definitely heed his or her advice. This chapter will provide some general advice for the computer expert or law-enforcement officer who may not have much experience in this area.

Depositions

Depositions are an integral part of our court system. A *deposition* is essentially sworn testimony taken before trial. Opposing counsel will ask you questions, which you will answer. Your own attorney will be present to advise you. The goal of a deposition is to gain information before a trial. Depositions are not frequently part of criminal proceedings, but are a standard part of civil litigation. An expert witness in a computer-related civil case can certainly expect to be deposed prior to the trial.

What Is a Deposition?

Using a strict legal definition, a deposition is a witness's out-of-court testimony that is reduced to writing for later use in court or for discovery purposes. A deposition is a part of the discovery process in which litigants gather information in preparation for trial. Some jurisdictions recognize an affidavit as a form of deposition; however, the norm is that a deposition is done in person via a formal interrogation by opposing counsel. The routine practice of obtaining the oral evidence of a witness before trial is foreign to common-law jurisdictions such as England, Australia, and New Zealand. Having the right to pose oral questions to opposing parties in litigation before trial developed in Canada and the United States in the 19th century.

Federal courts of the United States describe the procedure for taking depositions in Rule 30 of the Federal Rules of Civil Procedure. After we examine the nature of a deposition, we will look at the exact language of Rule 30.

If the party being deposed is actually a party to the case, either plaintiff, defendant, or witness, then often, simply a written notice of the deposition can be given to the person or his or her attorney. However, if the party to be deposed is not an actual party to the case, then a subpoena will probably be required to compel him or her to deposition. If you are the party being deposed, you should absolutely consult with your attorney before the deposition and have that attorney present during depositions.

Deposition testimony is taken verbally, with an attorney asking questions and the person being deposed (referred to as the deponent) answering them out loud. The proceedings are usually recorded by a court reporter. In the past few years, videotaping of depositions has become quite common. Deposition testimony is taken under oath, which makes statements in a deposition equivalent to statements taken during court testimony. This also means the laws regarding perjury apply to a deposition as well as court testimony. Usually, the court reporter and the deponent will sign affidavits attesting to the accuracy of the subsequent printed transcript.

Rule 30

First let's take a look at exactly what Rule 30 says, and then we can examine the implications. So let's begin with the actual text of Rule 30.

(a) When a Deposition May Be Taken.

(1) Without Leave. A party may, by oral questions, depose any person, including a party, without leave of court except as provided in Rule 30(a)(2). The deponent's attendance may be compelled by subpoena under Rule 45.

(2) With Leave. A party must obtain leave of court, and the court must grant leave to the extent consistent with Rule 26(b)(2):

(A) if the parties have not stipulated to the deposition and:

(i) the deposition would result in more than 10 depositions being taken under this rule or Rule 31 by the plaintiffs, or by the defendants, or by the third-party defendants;

(ii) the deponent has already been deposed in the case; or

(iii) the party seeks to take the deposition before the time specified in Rule 26(d), unless the party certifies in the notice, with supporting facts, that the deponent is expected to leave the United States and be unavailable for examination in this country after that time; or

(B) if the deponent is confined in prison.

(b) Notice of the Deposition; Other Formal Requirements.

(1) Notice in General. A party who wants to depose a person by oral questions must give reasonable written notice to every other party. The notice must state the time and place of the deposition and, if known, the deponent's name and address. If the name is unknown, the notice must provide a general description sufficient to identify the person or the particular class or group to which the person belongs.

(2) Producing Documents. If a subpoena duces tecum is to be served on the deponent, the materials designated for production, as set out in the subpoena, must be listed in the notice or in an attachment. The notice

to a party deponent may be accompanied by a request under Rule 34 to produce documents and tangible things at the deposition.

(3) Method of Recording.

(A) Method Stated in the Notice. The party who notices the deposition must state in the notice the method for recording the testimony. Unless the court orders otherwise, testimony may be recorded by audio, audiovisual, or stenographic means. The noticing party bears the recording costs. Any party may arrange to transcribe a deposition.

(B) Additional Method. With prior notice to the deponent and other parties, any party may designate another method for recording the testimony in addition to that specified in the original notice. That party bears the expense of the additional record or transcript unless the court orders otherwise.

(4) By Remote Means. The parties may stipulate—or the court may on motion order—that a deposition be taken by telephone or other remote means. For the purpose of this rule and Rules 28(a), 37(a)(2), and 37(b)(1), the deposition takes place where the deponent answers the questions.

(5) Officer's Duties.

(A) Before the Deposition. Unless the parties stipulate otherwise, a deposition must be conducted before an officer appointed or designated under Rule 28. The officer must begin the deposition with an on-the-record statement that includes:

 (i) the officer's name and business address;

 (ii) the date, time, and place of the deposition;

(iii) the deponent's name;

(iv) the officer's administration of the oath or affirmation to the deponent; and

 (v) the identity of all persons present.

(B) Conducting the Deposition; Avoiding Distortion. If the deposition is recorded nonstenographically, the officer must repeat the items in Rule 30(b)(5)(A)(i)-(iii) at the beginning of each unit of the recording medium. The deponent's and attorneys' appearance or demeanor must not be distorted through recording techniques.

(C) After the Deposition. At the end of a deposition, the officer must state on the record that the deposition is complete and must set out any stipulations made by the attorneys about custody of the transcript or recording and of the exhibits, or about any other pertinent matters.

(6) Notice or Subpoena Directed to an Organization. In its notice or subpoena, a party may name as the deponent a public or private corporation, a partnership, an association, a governmental agency, or other entity and must describe with reasonable particularity the matters for examination. The named organization must then designate one or more officers, directors, or managing agents, or designate other persons who consent to testify on its behalf; and it may set out the matters on which each person designated will testify. A subpoena must advise a nonparty organization of its duty to make this designation. The persons designated must testify about information known or reasonably available to the organization. This paragraph (6) does not preclude a deposition by any other procedure allowed by these rules.

(c) Examination and Cross-Examination; Record of the Examination; Objections; Written Questions.

(1) Examination and Cross-Examination. The examination and cross-examination of a deponent proceed as they would at trial under the Federal Rules of Evidence, except Rules 103 and 615. After putting the deponent under oath or affirmation, the officer must record the testimony by the method designated under Rule 30(b)(3)(A). The testimony must be recorded by the officer personally or by a person acting in the presence and under the direction of the officer.

(2) Objections. An objection at the time of the examination—whether to evidence, to a party's conduct, to the officer's qualifications, to the manner of taking the deposition, or to any other aspect of the

deposition—must be noted on the record, but the examination still proceeds; the testimony is taken subject to any objection. An objection must be stated concisely in a nonargumentative and nonsuggestive manner. A person may instruct a deponent not to answer only when necessary to preserve a privilege, to enforce a limitation ordered by the court, or to present a motion under Rule 30(d)(3).

(3) Participating Through Written Questions. Instead of participating in the oral examination, a party may serve written questions in a sealed envelope on the party noticing the deposition, who must deliver them to the officer. The officer must ask the deponent those questions and record the answers verbatim.

(d) Duration; Sanction; Motion to Terminate or Limit.

(1) Duration. Unless otherwise stipulated or ordered by the court, a deposition is limited to one day of seven hours. The court must allow additional time consistent with Rule 26(b)(2) if needed to fairly examine the deponent or if the deponent, another person, or any other circumstance impedes or delays the examination.

(2) Sanction. The court may impose an appropriate sanction—including the reasonable expenses and attorney's fees incurred by any party—on a person who impedes, delays, or frustrates the fair examination of the deponent.

(3) Motion to Terminate or Limit.

(A) Grounds. At any time during a deposition, the deponent or a party may move to terminate or limit it on the ground that it is being conducted in bad faith or in a manner that unreasonably annoys, embarrasses, or oppresses the deponent or party. The motion may be filed in the court where the action is pending or the deposition is being taken. If the objecting deponent or party so demands, the deposition must be suspended for the time necessary to obtain an order.

(B) Order. The court may order that the deposition be terminated or may limit its scope and manner as provided in Rule 26(c). If terminated, the deposition may be resumed only by order of the court where the action is pending.

(C) Award of Expenses. Rule 37(a)(5) applies to the award of expenses.

(e) Review by theWitness; Changes.

(1) Review; Statement of Changes. On request by the deponent or a party before the deposition is completed, the deponent must be allowed 30 days after being notified by the officer that the transcript or recording is available in which:

(A) to review the transcript or recording; and

(B) if there are changes in form or substance, to sign a statement listing the changes and the reasons for making them.

(2) Changes Indicated in the Officer's Certificate. The officer must note in the certificate prescribed by Rule 30(f)(1) whether a review was requested and, if so, must attach any changes the deponent makes during the 30-day period.

(f) Certification and Delivery; Exhibits; Copies of the Transcript or Recording; Filing.

(1) Certification and Delivery. The officer must certify in writing that the witness was duly sworn and that the deposition accurately records the witness's testimony. The certificate must accompany the record of the deposition. Unless the court orders otherwise, the officer must seal the deposition in an envelope or package bearing the title of the action and marked "Deposition of [witness's name]" and must promptly send it to the attorney who arranged for the transcript or recording. The attorney must store it under conditions that will protect it against loss, destruction, tampering, or deterioration.

(2) Documents and Tangible Things.

(A) Originals and Copies. Documents and tangible things produced for inspection during a deposition must, on a party's request, be marked for identification and attached to the deposition. Any party may inspect and copy them. But if the person who produced them wants to keep the originals, the person may:

(i) offer copies to be marked, attached to the deposition, and then used as originals—after giving all parties a fair opportunity to verify the copies by comparing them with the originals; or

(ii) give all parties a fair opportunity to inspect and copy the originals after they are marked—in which event the originals may be used as if attached to the deposition.

(B) Order Regarding the Originals. Any party may move for an order that the originals be attached to the deposition pending final disposition of the case.

(3) Copies of the Transcript or Recording. Unless otherwise stipulated or ordered by the court, the officer must retain the stenographic notes of a deposition taken stenographically or a copy of the recording of a deposition taken by another method. When paid reasonable charges, the officer must furnish a copy of the transcript or recording to any party or the deponent.

(4) Notice of Filing. A party who files the deposition must promptly notify all other parties of the filing.

(g) Failure to Attend a Deposition or Serve a Subpoena; Expenses. A party who, expecting a deposition to be taken, attends in person or by an attorney may recover reasonable expenses for attending, including attorney's fees, if the noticing party failed to:

(1) attend and proceed with the deposition; or

(2) serve a subpoena on a nonparty deponent, who consequently did not attend

You can see that Rule 30 is rather detailed and extensive. Rule 30 covers the transcript copies, the deposition itself, methods of recording, and notice of deposition. Of particular interest to testifying witnesses is the section regarding sanctions. Anyone who "interferes with the fair examination of the deponent" is subject to court sanctions; this can include the deponent themselves. That may seem odd, but occasionally a deponent will attempt to avoid direct answers to inconvenient or uncomfortable questions. Such tactics can only be taken so far before they constitute interfering with the fair examination of the deponent. It is best to simply answer questions truthfully and not rely on evasive tactics.

Rule 31

Rule 31 covers scenarios where the deposition is done via written questions. While this is not the standard way in which depositions are taken, this method may be used in certain exceptional circumstances. Rule 31 is provided in its entirety here.

(a) When a Deposition May Be Taken.

(1) Without Leave. A party may, by written questions, depose any person, including a party, without leave of court except as provided in Rule 31(a)(2). The deponent's attendance may be compelled by subpoena under Rule 45.

(2) With Leave. A party must obtain leave of court, and the court must grant leave to the extent consistent with Rule 26(b)(2):

(A) if the parties have not stipulated to the deposition and:

(i) the deposition would result in more than 10 depositions being taken under this rule or Rule 30 by the plaintiffs, or by the defendants, or by the third-party defendants;

(ii) the deponent has already been deposed in the case; or

(iii) the party seeks to take a deposition before the time specified in Rule 26 (d); or

(B) if the deponent is confined in prison.

(3) Service; Required Notice. A party who wants to depose a person by written questions must serve them on every other party, with a notice stating, if known, the deponent's name and address. If the name is unknown, the notice must provide a general description sufficient to identify the person or the particular class or group to which the person

belongs. The notice must also state the name or descriptive title and the address of the officer before whom the deposition will be taken.

(4) Questions Directed to an Organization. A public or private corporation, a partnership, an association, or a governmental agency may be deposed by written questions in accordance with Rule 30(b)(6).

(5) Questions from Other Parties. Any questions to the deponent from other parties must be served on all parties as follows: cross-questions, within 14 days after being served with the notice and direct questions; redirect questions, within seven days after being served with cross-questions; and recross-questions, within seven days after being served with redirect questions. The court may, for good cause, extend or shorten these times.

(b) Delivery to the Officer; Officer's Duties. The party who noticed the deposition must deliver to the officer a copy of all the questions served and of the notice. The officer must promptly proceed in the manner provided in Rule 30(c), (e), and (f) to:

(1) take the deponent's testimony in response to the questions;

(2) prepare and certify the deposition; and

(3) send it to the party, attaching a copy of the questions and of the notice.

(c) Notice of Completion of Filing.

(1) Completion. The party who noticed the deposition must notify all other parties when it is completed.

(2) Filing. A party who files the deposition must promptly notify all other parties of the filing.

What to Do, What Not to Do

One of the authors of this book received some excellent advice from an attorney before his first deposition: No one ever wins a case during a deposition, but many cases are lost during deposition. There are two key things to remember. The first is that a deposition is being conducted by the opposing counsel; that counsel wants to find information they can use to help their case. Also remember this is a part of discovery. The entire purpose of a deposition is for the attorney conducting the deposition to acquire information they do not currently have. There is no way you can provide opposing counsel details that will actually help your own case. This leads to two guidelines to follow: Answer truthfully and make your answers concise.

Because a deposition is a sworn statement, any prevarication can lead to perjury charges. You must be completely honest during a deposition—even if the answer is one you would prefer not to give. It is still better to give an honest answer. You can decline to answer a question, though in some cases opposing counsel can get an order from the presiding judge to compel you to answer. But you must never tell a lie. Your case might be able to recover from you being caught in an error, but it will never recover from you being caught in a lie. Generally, this basic rule of depositions is easy to grasp and easy to follow.

The second guideline in depositions is to be concise. This is an issue with which some experts have a real problem. Often, one wishes to assume a teaching role and to extol at length on the topic at hand. In a deposition, however, this is counterproductive. The opposing counsel is running the deposition because they are seeking additional information. By giving an excessively thorough answer, you may well alert them to facts they were not aware of. While it is your duty to answer honestly, it is not your duty to answer more than they asked. When possible, you should restrict your answers to yes or no. When that is not possible, make your answers as brief and direct as possible. It is also important to make certain you fully understand a question before you attempt to answer it. Don't be afraid to say "I don't understand the question."

These two rules—answer truthfully and concisely—lead to a few guidelines:

- **Be honest with all answers.** This is one that may seem obvious, but unfortunately is sometimes violated by people during a deposition. The opposing counsel may ask a question you were not prepared for, and the honest answer may be damaging to your case. However, under no circumstances can you give an answer that is not completely honest. Remember: The oath before testimony states you will "tell the truth, the whole truth, and nothing but the truth." You must absolutely stick to this rule.

- **Don't guess or speculate.** If you do not know the answer, say so. Some people, particularly experts in a given field, are uncomfortable admitting that they simply do not know an answer. That is natural, but unfortunately we all have gaps in our knowledge. Even a leading expert in a given field cannot know everything. If you guess or speculate, you are now stuck with that guess or speculation as your official position given under oath.

■ **Don't forget you have a right to confer with counsel.** If you have a question or concern, you are allowed stop the proceeding at any time and confer with your attorneys. This is your right and you should exercise it anytime you feel it necessary.

■ **Don't volunteer information.** Never give more information than you have been directly asked to give. It is the attorney's job to ask the right questions; they are here to find information to help their case. If you volunteer additional information that they did not think to ask for, you are helping their case. Keep your answers to exactly what they asked you without elaboration.

■ **Remain calm and polite.** Even if the other side attempts to fluster you, stay calm and stay polite. Your demeanor will tell the opposing counsel a great deal.

■ **Correct mistakes.** If at any time during the deposition you realize you have given an erroneous answer or you have misspoken, correct your answer as soon as you realize your error.

■ **Never joke in a deposition.** This may seem obvious to some readers. However, some people make jokes when they get nervous. A deposition is no place for levity, and that includes conversations before the deposition or during a break. Anything you say can and likely will be used against you by the opposing counsel.

■ **Be aware of traps.** A common lawyer trap is the question "Is that all?" They are seeking to limit your testimony. They want to pin you down to a limitation. A good answer is something along the lines of "That is all that comes to mind at this moment."

■ **Don't make small talk or chat.** You are probably a friendly and sociable person. You want to be polite. It may seem natural to chat with opposing counsel during breaks, before the deposition, or after. Never forget that everything you say can be used by the other side, so do not speak unless you absolutely must.

- **Don't waive the reading.** At the start of most depositions, counsel will agree on a variety of stipulations. One of the most common stipulations is that the deponent waives the right to read and sign the deposition transcript. The expert who is interested in accuracy should not agree to this waiver lightly. Experts who agree to waive the reading and signing are agreeing to a document's accuracy without even seeing the document.

Attorneys will often take one of two tactics with a deponent. The first tactic is to be overly cordial. They wish to make the deponent feel as if the attorney asking the questions is a friend. If they can lull the deponent into a more relaxed and informal mood, the deponent is more likely to give longer and more revealing answers, which has the potential of giving the attorney more information. Do not fall for this trap. The opposing counsel is most certainly not your ally. They want nothing more than to discredit your entire testimony. Barring that, they want to either catch you in any error, no matter now minor, or get you to make a false statement. Either way, they can then impugn your entire testimony and your character. You should be alert and wary during a deposition.

The opposite tactic is for the attorney to attempt to unsettle the deponent. This can be done by taking an abrasive attitude, being curt with questions, or purposefully trying to agitate the deponent. For example, suppose a professor is an expert witness in a trial and is being deposed. There are many ways opposing counsel might try to unsettle him or her. A few might include the following:

- Not call the professor by his or her proper title (i.e., Dr. or Professor). Frankly, some experts do have egos, and this sort of thing can cause some deponents to become agitated and lose focus.

- In response to every answer the deponent gives, the opposing counsel will ask something like "Are you sure about that?" In many cases, this leads deponents to doubt themselves.

- Ask questions about the deponent. An example might be, "Have you ever committed plagiarism in your academic work?" When the deponent answers in the negative, he will follow that with "Are you absolutely certain?"

▪ Ask questions about the deponent's background. For example, "I see you went to Northern University. Is it true that their computer-science department has a poor reputation?"

Now, there is a limit to how much of this sort of behavior opposing counsel can get away with. If they push these tactics too far, your own attorney will most likely end the deposition and complain to the presiding judge. However, you must simply keep in mind that the opposing counsel wants to discredit you. It does not matter how impressive your credentials are or how impeccable your background is. They will seek to undermine your credibility. Do not take this personally because it is not at all personal. It is simply the way these things work.

Trials

If you have never been a participant in a trial, the prospect of participating can certainly generate some anxiety. You may have seen courtroom dramas that were quite intense. The first thing you must realize is that courtrooms are rarely that intense and dramatic. In fact the proceedings can be quite dull. However, the courtroom is a place where minutiae are very important. From the papers filed with courts to the testimony given, every minute detail is critical. We need not concern ourselves with the documents that get submitted leading up to a trial, because that is a matter your attorney will deal with. But we must discuss your conduct in a trial.

First, you must follow the same rules we discussed about depositions: Always be polite, be honest, don't make guesses, and so on. However, there are some other factors that will play a role in regard to a jury trial. Let us discuss those.

Appearance is important. As much as we might like to believe otherwise, people do judge a person based on appearance. It may seem obvious to suggest people dress properly for court, but I know of at least one computer scientist who showed up to testify in court wearing casual pants and sandals. Now, if we were to be completely logical, we must realize that one's clothing does not change one's expertise. However, the reality is that if one does not look credible, one won't be perceived as credible. This usually means a suit and tie for men and a dress for women. But even that is not enough. It is important that you appear competent, not flashy. A nice gray, blue, or black suit with an average tie is an appropriate look for court. A $1,500 suit with a flashy colorful tie and matching pocket silk is not. The latter ensemble appears flashy and may generate some resentment from jurors.

You must speak clearly and confidently. When you speak, it must be in a clear and confident voice. If your tone of voice and inflection indicate uncertainty, then the jury will perceive that you are not sure about what you are saying. This can be difficult for scientists to adapt to. Scientists routinely couch conclusions in terms like "indicates," "appears to," and "may." That is because they are very much aware that future data may render their current position invalid. In a courtroom, though, you need to be definite whenever the current state of knowledge supports your statement. It is also critical that you speak clearly. If you speak too fast, mumble, or are not completely clear, that will damage your credibility with a jury.

Be understandable. When you speak, remember that the jury, the attorneys, and the judge are not colleagues of yours at some symposium. While they may be well educated and have expertise you do not possess, they are not experts in your field. When you speak, you need to avoid unnecessary jargon, and make sure you are speaking clearly. Think of testifying as teaching. You are teaching the jury why your position is correct. The other side of that is that you must never speak in a condescending manner. While the jurors may not be experts in your field, that does not mean you should speak as if they are unintelligent.

Now, this entire discussion of trial testimony may make some readers wonder about our court system. You might be thinking that all this seems to be totally irrelevant to issues of fact and determining guilt. But courtrooms are full of human beings, with all of our human frailties. People do form initial impressions and those impressions affect how they view evidence presented by a given expert. And in some cases, the technical issues are complex enough that the jury will have difficulty fully understanding them. In those situations, the impression the jury has of the expert is even more important.

The Daubert Decision and Trials

The case of Daubert v. Merrell Dow Pharmaceuticals (1989) is one that every potential expert witness must be intimately familiar with. This case was about minor children Jason Daubert and Eric Schuller, who were born with serious birth defects. They and their parents sued respondent Merrell Dow in California state court, alleging that the birth defects had been caused by the mothers' ingestion of Bendectin, a prescription anti-nausea drug marketed by Merrell Dow. Merrell Dow petitioned the court for summary judgment and in support of that Dow submitted an affidavit of Steven H. Lamm, a physician and epidemiologist, who was a well-respected expert on the risks of exposure to various chemical substances. Dr. Lamm fully supported his position by an extensive review of medical literature and concluded that the drug Bendectin could not cause birth defects.

The plaintiffs responded with reports from eight different well-respected experts. Each could only show some limited data that suggested Bendectin might be able to cause birth defects. This case ultimately led to a change in the way federal courts treat scientific evidence and testimony. The rule used now, referred to as the Daubert standard, states that in order for scientific testimony to be admissible, it must meet the following criteria:

- Has the technique been tested in actual field conditions (and not just in a laboratory)?

- Has the technique been subject to peer review and publication?

- What is the known or potential rate of error? Is it zero, or low enough to be close to zero?

- Do standards exist for the control of the technique's operation?

- Has the technique been generally accepted within the relevant scientific community?

Prior to the Daubert decisions, courts only required the final element, that the technique or finding has been generally accepted by the relevant scientific community. That was known as the Fry decision. It is important that any expert who intends to testify or to submit an expert report be certain that his or her methodologies meet the Daubert criteria. Failure to do so can lead to one's entire expert testimony being ruled inadmissible.

Use of Depositions at Trials

A deposition can be used at trial. Whatever you say during the deposition is admissible at trial. One common way attorneys will use depositions is to impeach trial testimony. If something you testify to at trial contradicts something you testified to during the deposition, this gives opposing counsel an opportunity to attack your credibility. This is one reason we stated that when being deposed, you must never guess. Imagine a situation in which you guess during a deposition, but then between that deposition and trial you discover your guess was wrong. Then, during trial, you testify to what you now know to be true, but it contradicts your deposition testimony.

Depositions are also used at trial when the witness who was deposed is not available. Generally, courts hold that being unavailable means due to circumstances that cannot be avoided, such as death, severe illness, or some similar extreme circumstances. A simple scheduling conflict on the part of the witness is usually not held to be a valid reason to be unavailable at trial. Federal Rule 32 provides the details for using deposition testimony at trail, and the exact wording of that rule is given here.

(1) In General. At a hearing or trial, all or part of a deposition may be used against a party on these conditions:

(A) the party was present or represented at the taking of the deposition or had reasonable notice of it;

(B) it is used to the extent it would be admissible under the Federal Rules of Evidence if the deponent were present and testifying; and

(C) the use is allowed by Rule 32(a)(2) through (8).

(2) Impeachment and Other Uses. Any party may use a deposition to contradict or impeach the testimony given by the deponent as a witness, or for any other purpose allowed by the Federal Rules of Evidence.

(3) Deposition of Party, Agent, or Designee. An adverse party may use for any purpose the deposition of a party or anyone who, when deposed, was the party's officer, director, managing agent, or designee under Rule 30(b)(6) or 31(a)(4).

(4) Unavailable Witness. A party may use for any purpose the deposition of a witness, whether or not a party, if the court finds:

(A) that the witness is dead;

(B) that the witness is more than 100 miles from the place of hearing or trial or is outside the United States, unless it appears that the witness's absence was procured by the party offering the deposition;

(C) that the witness cannot attend or testify because of age, illness, infirmity, or imprisonment;

(D) that the party offering the deposition could not procure the witness's attendance by subpoena; or

(E) on motion and notice, that exceptional circumstances make it desirable—in the interest of justice and with due regard to the importance of live testimony in open court—to permit the deposition to be used.

(5) Limitations on Use. (A) Deposition Taken on Short Notice. A deposition must not be used against a party who, having received less than 14 days' notice of the deposition, promptly moved for a protective order under Rule 26(c)(1)(B) requesting that it not be taken or be taken at a different time or place—and this motion was still pending when the deposition was taken.

(B) Unavailable Deponent; Party Could Not Obtain an Attorney. A deposition taken without leave of court under the unavailability provision of Rule 30(a)(2)(A)(iii) must not be used against a party who shows that, when served with the notice, it could not, despite diligent efforts, obtain an attorney to represent it at the deposition.

(6) Using Part of a Deposition. If a party offers in evidence only part of a deposition, an adverse party may require the offeror to introduce other parts that in fairness should be considered with the part introduced, and any party may itself introduce any other parts.

(7) Substituting a Party. Substituting a party under Rule 25 does not affect the right to use a deposition previously taken.

(8) Deposition Taken in an Earlier Action. A deposition lawfully taken and, if required, filed in any federal- or state-court action may be used in a later action involving the same subject matter between the same parties, or their representatives or successors in interest, to the same extent as if taken in the later action. A deposition previously taken may also be used as allowed by the Federal Rules of Evidence.

(b) Objections to Admissibility. Subject to Rules 28(b) and 32(d)(3), an objection may be made at a hearing or trial to the admission of any deposition testimony that would be inadmissible if the witness were present and testifying.

(c) Form of presentation. Unless the court orders otherwise, a party must provide a transcript of any deposition testimony the party offers, but may provide the court with the testimony in nontranscript form as well. On any party's request, deposition testimony offered in a jury trial for any purpose other than impeachment must be presented in nontranscript form, if available, unless the court for good cause orders otherwise.

(d) Waiver of Objections.

(1) To the Notice. An objection to an error or irregularity in a deposition notice is waived unless promptly served in writing on the party giving the notice.

(2) To the Officer's Qualification. An objection based on disqualification of the officer before whom a deposition is to be taken is waived if not made:

(A) before the deposition begins; or

(B) promptly after the basis for disqualification becomes known or, with reasonable diligence, could have been known.

(3) To the Taking of the Deposition.

(A) Objection to Competence, Relevance, or Materiality. An objection to a deponent's competence—or to the competence, relevance, or materiality of testimony—is not waived by a failure to make the objection before or during the deposition, unless the ground for it might have been corrected at that time.

(B) Objection to an Error or Irregularity. An objection to an error or irregularity at an oral examination is waived if:

(i) it relates to the manner of taking the deposition, the form of a question or answer, the oath or affirmation, a party's conduct, or other matters that might have been corrected at that time; and

(ii) it is not timely made during the deposition.

(C) Objection to a Written Question. An objection to the form of a written question under Rule 31 is waived if not served in writing on the party submitting the question within the time for serving responsive questions or, if the question is a recross question, within seven days after being served with it.

(4) To Completing and Returning the Deposition. An objection to how the officer transcribed the testimony—or prepared, signed, certified, sealed, endorsed, sent, or otherwise dealt with the deposition—is waived unless a motion to suppress is made promptly after the error or irregularity becomes known or, with reasonable diligence, could have been known.

Case Studies

In this section, we will look at a couple of actual cases. In these cases, there is some element that is of interest to our examination of expert-witness testimony. We will look at situations where an expert's actions were laudable and should be emulated, as well as situations where an expert may have harmed the case by a mistake.

Expert Performs Well

Let's start our examination of case studies by looking at a situation in which the testifying expert did well at trial. This will allow us to examine in what ways he performed well, and if you have to testify at trial, should give you some guidance on how you should conduct yourself. During the 2006 trial of Roger Duronio[1], the defense attorney subjected the prosecution's computer-forensics expert to an hour and a half of what witnesses describe as "contentious" cross examination. Mr. Duronio was accused of planting code that brought down the main server and 2,000 branches of UBS/Paine-Webber in 2002. The prosecution utilized Keith Jones, director of computer forensics and incident response at Mandiant, an information-security company based in Alexandria, Virginia, as their computer-forensics expert.

Mr. Jones first submitted 10 hours of detailed testimony regarding his findings in this case. This is the first item of note. While 10 hours may be a longer-than-average time for testimony, it is critical that one's testimony be detailed. You must meticulously cover all details and aspects of the investigation. In this case,

Mr. Jones showed that his investigation had pinpointed the attack to having originated from the defendant's home using the defendant's login. This level of specificity is important. You cannot simply show that it was likely the defendant committed a crime; it must be shown beyond a reasonable doubt.

When the defense began its cross examination, it immediately questioned the ethics of some of the individuals involved in the investigation. This is a common tactic. The key point here is that the expert witness did not allow this to disconcert him, or at the very least did not show it if it did. The defense counsel spent significant time questioning Mr. Jones about the specific forensic methods used and made several attempts to undermine those methods. As we have mentioned in previous chapters, your forensic methodology will be scrutinized at trial. You must ensure that it is impeccable, or at the very least defensible.

One particularly interesting part of the testimony came when the defense attorney questioned the expert witness about data he did not find. The expert witness handled this very well by simply responding that any amount of new data that might hypothetically be examined would not change what was actually found and examined. This is particularly interesting because it is an example of how to properly answer difficult questions. Clearly, the defense attorney was attempting to get Mr. Jones to speculate. Had Mr. Jones done so, that speculation could have opened entirely new avenues of argument for the attorney.

In general, this case illustrates the rules and guidelines we have been examining throughout the past several chapters. First and foremost, you must perform your forensic examination in a thorough and detailed manner by documenting every step. You can be assured that at some point, you will have your methodology scrutinized by hostile parties, such as opposing counsel or opposing witnesses. Furthermore, you must remain totally calm on the stand and truthfully answer questions. Don't let cross examination rattle you; stay calm, stay focused, and tell the truth.

Expert Makes Major Mistake

In the Texas appellate court case of Volkswagen of America v. Andrew Ramirez[2], the expert witness in this case made a fundamental mistake, one we discussed in Chapter 11 regarding expert reports. In this case, a Volkswagen Passat crossed the median and collided with an oncoming vehicle. Following the accident, the left rear wheel of the car was found completely detached from car's stub axle and lying on its side. The driver of the Passat did not survive the accident and his family sued Volkswagen claiming a design defect.

In this case, the expert witness failed miserably. Ronald Walker, who specializes in accident reconstruction, prepared the expert report for the plaintiff. In his expert report, Mr. Walker did not cite any literature supporting his opinions, nor did he conduct any tests. He simply relied on basic laws of physics to explain the accident. The jury did return a verdict for the plaintiff, but Volkswagen won a reversal on appeal based on the failure of the plaintiff's expert to properly support his opinions.

You must keep in mind that your opinion, even when based on years of extensive experience and training, is going to be challenged. You should never give an opinion that is not supported by either citations of reputable literature or your own experiments, and when possible supporting your claims by both experiment and citation is the ideal. Failure to fully support your conclusions can certainly lead to those conclusions being deemed inadmissible. Even if your statement is one that is common knowledge in your field of expertise, support it with a citation or two. And make sure the sources you cite are impeccable.

Expert Not Fully Qualified

The case of Wilson v. Bradlees of New England is very interesting in regard to expert testimony. In this case, a 12-year-old girl reached across a stove to turn off the burner, and her cotton-and-polyester–blend pajamas caught fire and caused third-degree burns. The plaintiff's expert witness, a chemist, testified to the chemistry and flammable properties of polyvinyl chloride and plastisols. However, he was not permitted to opine about the commercial feasibility of printing sweatshirt logos with flame-retardant ink. The reason was that the chemist admitted that he had no familiarity with the silkscreening industry, ink manufacture, or logo design, and that he never conducted comparison tests between flame-retardant and ordinary inks. His only knowledge regarding the use of flame-retardant ink in producing clothing was a phone conversation with an ink vendor.[3]

This example illustrates another pitfall for the testifying expert. Make absolutely certain that you are truly an expert in all facets of a case about which you might be asked to testify. In this case, the expert was clearly an expert in chemistry, but he attempted to testify on items beyond his personal expertise.

Conclusion

In this chapter, we have given you an overview of how depositions and trials work. We have also provided you with guidelines for testifying in depositions and trials. This chapter should not be construed as a substitute for legal advice. If you are testifying, then it is likely that your attorney will wish to discuss your testimony with you beforehand. This preparation is very important. However, after studying this chapter, you should have a working knowledge of how to conduct yourself in testimony and what pitfalls to avoid.

You should also carefully review the cases discussed here. They provide a practical view of how depositions and trial testimony work in the real world. By reviewing the mistakes and successes of other testifying experts, you can provide better testimony yourself.

Endnotes

[1] *Information Week.* "Defense Fails to Rattle Computer Forensics Expert in UBS Trial." http://www.informationweek.com/news/security/cybercrime/showArticle.jhtml?articleID=189602693

[2] Volkswagen of America v. Andrew Ramirez, Sr., et al. http://www.supreme.courts.state.tx.us/historical/2004/dec/020557.htm

[3] Wilson v. Bradlees. http://www.ca1.uscourts.gov/cgi-bin/getopn.pl?OPINION=99-1779.01A

CHAPTER 13

CIVIL MATTERS RELATING TO COMPUTER CRIME

Introduction

Our primary objective in this book is to deal with computer crime, which naturally leads to criminal cases. However, there are a number of computer crimes that either also entail civil litigation, or are often handled as a civil matter exclusively. For that reason, it is important that a computer-forensics investigator have a basic understanding of the civil process. If your investigations are related to a civil trial, you will most likely be working as an expert consultant for an attorney. In such cases, it is certain that the attorney who employs you will also prepare you for the litigation process. In this chapter, we want to give you an overview so that you will have a working knowledge of the process.

There are situations in which someone may choose to file in civil court rather than criminal court. For example, if theft of intellectual property is committed by a company or under the auspices of a company, the victim might choose to file a civil suit rather than criminal charges. The reason for this is that criminal charges won't get back the money the victim has lost; and if you do successfully convict someone and that person is incarcerated, it is likely he or she will have few if any assets to seize in civil litigation. It is also true that the burden of proof in civil litigation is lower than that of criminal court. In criminal court, one must prove one's case beyond a reasonable doubt. In civil court, you need only prove it by a preponderance of the evidence. The final reason someone might choose to proceed in civil court rather than criminal court is control of the proceedings.

If you elect to press criminal charges, the district attorney or U.S. attorney is in charge of the case. They decide what charges to file, whether or not to make a deal, and whether or not to even proceed with the case. If you file in civil court, you direct your attorney on whether or not to proceed, whether or not to make a deal, and how aggressively to pursue the case.

While there are certainly reasons one might choose civil court, one must remember that there are negative aspects of moving forward with civil litigation rather than criminal charges. One such aspect is the expense: You must pay the attorney's fees and filing fees up front. If you win the case, you may be able to recoup those expenses, but if you lose you will simply have lost that money. But the fact remains that civil litigation is often an option in computer-related crimes, and it will often be selected if one or both of the parties is a company with adequate resources for civil litigation. While criminal cases sometimes involve expert testimony, civil cases, at least those outside of small claims court, almost always do. One reason for this is that civil cases usually involve parties that are financially prepared to litigate and have budgeted for expert testimony. In criminal cases, it may often be the case that either party—the defendant or the prosecution—may not have the budget for an expert witness.

Finally, there is also the issue of time. The United States Constitution guarantees a defendant the right to a speedy trial. There is no such guarantee in civil courts. Civil cases often take many years to resolve. It can often be two years or more from initial filing date to the trial; in some cases, it can be much longer. Then, after the trial, the appellate process can last many more years. This is one reason that most parties to civil litigation are really seeking an out-of-court settlement. The vast majority of civil cases settle without an actual trial occurring.

From a legal perspective, the difference between civil and criminal law is really about the parties involved. Civil law pertains primarily to the duties of private citizens to each other. In civil cases, the disputes are usually between private individuals, businesses, or organizations, although a government agency may also sometimes be a party in a civil suit. Criminal cases always involve government prosecution of an individual or individuals for some infraction of the law.

Civil Law Related to Computer Crime

In this section, we will look at aspects of civil law as it relates to computer crime. We will examine categories of civil law that can intersect with computer crimes.

This should provide the reader with an understanding of what circumstances may lead to a computer crime being handled in civil court.

The Main Categories of Civil Law

The five main categories of civil law are contract law, tort law, property law, the law of succession, and family law. Family law and the law of succession are two areas we won't be examining as they have no direct relationship to computer crime. It is certainly possible that a case in one of those areas might peripherally involve computer crimes and forensics, but not directly. For example, in a family law case involving a divorce or child-custody issue, one party's possession of child pornography might have bearing on the outcome of the family-law proceedings. However, that computer crime, possessing child pornography, is tangential to the actual underlying family-law case.

Contract Law

Contract law is primarily concerned with voluntary agreements between two or more entities. Those entities can be individual people, businesses, or organizations, and such contracts can involve a wide range of subjects—for example, agreements by one party to perform some work for the other party or for one party to sell some item to another party. Often, acceptable-use policies, which are a form of contract, are related to computer cases. For example, a person's employment may be terminated because he or she violated the company's acceptable-use policy.

Although some contracts are relatively simple and straightforward, many can contain subtleties and complexities that are open to diverse interpretation. That difference in interpretation can sometimes be enough to lead to litigation. This happens frequently with contracts involving technology companies, and is often the basis of lawsuits.

Tort Law

Torts are the area of civil law most related to criminal law. A *tort* is usually described as conduct that in some way causes injury to another party. That injury could be a direct physical injury, monetary injury, or some other type of injury. If one person strikes another person, that act is both the crime of battery and a tort, and as such it can be dealt with either in criminal court or in civil court.

Many computer crimes can involve tort law. Identity theft can certainly be said to cause material harm to the victim; therefore, the act of identity theft would constitute a tort and could be addressed via civil litigation. Cyber stalking and harassment are also definitely torts as they cause psychological harm to the victim. It is not uncommon for a case such as this to be first prosecuted as a criminal matter and then, after the resolution of the criminal matter, further pursued as a civil tort. Sometimes that is because the plaintiff lost the criminal case and wants to try to get a better result with the less rigorous burden of proof in civil court. In other cases, the criminal conviction is used to bolster the civil case, and perhaps even force an out-of-court settlement.

Property Law

Property law may seem far removed from computer crimes, but it is not. We are not talking about real estate or personal property, but rather intellectual property. Cases of data theft and cyber espionage almost always involve a violation of property law, which can lead to civil litigation to address the issue.

Although not actually a computer crime, patent infringement is an important area of intellectual-property law, and it is at least related to computer crime in that similar investigative means are sometimes used. In the case of patent infringement, an expert working for the plaintiff may examine the product of the accused to gather evidence that it does indeed infringe upon the patent in question or to determine that it does not infringe. Such investigations must be conducted as scrupulously as criminal forensic investigations, and with just as much attention to detail.

What Court?

The first question is, which court should a case be tried in? The options are usually small-claims court, state district court, and federal district court. Fortunately, the guidelines for which court a case is filed in are very clear. In most jurisdictions, any litigation that is for an amount less than $10,000 goes to small-claims court. In a small-claims court case, you can have an attorney, but generally expert witnesses are not used. That does not mean you cannot consult an expert in advance to help prepare your case, but it is unusual for an expert to have any role in a small-claims case. There are multiple reasons for this. The first is that small-claims cases tend to be much simpler, and thus don't require experts to sift through the details. The second is expense: Expert witnesses usually charge significant amounts for their time. Rates from $150 to $300 per hour are common, and particularly renowned experts can charge significantly more. It usually costs more to hire an expert witness than the small-claims case is worth. The reason one elects to have their case in small-claims court, other than the $10,000 limit, is because the cases tend to be simpler and are usually resolved much more quickly.

If the case involves interstate or international commerce, then federal court is the appropriate venue. If it does not, then the state district court is the appropriate venue for that case. There is very little flexibility in choosing among small-claims, state district, or federal district court. The guidelines are clear. However, what constitutes interstate commerce can sometimes be a matter of interpretation. Generally, if the parties involved reside or work in different states, then it will likely be a federal matter.

It is also important to file in the right jurisdiction. For example, if both parties are in New York, and the activities in question took place in New York, you cannot file the case in Georgia state courts. When filing a case, one must show that the court one is filing in has jurisdiction. With state courts, the specific rules vary, but in general at least one of the parties must live or work in that court's jurisdiction. In some cases, certain courts can develop a reputation for being more favorable for a plaintiff, and then various plaintiffs will work to find some connection with that jurisdiction that would allow the case to be filed there.

The Process

A civil trial can often be a longer, more drawn-out process than a criminal trial. There are two reasons for this. The first is the lengthy discovery process, and the second is the lengthy appeals process. Each of these phases can take an enormous amount of time. For the computer-forensics expert, the pretrial discovery phase is the most important.

Pretrial

The first step in civil litigation is that one party, or that party's attorney, files a lawsuit with an appropriate court and has the other party served with notice of the filing. The person initiating the civil suit is known as the plaintiff, and the person being sued is the defendant or the respondent. A civil action is known by the names of the plaintiff and the defendant, such as Jones v. Miller, with the plaintiff's name appearing first. In some cases, the two parties have tried and failed to negotiate the matter before one party decides to file a lawsuit; in other cases, the defendant may not even be aware there is a dispute until they are served notice.

The U.S. legal system provides for discovery procedures; that is, each party is entitled to information in the possession of the other. The discovery in civil cases is a bit different than criminal trials. In a criminal trial, the prosecution is obliged to turn over to the defense any evidence that might be considered exculpatory. Exculpatory evidence is simply evidence that might demonstrate the defendant's innocence. The defense is not required to provide any of its evidence to the prosecution. There are several methods whereby parties can accomplish discovery:

- **Depositions.** We discussed depositions in depth in Chapter 12 , "Depositions and Trials." Just to summarize, a deposition is testimony of a witness taken under oath outside the court. While depositions usually do not play a prominent role in criminal proceedings, they are often critical to civil litigation. It is frequently the case that both parties, any experts they have retained, and any related parties may be deposed.

- **Interrogatories.** Interrogatories are written questions that must be answered under oath. Essentially, each side prepares a list of questions they want answered. The recipient must sign and notarize his or her response, swearing all answers to be true. Interrogatories can be submitted only to the parties in the case, not to witnesses. Often, the interrogatories are actually used to discover other evidence. For example, one party might ask the other party if there are any other computer systems he or she has access to. An affirmative answer might lead to subpoenas for those additional computers, which makes them available to be examined for evidence. You must remember that an interrogatory, like a deposition, is a sworn statement; thus, the rules of perjury apply.

- **Producing documents.** Production of documents may be requested by one of the parties in the suit if that party wishes to inspect documents, software source code, server logs, memos, e-mails, notes, company documents, photographs, or any other item that might provide evidence in the case. It is not uncommon for civil cases to involve thousands, and in some cases hundreds of thousands, of pages of documents.

The discovery phase is quite lengthy and involved. In many cases, this can be the most expensive part of the civil litigation. It is important that when examining evidence, you must be every bit as diligent as you would be when examining a crime scene.

In many cases, there may be judicial hearings to decide matters. One example involves discovery. It is commonplace for one party to object to some of the items the other party has requested in discovery. This usually leads to a hearing in which the judge will decide if the requested information is relevant to the case and if the requesting party has a right to such information.

Even terminology can be the subject of a hearing. During patent litigation, there is a process referred to as a Markman hearing. Holding a Markman hearing in patent-infringement cases has been common practice since the U.S. Supreme Court, in the case of Markman v. Westview Instruments, Inc., found that the language of a patent is a matter of law for a judge to decide, not a matter of fact for a jury to decide. In a Markman hearing, the two opposing parties submit arguments regarding the meanings of key terms in a patent. This is because the interpretation of these words can dramatically affect the outcome of the case. While Markman hearings are only pertinent to patent litigation, they do illustrate a point: Many aspects of civil litigation are debated in numerous motions and hearings long before a trial is even near. In civil cases, the pretrial phase is even more important than it is during a criminal case.

Motions

If you are ever involved in civil litigation, you should be aware that a certain type of document, called a motion, is often a major part of a civil case. A *motion* is literally a document that attempts to move the court to take some action. It might be a motion to dismiss the case, or a motion to compel the other party to produce evidence. In civil litigations, it is common for one party or the other to file a motion for summary judgment, which is essentially a claim that the other party's case fails as a basic matter of law and that the judge should simply rule in favor of the party filing the motion. Some attorneys make it a practice to file any motion that might have even a chance of success, the reasoning being that you have nothing to lose. And if one party has more financial resources than the other, then that party can overwhelm the other party with motions. Every motion has to be read, researched, and responded to. If a party fails to respond to a motion within the statutory time limits, the motion is probably going to be automatically granted by the judge.

It is also common for a defendant to file a motion to dismiss. In such a motion, the defendant must show that, as a matter of law, the plaintiff has no case. This is often based on some nuance of law such as a statute of limitations having expired. While it is common for such motions to be filed, it is not as common that they are granted. Unless a lawsuit is truly frivolous, it is not likely the judge will completely dismiss it. And, as with most motions, the judge's decision will only come after a hearing wherein both parties may argue the merits of the motion.

There may also be motions directly relating to your expert testimony. The opposing counsel may make a motion to have you disallowed as an expert based on any number of factors. However, two of the most common are as follows:

- **Lack of expertise.** The opposing counsel may argue that while you are a professional in your field, your expertise is either not directly related to the matters of this trial or not sufficiently extensive. For example, a nurse may be considered a medical professional, but might not be considered an expert on neurosurgery techniques.

- **Conflict of interest.** Any connection between the expert witness and either party can be interpreted as a conflict of interest, no matter how tenuous that connection is.

Don't be concerned about such motions. This is just a standard part of civil litigation, just like motions to dismiss and motions for summary judgment. Do not take these things personally. As a matter of course, the opposing counsel's view is that you are either not qualified or simply wrong. They cannot very well take the position that you are eminent in your field and exactly correct about the case. And remember, your party's attorney takes the very same position regarding the opposing expert. Your attorney will view their expert as incompetent, unqualified, or simply wrong. This is just the nature of the adversarial judicial system we have, and not a personal or professional reflection on you.

Trial

The actual trial is where it all comes together; this is true for both civil and criminal cases. Unfortunately, real trials are not at all like what you may have seen in television dramas. They are frequently quite tedious and boring. Each side methodically presents every piece of evidence and attempts to discredit the other party's evidence. For the computer-forensics expert, his or her own expert testimony and any rebuttal will be the key elements of the trial. We will examine this portion of the trial closely.

Your testimony will begin with you being sworn in. Then the attorney for the party you represent will question you. Throughout the questioning, it is possible that the opposing counsel may object to some questions, or even to your answers. Objections in real courts are rarely as dramatic as they are on television, however. It is likely that the attorney for your case will have gone over your testimony beforehand, so you should not have any unexpected questions from him or her. There are a few rules you should keep in mind when testifying in court:

- **You must speak clearly.** Don't rush your speech or use any speech patterns that might make it more difficult for the jury to understand.

- **Make eye contact with the jury.** People are more likely to trust you if you make and maintain eye contact. And in many cases, an expert's credibility is almost as important as the actual technical details of the testimony.

- **Think like a teacher.** Your job is to teach the jury your case. Remember that what may be common knowledge in your profession is probably not common knowledge among the laypeople of the jury. At the same time, you do not want to be perceived as condescending. Teach the jury as you would a freshman class. They are intelligent adults, just not professionals in your field.

- **Use only as much technical jargon as is necessary to make your point.** And make certain you define any and all technical terms.

The initial testimony will consist of you answering questions that your attorney asks you. This part should be relatively low stress. You have likely already gone over the questions and answers in advance. However, when your attorney is finished with his examination, then the opposing counsel will have a chance to cross-examine you. You can be assured that the opposing counsel has carefully studied any expert reports you have submitted, examined your curriculum vitae, and probably done a Web search to find out any information about you that might be available. Remember that the opposing counsel has one goal in cross-examining you, and that is to undermine the testimony you have just given. There are a few rules for cross-examination:

- Stay calm. No matter what the opposing counsel says or does, do not become agitated. Even if you are caught in an error, stay calm. Simply admit that error and move on.

- Just as with depositions, you must stick to the truth. Do not deviate or embellish.

- Remember that every question the opposing counsel asks is a chance for you to continue educating the jury about your case. Don't be anxious. Simply continue to provide the facts as you know them.

It is often the case that if you can simply stay calm, stick to the facts, and continue to provide facts to support your case, you will do well in cross-examination.

It is usually the case that an expert witness does not stay for the entire trial. Normally, you are there only for the duration of your testimony and then you are dismissed from the proceedings. You should not be overly concerned with the verdict. Your job is to present the facts as you know them as clearly as you can. The attorneys then will formulate arguments based on those facts, and the jury will make whatever decision it feels is appropriate. Your job is to carefully and diligently study the case, to gather evidence, and to present the facts. Your job is not to secure a specific verdict. Unlike an attorney, you are not an advocate for your client.

Post Trial

In many civil trials, there will be a mixed outcome, with neither side having a clear and unambiguous victory. This usually leads to appeals. In fact, many times, when there is a clear victory, the other side will still appeal if it can find the grounds to do so. An expert's role in the appellate process is minimal at best, as appeals are usually based on matters of law. At most, you may be asked to consult with the attorneys regarding some technical details. But your job is essentially done when the trial is done.

The major exception would be if an appeal is based on your testimony, such as if the opposing counsel is claiming there was a problem with your expert testimony. For example, they may claim to have evidence that you perjured yourself on the stand. In those cases, your involvement in the appellate process will be more extensive.

Real Cases

In this section, we will examine some computer-related cases that went to trial, and how that trial process flowed. We will look for any items that might be educational for you.

U.S. v. AOL

This case was quite interesting, and while it was a criminal case, not a civil one, it is worth examining here. There are two reasons for this. The first reason is that this was a criminal case that also involved civil litigation. The second reason is that the process of this trial is worth examining. The basic facts are that a number of America Online executives were accused of colluding with executives from PurchasePro, Inc. for the purpose of overstating revenue from software licenses that AOL sold for PurchasePro[1]. Both parties were accused of accounting deceptions that led investors to believe that PurchasePro had met its sales projections when it had not, which led to an inflation of PurchasePro, Inc. stock prices. Revenues were overstated by 37 percent in the first quarter of 2001.

America Online and several of its executives reached out-of-court settlements that included payment of a $210 million fine. This settlement allowed them to avoid criminal and civil prosecution. This is the first element of this case that is relevant to this chapter; it is frequently the case that both a civil and a criminal case is brought against a defendant in order to increase pressure on the defendant to settle. If a person or company is facing criminal charges in addition to potential losses in civil litigation, an early settlement may seem more advantageous.

A total of six individuals, including PurchasePro's former chief executive officer Charles Johnson, were indicted on federal charges of conspiracy, securities fraud, obstruction of justice, and wire fraud. This is the second element of this case that merits our examination, specifically the wire-fraud charge. Wire fraud is usually done via electronic trading means, thus it is a crime that is related to computer systems. It is one of those crimes in which the computer system is a means to commit the crime, not the goal of the crime itself. There are many computer crimes in this category, including cyber stalking and identity theft. It should also be noted that in any significant financial case, computer records are seized, including hard drives, e-mail records, and any other electronic-data storage medium. This necessitates the proper application of computer forensics.

Among the accused were former AOL business affairs executive director Kent Wakeford, who managed the company's relationship with PurchasePro, and John Tuli, who was a vice president in AOL's NetBusiness unit. Both of these individuals, along with PurchasePro's top executives, also faced civil litigation from the Securities and Exchange Commission. Here we see a combined threat of civil and criminal prosecution from the federal authorities.

Two of the former executives at America Online were acquitted on all counts of charges that they conspired with PurchasePro to inflate PurchasePro's revenue with secret side deals and back-dated contracts. John Tuli, a former vice president in AOL's NetBusiness unit; Kent Wakeford, a former executive director at AOL's business-affairs unit; and Christopher Benyo, a former senior vice president of marketing at PurchasePro had been accused of deceiving PurchasePro stockholders about the company's revenue in the first quarter of 2001 as the dot-com economy collapsed[2].

The final element of this case that is pertinent to our discussion is the outcome. As of this writing, the former CEO of PurchasePro is still awaiting trial, but Mr. Tuli and Mr. Wakeford of AOL were acquitted at trial. Even with what seemed like fairly substantial evidence, and with some of their co-defendants making settlement and plea agreements, these two were still found not guilty at trial. This illustrates a fact we mentioned earlier that the outcome of any trial is never certain, and is also why both parties in civil litigation often wish to come to some sort of out-of-court settlement. A compromising resolution is often perceived as better than risking a total loss.

eBay v. Bidder's Edge, Inc.

In April 1999, eBay granted permission to the company Bidder's Edge, Inc. to use a Web crawler to crawl its site for a period of 90 days[3]. A *Web crawler* is software that goes through Web pages and extracts some sort of data. Bidder's Edge, Inc. specializes in listing the prices from multiple auction sites so that users can find the best price, regardless of what site it is listed on. After this informal arrangement was approved, the two parties worked to find a formal agreement; however, when no agreement was reached, eBay insisted that Bidder's Edge cease its Web-spidering activities. Bidder's Edge did not comply. This is the first item that is pertinent to our discussions. Clearly, one can begin with access to a system and later be denied that access. It does not matter if you were previously given access; once the owner rescinds that access, you must comply.

On December 10, 1999, eBay filed a lawsuit against Bidder's Edge, Inc. alleging trespass to personal property, unfair business practices, copyright infringement, misappropriation, false advertising, violation of the Computer Fraud and Abuse Act, 18 U.S.C. § 1030 trademark dilution, injury to business reputation, and interference with prospective economic advantage. This is also interesting to our study of civil litigation as it is often the case that a single act can involve multiple legal infractions.

On May 24, 2000, U.S. District Court Judge Ronald M. Whyte issued a preliminary injunction ordering Bidder's Edge to stop spidering auction data from eBay and posting it on its site. In his ruling, the judge stated that the activities of the Web spider that Bidder's Edge, Inc. was using were a form of trespass against eBay's property. The court forbade Bidder's Edge from using the Web spider, or any other automated query program, to access eBay's computer systems. This is an example of the motions we discussed earlier. The plaintiff, eBay, made a motion for an injunction and it was granted.

Bidder's Edge also filed antitrust complaints against eBay. In March of 2001, eBay and Bidder's Edge settled these matters out of court. As part of the settlement, Bidder's Edge paid eBay an undisclosed amount and agreed not to access and re-post eBay's auction information. Countersuits are very common in civil litigation. Generally, when one party is sued, they will countersue if they believe they have any grounds for such action. Sometimes even very tenuous grounds are used in filing a countersuit. This also illustrates the fact that many civil suits end with a settlement rather than a jury verdict.

International Airport Centers, L.L.C. v. Citrin

This case is fascinating because it explores the breadth of coverage provided by the Computer Fraud and Abuse Act. In this case, Jason Citrin was a managing director for International Airport Centers, L.L.C., a real-estate business.[4] Mr. Citrin's job was to find potential real-estate purchases for International Airport Centers. In order to conduct his job functions, he was provided with a company laptop. At some point, Mr. Citrin decided to leave International Airport Centers and go into business for himself, which would effectively make him a competitor to his current employer. Prior to leaving International Airport Centers, he deleted all the data on his laptop. Rather than simply delete files, Mr. Citrin used a special program to completely erase all data, which meant the data was truly gone and not recoverable. A further complication of this case was the allegation that before terminating his employment, it was alleged that Mr. Citrin had engaged in various activities to steal customers from his employer. His employment agreement also specifically prohibited him from competing with his employer.

International Airport Centers decided to sue Mr. Citrin, citing the Computer Fraud and Abuse Act—specifically, its provision against transmitting a program in order to damage a computer. Mr. Citrin made a motion to dismiss in which he argued that he had authority to do what he did because his employment contract authorized him to "return or destroy" data on the laptop when his employment was ending. The court rejected his argument and stated that "his authorization to access the laptop terminated when, having already engaged in misconduct and having decided to quit International Airport Centers in violation of his employment contract, he resolved to destroy files that incriminated himself and other files that were also the property of his employer, in violation of the duty of loyalty that agency law imposes on an employee." The court further opined that it was unlikely that the provision authorizing him to destroy data on the laptop was intended to authorize him to destroy data that he knew the company had no duplicates of and would want to retain.[5]

Mr. Citrin's other argument was that simply erasing files is not a "transmission" within the meaning of the Computer Fraud and Abuse Act. A district court agreed with Citrin and dismissed the case. However, that decision was overturned upon appeal. The appellate court held that when Mr. Citrin installed this erasing software on the laptop, he had indeed transmitted it. It is this element that is most relevant to our discussions. It is frequently the case that a law may be interpreted a bit more broadly than a literal reading might indicate.

While the appellate decision was handed down in 2006, as of this writing the case has not been ultimately resolved. This aspect of the case illustrates just how lengthy a civil trial can be, which is another reason parties often settle.

Conclusion

In this chapter, we have examined civil trials. After reading this chapter, you should have a basic understanding of how civil trials work and the role that an expert witness, particularly a computer-forensics expert, plays in such a trial. You should also have an understanding of some of the nuances of civil law, including the role of motions and appeals. Should your investigations ever be a part of civil litigation, we trust that this chapter has given you enough information to navigate that process without too much difficulty.

Endnotes

1 LAW.com. "A Jury Without a Peer." http://www.law.com/jsp/PubArticle.jsp?id=1194429840779

2 *The Washington Times.* "AOL Executives Found Not Guilty of Fraud." http://www.washingtontimes.com/news/2007/feb/06/20070206-010949-8389r/

3 eBay v. Bidder's Edge, Inc. http://pub.bna.com/lw/21200.htm

4 The Metropolitan Corporate Counsel. "Computer Fraud And Abuse Act: Another Arrow In The Quiver Of An Employer Faced With A Disloyal Employee, Part II." http://www.metrocorpcounsel.com/current.php?artType=view&artMonth=June&artYear=2006&EntryNo=5065

5 The Metropolitan Corporate Counsel. "Computer Fraud And Abuse Act: Another Arrow In The Quiver Of An Employer Faced With A Disloyal Employee, Part II." http://www.metrocorpcounsel.com/current.php?artType=view&artMonth=June&artYear=2006&EntryNo=5065

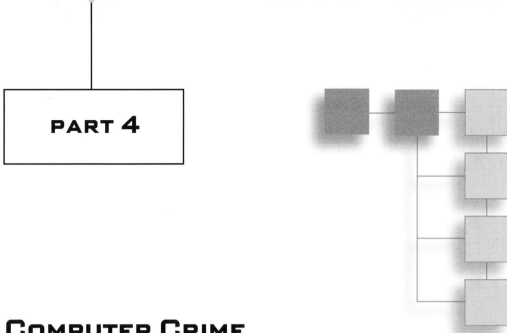

PART 4

COMPUTER CRIME AND INDIVIDUALS

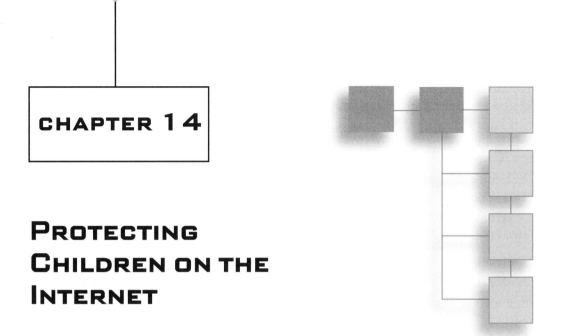

CHAPTER 14

PROTECTING CHILDREN ON THE INTERNET

Introduction

After reading this far into this book, you are clearly aware of the depth and breadth of computer crimes. But perhaps no computer crime is more disconcerting than pedophiles using the Internet to traffic in child pornography and to find new victims. In this chapter, we will examine this problem and also some practical steps one can take to protect one's children on the Internet. We will also examine tactics law enforcement can use to address this crime. The nature of this topic makes the material somewhat disturbing, even though we certainly won't be going into any specific or graphic details.

The Problem

One of the authors of this book is a police detective, and as such is unfortunately very aware of the scope of the problem of child pornography and the ways in which pedophiles try to lure children on the Internet. For the rest of us, you might simply look to your city's police department Web site or your state law-enforcement Web sites. In many cases, you will find that those agencies provide a utility for looking up registered sex offenders in your area. When you realize how many registered sex offenders live within a few miles of your home, you may be quite shocked. It must also be pointed out that such lists only contain the registered sex offenders. You might also gain an appreciation for the scope of this problem by watching television exposés such as the MSNBC News program

To Catch A Predator.[1] The first thing that stands out about such programs is they have yet to go to any city or town, regardless of the region or the size of the town, and fail to find predators who go online to attempt to arrange sexual liaisons with minors.

Programs like *To Catch a Predator* illustrate two important facts. The first is that every region contains sexual predators that use the Internet to find new victims. The second is that such predators come from all walks of life. They may be teachers, computer programmers, physicians, even police officers.

And of course, there are dangers other than a predator directly seeking out your child. As ProtectKids.com[2] points out, graphic and in some cases violent pornography is easily accessible to anyone on the Internet. It is entirely possible for your child to find such material on the Web, even accidentally. According to Enough Is Enough:

> Every second, $3,075.64 is being spent on pornography, 28,258 Internet viewers are viewing pornography, 372 Internet users are typing adult search terms into search engines, and every 39 minutes, a new pornographic video is made in the United States.[3]

It is not the purpose of this book, nor this author, to debate the morality of what adults view on the Internet. However, it should be clear from those statistics that pornography is very accessible via the Internet. It should also be obvious that pornographic Web sites cannot effectively prevent minors from accessing their material; the best they can do is ask the Web-site user if he or she is over 18 years old. Also according to Enough Is Enough, pornography is a $97 billion a year business, and child pornography is a $3 billion a year business.

How Online Predators Operate

It is important that both law enforcement and parents understand how online predators work. There are some common tactics that online predators use.

The first is to frequent places on the Internet that are likely to attract juveniles. They visit chat rooms or social-networking sites and strike up conversations with minors. Usually, these predators are very aware of the current trends among youths and know the latest movies, music, video games, and fads. The initial conversation the predator has with a minor will probably be about an innocuous topic that is of interest to a minor. During this initial phase, the predator is often looking for key signs that this child might be a likely target, including the following:[4]

- A child who is lonely or feels like he or she does not belong

- A child who feels he or she is not getting enough attention from his or her parents

- A child with significant problems such as parents divorcing, difficulties at school, or other life challenges

- A child with low self esteem

Once the predator has identified a potential target, he will then begin to try to extend the conversations outside the chat room or social page, taking them into private chats or e-mails. He will also likely act very sympathetic to whatever the child's problem is. Predators often use flattery with their intended victims. Children who feel like they don't belong or who have low self esteem are very susceptible to these sorts of tactics.

The next step is to begin easing sexual content into the conversation. The predator's intent is to gradually get the child comfortable discussing sexual topics. Usually, predators are careful to take this phase slowly so as not to cause the targeted child to panic. If this process proceeds to a point the predator feels comfortable, he will then suggest a face-to-face meeting. In some cases, the face-to-face meeting is expressly for the purpose of sex; in others, the predator lures the child to a location with the promise of some seemingly benign activity such as playing video games or seeing a movie.

Of course, there are sometimes deviations from this pattern. Some predators move much quicker to meet with the child face to face. They may also avoid sexual conversations at all and simply try to lure the child out of his or her house with the intent of forcibly molesting the child. Whether the predator chooses to lure the child and then force a sex act or attempts to seduce the child depends on how the predator views the act. It may surprise some readers to discover that some pedophiles actually view themselves not as child molesters, but rather as being in a relationship with the child. They actually think their behavior is acceptable and it is simply society that fails to understand them. This sort of pedophile is much more likely to use a method of gradually increasing the sexual content and explicitness of the online conversation. Their intent is to seduce the child.

Solutions for Parents

Before a parent can address this serious problem, he or she must be aware of the seriousness of the problem. Hopefully, this chapter has made you sufficiently aware. In this section, we will discuss ways you can work to prevent your child from becoming involved with an online predator.

You can do quite a lot to protect your children without using technological solutions. Just a few changes in your home could help ameliorate the danger. One common rule that is often recommended to parents is to control access to the computer. This primarily means keeping the computer in a common area. It is also important to establish clear rules on Internet use that include times it can be used and how it should be used. Setting rules for Internet usage should be accompanied by open, honest discussions about Internet use. Talk to your children about the dangers of the Internet; explain to them as much as is appropriate for their age. Most importantly, make certain they do not give out personal information on the Internet. If they have a Facebook or MySpace page, you should be listed as one of their friends so that you can see what they post on it.

Once you have implemented these non-technical means of protecting your children, you may want to consider some technological aids. The use of parental controls can be quite helpful. There are a number of software products one can purchase to help limit Internet activity. Some of the more well-known products are the following:

- Net Nanny, available at http://www.netnanny.com/alt_rotate. This product is an Internet filter available for Windows, Macintosh, and even mobile phones.

- B-Secure has a product called American Family Filter available at http://bsecure.com/offers/afafilter.aspx?13850. This product is available for Windows or mobile phone.

- CyberSitter is available at http://www.cybersitter.com/. This product is only available for Windows.

Windows Vista and Windows 7 have built-in parental controls that come with the operating system. The parental controls in Windows allow you to set up different controls for different users. Since these are available to anyone using Windows, we will look at how you set up these parental controls.

First, you must be logged on as an administrator. Then, go to Start > Control Panel > User Accounts. Select the individual user you wish to set up restrictions for, and then select Set Up Parental Controls. You should see something like what is shown in Figure 14.1.

Now you simply need to click the options to turn parental controls on, and to turn on activity reporting so that you can monitor how your child is accessing the computer and the Internet. You should see something like what is shown in Figure 14.2.

Next, you can select whether or not this user can play games on this computer. If you do allow games, you can allow or block specific games, and you can also allow or block certain games based on their rating (see Figure 14.3).

Controlling when the child can use the computer is very easy. You simply use your mouse to drag across blocks of time showing when the user can log on. If

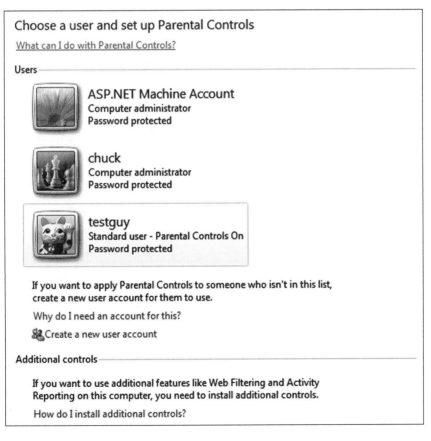

Figure 14.1
Select a user account.

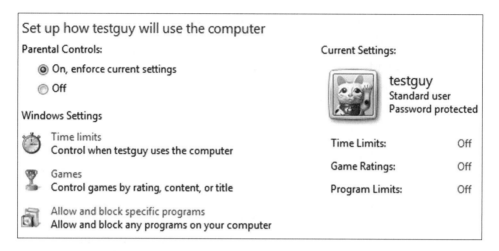

Figure 14.2
Turn on parental controls.

the child attempts to log on outside these established times, he or she will not be able to. This is shown in Figure 14.4.

Next, you can establish filters on Internet content, as shown in Figure 14.5. You can first choose to either block some content or allow all content. Then you have a choice to either block content by its rating or to only permit access to content that you have specifically allowed. This last option is more restrictive and will require the parent to approve any site the child wishes to visit and to add it to the list manually before the child can visit that site. Since this is labor intensive, many parents choose to simply block content based on rating. You can also block downloads on this screen. This can be a very good idea to prevent the child from downloading pornography and has the added benefit that it prevents him or her from accidentally downloading a virus or spyware.

These simple steps can help to reduce the chances of your child being exposed to objectionable content or from using the Web at odd hours when you cannot monitor what he or she is doing. However, some parents choose to go a step further and install software on the computer that monitors the details of their child's communication. This means installing spyware so that you can see the actual content of e-mails, chats, and other online communications, and you can view the actual Web sites your child visits. While some parents feel this is a responsible course of action, others feel it is an invasion of privacy. This is not a book about parenting, so a debate on the appropriateness of using spyware is outside the scope of this book. Whether this is an appropriate step to take or not

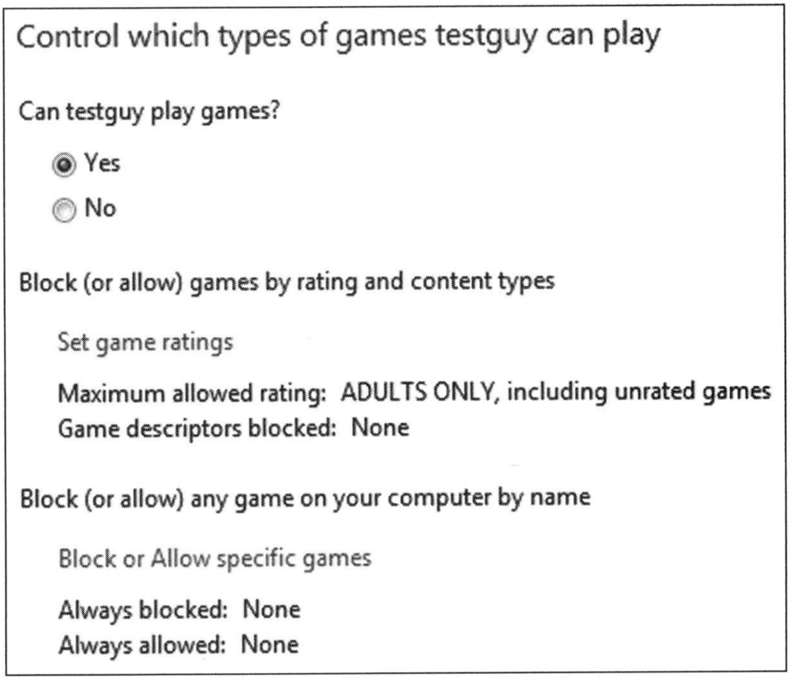

Control which types of games testguy can play

Can testguy play games?

◉ Yes

◯ No

Block (or allow) games by rating and content types

Set game ratings

Maximum allowed rating: ADULTS ONLY, including unrated games
Game descriptors blocked: None

Block (or allow) any game on your computer by name

Block or Allow specific games

Always blocked: None
Always allowed: None

Figure 14.3
Game controls.

is up to you. However, if you do decide to use this technology, you have several well-known options:

- SpectorSoft, available from http://www.spectorsoft.com/, monitors every detail of online activity. It is available for individual computers or for an

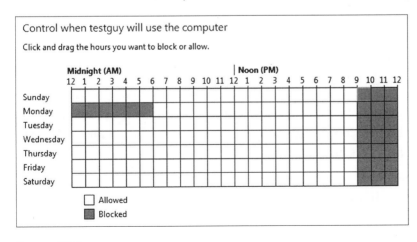

Figure 14.4
Time controls.

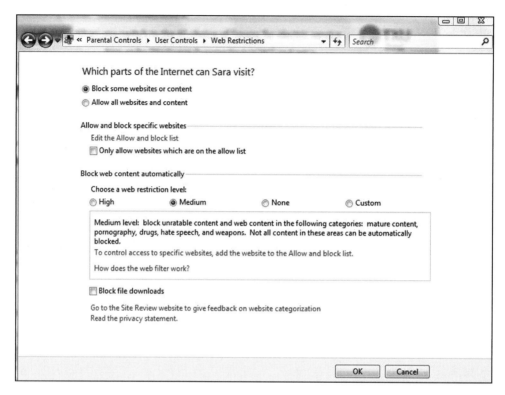

Figure 14.5
Internet filtering.

entire network (used by employers to monitor employee Internet use). You can also set it up to e-mail you activity reports. This product is available for Windows or Macintosh.

■ PC Tattle Tale, available from http://www.pctattletale.com/, is designed specifically for parental monitoring. They offer a free seven-day trial. It is available for Windows or Macintosh.

■ Safe Activity, available from http://www.softactivity.com/, has a free download. In addition to recording Internet activity, this product allows you to remotely monitor a computer live, while your child is using it.

These are just a few popular products you may consider using if you have decided to monitor your children's online activity. It is important to remember that no measures are foolproof, but you can take steps to ameliorate the danger. It is also critical that parents keep in mind that the most important step you can take is to talk to your children. Communication is critical in addressing most issues with children.

How to Know if Your Child Is Already in Danger

So far we have discussed how to prevent your child from becoming at risk to pedophiles on the Internet. But what do you do if your child has already been contacted by an online predator? It is critical that parents be aware of signs that their child is already in danger, as well as what steps to take to get him or her out of danger. Whatever approach the predator uses, there are some signs that a child might be involved with an online predator. Let's examine the most common signs that a child might have ongoing contact with an online predator. But be cognizant of the fact that any of these signs by themselves don't necessarily mean your child has been contacted by a pedophile. One needs to look at the entire spectrum of your child's behavior.

- **Does your child spend a lot of time on the computer?** Obviously, there are completely innocuous reasons a child might be on the computer, including playing online games, chatting with friends, or surfing the Web. So this particular sign, in and of itself, is not one to be overly concerned with. But when it is combined with one of the following signs, it should be taken seriously.

- **Does your child receive any communication from people you do not know?** Phone calls, e-mails, or letters from strangers should be a matter of grave concern, particularly if the child seems reluctant to tell you who the person is or seems to be making up lies to hide who the person is. This particular sign should be considered very serious. If it does involve an online predator, then this sign indicates that either this situation is almost to the point of an in-person meeting or that such a meeting may have already occurred.

- **Do you find pornography on your child's computers?** This is a sign that, while always a concern for a parent, may or may not indicate an online predator. It is entirely possible that a child, particularly a teenager, may have found pornographic materials on his or her own. At issue would be the content of the materials. Particularly graphic material or material that depicts an older person with a younger person should raise a red flag. You should also examine the source. If the pornographic materials were e-mailed to your child by someone you don't know or who is not in his or her same age range, that would be a clear indication of an online predator.

- **Does your child suddenly have items that you did not purchase for him or her?** A new iPod, game, or CD whose source is unexplained could be a gift from a pedophile. And if the child is receiving gifts, it is entirely possible that in-person meetings have already occurred. Any time your child has items of value that you don't know about should be a concern.

- **Has your child withdrawn from normal activities?** Whether the cause is the influence of an online predator or not, any time your child withdraws from his or her normal activities should be a matter of concern. It can mean an online predator, or it could mean drug use, depression, or some other serious problem. Under no circumstances should it be ignored.

- **Does your child hide his or her computer screen when you come by?** Quickly switching to another screen or hiding the monitor is a sign that something is occurring on the computer that the child doesn't want you to see. It may or may not be communication from an online predator, but whatever it is warrants parental attention.

- **Have you discovered alternate Internet accounts?** Does your child have new or secret e-mail addresses or Internet accounts? That could be a sign of communication channels established with an online predator. Much like the other signs we have discussed, this may be due to some other cause, but it certainly warrants parental attention.

If you suspect your child has already been contacted by an online predator, the most important thing is to stay calm. Obviously, you will be concerned, but this is not a time to panic. If you have not previously installed monitoring software on your child's computer, you should do so now. This can not only confirm (or refute) your suspicion, but it can also gather evidence for law enforcement. It is also important that you begin to closely monitor your child's physical location to prevent him or her from meeting the online predator.

If you confirm your child has been approached by an online predator, do not respond to the predator yourself. Immediately stop using the suspect computer, and contact law enforcement. By this point in this book, you should be well aware of the issues of handling forensic evidence. You should also know that even if you are a computer-forensics expert yourself, any evidence you personally obtain is likely to be viewed differently because of your conflict of interest. Do not try to perform the forensics yourself. Let the police handle the forensics and the investigation. You need to devote your time to your child's well being. You should also seek professional counseling to assist in this matter.

Solutions for Law Enforcement

Investigating and dealing with online predators is a challenging issue for law enforcement. It is important that you first and foremost deal with the victim appropriately. It is possible that an overzealous investigator can plant suggestions with a child about things that may not be accurate. You must avoid this when talking to the minor. It is best that an officer with experience dealing with child-related crimes handle the questioning of the minor child. The next issue is the forensics. As we have discussed throughout this book, you need to be very careful in dealing with the computer forensics to ensure the case is handled properly.

A major issue for law enforcement is the use of sting operations. These can be controversial. We have previously mentioned the program *To Catch a Predator*, which utilized sting operations to catch online predators. The group Perverted Justice[5] specializes in performing stings to catch online predators. They work exclusively with law-enforcement agencies and their volunteers are screened and trained. Particularly if your agency does not have experience with this sort of operation, or is simply under resourced, using a group like Perverted Justice can be a benefit to your agency.

The Perverted Justice group is considered controversial by some. They use adult volunteers who go online posing as children and engage in sexually explicit conversations with adults. Perverted Justice was set up in 2002 by Frank Fence-post and Xavier Von Erck. They claim that their actions have led to more than 300 convictions so far. The group is operated by volunteers, all of whom are first carefully screened and then given training. Once a volunteer has engaged in explicit conversations with an adult online, the next step is to get identifying information from that adult. That information and complete transcripts of all communication is then turned over to a law-enforcement agency. They do not attempt to directly contact or to apprehend the suspect themselves. Prior to 2003, the group would often simply post the logs to their Web site and/or contact the family of the intended victim. However, they have changed their policy and now contact a local law-enforcement agency.

It should also be noted that while some have charged the group with entrapment, they make it a policy to not send information on to law enforcement unless the adult in question has been very explicit and graphic in his or her communication, and the decoy has repeatedly made it clear that he or she is a minor. A reading of any transcripts (some can be found on the *To Catch a Predator* Web site, http://www.msnbc.msn.com/id/10912603/) makes it very clear that the adult was indeed soliciting sex with someone he thought was a minor. Such transcripts are much too graphic to be repeated in this book, but it should be emphasized that it is impossible to mistake the adult's intent.

The group also maintains a site called Wikisposure[6] where they track pedophile activists. It may be a shock to some readers to realize that there are pedophiles who hold that their pedophilia is merely a lifestyle choice and one that should be legal. Most notable among these activists is the group NAMBLA (North American Man-Boy Love Association)[7], which publicly advocates what they term "the decriminalization of relationships between adult males and minors."

Many law-enforcement officers and agencies that have worked with Perverted Justice have very positive comments to say about them. However, there has been some criticism. Not surprisingly, some of the most vocal criticism has come from defense attorneys and relatives of men arrested due to Perverted Justice's investigations.

Some law-enforcement agencies may laud the goals of Perverted Justice but may be concerned about issues such as entrapment and chain of custody. If a law-enforcement agency has such concerns, there is no reason that agency cannot conduct their own sting operation. Using only trained law-enforcement officers in the sting can help alleviate these concerns. One law-enforcement agency that has done just that is the Alken County Sheriff's office in South Carolina.[8] They established a sting operation of their own. The Sheriff's department has reported a great deal of success in this operation. In many cases, when they catch a pedophile through a sting operation, they find other victims. Nearby counties in South Carolina are now planning similar operations of their own.

Conclusion

Clearly, online predators are a serious problem. Both parents and law enforcement must take steps to combat this issue. Parents have at their disposal a number of technical and non-technical means to protect their children from this threat, and to help deal with the issue if their child is approached by an online predator. Law-enforcement agencies have many options in combating this problem as well. One option is a sting operation. Sting operations have been used to catch drug dealers, thieves, and other criminals, and there is no reason to assume they would not be effective in dealing with online predators.

Endnotes

[1] MSNBC. "To Catch a Predator." http://www.msnbc.msn.com/id/10912603

[2] ProtectKids.com. http://www.protectkids.com/dangers/onlinepred.htm

[3] Enough Is Enough. http://enough.org/inside.php?id=2UXKJWRY8

[4] How Pedophiles Operate. http://www.section21.m6.net/prf-how.php

[5] Perverted Justice. http://www.perverted-justice.com/

[6] Wikisposure. http://www.wikisposure.com/Main_Page

[7] NAMBLA. http://www.nambla.org/

[8] WRDW Channel 12, August Georgia. "Local Law Enforcement Targeting Online Predators." http://www.wrdw.com/home/headlines/46845787.html

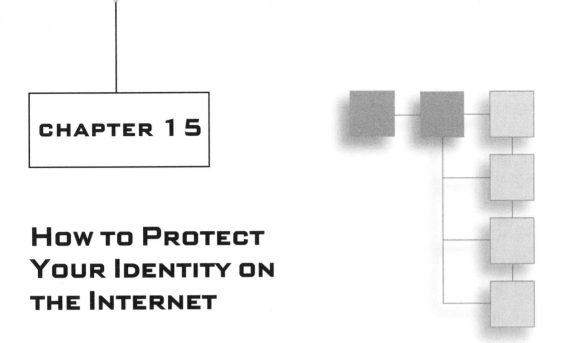

CHAPTER 15

How to Protect Your Identity on the Internet

Introduction

In preceding chapters, we have already seen that identity theft is a serious problem. We have also looked at the techniques that identity thieves use. In this chapter, we will examine some countermeasures you can take to prevent identity theft. We will also look at techniques law enforcement can use to investigate identity theft.

According to the Federal Trade Commission's 2006 report on identity theft,[1] approximately 8.5 million Americans were victims of identity theft in a single year. Of those victims, 1.8 million discovered that their stolen identities had been used to open new credit accounts. The rest had existing accounts compromised and used by the thieves. That report further states that the median amount stolen was $500, while 10 percent of the cases involved amounts in excess of $6,000. These numbers tell us a couple of things:

- Identity theft is a growing problem. 8.5 million victims means that in a single year, about 2.8 percent of the United States population was the victim of identity theft. This means your odds of being a victim in any given year are about 1 in 30.

- Most identity thefts involve small amounts. This can lead to people taking the problem less seriously and being less aggressive in countermeasures.

However, a significant number of cases, about 850,000, involved more than $6,000.

These figures should be a bit alarming to you. It should also be pointed out that in addition to the actual money stolen is the time and effort the victims must spend trying to sort out the problem and repair their damaged credit. These damages are harder to calculate but are just as significant.

What You Can Do

We will begin by looking at what you can do to protect yourself from identity theft. Rather than simply list a number of actions you can take, we will examine each technique that identity thieves use and then look at the specific counter-measures for that technique. Then we will look at general defense measures that will apply to all forms of identity theft, and finally we will examine what you should do if you think you have been the victim of identity theft.

Phishing

As we have examined earlier, phishing is an attempt to get you to provide the perpetrator with personal information that can be used to steal your identity. Phishing uses spoofed e-mails and Web sites to try to lure the victim into divulging personal data. This is perhaps the most common way to perpetrate phishing. The good news is that it is also the easiest to defend against. It relies totally on you being willing to give up personal information. A little caution can help you avoid this.

Phishing E-mails

Let's begin by addressing phishing e-mails. As we discussed earlier in this book, a phishing e-mail will purport to be from a legitimate source. It will try to convince you there is a problem with a particular account of yours, and in order to correct the mistake you have to click on the link in the e-mail and fill out some form. But rather than take you to a legitimate site, if you click that link, it will take you to a site set up by the criminals in order to gather your personal information.

During the writing of this book, a new e-mail phishing scheme was becoming widespread. This particular scheme capitalized on the popularity of Facebook. This e-mail claimed there was a problem with your Facebook account that you needed to correct. You can see an example of this e-mail in Figure 15.1.

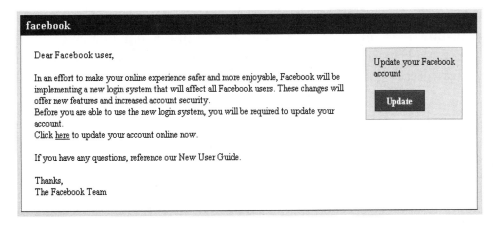

Figure 15.1
Facebook phishing e-mail.

In this case, the perpetrators have done a good job of making the e-mail look like it is from Facebook. They have taken the time to completely emulate Facebook's fonts, graphics, and format. However, there are some telltale signs that this is not legitimate. If you move your mouse over either the "Click here" link or the Update button without clicking them, the actual Web address they point to will pop up. You can see that in Figure 15.2.

Notice the long string of characters after the "www.facebook.com" part: That is a clear indication that this link will actually take you to a different Web site, not to Facebook. In this case, the actual address is www.facebook.com.sazzawy.eu. It is

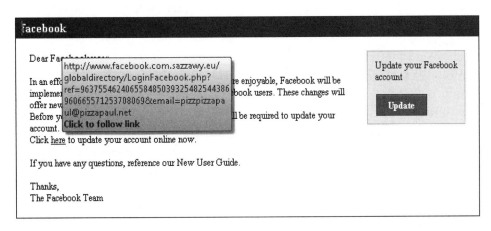

Figure 15.2
View the Web address to which a link in an e-mail points.

also common for these sites to be up for only a very short time. One of the authors of this book intentionally clicked on the link about four weeks after getting the e-mail (he keeps these sorts of things for research purposes), and the Web site was already gone.

Note

An interesting thing to note about phishing sites is how they get their domain names. If one does a Whois or domain lookup on www.facebook.com.sazzawy.eu it is, as of this writing, available. One technique phishing perpetrators try is a variation on what is called domain kiting. *Domain kiting* is a process that takes advantage of a weakness in the domain registry system. When one purchases a domain name, one has a five-day grace period to decline it for a full refund. Domain kiting is the process of registering a number of domains that are very close to popular domain names. For example, you might register www.microsof.com (note the missing "t" at the end). Then, if people misspell the real domain, they accidentally go to yours instead. The domain site is filled with click-through and pay-per-click ads. The perpetrator has dozens of these up for a few days just to scam the ad money. In the case of phishing, they use the same scheme to temporarily register a domain name for use in their phishing scheme.

These phishing Web sites tend to be up for only a short time. But as you have seen, simply putting your mouse over the link and seeing what it actually links to can be a great benefit in avoiding phishing e-mails.

It is also important for you to be aware that most organizations, particularly banking and credit institutions, will not send you e-mails asking you to follow a link to your account. If you think the message might be legitimate, then open your browser and type in the address of the Web site manually. For example, if you get an e-mail purporting to be from your Visa card, open your browser and type in the address that is on the back of your credit card. Then log in via that Web site and see if there is a problem.

You should also consider reporting these phishing attempts to the organization in question. If you have a suspicious e-mail from your bank, call your bank and ask them about it. It is very likely that they will forward you to their fraud department, who will ask you to forward the e-mail in question to them. This allows them to use their resources to attempt to catch the perpetrators, or at least to warn other customers of the scam.

Phishing Web Sites

Web sites play a role in phishing scams. The most common way is for the Web site to be the target of a phishing e-mail. Even if you do follow a link to a Web site, there are ways you can tell if the site is legitimate. One such way that is becoming increasingly popular with financial institutions is the site key. In Figure 15.3, you can see an example of a Bank of America site key.

The way a site key works is that when you open an account you are asked to select an image from a random group of images, and then to select a pass phrase, which can be anything you want. In the image shown in Figure 15.3 there is a pair of goggles. You can add to that any random pass phrase. Then when you log in to the Web site, the first step is to enter just your ID, not your password. After your ID is entered, the Web site will show you your image and pass phrase; this is your site key. If you do not see the image and pass phrase you selected, then this is not a legitimate site and you should not enter your password. You should instead report that site's address to your financial institution's fraud department so that they can initiate an investigation.

Another way phishing can work is the use of fake sales sites. These are far less common than phishing e-mails. Essentially, the perpetrator sets up a Web site much as they would for other types of phishing. The Web site is probably hosted

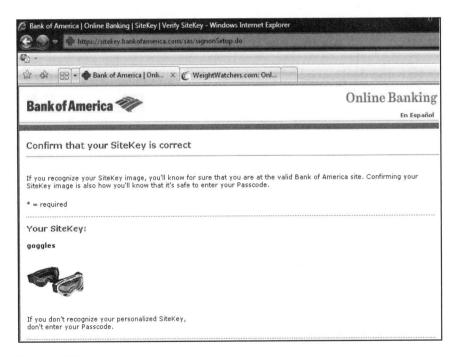

Figure 15.3
Site key.

on a compromised zombie server (i.e., the perpetrator has hacked into someone else's system and set up the Web site there), or on an anonymous hosting site. One can host on most public hosting companies servers with just a credit card, including a pre-paid credit card. Then the site purports to sell some item at a very low price, for example Blu-ray players for $40. The perpetrator then sends out spam enticing people to visit the site. If you visit the site and fill out an order form, you will never get the product, but you have just given your personal information and credit-card number to the perpetrator.

The best way to protect yourself against this sort of scam is to simply be wary when shopping online. You are usually safe ordering from well-known online shopping sites such as Amazon.com. However, before you order from a new or unknown site, take a few steps to check out the site:

- Run the site address through Whois. Find out who owns the site and where it is registered.

- You can run the site through www.netcract.com and find out how long the site has been up and information about the server.

- Look for some information on the Web about the company. If there are zero references to the company, this is a sign it may be a scam.

- Ask yourself: Is the deal too good to be true? If it seems too good to be true, it probably is.

Following just a few simple rules for online shopping can help you avoid a great many problems. And for those readers who want an extra layer of protection, there is another step you can take. Get a pre-paid Visa credit card; many places sell them at the checkout counter, including major retailers such as Walmart. Use that pre-paid card for all online shopping. If your card is compromised by a criminal, the most he or she will be able to steal is the amount on your pre-paid card. If you are using a debit card, he or she could potentially drain your entire checking and savings accounts.

Spyware

Another way that perpetrators gather personal information is by using spyware. In previous chapters, we discussed what spyware is and some of the ways it can get on your system. Perhaps the most common way is via an e-mail attachment. The goal of the perpetrator is to entice you into opening the e-mail so that

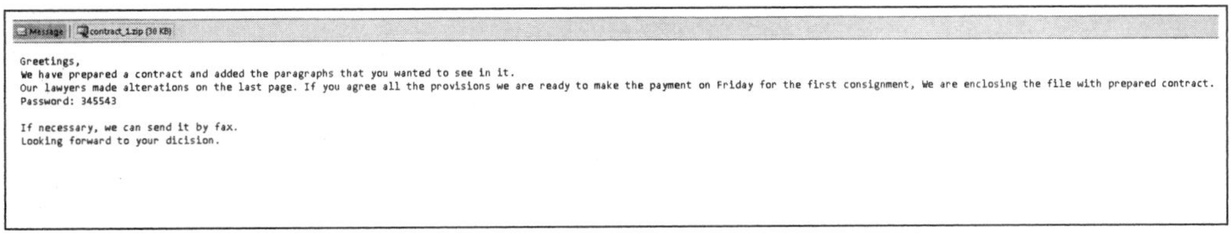

Figure 15.4
Spyware e-mail.

the spyware can be delivered. Let's look at a typical e-mail of this sort (see Figure 15.4).

This is an e-mail one of the authors received. This one is not quite as sophisticated as some, because it would not attract a wide audience. However, it is likely that the perpetrators are attempting to target business owners in the theory that stealing their identities would yield more reward. So this e-mail purports to have contract documents for you to review and sign. If you imagine yourself as a busy business owner or executive, you can see how one might open the attachment without first looking closely. However, this e-mail has some telltale signs:

- Notice the signature block. Most business e-mails have a signature block with the person's name, title, company, and contact information. If this e-mail had those elements, you would know whether or not it was a company you were doing business with.

- Take note of the greeting. It is generic and not specifically addressed to you. This is common for e-mails that contain viruses and spyware.

- Finally, you may notice a few spelling errors. Certainly, anyone can misspell a word, and by itself a misspelling should certainly not be taken as a sign that the e-mail is spyware or a virus. However, when added to the other items, this is a warning sign.

Simply being careful about opening attachments will help you to avoid most spyware. It is also critical that you run some sort of antivirus and anti-spyware. It is also important that you use a well-known and respected antivirus tool. Any of the following are good choices:

- **Norton.** Available at http://www.symantec.com/index.jsp

- **Kaspersky.** Available at http://www.kaspersky.com/

- **AVG.** Available at http://www.avg.com/

- **McAfee.** Available at http://www.mcafee.com/us/

We should also note that a number of people highly recommend Malware Bytes from http://www.malwarebytes.org. However, because neither of the authors has had direct experience with that product, we cannot recommend it. It might well be an excellent product, but we have not examined it in order to make our own evaluation.

There are certainly other antivirus products, and even a number of free ones. However, there are issues with relying on less well-known products. To begin with, there are questions as to how often they will update their virus lists, as well as questions about the financial stability of the vendor. So as a general rule, it is best to rely on well-known antivirus products.

Gathering Personal Data

Another way that identity thieves work is simply by gathering as much personal data about a person as they can. To some extent, it is impossible to avoid personal data about you being made public. For example, court records are public records and many courts now have records available online. It is probably not possible for you to prevent this. Someone could use the Internet to find out about any litigation you have been involved in, any criminal charges, even traffic tickets. However, this is not enough information to steal your identity.

Other places perpetrators can find personal data is via social-networking sites. Sites such as MySpace and Facebook were designed for people to connect and to share information. Therefore, they tend to be target-rich environments for personal information. There are a few things you can do to decrease the chances of an identity thief getting personal information about you via a social-networking site:

- Keep most of your information private and share it only with friends. Someone who has not friended you should only see your name and possibly a single photo of you, nothing more. They should not see your address, birthday, or any other information about you. Figure 15.5 shows Facebook privacy settings.

- Do not give specifics. For example, you might say you live in Chicago, but do not post a street address. You might give your birthday, but not the year.

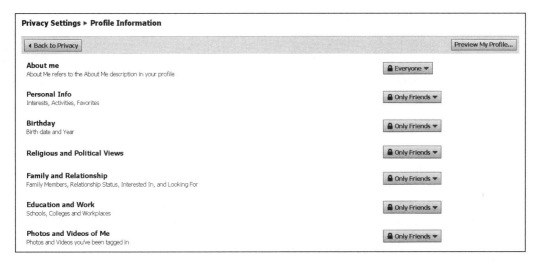

Figure 15.5
Facebook privacy settings.

Anyone who knows you probably already knows your address, and anyone celebrating your birthday only needs month and day, they don't need a year.

- Be careful of who you let become a friend. You may receive friend requests from strangers. In that case, just e-mail them back asking them where you know them from.

It should be noted that one of the authors of this book keeps a Facebook page specifically for interacting with students and readers. For that reason, it is much more accessible than we normally recommend. However, there is no information on that page that would be of use to an identity thief. But if you do want to find that author on Facebook, just search for *Chuck Easttom.*

Also be careful of information you give out in any public forum. This includes bulletin boards and chat rooms. Many neighborhood homeowners' associations now have Web sites with bulletin boards, and all too frequently people reveal personal information on such Web sites. Simply restricting what you make available online can do a great deal to protect your identity.

General Countermeasures

There are some general countermeasures you can take to avoid becoming the victim of identity theft. These are not for any specific type or technique of identity theft, but are general guidelines that can help ensure your safety.

- Destroy sensitive documents completely; do not simply throw them in the trash. For about $20, one can purchase a paper shredder at any office store or retail store. Use that to shred any old documents before you throw them out. Some identity thieves use a tactic called Dumpster diving, which literally means combing through trash for personal data.

- If you throw out old computer media, destroy it thoroughly. For example, old CDs, floppy disks, hard drives, tapes, and so on should be physically destroyed before they are thrown out.

- Check your credit periodically. If someone steals your identity, it is likely for a financial motive. They want to obtain credit and make purchases in your name. If you are routinely checking your credit, you might be able to catch it early and stop it.

- Put a notice on your credit report. Most credit-reporting agencies will place a notice on your report that no new credit is to be issued to this identity without first calling the home number and verifying. This will add a bit of an inconvenience if you are purchasing a new car or getting furniture on credit, but it can help avoid someone else making purchases in your name. It should be noted that not all retailers will honor that credit-report notice, but since many will, it is a good idea.

It is recommended, however, that you avoid the commercial identity protection tools such as LifeLock and IdentityProtect.com. They offer very minimal protection, and what protection they do offer comes primarily in the form of things you can do yourself for free. For example, putting a notice on your credit report is one of the steps they take. You can do this for free. *Consumer Reports* did a thorough examination of LifeLock[2] and did not give them a favorable recommendation. Also according to *Consumer Reports,* the protections offered by LifeLock should your identity be stolen are rather vague. The contract is not clear on exactly what they will or will not reimburse. And while the television commercials feature a man displaying his Social Security number publicly, LifeLock's contract specifically forbids its customers from publicly divulging private information such as their Social Security number; doing so nullifies the contract.

What to Do If You Become a Victim

In the unfortunate event that you become a victim of identity theft, there are some key steps you should take. The very first step is to notify all of your banks and credit cards of what has transpired. They will often give you some re-commendations, many of which we will also give you here. You must im-mediately close those accounts that you believe have been compromised. This may be quite inconvenient, but the alternative is much worse.

You should immediately contact all three credit-reporting bureaus and place a fraud alert on your credit report. Here is the contact information for those bureaus:

- **TransUnion:** 1-800-680-7289; http://www.transunion.com; Fraud Victim Assistance Division, P.O. Box 6790, Fullerton, CA 92834-6790

- **Equifax:** 1-800-525-6285; http://www.equifax.com; P.O. Box 740241, Atlanta, GA 30374-0241

- **Experian:** 1-888-EXPERIAN (397-3742); http://www.experian.com; P.O. Box 9532, Allen, TX 75013

According to the Federal Trade Commission, there are two types of alerts you can put on your credit file. This quote from the FTC Web site[3] will explain that more thoroughly:

> There are two types of fraud alerts: an initial alert and an extended alert. An initial alert stays on your credit report for at least 90 days. You may ask that an initial fraud alert be placed on your credit report if you suspect you have been, or are about to be, a victim of identity theft.
>
> An initial alert is appropriate if your wallet has been stolen or if you've been taken in by a "phishing" scam. Phishing occurs when scam artists steal personal information from you by sending e-mail that claims to be from a legitimate company and says you have a problem with your account. When you place an initial fraud alert on your credit report, you're entitled to one free credit report from each of the three nationwide consumer-reporting companies.
>
> An extended alert stays on your credit report for seven years. You can have an extended alert placed on your credit report if you've been a victim of identity theft and you provide the consumer-reporting company with an "identity theft report." When you place an extended alert on your credit report, you're entitled to two free credit reports within 12 months, after placing the alert, from each of the three nationwide consumer-reporting

companies. In addition, the consumer-reporting companies will remove your name from marketing lists for prescreened credit offers for five years unless you ask them to put your name back on the list before then.

This is a critical step. This notice may prevent further damage by alerting financial institutions that a fraud has occurred.

The next step is to report the crime. You should report it either to your local police department or to the police in the city where the theft occurred (if you know where). Then you should also file a complaint with the Federal Trade Commission. You can file a complaint at the Web site or by calling 1-877-438-4338. You should be aware, however, that investigating these sorts of crimes is not always successful. One reason for the difficulty in investigating these crimes is that sometimes these crimes involve perpetrators in other countries. However, it would be a serious mistake to not report the crime. First of all, there is always a chance that law enforcement will catch and be able to convict the perpetrator. Many identity thieves have been caught and convicted. Often, these criminals have an ongoing criminal enterprise. An individual reported incident may not lead to a capture and conviction, but multiple incidents that get reported probably will.

Law Enforcement and Identity Theft

For the law-enforcement office, the issue is how to properly investigate identity theft. This crime requires some specific law-enforcement steps in order to successfully investigate it.

The first step is to attempt to trace the phishing e-mail and the Web site. We discussed some of these techniques in Chapter 10, "Collecting Evidence from Other Sources." If you can trace the IP address for the e-mail and/or the Web site, you will then need to ascertain who registered that domain name. This may require a subpoena for the Internet service provider or hosting company. If the phishing Web site was hosted on a zombie server (a third-party server that has been hacked and used for this purpose), then you will need to investigate the hacking of that server and attempt to ascertain who is responsible for it. If the phishing site was hosted with a hosting company, they should have access logs that record the username, password, and IP address of whoever established this site. They may also have logs of the IP addresses that have accessed the site. You can then try to track down additional victims, or at least warn people of the possible danger.

It is also important to attempt to track the case from the other end. That means starting from the use of the data. Often, identities are stolen to make illicit purchases. If, for example, a credit-card number was stolen, then the credit-card company should have some records of the purchases made. You can investigate those purchases in order to gain clues about the perpetrator.

Let's take a hypothetical scenario. Let's assume John Doe has had his identity stolen and his Visa card compromised after he responded to an e-mail purporting to be a security bulletin from his bank. You should investigate this in two ways. The first is to try to track down who sent that e-mail and who set up the Web site. Even if Mr. Doe has already deleted the e-mail, his browser history might still have that Web site in it. Try to track down the site. Then use the techniques already mentioned to try to gather more information about who was hosting this site. At the same time, you should try to track purchases made with that credit card. For example, perhaps someone purchased products online and had them shipped to some address, or perhaps they downloaded products (such as songs). That can give you yet another lead on who the perpetrator is. Just keep in mind that you will probably have to utilize several diverse investigative paths to find the criminal.

The biggest mistake an investigator can make is taking the situation too lightly. A single individual who has had $400 stolen via his or her credit card being compromised may not seem like a major crime. And the fact that the perpetrator may have used overseas servers, or even be overseas, may make this seem like an unsolvable case. But remember that identity theft is rarely an isolated crime. Chances are that if one victim has been reported, there are hundreds others. And remember that while multiple victims might make a case more complex, it also means more clues to help find the perpetrator.

Conclusion

Identity theft is clearly a serious problem, and it is one that is growing. However, there are steps you can take both to prevent identity theft and to deal with it once it has occurred. This is a crime that can affect anyone, so it is critical that you learn the steps required to prevent identity theft and that you implement those steps.

Endnotes

[1] FTC Identity Theft Statistics for 2006. http://www.ftc.gov/os/2007/11/SynovateFinalReportIDTheft2006.pdf

[2] *Consumer Reports.* "LifeLock's Ads Are Bold, Its Protection Less So." http://www.consumerreports.org/cro/money/credit-loan/questionable-id-theft-protection-3-08/overview/questionable-id-theft-protection-ov.htm

[3] FTC Identity Theft Recommendations. http://www.ftc.gov/bcp/edu/pubs/consumer/idtheft/idt07.shtm

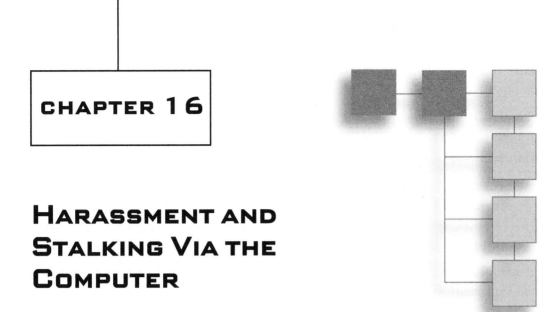

CHAPTER 16

HARASSMENT AND STALKING VIA THE COMPUTER

Introduction

We have mentioned the issue of cyber stalking and harassment in previous chapters. We even discussed a few prominent cases and the relevant state laws regarding this issue. In this chapter, we will go into more depth on the topic. We will also discuss what you can do to prevent stalking and harassment from occurring and what you can do if it does occur.

What Is Cyber Stalking and Harassment?

Many years ago, the saying became common on the Internet that WWW did not really stand for World Wide Web; instead, it stood for "Wild Wild West." While that was originally meant facetiously, it is probably an accurate evaluation of the Internet. The Internet is a largely unregulated communication medium in which almost anything goes. Anyone can post anything they want. If you have any experience with public boards such as usenet groups, Amazon communities, or similar groups, you already know the diversity of postings one can find on the Internet. To some extent, this is a positive thing. The Internet provides myriad free and open discussion forums. It is not at all uncommon for someone to get overzealous in defending their viewpoint and to post rather hostile and derogatory statements about their ideological opponents. However, this almost never escalates beyond that level, and therefore does not constitute harassment. There are even those who like to post extremely offensive things simply because they enjoy watching the ensuing reactions. This also does not rise to the level of harassment.

So what is harassment? It is a sustained and targeted attempt to intimidate or frighten the target through intentional conduct. The Criminal Justice Intervention Web site posts this definition of harassment:

> engaging in intentional conduct which the actor [harasser] knows or has reason to know would cause the victim, under the circumstances, to feel frightened, threatened, oppressed, persecuted, or intimidated; and causes this reaction on the part of the victim.[1]

It would be quite difficult to make the claim that a rude comment on a public communications forum meets this definition.

The U.S. Legal Definitions Web site defines harassment as follows:

> A person is guilty of harassment in the first degree when he or she intentionally and repeatedly harasses another person by following such person in or about a public place or places or by engaging in a course of conduct or by repeatedly committing acts which place such person in reasonable fear of physical injury.[2]

Obviously, this definition applies to actual physical harassment, but the same concept applies to online harassment as well. Notice the requirements that the acts be intentional and repeated and the requirement that the perpetrator's actions place the person in reasonable fear of personal injury. Insults in an online forum simply do not meet this definition.

So what might constitute online harassment? Let us look at a scenario. Suppose you are in an online discussion board and you interact with a hostile person. Then the person begins e-mailing you repeated threats. You ask the person to stop, yet the person persists. You put the person on your blocked e-mail list, but the person uses a different e-mail to send you more threats. It is now likely that this may fit your state's definition of online harassment. It is usually important to at least report this action to the police.

Cyber stalking is a more serious version of harassment. It usually involves a sustained pattern of harassment. The Wired Safety Web site[3] defines cyber stalking in the following way:

> When identifying cyberstalking "in the field," particularly when considering whether to report it to any kind of legal authority, the following features or

combinations of features can be considered to characterize a true stalking situation:

- Malice

- Premeditation

- Repetition

- Distress

- Obsession

- Vendetta

- No legitimate purpose

- Personally directed

- Disregarded warnings to stop

- Harassment

- Threats

Notice the requirements of malice and premeditation. These are key elements to the case of criminal cyber stalking. Furthermore, the perpetrator's actions must be such that a reasonable person would feel distress. Other important elements to note are that the person has disregarded warnings or requests to stop. The difference between harassment and cyber stalking is more a matter of degree, so there is no clear line of demarcation between the two. However, the Justice Department conducted a report in 1999[4] and in that report had this to say about cyber stalking:

Although there is no universally accepted definition of cyberstalking, the term is used in this report to refer to the use of the Internet, e-mail, or other electronic communications devices to stalk another person. Stalking generally involves harassing or threatening behavior that an individual engages in repeatedly, such as following a person, appearing at a person's home or place of business, making harassing phone calls, leaving written messages or objects, or vandalizing a person's property. Most stalking laws require that the perpetrator make a credible threat of violence against the victim; others include threats against the victim's immediate family; and still others require only that the alleged stalker's course of conduct constitute an implied threat. While some conduct involving annoying or menacing behavior might fall short of illegal stalking, such behavior may be a prelude to stalking and violence and should be treated seriously.

Notice the warning at the end about the possibility that cyber stalking could be a prelude to actual violence. This is the real concern about online harassment and stalking: that it might not simply be online. Also note that the Department of Justice, like the other sources we have examined, includes in its definition the issues of repeating the behavior and a credible threat of violence. The real issue with all of these attempts to define cyber stalking is that the conduct must be directed at you, be repeated, be threatening, and that you have asked that they stop on more than one occasion. In these cases, the harassment may have crossed the line to the level of stalking.

It is important to keep in mind, though, that someone being hostile toward you online is not the same as harassment or stalking. Can you easily avoid the person by simply blocking their e-mail or not rejoining that particular forum? If so, and if such acts stop the communication, then it is unlikely this scenario would be considered a serious problem by law enforcement. However if you make reasonable steps to avoid that person and that person takes conscious and deliberate steps to circumvent your measures to avoid him or her, then you probably have a harassment or cyber-stalking case going on.

It should also be noted that cyber stalking and harassment is not limited to e-mail and Web pages. A person can use a cell phone or any communications device to harass someone else. The Department of Justice[5] has catalogued cases in which the perpetrator text messages "187" to the victim repeatedly (187 is the California penal code for murder). The Department of Justice Web site discusses how stalkers might use a Web site or chat room to entice others to harass the targeted victim, as well as state and federal laws against cyber stalking and harassment. In particular, it discuses United States Code 875, which states that:

> Under 18 U.S.C. 875(c), it is a federal crime, punishable by up to five years in prison and a fine of up to $250,000, to transmit any communication in interstate or foreign commerce containing a threat to injure the person of another....

Why Cyber Stalkers Do It

Many readers may be puzzled by online harassment and cyber stalking. Unlike other computer crimes we have examined in this book, this one does not have a clear motive. Many computer crimes are financially motivated, and while obviously most people disapprove of identity theft, it is easy to understand the financial motives behind it. There can be any number of motivations for cyber stalking, including:

- **Low self esteem.** Some people have very low self esteem, and they get a sort of ego boost by denigrating others. The Internet allows them to do this remotely with complete strangers. By harassing another person, they feel they have elevated themselves. It is the same motivation that drives schoolyard bullies.

- **Obsession.** Some cyber stalking begins with unrequited romantic feelings or a relationship that ended against the stalker's wishes. In these cases, the stalker is obsessed with the target of the harassment.

- **Revenge.** In some cases, the cyber stalker wants to extract revenge for some grievance, whether real or imagined. This person believes that by causing the victim significant distress via online harassment, he or she will have been avenged of this wrong.

- **Insanity.** In some cases, the perpetrator is mentally unstable and may have targeted a victim because of delusions. In these cases, there is very little the victim can do to dissuade the perpetrator, and the harassment is likely to escalate.

Regardless of the motive behind the harassment, it must not be dismissed lightly. Unfortunately, some cases of cyber stalking escalate to real-world violence. It is important that you be aware of this fact and take precautionary steps.

Real-World Cases

Let's look at a few examples of cyber stalking. By studying these real-world cases, it is likely you will gain a better understanding of what constitutes online harassment and cyber stalking, as well as a better understanding of the seriousness of the problem.

England's Most Obsessive Stalker

In England, Jason Smith continually harassed college student Alexandra Scarlett.[6] He would send her as many as 30 messages a day threatening to slash her face, sexually assault her mother, or shoot her father. He was convicted and given a 12-month suspended sentence and a restraining order. Within a week of his conviction, however, he used social-networking sites to track down Ms. Scarlett and continue the campaign of harassment.

This case is also an example of stalking in response to unrequited romantic feelings. Mr. Smith had met Ms. Scarlett at a night club. She had given him her phone number. He then became convinced that they were in love and that they must be together. This led him to extreme jealousy, and eventually to the obsessive stalking. As of this writing, the final resolution of this case is unkown. But it clearly shows how easy it is to attract the attention of a stalker. The victim did nothing wrong. She behaved completely normally, yet still became the target of a stalker.

70-Year-Old Man Stalks 16-Year-Old Girl Online

Seventy-year-old Joseph Medico met a 16-year-old girl at his church.[7] The girl was at the church volunteering, helping to prepare donations for homeless shelters. Mr. Medico followed the girl to her car and tried to talk her into going to dinner with him and then back to his home. When she spurned his advances, he began calling and texting her several times a day.

When she realized he was not going to stop, she called the police. Mr. Medico was arrested and charged with stalking. As of February 10th, 2010, Mr. Medico was out on bail. The trial has not occurred as of this writing. This case illustrates how easy it is for an unstable person to become obsessed with his or her victim. It also demonstrates the proper way to handle this sort of situation. This is definitely a case to report to the police. An adult who is making romantic overtures to a minor is a matter of grave concern.

These are just two cases, and we presented a few other examples earlier in this book. Together, these cases should help you to understand what constitutes harassment and stalking.

Protecting Yourself

As we have seen, not all hostile encounters on the Internet are cyber stalking or harassment. But you should be aware that the Internet allows access to everyone, including unstable and potentially violent people. There are steps you can take to avoid engaging with such people on the Internet. There are also steps you can take to avoid having someone who knows you personally use the Internet to harass or stalk you.

What do you do if you encounter a stranger on the Internet who is bothering you? A few simple steps can help you to resolve the situation:

- Place that person's e-mail address on your blocked e-mail list.

- Stop posting in the forum in which you encountered the person.

- Do not communicate with the person under any circumstances.

- Do not post in any forum that references the person.

If the person is simply overly aggressive, these tactics will probably dissuade him or her. If the person persists, then you can show law enforcement (and eventually perhaps a jury) that you took all reasonable steps to avoid the person.

There are also steps you can take to avoid this situation in the first place:

- Never use your real identity on any public forum. Do not use your real name, or provide any identifying features.

- If you are on a public forum and someone is posting an overly hostile manner, erratically, or in any way that makes you uncomfortable, simply avoid that person. Do not engage him or her in any way.

- If you feel you must have a public e-mail address when using a public forum, then set up a separate account using Hotmail, Google, Yahoo!, or a similar free service and use that e-mail on public forums. Then, if you must, you can always delete that account without inconveniencing friends and colleagues who use your real e-mail address.

If you take these steps, you will probably be able to avoid the issue of strangers stalking you. The fact is that with so many millions of people on the Internet, and such free and open avenues of communication, it is not at all unlikely that you would encounter someone on the Internet who is genuinely mentally ill and/or violent. These simple steps can help you to protect yourself.

Online harassment from someone you know, on the other hand, is both more complicated and more serious. It is more complicated because the line between legitimate but rude communication and harassment is much less clear. It is more serious because this person knows you, and if the situation escalates, violence can be a real possibility. If you feel someone you know is harassing you online, the first step is to calmly but politely e-mail that person and ask him or her to stop the activities. Tell the person clearly but politely that his or her actions are making you uncomfortable and request that he or she cease all communication with you. Then do not respond to any communications from that person. After that, the steps are much like what you would do with a stranger. Block the person's e-mail and make all reasonable efforts to avoid that person.

If the preceding steps do not remedy the situation, whether it is a stranger or someone you know, you should take the situation seriously. At this point, make sure you retain all e-mails or other online communications between you and that person and keep a log of when he or she contacts you in person or by phone. If there is a witness to any such events, log that person's name and contact information. Then contact your local police department and give them all of the data you have collected. You help the police immensely if you do the following:

- Retain all evidence, including e-mails, voice mails, or other communications.

- Take all reasonable steps to avoid the perpetrator.

- Do nothing that might escalate the situation.

Following these guidelines makes the investigation easier for the police. You should be aware that when police contact the alleged stalker, that person will have a very different story. It is likely he or she will claim either that all communications were by mutual consent or that he or she never threatened you or it was a joke. When you keep all the evidence, you help police to see the truth on the issue of whether or not the communications were a threat. When you take all reasonable precautions to avoid the person, you help the police to see that the communication was not by mutual consent and that you did nothing to escalate the situation.

All too often, the original victim in these situations decides either to "get even" or to try to talk to the person in question. If you do anything—even so much as respond with a hostile e-mail of your own—you make it difficult for the police to see who is really at fault. Even if you simply try to talk the other person out of bothering you, you will have made it difficult not to view the communications as mutually consented.

Guidelines for Law Enforcement

Obviously, if there is evidence that an individual is in danger, then law enforcement should take the situation very seriously. The question is how to determine whether someone really is in danger. We touched on this briefly early in this book, but we'll examine the criteria in more detail here.

The first thing to consider is the likelihood that the person making a threat can actually carry it out. If you are investigating possible harassment or cyber stalking and all the communication is traced back to an IP address on the other side of the world, it is far less likely that the person making the threats can actually carry them out. A person living in California may become quite angry with a person living in Spain, but probably lacks the capacity to physically harm that person.

The next thing to consider is whether or not this really is a threat. People make rash comments in the heat of emotion. How often of you heard someone say "Oh I could just kill....."? It is probable that in most of these situations, the person had no intention of killing anyone; he or she was simply exasperated or angry. However, an exasperated person usually does not persist in such comments or become increasingly graphic. A person repeating a threat is no longer acting in the heat of emotion. A person who makes very graphic or specific threats is far more likely to act on those threats.

You do have to determine the underlying facts. Is the person making the complaint the victim or did the person instigate this encounter? Consider an analogy: Suppose you are on patrol and you see a man strike another man. You might assume he has just committed assault. But what if on further investigation you discover the second man was actually attempting a robbery with a knife, and the first man struck him in self defense? The same holds true with online harassment, though to a lesser extent. Someone may send a rude and hostile e-mail to someone else, but it could be in response to threatening comments from that person. In those situations, the best approach may be to inform both parties that they are in danger of being arrested and that they both need to cease and desist all communications with each other. There may be no clear victim in the matter.

Of course, stalking is a different matter. While it is certainly possible to imagine someone sending a heated e-mail in response to some provocation, it is difficult to imagine a normal person engaging in a pattern of repeated and sustained threatening behavior in response to provocation. In the case of genuine stalking, there is really no valid provocation that would justify this.

The key in investigating such matters is to first collect all the evidence either party may have: e-mails, text messages, voice mails—anything that might support their claims. Then, of course, you need to get statements from both parties. How aggressively you pursue the issue should be related to how credible the threats are. And while we have discussed some guidelines on this issue, this still comes down to a judgment call that will depend on your experience as an officer. It is often a good idea to consult with your superior on these matters. You might also recommend that the complainant obtain a restraining order while the investigation is ongoing. That would at least provide clear legal grounds to arrest the alleged perpetrator should they persist in their communications.

The previously mentioned 1999 report by the Department of Justice also had some advice for local law enforcement:

- The report specifically takes some law-enforcement officials to task for sometimes ignoring the problem. It specifically cites a case in which a couple was receiving phone threats and the local police response was simply to advise them to change their number. It is never a good idea to simply ignore a citizen's concerns for his or her safety. A preliminary investigation may reveal there is no credible threat, but you should not simply ignore their concerns.

- Ensuring that officers are aware of the problem and trained to handle online stalking cases is critical. The report stated that some police departments have no officers on staff with any training in investigating computer crimes. Hopefully, books such as this one will help ameliorate this problem.

- The anonymity of the Internet can make these investigations difficult. The Department of Justice report acknowledged the challenge that police officers face in investigating these matters.

- The report also discussed First Amendment issues at some length. It is important that police officers do not step over the line from stopping online harassment to restricting free speech. And this further complicates these investigations. What is protected free speech, and what is harassment? This can only be addressed by properly educating and training officers.

The real issue for all law-enforcement officers is training in this area. By reading this book, you are taking an important step in that direction. Obviously, the best approach is for agencies to provide formal training for their officers, but budgetary and time constraints sometimes make this impractical. But one can certainly take the time to read and educate oneself on these issues.

Conclusion

Harassment and cyber stalking are serious problems. However, it is important to differentiate between simple rude communications and genuine harassment. There are many steps you can take to first avoid engaging people who are likely to harass, and then to disengage if the harassment has already begun. In many cases, you can simply block the person's communication and resolve the problem yourself. However, if the problem persists, or you genuinely feel you are in real physical danger, you must contact law enforcement.

For officers, there are some guidelines that will help you determine if a case is a genuine, real threat or simply an exchange of rude commentary. You should consider these guidelines when determining how much real danger exists. However, you must also rely on your years of experience in law enforcement. It is always better to err on the side of caution when the physical safety of people is in question.

Endnotes

[1] The Criminal Justice Intervention Web site. http://www.letswrap.com/legal/harass.htm

[2] The U.S. Legal Definitions Web site. http://www.definitions.uslegal.com/h/harassment/

[3] The Wired Safety Web site. http://www.wiredsafety.org/cyberstalking_harassment/definition.html

[4] Justice Department Report on Cyber Stalking. http://www.justice.gov/criminal/cybercrime/cyberstalking.htm

[5] Justice Department Cyber Stalking. http://www.cyberguards.com/CyberStalking.html

[6] Mail Online. "'I Will Slash Your Face': Britain's Most Obsessive Stalker Jailed for Terrorising Student on Facebook." http://www.dailymail.co.uk/news/article-1253647/Cyber-stalker-ignored-restraining-order-terrorise-girl-turned-Facebook-death-threats.html?ITO=1490

[7] KALB Alexandria Louisiana. http://www.cenlamedia.com/alb/index.php/site/article/may-december-stalker/

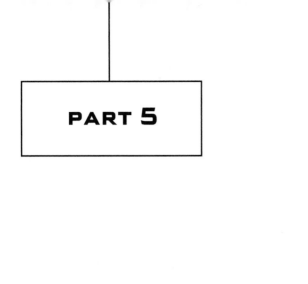

PART 5

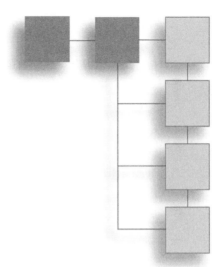

TECHNIQUES

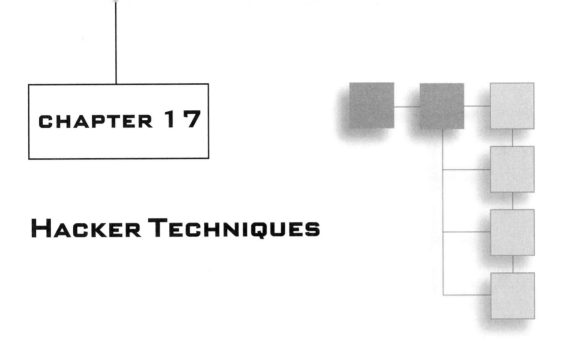

CHAPTER 17

Hacker Techniques

Introduction

Throughout this book, we have looked at a variety of computer crimes. We have examined forensic techniques, laws, actual case studies, and preventative measures. In this chapter, we will examine some of the actual techniques that hackers might use to gain access to a system. It is important to realize that these techniques could be used to commit these acts, and we are providing them here so that investigators (either law enforcement or network administrators) will understand how the hackers work and be better able to stop them or catch them. Some colleges now offer courses in hacking techniques for this very reason. (One of the authors of this book, Chuck Easttom, teaches such courses.) The philosophy behind teaching such skills is that it is very difficult to catch the bad guys if you don't know what they know. We have briefly touched on some of these issues in previous chapters. In this chapter, we will be discussing them in depth.

One chapter will not make you a skilled hacker. However, one chapter can definitely make you familiar with common hacking techniques. We will look at a sampling of techniques that are used in various phases of hacking. In each case, we will explain how the technique works and, if appropriate, why it works. This should give you a working understanding of what hackers do, and hopefully a better idea of how to prevent them from doing it to your system. It should also help law-enforcement officers improve their investigative approach by providing insight into how hackers work.

The Pre-Attack Phase

Before a hacker will actually attempt to hack into a site, there is a pre-attack phase during which the hacker will attempt to gain as much information as possible about the target before the attack. For a network administrator, this phase can alert you to an upcoming attack and perhaps enable you to thwart it. For law-enforcement officers investigating the attack after the fact, you may find evidence of this planning phase, both on the suspect's computer and on the victim's system. In hacker terminology, this phase often referred to as *scanning* or *footprinting*. In some instances, it is simply called reconnaissance. Whatever the terminology, it is essentially the same as when a bank robber assesses the vulnerabilities of bank prior to robbing that bank.

Some security experts would say that this is the most important phase of the attack. The more that the attacker learns during this phase, the more likely he or she is to be able to breach the target system, and the more likely he or she is to do so surreptitiously. It is important to be aware of what information you are making public about your system and its security. Some things you cannot prevent from becoming public knowledge, but others you can.

The Passive Search

The first step in any computer attack is a passive search. This does not involve actually connecting to the target system. For that reason, it won't leave any evidence on the victim's computer; however, it is very likely to leave some evidence on the suspect's computer. It usually begins with the attacker trying to find out about the target system. There are actually several Web sites that can help with this. The Web site www.netcraft.com, shown in Figure 17.1, will provide information about a target Web server.

At this Web site, the attacker may be able to find out what Web server and what operating system the target is using. This will help the attacker to decide what sort of attack to attempt. The attacker may also be able to see the last time the system was rebooted. Patches and upgrades often require a reboot, so this information will tell the attacker if the system has been patched recently. Best of all, from the intruder's point of view, this can all be done without the attacker directly accessing the target system.

The attacker may also gain a lot of information from the Web site www.archive. org. This Web site archives all the Web sites on the Internet, which enables you to

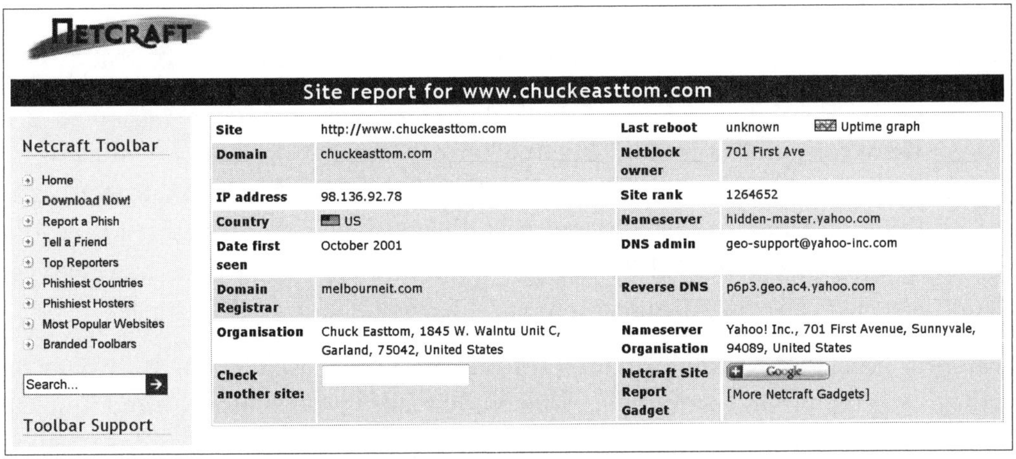

Figure 17.1
www.netcraft.com.

see what that Web site looked like at a previous point in time. This is shown in Figure 17.2.

In many cases, company changes, new technologies, new hires, and so on can all be found by looking at old versions of the company Web site. This gives the attacker valuable information that he or she can use to attack the system.

Another piece of valuable information the attacker may be able to get from www.archive.org is the names of former employees. One of the authors of this book has personally seen networks that still had active user accounts for people who had left the company as much as two years prior. If one can find the

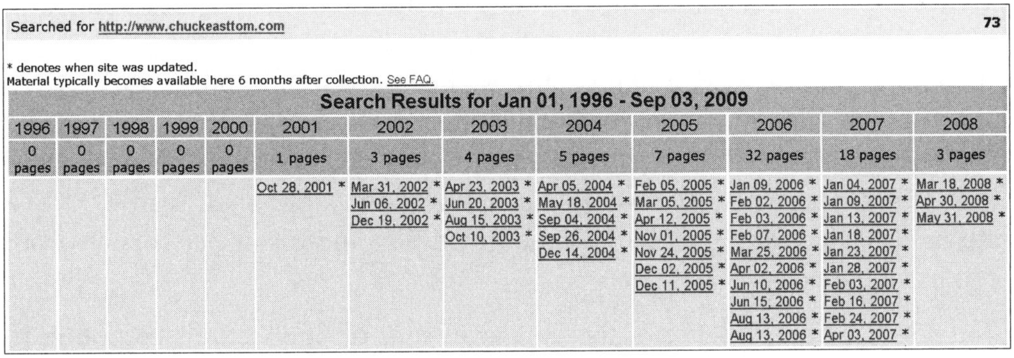

Figure 17.2
www.achive.org.

names of former employees, it is then possible to try to log in using their accounts. If the network administrator has not been diligent in deactivating such accounts, it may be possible to log in.

Using these two sites together, the attacker may be able to get some idea of the technologies used on the target system. He or she can then focus only on vulnerabilities in those systems. For example, there are vulnerabilities in a Windows 2003 server that are very different from the vulnerabilities in a Linux server. Knowing the target operating system is a significant step in the attack.

Another place that hackers will look for information is on job boards. By viewing job ads for the target company and carefully reading the skills required, one can learn about what technologies an organization is using. Even old job ads can be treasure troves of information. For example, suppose the attacker finds an older job ad in which the target was seeking a Linux administrator with knowledge of Apache Web server. Then he or she finds a newer ad in which the same organization is looking for a PHP programmer. Now the attacker knows that the organization's Web applications are written in PHP and deployed on a Linux server using Apache Web service. That gives the attacker a specific target to try to exploit and narrows his or her focus. This is one of the things you won't be able to hide from public scrutiny. You have to put complete job descriptions in ads or else you won't get resumés from qualified candidates.

Whois databases are another place that hackers will seek knowledge. A Whois entry contains information about who registered a domain or IP address and the administrative contact. It is usually best to have generic contact information such as the e-mail address admin@mycompany.com. If you use specific information, such as actual names, that is more information an attacker might use to try to compromise your system. For example, if the attacker finds out via Whois that your network administrator's name is John Doe and he works at your Seattle office, that information can be used to make a more credible attempt at social engineering. When the attacker calls your Dallas office pretending to be from tech support, he can now say "Yeah, I work for John, up in Seattle...." The attacker's believability just increased dramatically and his or her chance of success has increased accordingly.

You will not find evidence of these passive scans on the victim's computer because it is all done without directly connecting to the victim's computer. However, when you have a suspect, his or her computer might very well have evidence of this activity. It is likely that the suspect's Web browser will contain evidence that he or she performed these searches. Obviously, these searches are not, in and of themselves, illegal. But they may help build a case against the hacker by showing the planning he or she put into the attack. It can also show that the attack was one that the person consciously committed, and was not because his or her computer was used as a zombie (i.e., under someone else's control). It is well worth the time to look for such evidence on a suspect's computer.

The Active Scan

Passive searches can yield a wealth of information, but they do have limits. At some point, the attacker will need to actually scan the target system. There are several ways to do this, and there are several tools freely available on the Internet to assist in this process. There are several things an attacker will want to do in this phase, including the following:

- **Port scanning.** This is a process of scanning the well-known ports (there are 1,024) or even all the ports (there are 65,535) to find out which ports are open. This can tell an attacker a great deal. For example, port 445 would indicate that the target is running Active Directory and is therefore a Windows machine—in fact, Windows 2000 or later. Port 88 would tell an attacker that the target system is using Kerberos authentication. All of this information helps the attacker narrow down the attack vectors to use.

- **Enumerating.** This is a process whereby the attacker tries to find out what is on the target network. Items such as shared folders, user accounts, and similar items are sought after. Any of these may provide a point of attack.

- **Vulnerability assessment.** This is the use of some tool to seek out known vulnerabilities, or the attacker may try to manually assess vulnerabilities. The latter can be done in many ways. We will discuss one of these methods later in this section.

There are a number of tools freely available on the Internet for active scanning. They range from the very simple to the complex. Anyone involved in preventing computer crimes or investigating computer crimes should be familiar with a few of these. We will examine a few of them later in this section.

There are many types of scans, and some are more successful than others. Some are also very likely to alert the target network. The most common types of scans and their limitations are as follows:

- **ping scan.** This is sending a ping packet to the target IP address to check to see if a given port is open. The problem with ping scanning is that many firewalls block ICMP packets. ICMP, or Internet Control Message Protocol, is the protocol used by `ping` and `tracert`.

- **Connect scan.** This type of scan actually tries to make a full connection to the target IP address at a given port. This is the most reliable type of scan; it will not yield false positives or false negatives. However, it is the scan most likely to be detected by the target network.

- **SYN scan.** This scan is based on knowledge of how network connectivity works. Any time you connect to any server, there is an exchange of packets that negotiate the connection. Your machine sends a packet with a SYN flag. (That means *synchronize.*) Basically, you are asking permission to connect. The server responds with a packet that has a SYN-ACK flag. (That means *synchronize-acknowledge.*) That is the server saying "Okay, you can connect." Your computer then sends a packet with an ACK flag, acknowledging the new connection. A SYN scan simply sends a connection request to each port to check to see if the port is open. Because servers and firewalls routinely get SYN packets, this is unlikely to trigger any alarms on the target system.

- **FIN scan.** This scan has the FIN flag, or connection finished flag set. This is also usually not going to attract unwanted attention at the target network because connections are being closed routinely, so packets with the FIN flag set are not unusual.

There are other scans, including the XMAS scan. It has several flags set. The point here is that a potential attacker has several ways to probe the ports of a network. As a network administrator, the challenge is to make sure your system will alert you to suspicious activity. As an investigator, the challenge will be to scan the system logs for many weeks preceding the actual attack to see if there are signs that the suspect performed active scans on the system. Network servers, firewalls, and routers all have logs that should be examined for evidence.

To perform these active scans, the perpetrator may choose to do so manually or to use one of the many tools available for download on the Internet. It is important that you be basically familiar with these tools so that you will know how the hackers work.

Angry IP

This is one of the simplest port scanners. It can be downloaded for free from http://www.angryip.org. This tool does not allow you to choose which of the previously mentioned scan types you wish to execute; it simply does a ping scan and reports the results. However, it is very easy to use and has an intuitive interface, as shown in Figure 17.3.

There are not many options for the user to pick, but it is easy to see that you simply type in the IP address then click on the button labeled Scan. This tool only does port scanning; it does not do any enumeration at all.

NSAuditor

NSAuditor is a much more robust tool, offering many options. However, it is also more difficult to use. You can download it for free at http://www.nsauditor.com/. The opening screen, shown in Figure 17.4, should make obvious the additional choices you have available.

We will examine some of the more commonly used options. Let us begin by clicking on the fourth button down on the left, the one labeled Network Scanner. You will be presented with a window like the one shown in Figure 17.5.

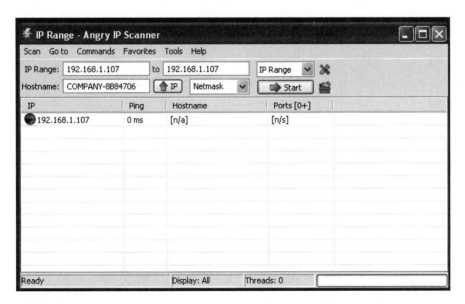

Figure 17.3
Angry IP.

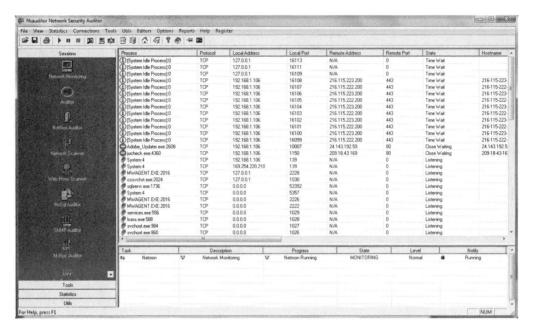

Figure 17.4
NSAuditor opening screen.

You should immediately notice that you can choose the type of scan you wish to perform in the top-left corner in the Scan Mode section (see Figure 17.6). This is very valuable to the intruder as it enables him or her to choose scan options that are less likely to cause an alert on the target system.

Also, in the upper-right corner of the Advanced Network Scan Dialog window, you can select how aggressively you want to scan. You can see this option in Figure 17.7. The aggressiveness level determines how many times per minute to scan ports, as well as how many ports to simultaneously scan. The more aggressive the scan, the quicker the results, but the more likely one is to trigger an alarm on the target system.

This flexibility in NSAuditor is one reason it is such an effective tool for scanning a target system. Incidentally, it is also an effective tool for network administrators to scan their own networks in order to find vulnerabilities.

Back at the main window shown in Figure 17.4, if you open the Tools menu, you will find a tool named Remote Explorer. You can see Remote Explorer in Figure 17.8. This tool allows you to attempt to connect to another computer either using either your current logon credentials or some others. This is an

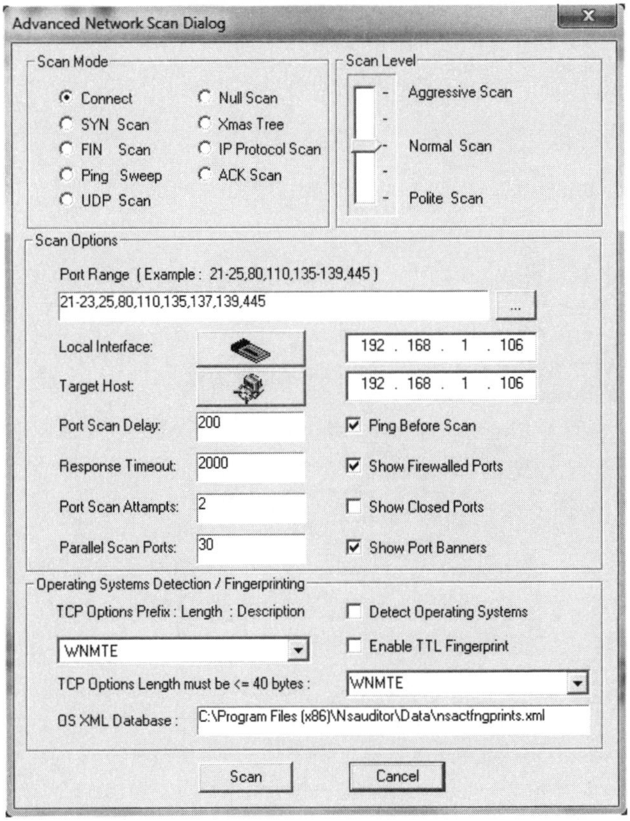

Figure 17.5
NSAuditor's Advanced Network Scan Dialog window.

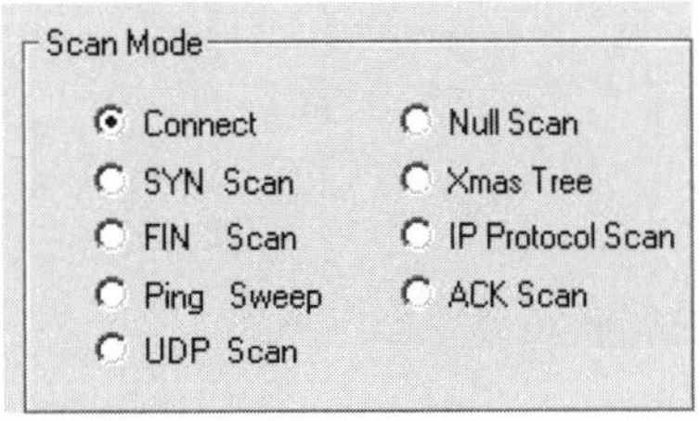

Figure 17.6
Selecting the scan type.

excellent tool for simply trying to connect to see if you can access a remote system.

There are many other tools in NSAuditor, but our goal in this section is to simply make you familiar with the basics, as well as to show you one of the many tools available to people who may want to break into a network.

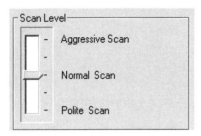

Figure 17.7
Choosing a scan aggressiveness level.

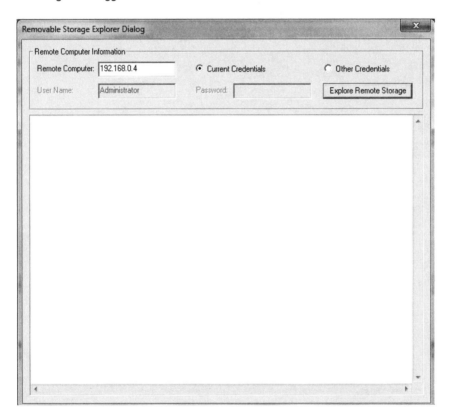

Figure 17.8
Remote Explorer.

Microsoft Baseline Security Analyzer

This tool is remarkably simple to use, and extremely helpful. It scans a target system and reveals any flaws in that system if that system is running Windows. This tool is available from http://technet.microsoft.com/en-us/security/cc184923.aspx. This tool has an easy-to-use interface, as you can see in Figure 17.9.

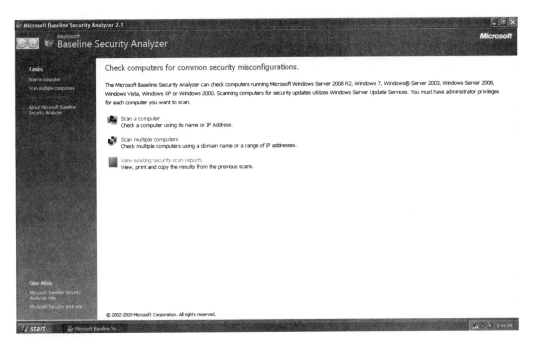

Figure 17.9
Microsoft Baseline Security Analyzer.

You can choose to scan one machine or many, and you can select which vulnerabilities you want to scan for (see Figure 17.10). Then, when the scan is finished, a complete report is shown to the user, as you can see in Figure 17.11.

This is a very user-friendly tool that gives you a clear overview of a given system's vulnerabilities. The tool will not only tell you what vulnerabilities your system has, but it will give you specific details. This would make it easy for an attacker to exploit those vulnerabilities, but it would also make it easy for you to correct them. This is the sort of tool someone might use to find possible attack vectors into your system. It is also an excellent tool for system administrators to use to check their systems for vulnerabilities.

There are many other tools available on the Internet to use in scanning a target system. These three were examined as an example of the concept. You should be aware that an attacker who targets your system has a great many tools in his or her arsenal.

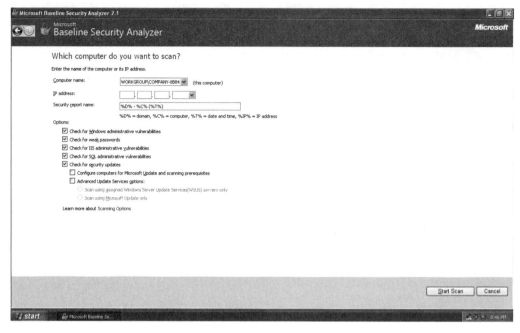

Figure 17.10
Microsoft Baseline Security Analyzer scan selection.

Figure 17.11
Microsoft Baseline Security Analyzer results.

Enumeration

Enumeration is the process of finding out what computers, shared folders, and users are on a given network or machine. It requires connection to that target machine or network. Many of the port scanners mentioned previously also allow the attacker to perform enumeration; there are also tools that just do enumeration. Let's first look at the enumeration capabilities within NSAuditor. If you look again under Tools, you will find an option labeled Enumerate Computers. This is shown in Figure 17.12. When you select this option, you are given a number of choices as to what you want to enumerate. This is shown in Figure 17.13.

Figure 17.12
NSAuditor's Enumerate Computers option.

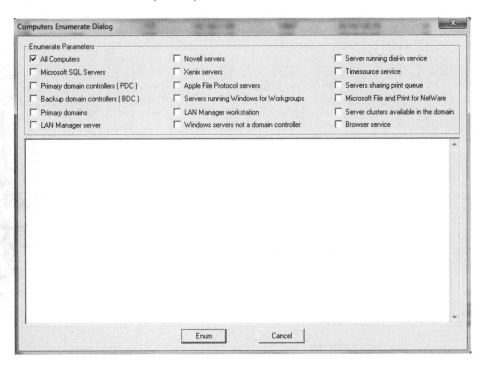

Figure 17.13
The NSAuditor Computers Enumerate Dialog screen.

You can choose to enumerate all computers, just the domain controller, just servers, or MS SQL database servers; there are many choices. When you run the enumerator, the output is in XML format, as shown in Figure 17.14.

You can see that a great deal of information is provided about every computer on that network. First, you get a list of all the computers on the network. Then you can see what services they are running. Any running service is a potential attack vector.

There are other enumeration products that only enumerate one thing. For example ShareEnum, available for download from http://technet.microsoft.com/en-us/sysinternals/bb897442.aspx, will simply try to find all shared folders on the network. This can be useful because a shared folder is a possible attack vector for the hacker to use. You can see ShareEnum in Figure 17.15.

Another good enumeration tool is FreeNetEnumerator, which is also available from the NSAuditor Web site. It has a simple, easy-to-use interface, which you can see in Figure 17.16.

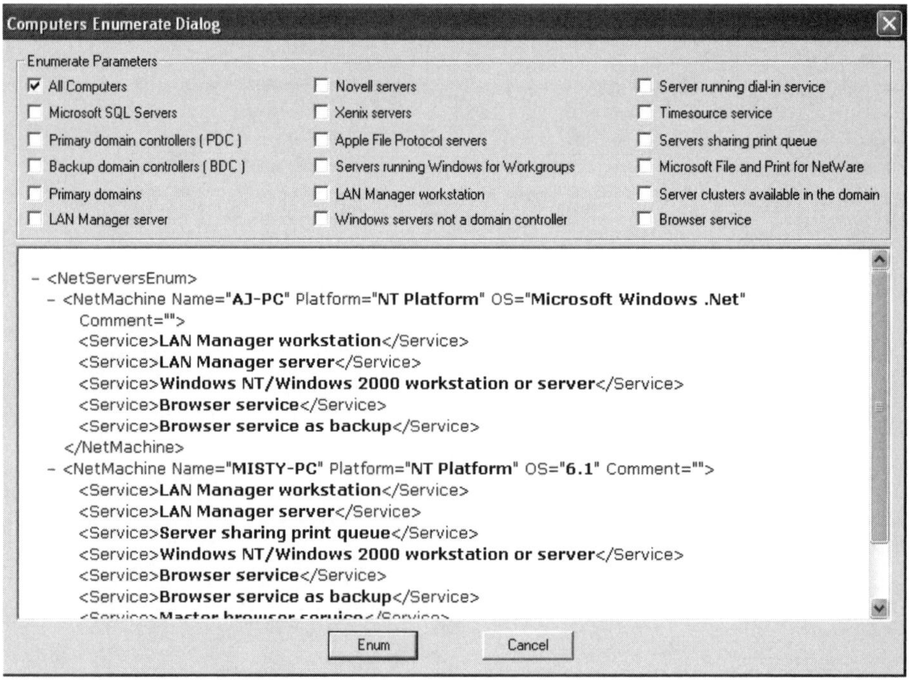

Figure 17.14
NSAuditor enumeration results.

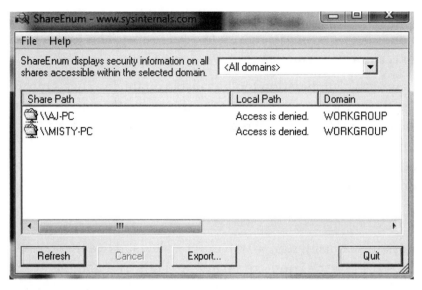

Figure 17.15
ShareEnum.

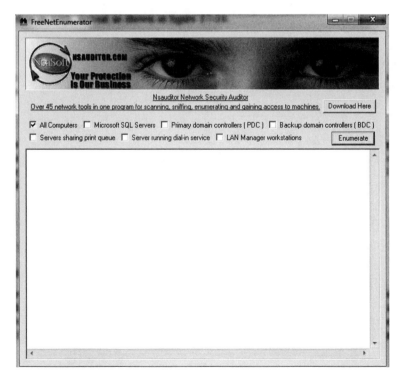

Figure 17.16
FreeNetEnumerator.

You can see in Figure 17.17 that FreeNetEnumerator provides the same information NSAuditor provides, but in an easy-to-read format. This tool is made for someone who is a novice at enumeration.

These are just a few of the enumeration tools available on the Internet. Once an attacker has access to your network, he or she can use one of these tools to map out the rest of the network: the computers that are on the network, the servers, shared folders, and users. The attacker can also learn what operating system is being used on each machine. This is valuable information that allows the attacker to plan out his or her attack.

Manual Scanning

There are also ways to manually scan a system for vulnerabilities. Perhaps the most commonly used is the `telnet` command. `telnet` is a command that works in Linux or Windows, and is used to attempt to connect to a machine in order to perform administrative tasks. By default, `telnet` uses port 23, but you can attempt to telnet into any port you wish. You simply open a command

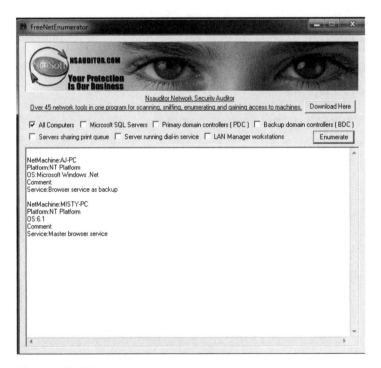

Figure 17.17
FreeNetEnumerator results.

window, type in `telnet` and the address or URL you wish to telnet into, and then the port number. It will look something like what you see in Figure 17.18.

This is an excellent scanning tool because not only does it tell you if a port is open, but it also tells you if you can log on to that port, thus providing the attacker a way into the system. The results could be one of the following:

- You are informed you could not connect.

- The screen goes blank, indicating it is ready for commands (i.e., you did connect).

If you can connect, you still may only have very limited access. The next thing a hacker will attempt, if this is a Web server, is to retrieve the banner so that he or she knows for certain what operating system is being used. You do that by typing `HEAD /HTTP/1.0` and then pressing Enter twice. If it is successful, the hacker will now know precisely what operating system is being used.

This is just one of many techniques a hacker could use to find out more information about your system. This technique is simple, whereas some of the others are much more complex. That is why we have focused here on the tools that do the scanning for you. As those tools become more common, there are more people trying to hack systems.

The Attack Phase

After an attacker has scanned your system and determined the vulnerabilities the system has, that person will begin his or her attack. There are many ways to attempt to attack a system. Some depend on having physical access; some do not.

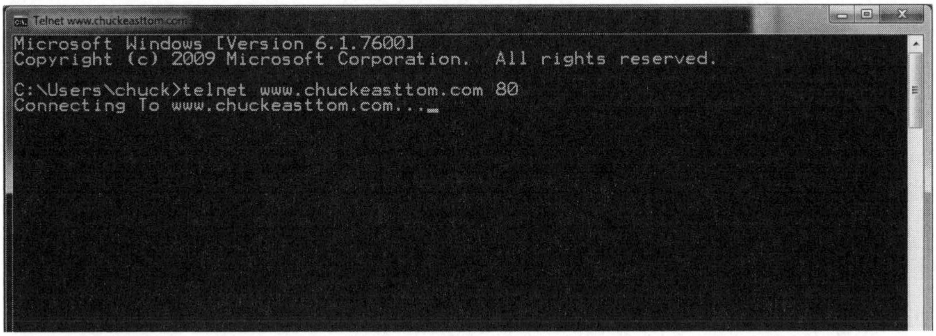

Figure 17.18
telnet.

Let's start with those that depend on physical access. This may seem odd to some readers. You may not envision hacking beginning with someone being able to sit down at a computer on your network. But consider how many large office buildings have minimal security and how easy it would be to simply go in and sit in an empty office and get on the computer. Or consider the many public-access computers that exist at places such as libraries and college campuses. It is often easy to find a computer that is connected to a network; the only challenge is being able to get onto that computer.

Physical Access Attacks

If an attacker can physically sit in front of any machine connected to your network, there are a number of ways he or she can gain access to your entire network. Their first step is simply to log on to that machine. The attacker need not be able to log on to the network yet, just that machine. Let's look at a few techniques that would enable an attacker to log on to a machine, even if that person does not have a password.

OphCrack

One very popular tool for getting into a machine locally is OphCrack, which can be downloaded from http://ophcrack.sourceforge.net/. This tool is based on an understanding of how Windows passwords work. Windows passwords are stored in a hash file in one of the system directories, usually C:\WINDOWS\system32\config\, in a SAM file. (SAM is an acronym for Security Accounts Manager.) Now, because the file contains hashed entries, you cannot simply read the usernames and passwords, and if you simply try random passwords, most systems will lock you out after a few tries. It would be great if you could get the SAM file away from Windows and try to crack it, but it is a locked file; the operating system will not let you copy it or do anything with it. What OphCrack does is boot the system in Linux so that the Windows operating system is not loaded, and thus the SAM file is not protected. Then it uses what's called a rainbow table to crack the entries in the SAM. A rainbow table is a table of all possible hashes of all possible character combinations. OphCrack just searches the SAM for a match. When it finds it, it knows the username and password. You can see this in Figure 17.19. (Note that we have obscured the passwords that OphCrack found.)

To make this work, all you have to do is put the CD into the computer and reboot. Then, during the boot-up process, press F12 for a Boot menu, and then choose Boot from CD.

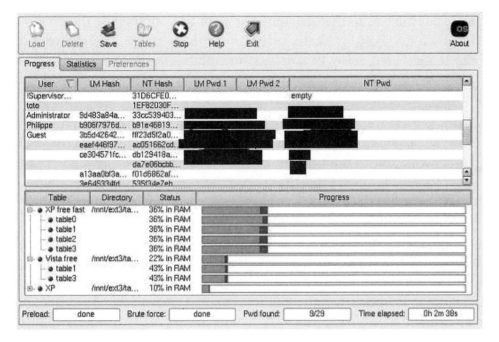

Figure 17.19
OphCrack.

Once the attacker has accessed a valid login account, particularly an administrator account, he or she can log on to that computer. This won't let that person join the domain, but he or she now has a foothold on your network.

There are other tools for bypassing the Windows password. KonBoot, available at http://www.raymond.cc/blog/archives/2009/05/11/burn-iso-image-to-usb-flash-pen-drive-kon-boot-to-usb/, is a tool similar to OphCrack that works on Windows and Linux machines.

It is also possible on some Windows systems to manually bypass the password. When the machine is booting up, press F8 for Safe mode. In Windows 2000 and XP, Safe mode will not ask for a password. So when the system boots into Safe mode, the attacker can simply add a new user account for himself and then re-boot the machine.

As you can see, there are many ways an attacker can log on to a computer if he or she can simply get physical access. This is why physical security is such a critical part of network security. If you have machines that can be readily accessed by unauthorized personnel, this is an open invitation to hackers. And once the hacker has gained access to that machine, they can then enumerate the network from that machine, look for shared drives, and then copy a Trojan horse or spyware to those shared drives or conduct any number of malicious acts.

Cain and Abel

Once an attacker has gained access to even one machine, even if it is not part of the domain, he or she can use a tool called Cain and Abel to discover quite a bit about the network and to advance his or her attack. Let's look at a few of the things an attacker can do with this tool.

Retrieve Login Accounts

If the attacker used a method such as booting into Safe mode and creating an account or simply logging on with a guest account, Cain and Abel will help that person find all the passwords for all the other accounts on that computer. After you open Cain and Abel, select the Cracker tab, and then select LM Hashes on the left and click the plus sign. You will then be asked what you want to crack; make sure the top two options are selected, as you see in Figure 17.20.

Cain and Abel will then pull all the usernames and list them for you. You can then right-click on the one you want to crack and choose how you want it to be

Figure 17.20
Retrieving logons with Cain and Abel.

cracked. You can choose a dictionary attack, a rainbow table, or brute force, as shown in Figure 17.21.

It may take quite some time, but Cain and Abel will eventually crack the password. In some cases, if the password is complex enough, it may take hours, but it will eventually crack the password. This gives an attacker who is just using a guest login account the opportunity to find out every password on the system. But that is only one of the things Cain and Abel can do.

Get Other Passwords

If you select the Decoder tab, you have the option of finding and displaying any stored passwords on that machine. People often save passwords to e-mail accounts and Web sites. If you select the IE (Internet Explorer) option on the left and then click the plus sign at the top to add it to the workload, Cain and Abel will attempt to retrieve all stored browser passwords. This is shown in Figure 17.22. Because this image was taken by running Cain and Abel on a real computer, we have covered up the passwords it retrieved.

Get a Wireless Key

When one sets up a wireless connection on a client machine, it is common practice to save the wireless key on that machine. You don't want users to have to enter that every time they want to get on the network. Well, Cain and Abel can

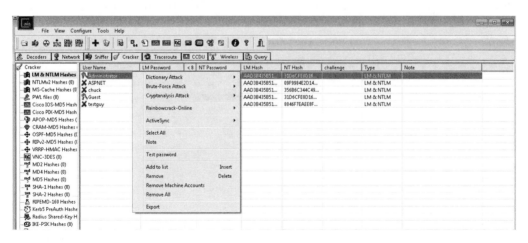

Figure 17.21
Cracking passwords with Cain and Abel.

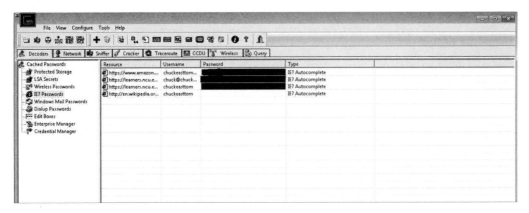

Figure 17.22
Browser passwords with Cain and Abel.

grab those, too. Just select Wireless and click the plus sign and you will see any wireless passwords/keys that have been stored on that computer. You can see an example of this in Figure 17.23. As before, we have blocked out the passwords discovered, as well as the wireless network's SSID.

You can see that Cain and Abel is a powerful tool. If an attacker gains access to any machine on your network and then runs Cain and Abel on that machine, it is likely that they will have all the information they need to access your systems at will. And this is only one of many tools available on the Internet.

If you are investigating a suspect who is accused of hacking into a system, you should examine their computer systems and removable media (i.e., CDs, USB

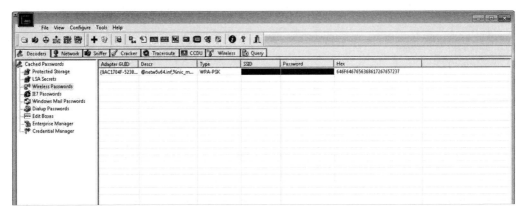

Figure 17.23
Retrieving wireless keys with Cain and Abel.

drives, etc.) for any of the tools we have mentioned here. But remember that simply possessing these tools is not a crime; some network administrators use them for legitimate purposes such as scanning their own network for vulnerabilities or to log on to a machine if the password has been lost. However, the possession of these tools along with evidence from the target system on which these tools were used can be an important part of a case. It cannot, by itself, be enough to secure a conviction, but clearly you have other evidence already or you would not have identified a suspect. It is important to keep in mind that every piece of evidence, even circumstantial evidence, can help build a stronger case.

If you are a network administrator, it is probably a wise choice to try each of these utilities on your own systems to find the vulnerabilities and try to correct them before someone breaks into your system.

Remote Access Attacks

If the attacker cannot gain physical access to your computer, there are still other techniques he or she might be able to use. These techniques usually don't involve tools, but rather are complex exploits of some vulnerability in either the operating system or the communications used. Often, these attacks utilize a very specific weakness in a particular system. There is not a single commonly used approach or tool, which makes it difficult to discuss these as specifically as we did attacks based on physical access. However, we can discuss generally how these attacks are conducted.

- **Operating-system exploits.** During the pre-attack phase, one of the things the hacker is attempting to learn is what operating system the target is running. Knowing this can help him or her find vulnerabilities. For example, if the target system is a Web server running Windows Server 2003 and IIS 6.0, then the hacker will probably begin with a Web search for known vulnerabilities in either product. This is why it is so critical to keep operating systems patched and updated. Any vulnerability that is not corrected is an opening that hackers can and will use.

- **Session vulnerabilities.** When anyone connects to a system remotely, he or she initiates a communications session. There are various techniques a person can use to compromise that communication, such as session hijacking. These techniques are rather complex and require a significant amount of skill. If you are using encrypted transmissions such as in a virtual private network (or VPN) and secure authentication such as CHAP or Kerberos, then your danger from these attacks is minimal.

▪ **System flaws.** Many systems have significant flaws in their default config-urations. For example, most FTP servers have a default anonymous login account. That account has very few privileges, but anyone can log into it. Most hackers, if they find ports 20 and 21 open, thus indicating the presence of an FTP server, will at least attempt anonymous logon. If they are suc-cessful, then they have gained a foothold on your system. The same is true for any type of connectivity, including `telnet`.

▪ **Trojan horses.** One of the most popular ways to gain access to a target system is via a Trojan horse. If, during the passive search phase, the attacker can get e-mail addresses for people inside the targeted network, then he or she can send them e-mails with a Trojan horse attached. If the Trojan horse is opened by the targeted party, then some device such as a rootkit or spy-ware can be deposited on that computer. This can give the attacker a way into the system.

▪ **SQL injection.** This is a popular attack against Web applications. If there is a login screen, it requires a username and password. That username and password will have to be checked against a database to see if they are valid. All databases speak Structured Query Language (SQL); SQL looks a lot like English. If the programmer who created the login is not careful, it may be susceptible to SQL injection. Here is how that attack works. For example, to check a username and password, you might want to query the database and see if there is any entry in the users table that matches the username and password that was entered. If there is, then you have a match. Now, the SQL in the programming code for the Web site has to use quotation marks to separate the SQL code from the programming code. So you might have something that looks like this:

```
'SELECT * FROM tblUsers WHERE USERNAME = '" + txtUsername.Text +' AND
PASSWORD = '" + txtPassword.Text +"'"
```

If you enter username `'admin'` and the password `'password'`, this code produces the SQL command:

```
SELECT * FROM tblUsers WHERE USERNAME = 'admin' AND PASSWORD =
'password'
```

SQL injection has you add something at the end of the password. For example you enter in `'password ' OR X=X '`. This will cause the program to create this query:

```
SELECT * FROM tblUsers WHERE USERNAME = 'admin' AND PASSWORD = 'password' OR X=X'
```

So you are telling the database and application to let you in if there is a match for your username and password, or if X=X, which it always will. Now, if the programmer wrote the login properly, this will not work. But in all too many cases it does work. And then the intruder has logged into your network and can do whatever any authorized user can do.

Countermeasures

By this point, you are probably feeling a bit concerned about the security of your own systems. Clearly, there are a number of tools and techniques that can be used to breach your system's security. And you may have learned about vulnerabilities in this chapter that you had not previously known about. But there are ways to counter these attacks; some are common knowledge, others are not. Let's look at the major countermeasures:

- **Antivirus/spyware.** In this day and age of computer-security breaches, it is extremely negligent not to have a robust antivirus or anti-spyware program running on your system. We have discussed this in previous chapters. You must run antivirus software and you must keep it updated.

- **Update your software.** Hackers frequently use known vulnerabilities in operating systems and other software. Keeping your software updated and patched will prevent a number of attacks. Any patch you don't apply is an opening for a hacker.

- **Firewalls.** Firewalls are devices that block traffic based on some particular set of rules. Windows XP, Vista, and 7 all ship with a basic firewall. It should be turned on and configured. Most routers have built-in firewalls; they should be turned on and configured. And if you are administering a network, it should have a dedicated firewall between it and the Internet. Properly configured firewalls also log activity. Such logs can be a valuable piece of evidence in prosecuting someone who illegally hacks into your system.

- **Policies.** It is absolutely critical that you have policies covering all aspects of network security. Among the most important policies would be policies handling the terminating of access for former employees and educating employees on the danger of opening suspicious attachments.

- **Physical security.** You have already seen that if a person can get physical access to any machine, this can be the first step in completely breaching the system. You must restrict physical access to your computers and monitor them closely.

- **IDS.** Intrusion-detection systems are programs that look for signs of an intrusion. For example, an IDS might notice that a port scan is occurring or that someone is trying to log on with SQL injection. Intrusion-detection systems can then alert the administrator about the attempted breach and log details of the event such as the source IP address. This can not only allow you to thwart the attack, but also provide evidence for later prosecution. There are many different types of IDS, each with varying degrees of efficacy. It is beyond the scope of this book to explore them all, but you should be aware that you can implement an IDS and improve the security of your system significantly. The logs of an IDS, like firewall logs, can provide valuable evidence in the investigation and prosecution of any computer crimes.

- **Honey pots.** A honey pot is software you run on a given machine that makes that machine look more attractive to intruders. The honey-pot software can appear to be a high-value database server or an entire subnetwork. It can be complete with fake data. This is used in case someone does breach your network security. Because no real users access this system, as soon as it is accessed, you know it must be an intruder. The appearance of high-value data can keep the intruder focused on the honey pot rather than the rest of your network, which gives you time to secure your system and stop the attack. Honey pots also log information, which provides additional evidence for criminal investigations.

No single security measure can ensure the safety of your network. Each attack countermeasure you implement makes your system a bit more secure. The cumulative effect of implementing multiple countermeasures is that your system is much harder to breach. No system is totally safe and protected, but you can dramatically increase the security of your system and at the same time provide more evidence should a breach occur. All of the logs of all these systems will help in the investigation of any breach that might occur.

Conclusion

In this chapter, you have seen a number of interesting tools and techniques that can be used to breach system security. However, we have only scratched the surface. There are many other tools and techniques available. If you are in law enforcement, you will want to be as aware of the techniques of hackers as you can be. Only by knowing how they operate can you properly investigate these sorts of crimes. If you are a network administrator, then this chapter is information you can use to know your enemy and to improve your network's security.

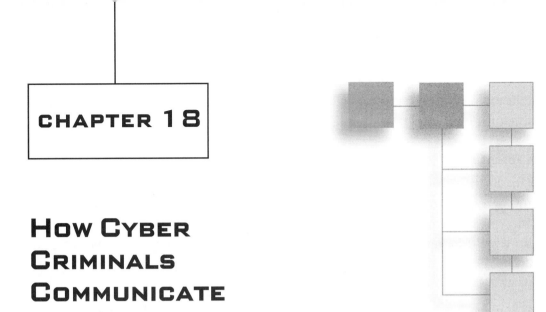

CHAPTER 18

How Cyber Criminals Communicate

Introduction

Understanding how computer criminals communicate is vital to investigating computer crimes. There are methods that computer criminals can use to hide their communications. These methods are not used only by computer criminals, but also by non–computer-based criminals and terrorist groups as well. Understanding how computer technology can facilitate illicit communication will make you better able to investigate such communications.

Encryption

The most obvious way to hide the content of communications is through encryption. There are a number of products that allow one to encrypt messages, including e-mails. There are also tools that allow one to obfuscate a message by hiding it in something innocuous. In this section, we will look at these techniques. Our goal is not to make you a cryptographer, but rather to give you a working understanding of cryptography.

History of Encryption

Let's begin with a discussion of the history of encryption. The methods discussed in this section are presented for historical purposes and are not considered secure. But they will help you to understand how the encryption process works. Most modern encryption methods use rather advanced mathematics, so it becomes difficult to teach the fundamentals of cryptography to those who may not have that mathematical background. By examining historical methods, you can get a feel for how cryptography works without needing to know any significant math.

Caesar Cipher

One of the earliest encryption methods known is called a Caesar cipher. It has this name due to the fact that Romans in Julius Caesar's time used this method to encrypt messages. This is probably the easiest type of encryption to learn. The principal is simply to shift each letter in a message by a given number of characters. For example, if you shift each letter two characters to the right, you get what is shown in Figure 18.1.

If you reach the letter Z, then you start over at A. You can shift any number of letters you like and in either direction. For example, if you chose to shift one to the left, you would see what is shown in Figure 18.2.

The weakness of this cipher has to do with letter frequency distribution. In any language, certain letters appear more often than others. For example, in English, if you see a one-letter word, it will most likely be the word "a," and the second most likely word would be "I." If you see a three-letter word, the two most likely results are "and" and "the." Using these facts about a language makes

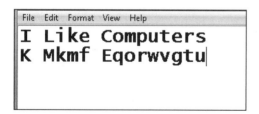

Figure 18.1
Caesar cipher: Shift two right.

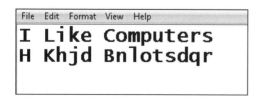

Figure 18.2
Caesar cipher: Shift one left.

deciphering a message encrypted with the Caesar cipher a trivial task. In fact, complete novices at cryptography are often able to decrypt Caesar cipher messages in a matter of minutes simply using a pencil and paper.

There are special versions of this cipher, such as ROT 13 (short for Rotate 13 spaces), in which one would shift all letters by 13. Both ROT 13 and the Caesar cipher are referred to as single-alphabet–substitution ciphers because they use a single substitution alphabet. The alphabet is the the number of times you choose to shift each letter. Since all letters are shifted the same amount (to the right two, to the left one, or any other amount you like), this is a single-substitution alphabet.

Multi-Alphabet Substitution

Over time, single-substitution alphabets were improved with the introduction of multi-substitution alphabets. For example, you might choose to use +2 and −1. That would mean the first letter is shifted two to the right, the next letter one to the left, then the next two to the right, repeating that pattern until the message is encrypted. You can see an example of multi-alphabet substitution in Figure 18.3.

You can use any number of substitutions you want. Each substitution is referred to as a *substitution alphabet.* So if you use +1, −3, +4, that would be a three-substitution alphabet. If you use +2, −1, −2, +3 that would be a four-substitution alphabet. This is obviously a bit more complex than the single-substitution alphabet, but this is still not secure by modern standards. It would probably take an amateur cryptographer more time to crack, but modern computers would crack such codes in a very short time.

Binary Operations

Another simple method is to just combine the message with a random string of bits. Binary numbers can be combined in one of three ways: a binary AND, a binary OR, or a binary XOR.

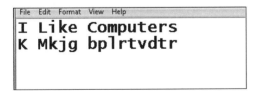

Figure 18.3
Multi-alphabet encryption.

With the binary AND, you take two binary numbers and compare them one digit at a time. If both numbers have a one in that digit, then the result is a one. If not, then the result is a zero. You can see this in Figure 18.4.

Another operation is the binary OR, in which you take two binary numbers and compare them one digit at a time. If either number in that digit is a one, then the result is a one. If not it is a zero. You can see this in Figure 18.5.

The final operation we will examine—and the one most important for our discussion of encryption—is the XOR, which means exclusively or. In this case, you take two binary numbers and compare them one digit at a time. If there is a one in only one of the numbers at that digit, then the result is a one. If not (i.e., there is a one in both numbers or a zero in both numbers) then the result is a zero. You can see this in Figure 18.6.

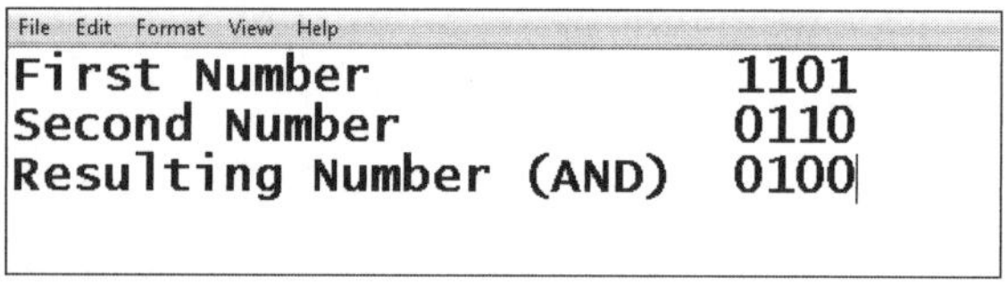

```
File  Edit  Format  View  Help
First Number               1101
Second Number              0110
Resulting Number (AND)     0100|
```

Figure 18.4
Binary AND.

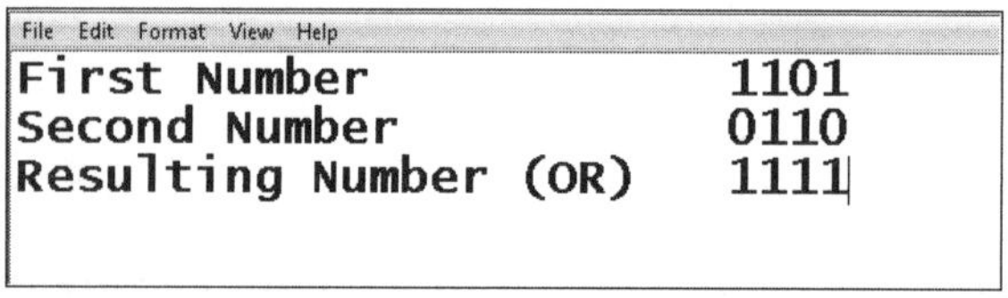

```
File  Edit  Format  View  Help
First Number               1101
Second Number              0110
Resulting Number (OR)      1111|
```

Figure 18.5
Binary OR.

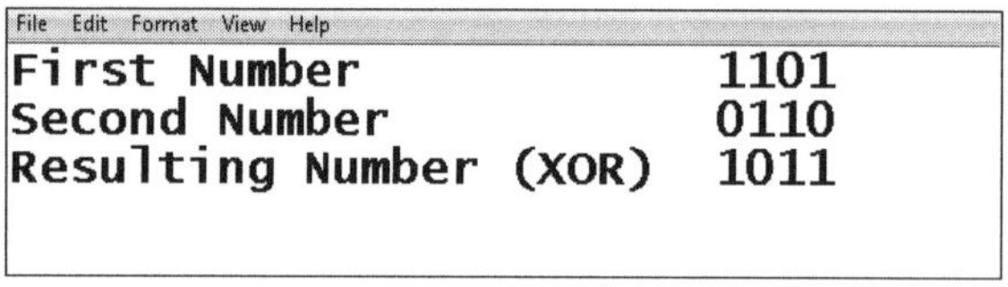

```
File  Edit  Format  View  Help
First Number               1101
Second Number              0110
Resulting Number (XOR)     1011
```

Figure 18.6
Binary XOR.

The binary XOR has an interesting property. If you take the result from the previous example and XOR that number with the second number from the previous example, you will get back the original number, as shown in Figure 18.7.

This is a simple form of encryption. If you use the second number as the key, then the first time you apply it, the original numbers are encrypted. If you then apply that key to the encrypted numbers, you get the original number.

As with the other encryption algorithms we have examined in this section, this is just meant to help you understand how encryption works. This is not meant to be used for actual encryption because it is not secure. But it can be useful in illustrating the principles of encryption to someone who does not have an advanced-mathematics background.

Modern Encryption Methods

In this section we will examine modern methods of encryption. Modern methods fall into one of two categories: symmetric algorithms and asymmetric algorithms. In *symmetric algorithms,* the same key is used to encrypt and decrypt a message. In *asymmetric algorithms,* two keys are used: One key is used to encrypt a message, and the second is used to decrypt it.

Symmetric encryption algorithms have a major weakness: the manner in which one distributes the key. Because the same key can be used both to encrypt and decrypt messages, if it should fall into the wrong hands, that person could read all encrypted messages made with that key. Asymmetric algorithms seek to overcome this problem. With an asymmetric algorithm, one key is used to encrypt messages and a different key is used to decrypt them. A person can widely distribute his or her public key (the one used for encrypting messages) and not be concerned about it falling into the wrong hands. Even if it does fall into the

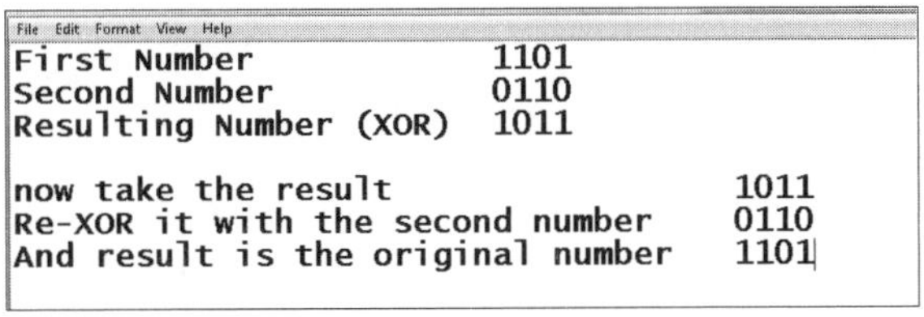

```
File  Edit  Format  View  Help
First Number                    1101
Second Number                   0110
Resulting Number (XOR)   1011

now take the result                   1011
Re-XOR it with the second number      0110
And result is the original number     1101
```

Figure 18.7
Binary XOR again.

wrong hands, it can be used only to encrypt messages, not decrypt them. The private key (the one used for decrypting) is kept secure.

Another way to classify encryption algorithms is to categorize them as either block or stream ciphers. *Block ciphers* encrypt a block of data at a time, whereas *stream ciphers* encrypt each bit one at a time in a stream. We will look at asymmetric, symmetric, block, and stream ciphers in the following sections.

Data Encryption Standard

One of the most widely known symmetric-key algorithms is the Data Encryption Standard, or DES. DES was developed by IBM in the early 1970s. The keys are 56 bits in length. While the details of the process are complex and beyond the scope of this chapter, the essentials are as follows:

■ The data to be encrypted is divided into 64-bit blocks. Entire 64-bit blocks are encrypted at a time, making DES a block cipher.

■ The data is then manipulated by 16 separate steps of encryption, involving substitutions, bit-shifting, and logical operations using that 56-bit key.

DES is fairly fast, and was, at one time, one of the most common symmetric-key encryption algorithms. It has since been supplanted by a stronger version called 3DES, or triple DES. Triple DES is a symmetric encryption algorithm that uses 168-bit encryption keys, which are used in sets of three independent keys. 3DES is more secure than DES but also considerably slower.

RSA

RSA is perhaps one of the most widely known asymmetric-key encryption algorithms. This algorithm was developed in 1977 by three mathematicians: Ron Rivest, Adi Shamir, and Len Adleman. The name "RSA" is derived from the first letter of each mathematician's last name. Some readers may be interested in seeing the fundamentals of the mathematics behind the RSA algorithm. So let's take a brief look at just the broad strokes of the RSA mathematics.

You start with two large prime numbers and multiply them together: $n = p^*q$. Then you let $f(n) = (p-1)\ (q-1)$, and $e > 1$ such that greatest common denominator $(e, f(n)) = 1$. If n is large enough and e is part of the key, then e will have a large probability of being co-prime to $f(n)$. Then linear algebra is used to solve the equation for *d*. The pair of integers *(e, n)* are the public key and *(d, n)* form the private key.

Others

DES and RSA are great examples of symmetric and asymmetric encryption. However, there are other popular encryption algorithms:

- *Blowfish* is a symmetric encryption algorithm (block cipher) with a variable-length (up to 448 bits) key. It operates on 64-bit data blocks. Blowfish was designed by Bruce Schneier and is optimized for applications where the key does not change often.

- *Elliptic Curve PSEC–3* is a public-key encryption system that uses the elliptic curve ElGamal trap-door function and two random functions as well as any secure symmetric-encryption scheme, such as a block cipher. This method is quite complex and very secure, but also very slow.

- *IDEA* is the International Data Encryption Algorithm designed by Xuejia Lai and James Massey. IDEA is a symmetric-key encryption algorithm that uses 128-bit long keys. IDEA, like DES, is a block cipher and operates on 64-bit data blocks. IDEA is much faster than DES and is considered to be quite secure.

- *AES* is the Advanced Encryption Standard. It is a symmetric-key algorithm that uses a block cipher. It can use keys that are 128, 192, or 256 bits, and it uses 10, 12, or 14 rounds of encryption. It is widely used as a replacement for DES.

- *PGP*, which stands for Pretty Good Privacy, was invented by Phil Zimmerman in 1991. The PGP algorithm uses a series of hashing, data compression, symmetric-key cryptography, and public-key cryptography. This means it is literally a combination of several methods. The keys are bound to a user-name or e-mail address, thus making PGP an excellent choice for e-mail encryption.

How Criminals Use Encryption

Now that you have a basic understanding of some of the more common encryption methods, we can discuss how criminals use encryption. The primary applications of encryption would be to encrypt e-mails before sending them or to encrypt files on a computer. In the first case, the goal is to communicate with other criminals, often to conspire. They want to make sure law-enforcement officers cannot read the communications. In the second case, the object is to protect files that might contain incriminating evidence. For example, if an identity thief steals credit-card numbers, he or she may store them in an encrypted file on a hard drive. That way, if the person is arrested and his or her computer is searched, it may be difficult or impossible for the police to read the file and gain evidence against the perpetrator.

There are a number of software packages that can be used to encrypt e-mail. Most of these are inexpensive or free. A few popular ones are listed here:

- Free e-mail encryption is available at Encrypt the Planet http://www.encrypt-the-planet.com/freeemailencryption.htm.

- PGP is a popular public-key encryption system and is available for e-mail from http://www.pgp.com/products/desktop_email/index.html.

- Entrust is a well-known manufacturer of security software. Their e-mail encryption software is available from http://www.entrust.com/email-encryption/index.htm.

If the goal is to encrypt files on a hard drive, one has several options:

- Encrypt Files is a free program that you can download from http://www.encryptfiles.net/.

- FileFlash is specifically designed to encrypt PDF files. It is available from http://www.fileflash.com/allfiles/encrypt/.

- Encrypt4All is a popular file- and folder-encryption tool. You can find it at http://encrypt4all.com/.

In addition to these options, Windows has file encryption built into the NTFS file system. It is pretty simple. First, find a file or folder you want to encrypt and right-click on it. Then select Properties (see Figure 18.8). In the dialog box that appears, click the Advanced button and you will see a check box to encrypt the file. This is shown in Figure 18.9. Check that box, click OK to close the dialog box, and your file will be encrypted. Encrypted files in Windows show up with green text (see Figure 18.10).

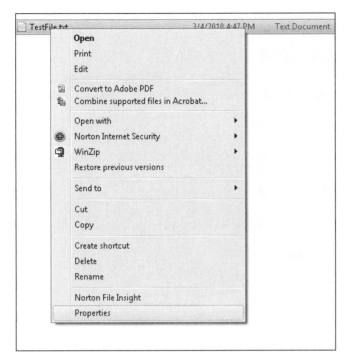

Figure 18.8
Windows File Properties.

The user login information is part of the key, so if you are logged on with the same account used to encrypt the file, it will automatically decrypt the file for you. If someone logs in with a different account, however, that person will not be able to view the file or folder contents.

As you can see, there are many ways to encrypt messages and files. It is important for computer-crime investigators to be aware that some incriminating communications may be encrypted. It is always possible to crack encryption, but it is usually quite time consuming and requires significant computer resources.

Steganography

Steganography is a different way of keeping messages secret. Rather than hide it through encryption, it protects communication by obscuring it. Messages are hidden within images, and in some cases other images are hidden within images.

Figure 18.9
Windows encryption.

The word steganography comes from the Greek *steganos,* meaning covered or secret, and *graphy,* meaning writing or drawing. There are several technical means to accomplish this:

■ Concealing messages within the images or sound files by inserting additional bits.

■ Embedding pictures in video material. Because all video formats send several frames per second, adding one hidden frame would not be immediately obvious to an observer who was not looking for it.

Steganophony is the concealment of messages inside Voice-over-IP conversations. In some cases, the messages are stored in delayed or corrupted packets normally ignored by the receiver or in unused header fields.

It is even possible to first encrypt a message and then embed it in an image. In World War II, the Nazis used a form of steganography called the microdot. The microdot was a photograph that was reduced to the size of a typewritten period.

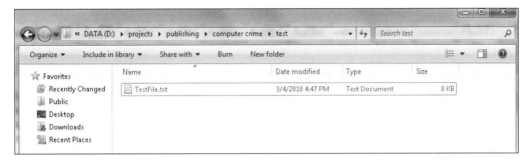

Figure 18.10
An encrypted file.

You might think that steganography requires a great deal of technical knowledge to accomplish, but there are many software packages available that will perform the steganography for you. We will examine one of the easiest to use, and that is QuickStego. It is available for free from http://www.quickcrypto.com/page22. htm. This software has a very simple and intuitive interface, as you can see in Figure 18.11.

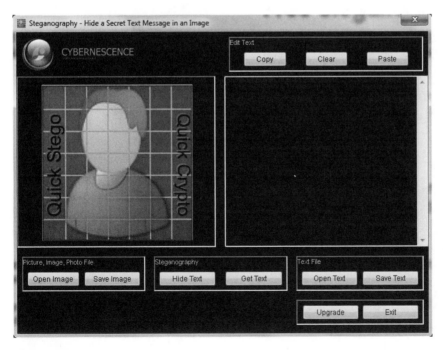

Figure 18.11
QuickStego.

Simply click the Open Image button on the left to find any picture you want to embed a message in (see Figure 18.12). Then, you can either embed the entire contents of a text file in the image or simply write something in the box on the right side, as shown in Figure 18.13. Now simply click the Hide Text button, and the message is hidden in that picture. It can then be retrieved by anyone who knows it is there and looks for the message using steganography software.

QuickStego is just one choice; there are many other steganography tools available, some with more robust features. Here are a few:

- MSU Stego Video, available from http://compression.ru/video/stego_video/index_en.html, is designed to embed messages into video files.

- Steganography 4.0 is available from http://www.clickok.co.uk/steg/. It is also quite easy to use.

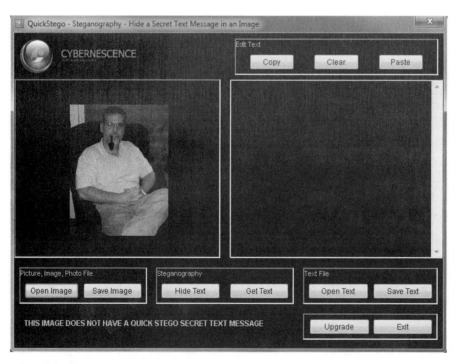

Figure 18.12
QuickStego selected image.

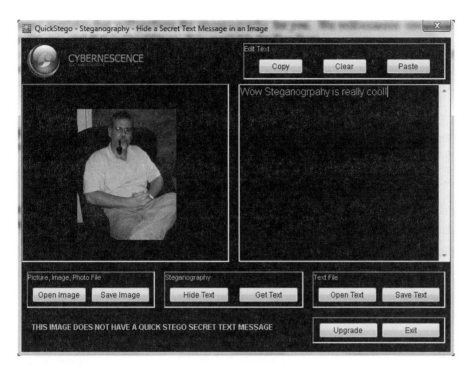

Figure 18.13
QuickStego inserting text.

- Invisible Secrets, available from http://www.invisiblesecrets.com/. This tool can hide entire files in an image.

If you are investigating any sort of computer crime, you should be aware that any images on a device could potentially have evidence hidden within them. It is not at all uncommon for child pornographers to hide illegal images inside of innocuous images.

Leet

Most readers are probably familiar with the fact that various subcultures often have their own slang terms that almost create a new language. The same holds true with cyber criminals and traditional (i.e., non-cyber) criminals using cyber space to communicate. In fact, there are a few sublanguages that have developed in recent years. Let's take a look at *leet,* which is commonly used as the language of hackers and online gamers.

Leet, also known as l33t, 1337, eleet, or leetspeak, is an alternative alphabet used on the Internet. It should first be noted that this is not only used by computer criminals. It is quite popular with hackers in general, including those who are completely law abiding. However, it is also widely used among cyber criminals. This language is based on a combination of alternative spellings, abbreviations, and ASCII code derivatives.

Note

ASCII, or American Standard Code for Information Interchange, is a set of codes for every key on your keyboard. For example, ! is ASCII code 33 and capital A is ASCII code 65. Programmers often use ASCII codes to represent characters.

The exact origin of leet is unknown, but it can be traced back to online bulletin boards of the 1980s. Using abbreviations and ASCII code derivatives was one way to know who was truly computer knowledgeable and who was not.

An example of leet is the term l33t, where the "e" is replaced with the number 3. There are few firm rules in leet, and much variation. A few widely used substitutions are shown in Table 18.1

Table 18.1 Leet Substitutions

English Letter(s)	Leet Equivalent
A	4
E	3
I	1
O	0 or ()
T	7
D	l)
S	$
-ed or –er	0r
s (as in making something plural)	z
B	8
G	6
H	#
V	V
W	\/\/

Leet has also been widely embraced by the online gaming community. Here is a list of common leet words used by hackers and in some cases gamers:

- **0w|\| or 0wn3d:** Owned or pownd means to have completely beaten the other person in a devastating or humiliating fashion. For example, if a hacker completely takes over a server and is able to do anything at will, he may say he has own3d the network or pownd the administrator.

- **w00t:** Derived from "hoot," this is an exclamation of joy or victory.

- **13wt:** This is a misspelling of the word "loot." It literally means something gained. In gaming, it can refer to online rewards. In hacking, it refers to data or software that has been plundered.

- **h4x0r:** A misspelling of hacker. This is a common designation for a skilled hacker. Note the use of the 0r clause mentioned in Table 18.1.

- **ph33r:** Fear, as in "ph33r me." Sometimes also written as "ph34r."

- **sk1llz:** Skills. This term is often used to refer to hacking or gaming skills.

- **m4d:** This is a spelling for mad. It is not usually meant to denote anger, but rather an extreme degree, as in "that h4x0r has m4d sk11lz" ("that hacker has mad skills").

- **j00:** You.

- **f00:** Fool, an obviously derogatory term denigrating the other person's intellect or, more likely, their hacking or gaming skills.

- **j0:** Yo, used as a greeting.

- **d00d:** Dude, a generic expression for another person.

- **sux0r:** Sucks, as in "this sux0r."

- **14m3r:** Lamer, someone who simply is not a real member of the community. In gaming, it can refer to a cheater. In hacking, it can refer to someone who has no real skills but likes to pretend.

- **n00b:** Short for noobie, misspelling of newbie. This is a derogatory term for someone who is new to gaming or hacking or simply lacks any real skills.

- **Pr0n:** This term is for pornography.

- **Warez:** This is a term for pirated software. There are warez Web sites that allow one to download pirated software or keys for software.

It is absolutely vital that you keep in mind that many law-abiding people use leet simply to communicate in a given community such as the online gaming or hacking communities. And as we have pointed out before, even many hackers are not criminals. It is also true, however, that the criminal element of the hacking community does use leet, so being able to decipher leet can be critical to investigating computer crimes. There are online leet translators that you can use to assist you in this, including the following:

- Jay's Site Leet Translator (http://www.jayssite.com/stuff/l33t/l33t_ translator.html)

- D00d's Leet Translator (http://www.albinoblacksheep.com/text/leet)

- English-to-Leet Translator (http://www.plasticnipple.com/translator.shtml)

Meeting

At some point, it may become important for cyber criminals to interact directly with each other. Some sort of personal meeting may be required. There are several ways this can happen; some occur online and some in person.

Online Discussions

It has been known for some time that terrorists have used private online chat rooms to plan terrorist activities and to coordinate operations. However, a new twist has emerged: online training.[1] It has always been possible to search online and perhaps find instructions to make an explosive device or to mix household chemicals to make a poison. But now terrorists are setting up online training camps for the express purpose of training new terrorists. They literally meet online, often in private chat rooms, and teach the new terrorists how to make and plant explosives and conduct other terrorist activities.

Terrorists are also now using social networks to make connections with likely recruits and with current terrorists.[2] By observing online profiles, discussions, and other personal expressions, the terrorist group can identify potential recruits. Then the recruiter will begin talking with potential recruits, trying to gauge the extent of the target's views. Little by little, the attempt is made to bring the target to a more radical viewpoint and ultimately to recruit him or her as a terrorist.

The fact that terrorists use online communications to recruit, plan, and train reinforces a fact we mentioned earlier: Cyber investigations are often an aspect of more traditional crimes. Even terrorist investigations have a cyber component. This means that if you are a law-enforcement officer, tracking down hackers and identity thieves may not be your only assignments. Your skills could be required with organized crime, espionage, and terrorist investigations.

We have previously discussed how pedophiles stalk new victims online, but that is just the beginning of their online activities. The steganography techniques we mentioned earlier are a common way pedophiles store and distribute child pornography.[3] Unfortunately, many pedophiles are quite computer savvy. It is not uncommon for investigators to find that a pedophile's hard drive is encrypted, and that even once that encryption is broken, the child-pornography images are actually stored inside of innocuous images using steganography.

Conclusion

We have examined some of the ways that criminals can utilize the Internet to communicate. After reading this chapter, you should have a basic idea of how cryptography works and be basically familiar with steganography and steganophony. You should also understand how criminals, including terrorists, can use chat rooms and other online resources to facilitate their criminal activity. And you have now been introduced to leet.

It is also important to realize that the more clever a criminal is, the more likely he or she is to use multiple methods in concert—for example, a message written in leet, that is then encrypted, and then buried in an image using steganography. It is important that as a criminal investigator, you have skills that are equal to the computer criminals' skills, or at least you know how to find someone who does.

Endnotes

1 *SoftPedia*. "Terrorists Setup Online Training Camps." http://news.softpedia. com/news/Terrorists-Building-Online-Training-Camps-71521.shtml

2 *PC World*. "Social Networks Link Terrorists." http://www.pcworld.idg.com. au/article/272364/social_networks_link_terrorists/

3 Anti Child Porn. "STEGANOGRAPHY: Hidden Images, A New Challenge in the Fight Against Child Porn." http://www.antichildporn.org/steganog.html

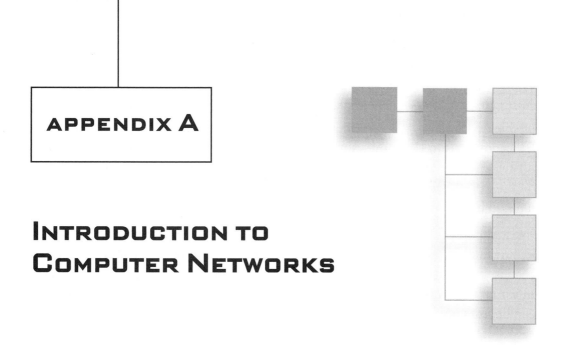

APPENDIX A

INTRODUCTION TO COMPUTER NETWORKS

Introduction

Investigating computer crime requires a solid knowledge of computer systems. The best scenario is when an investigator has a background in network administration or technical support. However, the fact is that sometimes law-enforcement officers are assigned to computer-crime investigations without that background. This appendix is meant to give you a brief introduction to network operations. Clearly, this is just an introduction, and you should absolutely go further in your network and systems education if you intend to investigate computer-related crime as a vocation.

Network Basics

The basic concept of networking is actually very simple. You need to get data from one computer to another. There are a number of parts involved in this effort: the physical connection, the protocols for transmissions, the data packets, and the devices used to route the packets. We will examine all of these facets of network communication in this appendix.

The Physical Connection

The physical connection starts with the actual cable that is connected to the computer. The cable connection used in most networks is called twisted pair cable. *Twisted pair cable* is literally cables twisted together inside a plastic sheath.

There are two varieties of twisted pair cabling: shielded and unshielded. The shielded cabling experiences less interference but is much more expensive, so unshielded twisted pair is more common. Both types of twisted pair cable use an RJ 45 connection (RJ is an abbreviation for *registered jack*). RJ 11 is the jack used for telephones. The RJ 45 looks just like the phone jack only a bit bigger. This is because phone lines have four wires, whereas standard network cable connectors have eight.

Twisted pair cabling is categorized by its speed. There are currently six categories in production, although category 7 is supposed to be released soon. The cable used in most networks today is a category 5 cable (abbreviated as a cat-5 cable) or in some cases category 6 cable. Now, there are certainly other types of cable that can be used, including coaxial, fiber optic, and others. However, the twisted pair cable (cat-1 through cat-6) is by far the most commonly used. If you look at the back of most computers, you will probably find two ports that look like phone jacks. The first port is probably for a traditional modem and has a standard RJ 11 jack. The second port is larger; this is an RJ 45 jack. Not all computers come with a network interface card (NIC), but most modern computers do. A network interface card is simply the card used to connect a network cable to your computer. Table A.1 summarizes the various categories of cable and their uses.

Notice the speeds listed in Table A.1. Mbps stands for megabits per second. Many readers are probably already aware that ultimately, everything in the computer is stored in a binary format, a 1 or a 0. These units are called bits. It follows, then, that a category 5 cable can transmit up to 100 million bits per second. It takes eight bits, or one byte, to represent a single character such as a letter, number, or carriage return.

Table A.1 Categories of Cable

Category	Specifications	Uses
1	Low-speed analog (less than 1 MHz)	Telephone, door bell
2	Analog line (less than 10 MHz)	Telephone
3	Up to 16 MHz or 100 Mbps	Voice transmissions
4	Up to 20 MHz or 100 Mbps	Used in data lines, Ethernet networks
5	100 MHz or 100 Mbps	The most common type of network cable
6	1,000 Mbps	Used in very high-speed networks

The Hub

The simplest connection device is the hub. A *hub* is a small box-shaped electronic device into which you can plug in network cables. It will have four or more (commonly up to 24) RJ 45 ports into which one can plug in the RJ 45 connectors at the end of twisted pair cable. You can also connect one hub to another; this strategy is referred to as *stacking* hubs. Hubs are quite inexpensive and simple; just plug the cable in. However, hubs have a downside. If you send a packet from one computer to another, a copy of that packet is actually sent out from every port on the hub. These copies can lead to a lot of unnecessary network traffic. This situation is due to the fact that the hub, being a very simple device, has no way of knowing where a packet is supposed to go. Therefore, it simply sends copies of the packet to all of its ports.

The Switch

A *switch* is basically an intelligent hub. A switch works and looks exactly like a hub, with one significant difference. When it receives a packet, it will send that packet only to the port it needs to go to. A switch is essentially a hub that is able to determine where a packet supposed to go.

The Router

A *router* traditionally was defined as a device for connecting two diverse networks. For example, you may have a router in your home that connects your home network to your Internet service provider's network. However, modern routers usually also function as a switch, a firewall (which we will discuss later in this appendix), and often a wireless access point.

The Data Packets

All network communication depends on packets. All data is parsed into individual packets and sent to its destination. What, exactly, is a packet? As you probably know, everything in a computer is ultimately stored as 1s and 0s, called bits. These 1s and 0s are grouped into groups of eight bits, called a byte. A *packet* is a certain number of bytes divided into a header and a body. The header is 20 bytes at the beginning and gives the source address, the destination address, the type of content in the packet, how many packets total, and which one this packet is (i.e., packet five of eight). The body contains the actual data, in binary format, that you want to send. The aforementioned routers and switches work by reading the header portion of any packets that come to them.

There are different types of communications that serve different purposes. The different types of network communications are called protocols. A *protocol* is, essentially, an agreed-upon method of communication. In fact, this definition is exactly how the word "protocol" is used in standard, non-computer usage. Each protocol has a specific purpose and normally operates on a certain port (more on ports in a bit). Some of the most important protocols are listed in Table A.2.

There are many more protocols, but these are some of the most commonly used. The term *port* is often confusing for those new to networking. This is because you may think of a port as some opening on the computer you plug something into, such as a USB port, and that is a logical deduction. However, in this case, a port is

Table A.2 Protocols

Protocol	Purpose	Port
FTP (File Transfer Protocol)	Used for transferring files between computers.	21
Telnet	Used to remotely log on to a system. You can then use a command prompt or shell to execute commands on that system. Popular with network administrators.	23
SMTP (Simple Mail Transfer Protocol)	Sends e-mail.	25
Whois	A command that queries a target IP address for information.	43
DNS (Domain Name Service)	Translates URLs into Web addresses.	53
tFTP (Trivial File Transfer Protocol)	A quicker, but less reliable, form of FTP.	69
HTTP (Hypertext Transfer Protocol)	Displays Web pages.	80
POP3 (Post Office Protocol Version 3)	Retrieves e-mail.	110
NNTP (Network News Transfer Protocol)	Used for network newsgroups (usenet newsgroups).	119
NetBIOS	An older Microsoft protocol that is for naming systems on a local network.	137, 138, 139
IRC (Internet Relay Chat)	Chat rooms.	194
ICMP (Internet Control Message Protocol)	These are simply packets that contain error messages, informational messages, and control messages.	No specific port

more like a channel. All network communications are coming through the cable (or wireless connection) through a single physical connection on your computer. But each port in this case is much like a channel on TV.

IP Addresses

The most basic issue in networking and the Internet is how to get packets to the right place. Just as a letter or package requires a mailing address to be sent successfully, packets also require an address. Computers use an IP address. An IP address is made up of four numbers, 0 to 255, separated by periods—something like 192.58.99.03. The reason they must be 0 to 255 is because what you see as a decimal number the computer sees as a byte, and if you take eight bits (one byte), the largest decimal number that can be stored in it is 255.

Now, each computer needs an IP address to send and receive, and most people use an Internet service provider to connect to the Internet. For most home users, their computer is assigned an IP address by their ISP and it is used as long as it is needed. That means it is possible that an IP address used by one person today would be used by another person next week. The ISP servers know where to route the packets. This is critical in criminal investigations because if you trace an IP address, you may well have only traced it back to the Internet service provider and not to an individual. The next step would be to subpoena that ISP's records to verify who was assigned that IP address at the time in question.

Now, some readers may be thinking that they never enter IP addresses; they enter names like http://www.charlesriver.com. These are *uniform resource locators* (URLs). They are names, which we people understand better. The computer systems use *domain name service* (DNS) to translate those names into the numeric IP address.

Basic Network Utilities

There are several basic network utilities you should be familiar with. To use any of these you will need a command prompt. In Windows XP, Vista, or Windows 7, you get pull up the command prompt by clicking on Start and typing in cmd, as shown in Figure A.1. That will get you the command prompt shown in Figure A.2. This is where you will go to use any of these utilities we will be exploring next.

Figure A.1
Getting the command prompt.

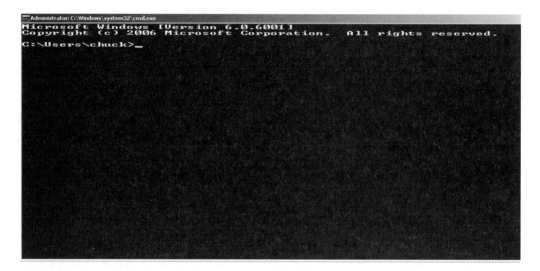

Figure A.2
The command prompt.

IPConfig

`IPConfig` is an important utility. It basically gives you all the essential information about your computer, such as the IP address, what DNS server it is using, what gateway it is using to get to the outside (i.e., the Internet), and other information. You can see the results of `IPConfig` in Figure A.3.

All the command-line utilities have optional parameters you can pass to them. For example, with `IPConfig`, you can type in `IPConfig/All` and get even more detailed information. You do not have to memorize the various command parameters. With any command you can type *command*/?—in this case `IPconfig/?`—and you will see all the parameters available. This is shown in Figure A.4.

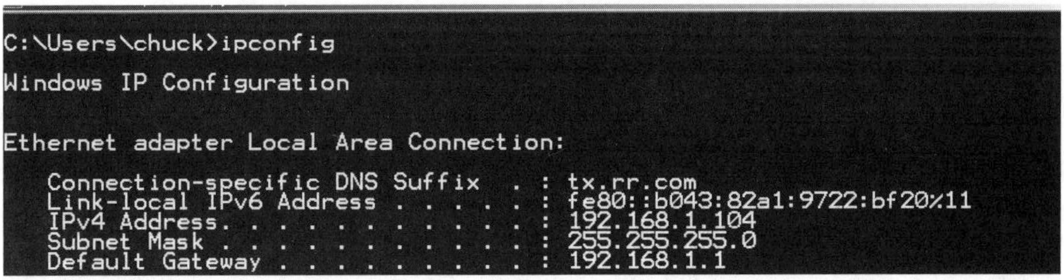

```
C:\Users\chuck>ipconfig

Windows IP Configuration

Ethernet adapter Local Area Connection:

   Connection-specific DNS Suffix  . : tx.rr.com
   Link-local IPv6 Address . . . . . : fe80::b043:82a1:9722:bf20%11
   IPv4 Address. . . . . . . . . . . : 192.168.1.104
   Subnet Mask . . . . . . . . . . . : 255.255.255.0
   Default Gateway . . . . . . . . . : 192.168.1.1
```

Figure A.3
IPConfig.

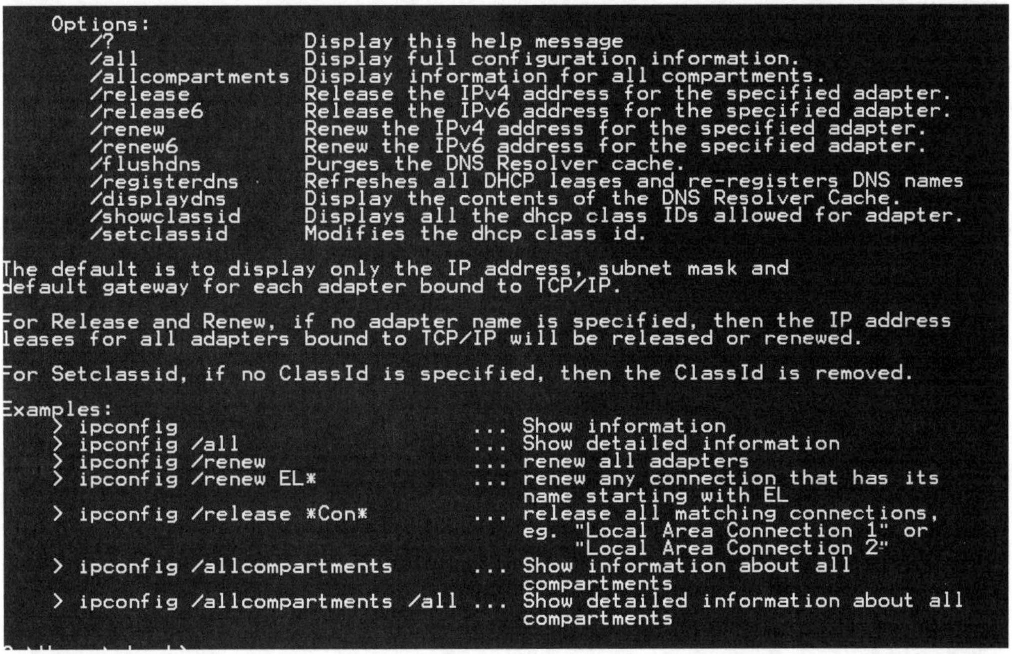

```
   Options:
      /?               Display this help message
      /all             Display full configuration information.
      /allcompartments Display information for all compartments.
      /release         Release the IPv4 address for the specified adapter.
      /release6        Release the IPv6 address for the specified adapter.
      /renew           Renew the IPv4 address for the specified adapter.
      /renew6          Renew the IPv6 address for the specified adapter.
      /flushdns        Purges the DNS Resolver cache.
      /registerdns     Refreshes all DHCP leases and re-registers DNS names
      /displaydns      Display the contents of the DNS Resolver Cache.
      /showclassid     Displays all the dhcp class IDs allowed for adapter.
      /setclassid      Modifies the dhcp class id.

The default is to display only the IP address, subnet mask and
default gateway for each adapter bound to TCP/IP.

For Release and Renew, if no adapter name is specified, then the IP address
leases for all adapters bound to TCP/IP will be released or renewed.

For Setclassid, if no ClassId is specified, then the ClassId is removed.

Examples:
   > ipconfig                     ... Show information
   > ipconfig /all                ... Show detailed information
   > ipconfig /renew              ... renew all adapters
   > ipconfig /renew EL*          ... renew any connection that has its
                                      name starting with EL
   > ipconfig /release *Con*      ... release all matching connections,
                                      eg. "Local Area Connection 1" or
                                          "Local Area Connection 2"
   > ipconfig /allcompartments    ... Show information about all
                                      compartments
   > ipconfig /allcompartments /all ... Show detailed information about all
                                      compartments
```

Figure A.4
IPConfig parameters.

ping and tracert

These are very commonly used commands. ping basically sends a packet to an IP address or URL to verify whether or not that IP address or URL is reachable. You can see this in Figure A.5.

A closely related utility is tracert. This utility not only tells you if an IP address was reachable, but also what route was taken by the packet to reach the destination.

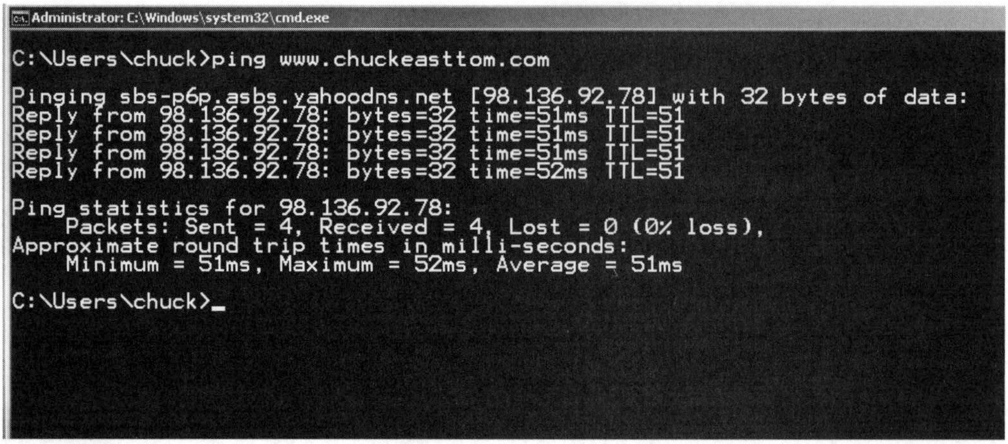

Figure A.5
ping.

This can be very important when conducting an investigation and trying to ascertain where exactly an e-mail or other transmission came from (see Figure A.6).

It is a good idea to take some time and simply experiment with these utilities.

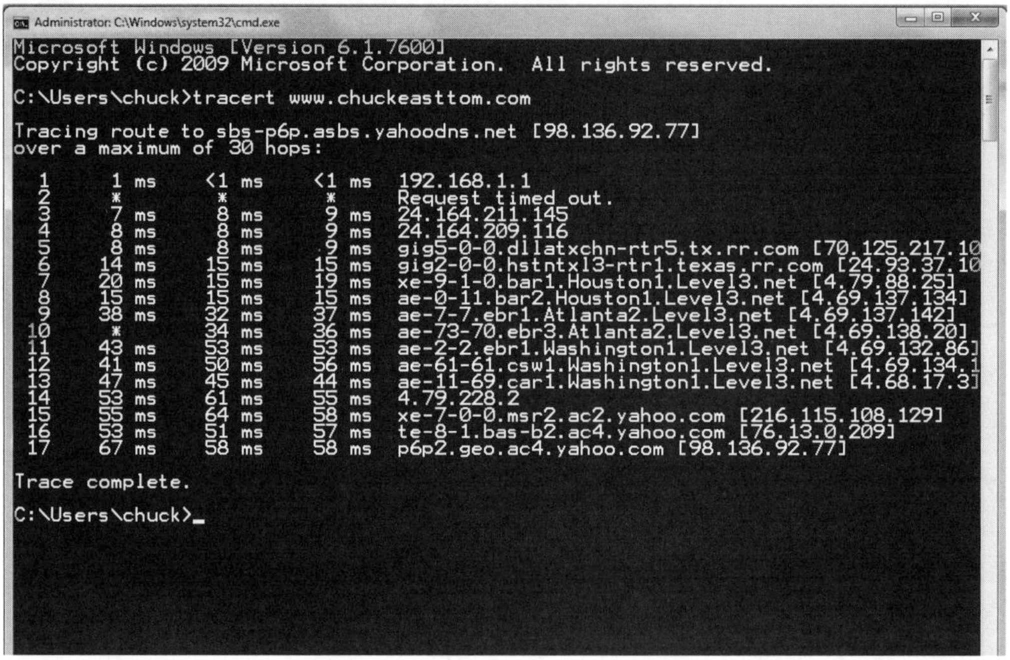

Figure A.6
tracert.

Network Security Measures

There are a number of security measures and devices used on modern networks. The most basic is the firewall. A *firewall* is a device or software that blocks incoming traffic based on some criteria. It might block traffic coming to a certain port or using a certain protocol. Windows XP, Vista, and 7 all have software firewalls as part of the operating system. Most modern routers also have firewall capability. One can also get very advanced firewalls with rather complex schemes for filtering traffic.

Another useful security tool is the virus scanner and/or spyware scanner. These types of software attempt to prevent viruses and spyware from infecting a machine. They work in essentially two ways. The first is by having a list of all known viruses and spyware. They then compare files on the computer to that list. The other way they work is by watching the behavior of a given program. If it behaves like a virus (trying to alter system settings, copy itself, and so on), it is flagged as a possible virus.

There are many more advanced security measures, such as intrusion-detection systems (IDSes). These systems monitor all traffic and look for anything that might be a prelude to an attack. For example, if someone starts pinging each port on a firewall, that is often a hacker looking for vulnerabilities. An IDS will detect that activity and alert the administrator.

This appendix is just meant to give the networking novice enough information to follow the material in this book. However, if you intend to have a career related to investigating computer crimes, it is highly recommended that you learn as much as you can about networks and operating systems.

APPENDIX B

GLOSSARY

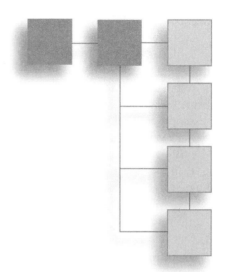

This appendix is meant to give you a general glossary. Clearly defining terms used in this book is the primary goal, but this glossary will also define terms that are generally used in the hacking and legal communities.

A

acquittal: Being found not guilty, or to be acquitted of a crime. It is the opposite of a conviction.

admin: Short for system administrator.

adware: Software loaded onto your machine, often without your knowledge, that causes ads to pop up onto your screen. This technology often works in a different manner than Web page pop-ups, thus pop-up blockers won't stop them.

affadavit: A sworn statement. Usually given in lieu of in-person testimony.

appeal: A request to a higher court to overturn the decision of a lower court.

audit: A check of system security. This usually includes a review of documents, procedures, and system configurations.

authentication: The process of verifying that a user is authorized to access a given resource. This is part of the logon process. There are many different authentication protocols. Two of the most famous are CHAP and Kerveros.

B

back door: A hole in the security system deliberately left by the creator of the system or by a hacker who wants to ensure they can return to the system.

bagbiter: Something, such as a program or a computer, that fails to work, or works in a remarkably clumsy manner.

black-hat hackers: Hackers with malicious intent, synonymous with *cracker*.

block cipher: Ciphers that encrypt blocks of text at a time—for example 64 bytes at a time.

BlowFish: A well-known encryption algorithm.

brain dump: The process of telling someone everything one knows about a given subject.

breach: To successfully break into a system, to breach the security.

brute force: To try to crack a password by simply trying every possible combination.

buffer overflow: An attack that involves loading a memory buffer with more data than it is designed to hold.

bug: A flaw in a system.

C

Caesar cipher: One of the oldest known encryption methods that simply shifts each character by a given number. It is not secure and should not be used anymore.

cipher: A method for encrypting messages. It is the algorithm or process you apply to the message in order to encrypt it. Synonym for *cryptographic algorithm*.

cipher text: Encrypted text.

code: The source code for a program, or the act of programming, as in "to code an algorithm" or "let's review the code for that application."

cookie: A small file containing information from a Web site. It resides on a person's computer, not on the Web server.

cracker: A person who breaks into a system in order to do something malicious, illegal, or harmful. Synonymous with *black-hat hacker*.

crash: A sudden and unintended failure, as in "my computer crashed."

cross examination: The process of an attorney asking questions of the other attorney's witness. For example, the defense attorney may cross examine the prosecution's witness.

cryptography: The study of encryption and decryption.

cyber fraud: Using the Internet to defraud someone.

cyber stalking: Using the Internet to harass someone.

cyber terrorism: Using Internet attacks with the intent of causing fear and/or panic.

D

data encryption standard (DES): A widely used block cipher encryption algorithm that uses a 56-byte symmetric key.

datagram: A packet sent using the TCP protocol.

decryption: To reverse encryption and discover the underlying message.

demigod: A slang term for a hacker with years of experience and a national or international reputation.

denial of service (DoS): An attack that prevents legitimate users from accessing a resource.

deposition: Sworn testimony taken outside of a court. Usually done in the pre-trial phase.

distributed denial of service (DDoS): A denial-of-service attack launched from multiple machines, often without the knowledge of the owners of those machines.

domain name service (DNS): A protocol that translates names such as www. ChuckEasttom.com into IP addresses.

domain name server (DNS server): A server that provides DNS service.

Dumpster diving: The process of searching through trash looking for information that might be useful in hacking (particularly social engineering) or identity theft.

E

echo/chargen attack: A type of denial-of-service attack that attempts to build up too much CPU activity by using sending repeated echo packets.

encryption: The act of applying a cryptographic algorithm to a message so that its message cannot be read without having the key to decrypt the message.

espionage: Spying, the act of illicitly gaining confidential information.

ethical hacker: One who hacks into systems in order to accomplish some goal that is both legal and is ethically valid. This is synonymous with *white-hat hacker*.

F

firewall: A device or software that provides a barrier between your machine or network and the rest of the world.

flood attack: An attack that involves sending a large number of packets to a server in an attempt to overload the server. There are several types of floods, including as syn floods and ping floods.

footprinting: A term hackers use for assessing a system looking for vulnerabilities.

G–H

gray-hat hackers: Hackers who normally behave legally but who may, for certain reasons and in limited situations, conduct illegal activities, usually for reasons they feel are ethically compelling. Note that some sources define gray-hat hacker as a former black-hat hacker who is no longer engaging in illegal acts.

hacker: One who tries to learn about a system by examining it in detail by reverse engineering it.

hacking: The process of attempting to learn about a system by examining it often by exploiting flaws. This usually involves attempts to compromise the target system in some way.

hactivism: Hacking conducted for ideological purposes.

hardening: The process of securing all aspects of a system. This includes adding patches, shutting off unnecessary services, making sure all settings are secure, and any other step that would fundamentally secure the operating system.

hub: A device for connecting computers. It has a number of ports into which you plug cables that connect to the computer(s). This is the simplest of connection devices. More advanced devices that also connect computers include bridges and switches.

I

ICMP flood attacks: An attack that attempts to overload the target system with more ICMP packets than it can respond to. This is also referred to as a ping flood because it is often done with the ping utility, which sends ICMP packets.

identity theft: The process of getting enough of a person's personal information that you might be able to pose as that person. Often done to secure credit or make purchases in the victim's name.

industrial espionage: The use of espionage for purely economic purposes.

information warfare: The use of information in any conflict. This often involves propaganda and disinformation campaigns.

Internet service provider (ISP): A company that provides Internet access for clients.

intrusion-detection system (IDS): A system that is designed to detect signs of attacks in progress and to notify the administrator.

IP address: A numerical designation for a computer consisting of four, one-byte binary numbers.

IPConfig: A utility that provides extensive information about a computer's network connection.

K–L

keylogger: Software that logs keystrokes on a computer.

loopback address: An address used to test a machine's own network card, 127.0.0.1.

M

MAC address: A unique 6-byte hexadecimal number that is used to identify a network interface card.

malware: Any software that has a malicious purpose, such as a virus, worm, or Trojan horse.

motion: A legal filing requesting the court take some action. It is literally an attempt to *move* the court to do something.

N

network interface card (NIC): The card that allows network connectivity for a computer.

network scanning: The process of scanning a network looking for vulnerabilities.

P

packet: A binary piece of data prepared for transmission over a network.

perjury: Lying while under oath. There is usually a significant legal penalty associated with committing perjury, which can include prison time.

penetration testing: Assessing the security of a system by attempting to break into the system. This is the activity most sneakers engage in.

phishing: The process of sending e-mails to people, where the e-mail purports to be from some legitimate financial institution such as a bank or credit-card company, and induces the recipient to provide personal information.

phreaking: The process of hacking phone systems.

ping: Sending a single ICMP packet to a destination, usually in order to confirm the destination can be reached. It also refers to the utility ping, which sends one or more ICMP packets to a destination to confirm it can be reached.

ping of death (PoD): Sending an extremely large packet to a target. For some older systems, this would cause the target to crash.

plaintiff: The party who files a civil lawsuit.

port: A numerical designation for a connection point on a computer. There are well-defined ports for specific protocols. For example, FTP is port 21, HTTP is port 80, SMTP is port 25, etc.

port scanning: Scanning a target machine to see what ports are open in an attempt to assess vulnerabilities.

protocols: Agreed-upon methods of communication. In networking, protocol refers to ways of performing certain types of communication, such as the hypertext transfer protocol for Web pages.

public-key encryption: Encryption algorithms that use two keys. One is publicly distributed and is used to encrypt messages. The other is kept private and is used to decrypt the messages.

pump and dump: Artificially inflating the price of a stock so that you can sell your shares at a much higher value than they should have.

R

respondant: The person who has been served a civil lawsuit or some other court action such as a subpoena or restraining order.

router: A device that separates networks.

RSA: A widely used public-key encryption algorithm.

S

script kiddie: A hacker term for one who claims much greater hacking skill than he or she actually has.

single-key encryption: Also called symmetric key encryption. The same key is used both to encrypt and decrypt the message.

smurf: A specific type of distributed denial-of-service attack. This attack essentially tricks a network into flooding one of its own nodes.

sneaker: Someone who is attempting to compromise a system in order to assess its vulnerability.

social engineering: Using interpersonal skills to extract information about a computer system and its security.

spoofing: Pretending to be something else, such as when a packet might spoof another return IP address (as in the smurf attack) or when a Web site is spoofing a well known e-commerce site.

spyware: Software that monitors computer use.

stream cipher: A type of cipher where the original text is encrypted one byte at a time in a stream of bytes.

subpeona: A court order to take some action, usually to testify or to hand over evidence in a case, as in "the court issued a subpoena for the server logs."

substitution alphabet: The characters used to replace plain text in a substitution or multi-substitution encryption algorithm.

switch: A device that works like a hub, only it routes packets only out the port that they need to go to rather than to all ports. It is essentially an intelligent hub.

SYN flood: A denial-of-service attack wherein the target is flooded with connection requests that are never completed.

SYN/ACK: The response a server sends back to a connection request from a client.

T

terminate and stay resident (TSR): Software that stays loaded in memory even if the computer is shut down.

tort: A civil wrong related to some act that has caused injury (either physical or financial) to another person.

tracert: A utility similar to ping, but it also tells you what hops it made getting to the destination and how long it took to get there.

Trojan horse: Software that appears to have a valid and benign purpose but really has another, nefarious purpose.

U

UDP flood attack: A denial-of-service attack based on sending a huge number of UDP packets.

uniform resource locator (URL): An Internet address, such as http://www.chuckeasttom.com.

user datagram protocol (UDP): A protocol very similar to TCP, except that transmissions are merely sent without any attempt to confirm their arrival at the destination.

V

virtual private network (VPN): A connection that is encrypted/tunneled so that all the communications are secure. It gives the client the same access as they might have if they were physically at the server, with all communications being secure via encryption.

virus: Software that is self replicating and spreads like a biological virus.

W

war dialing: Dialing phones waiting for a computer to pick up. This is usually done via some automated system.

war driving: Driving and scanning for wireless networks that can be compromised.

white-hat hackers: Hackers who only hack for legal/ethical purposes.

Z

zone transfers: DNS servers must update their list of what IP addresses go with what URL (uniform resource locator). They periodically perform zone transfers to synchronize those lists.

INDEX